Save OVER **50%** off the cover price!

S0-AUK-041

Shojo Beat
MANGA from the HEART

The Shojo Manga Authority

This monthly magazine is injected with the most **ADDICTIVE** shojo manga stories from Japan. PLUS, unique editorial coverage on the arts, music, culture, fashion, and much more!

☑ **YES!** Please enter my one-year subscription (12 GIANT issues) to *Shojo Beat* at the LOW SUBSCRIPTION RATE of **$34.99!**

Over **300 pages** per issue!

NAME

ADDRESS

CITY   STATE   ZIP

E-MAIL ADDRESS   P7GNC1

☐ **MY CHECK IS ENCLOSED** (PAYABLE TO *Shojo Beat*)   ☐ **BILL ME LATER**

CREDIT CARD: ☐ **VISA**   ☐ **MASTERCARD**

ACCOUNT #   EXP. DATE

SIGNATURE

CLIP AND MAIL TO ➤

SHOJO BEAT
Subscriptions Service Dept.
P.O. Box 438
Mount Morris, IL 61054-0438

RATED
T+
FOR OLDER TEEN
ratings.viz.com

Shojo Beat™

MANGA from the HEART

The Shojo Manga Authority

The most **ADDICTIVE** shojo manga stories from Japan **PLUS** unique editorial coverage on the arts, music, culture, fashion, and much more!

12 GIANT issues for ONLY $34.99*

That's 51% OFF the cover price!

Subscribe NOW and become a member of the 🅑 Sub Club!

- **SAVE** 51% OFF the cover price
- **ALWAYS** get every issue
- **ACCESS** exclusive areas of www.shojobeat.com
- **FREE** members-only gifts several times a year

Strictly VIP!

3 EASY WAYS TO SUBSCRIBE!

1) Send in the subscription order form from this book OR
2) Log on to: www.shojobeat.com OR
3) Call 1-800-541-7876

Backstage Prince

By Kanoko Sakurakoji

Drawn into the exciting world of kabuki theatre, young Akari spends her time after school assisting the famous actor, Shonosuke Ichimura. In the real world, however, this prince of kabuki is actually a high school cutie named Ryusei. The pair's relationship gets off on the wrong foot, but eventually, with the help of a cat known as Mr. Ken, the two teenagers fall in love!

Backstage Prince 1

Kanoko Sakurakoji

Shojo Beat

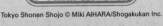

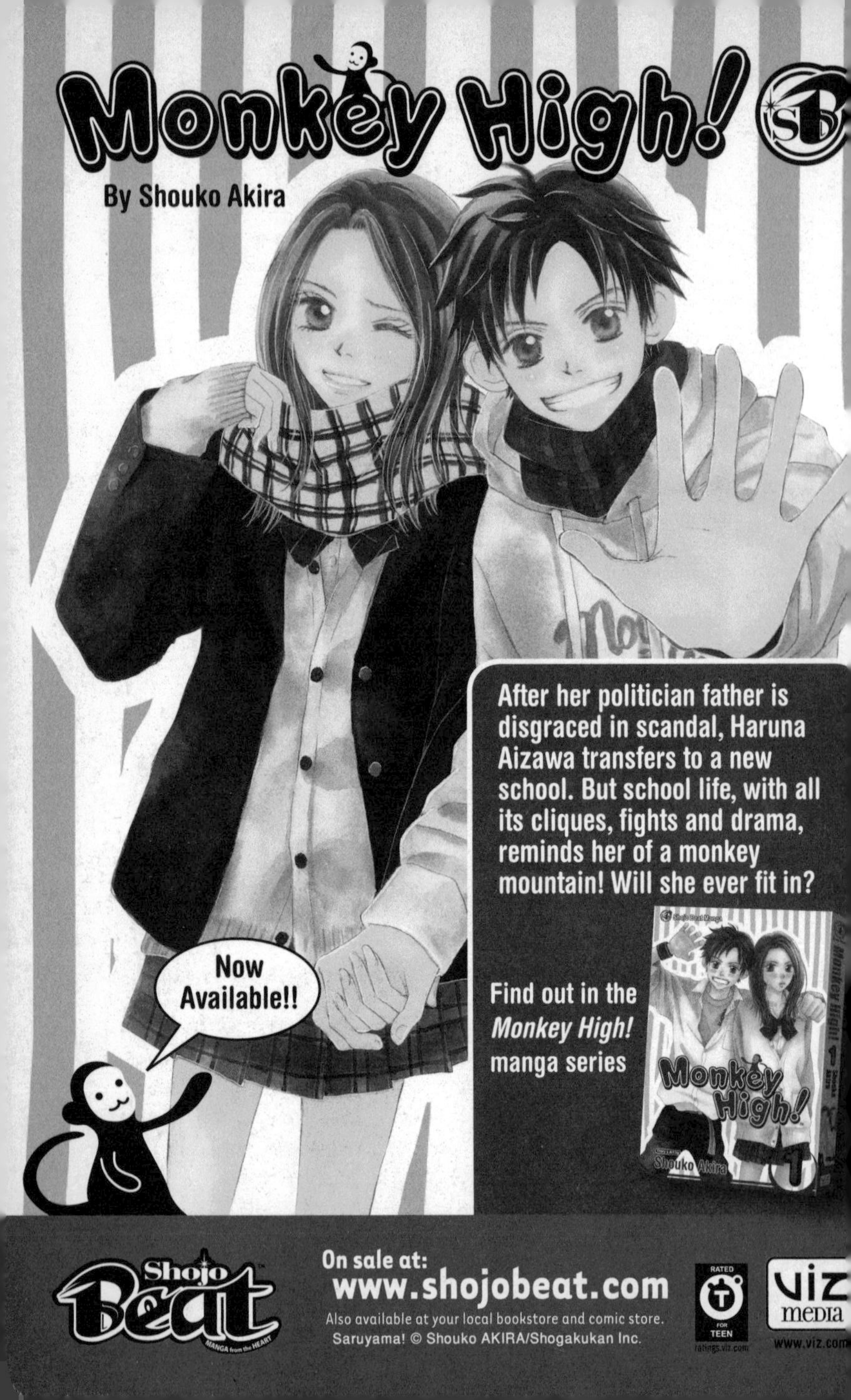
Monkey High!
By Shouko Akira
Now Available!!
After her politician father is disgraced in scandal, Haruna Aizawa transfers to a new school. But school life, with all its cliques, fights and drama, reminds her of a monkey mountain! Will she ever fit in?
Find out in the Monkey High! manga series
Shojo Beat Manga
Monkey High!
Shouko Akira
1
Shojo Beat
MANGA from the HEART
On sale at:
www.shojobeat.com
Also available at your local bookstore and comic store.
Saruyama! © Shouko AKIRA/Shogakukan Inc.
RATED
T
FOR TEEN
ratings.viz.com
VIZ media
www.viz.com

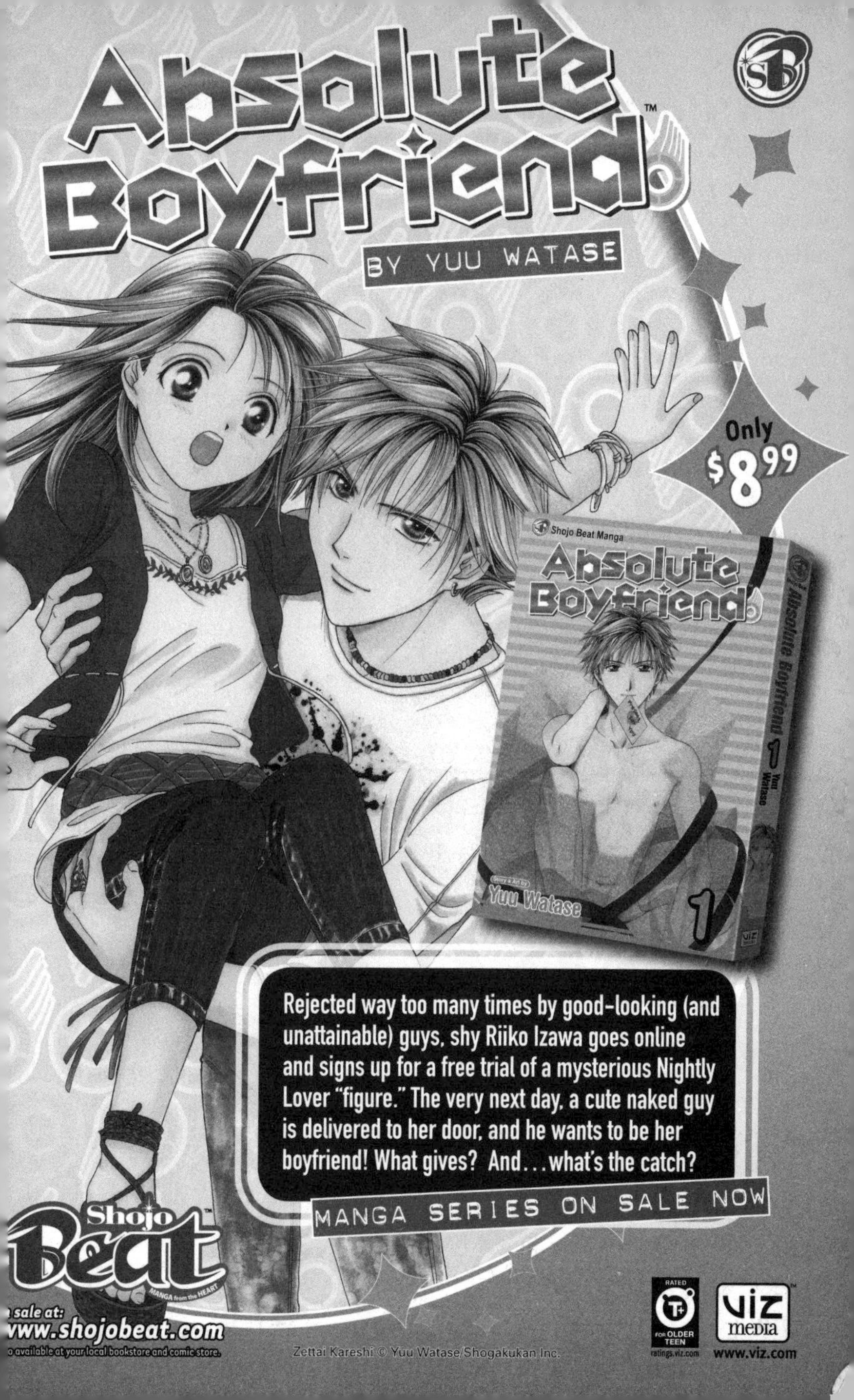

Absolute Boyfriend™
BY YUU WATASE
Only $8.99
Shojo Beat Manga
Absolute Boyfriend
Absolute Boyfriend 1 Yuu Watase
Story & Art by Yuu Watase
1
Rejected way too many times by good-looking (and unattainable) guys, shy Riiko Izawa goes online and signs up for a free trial of a mysterious Nightly Lover "figure." The very next day, a cute naked guy is delivered to her door, and he wants to be her boyfriend! What gives? And…what's the catch?
MANGA SERIES ON SALE NOW
Shojo Beat™
MANGA from the HEART
n sale at:
www.shojobeat.com
o available at your local bookstore and comic store.
Zettai Kareshi © Yuu Watase/Shogakukan Inc.
RATED T+ FOR OLDER TEEN
ratings.viz.com
VIZ media
www.viz.com

SAND CHRONICLES

Vol. 2

The Shojo Beat Manga Edition

This manga volume contains material that was originally published in English in *Shojo Beat* magazine #30 through #33. Artwork in the magazine may have been slightly altered from that presented here.

STORY AND ART BY HINAKO ASHIHARA

English Adaptation/John Werry
Translation/Kinami Watabe
Touch-up Art & Lettering/Rina Mapa
Additional Touch-up/Rachel Lightfoot
Design/Yukiko Whitley
Editors/Pancha Diaz & Annette Roman

Editor in Chief, Books/Alvin Lu
Editor in Chief, Magazines/Marc Weidenbaum
VP of Publishing Licensing/Rika Inouye
VP of Sales/Gonzalo Ferreyra
Sr. VP of Marketing/Liza Coppola
Publisher/Hyoe Narita

Printed in Canada

store.viz.com

Published by VIZ Media, LLC
P.O. Box 77010
San Francisco, CA 94107

Shojo Beat Manga Edition
10 9 8 7 6 5 4 3 2 1
First printing, May 2008

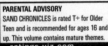

Sand Chronicles

Shojo Beat

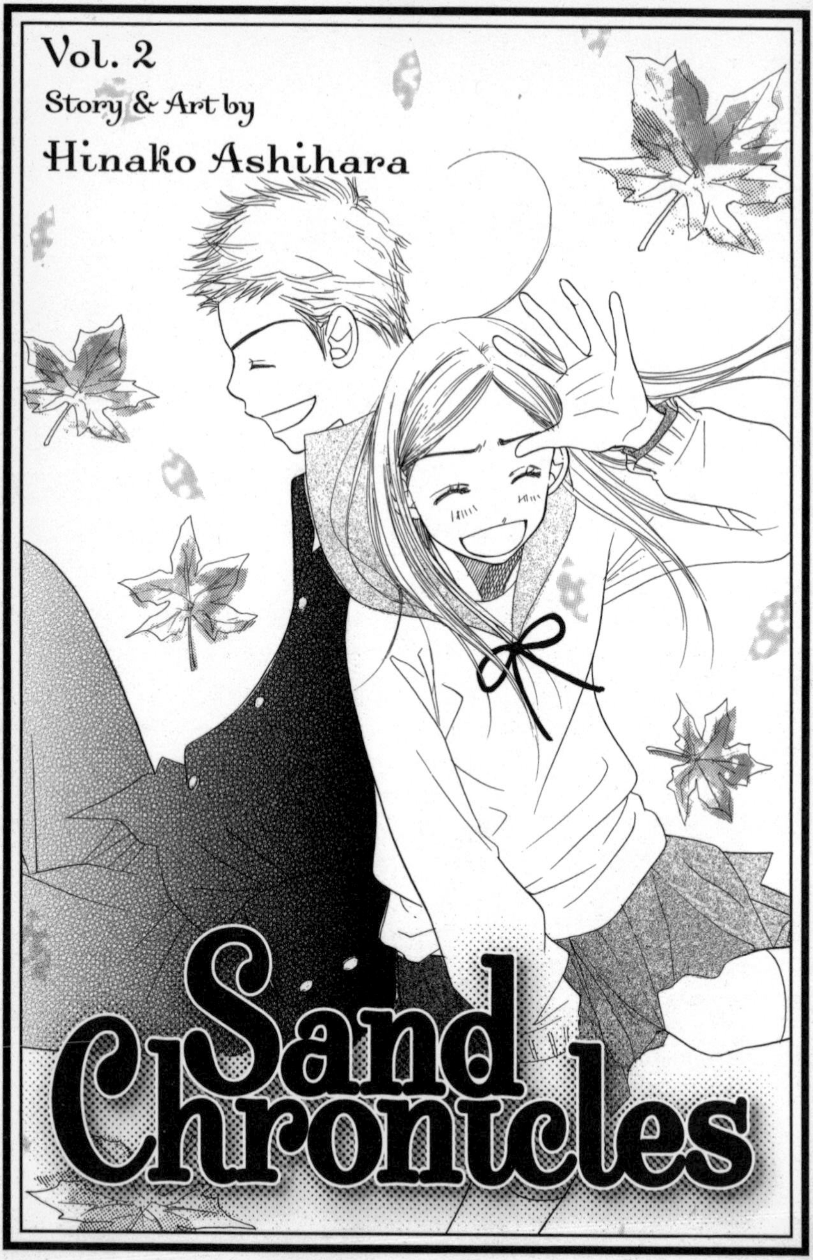
Vol. 2
Story & Art by
Hinako Ashihara
Sand Chronicles

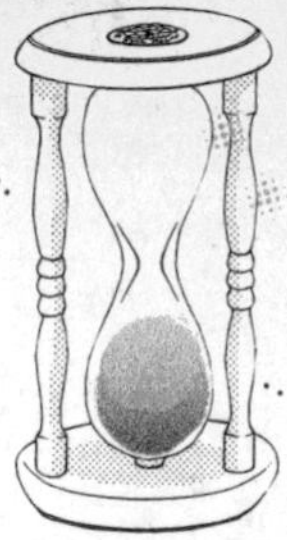

Sand Chronicles

Volume 2

Contents

Story thus far...

After her parents' divorce, Ann moved to Shimane with her mother. At first Ann didn't like living in the country, but then she met Daigo and other kids her age and found a place for herself. After her mother's suicide, she started dating Daigo…

Main characters

Shika Tsukishima
Fuji's younger sister. Soft-spoken and popular with boys.

Fuji Tsukishima
The son of an important family. Doesn't like group activities.

Daigo Kitamura
Boyish and rough but also kind.

Ann Uekusa
Strong-willed, but sensitive like her mother.

AUTUMN, AGE 15: TWILIGHT (WHO IS THAT?)

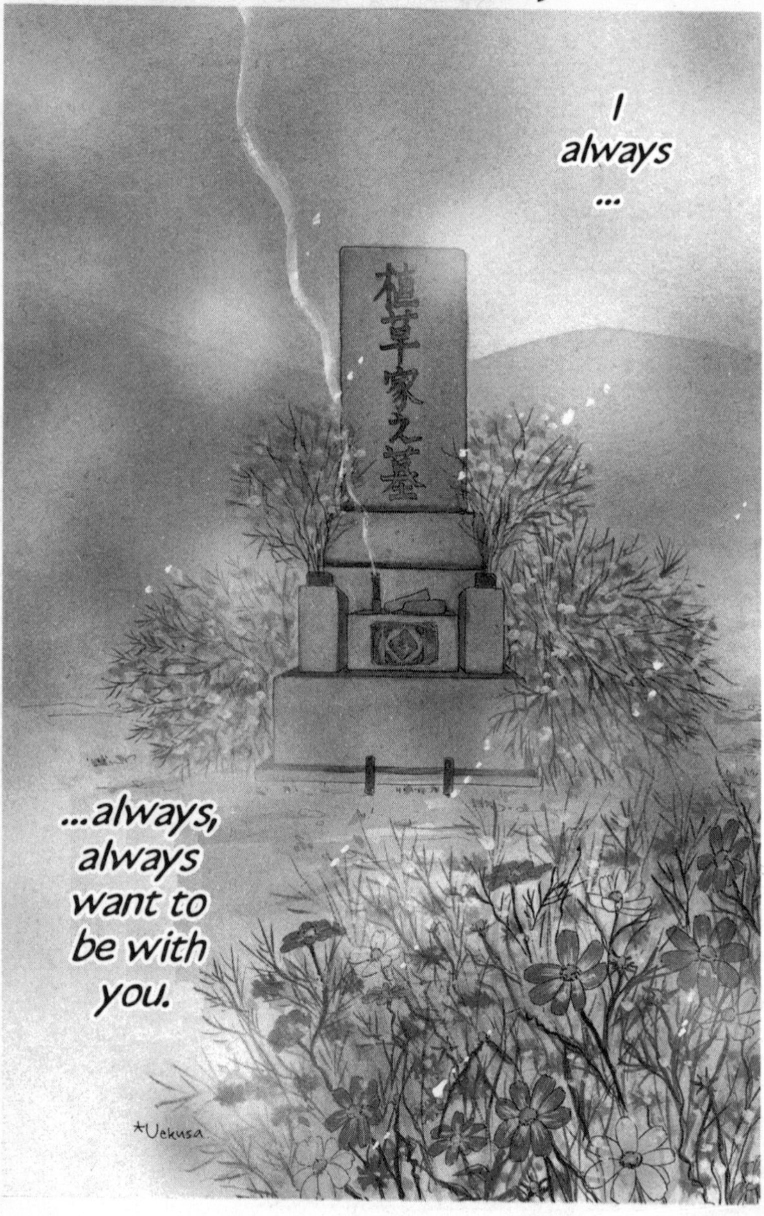
I always ...
植草家之墓
...always, always want to be with you.
*Uekusa

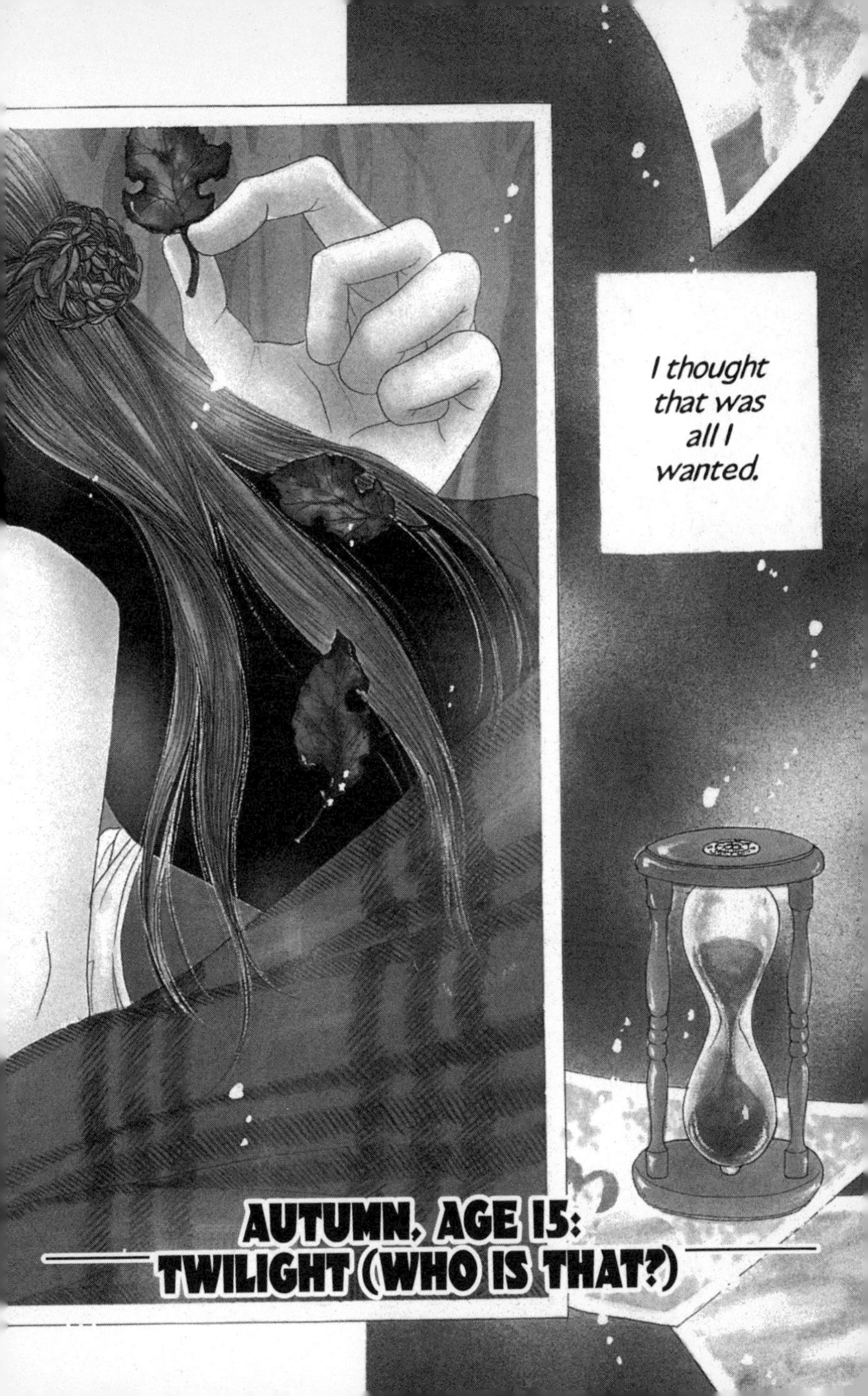
I thought that was all I wanted.
AUTUMN, AGE 15:
TWILIGHT (WHO IS THAT?)

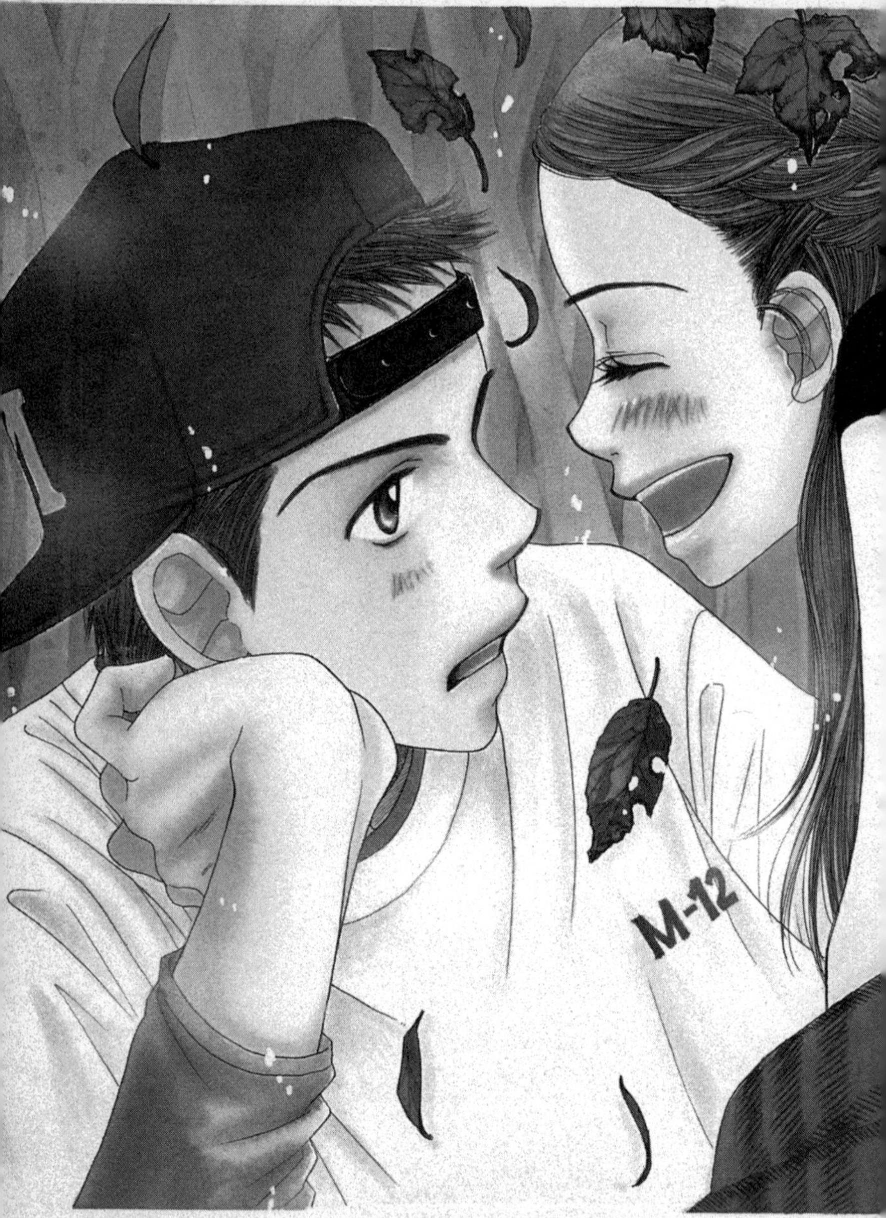
M-12

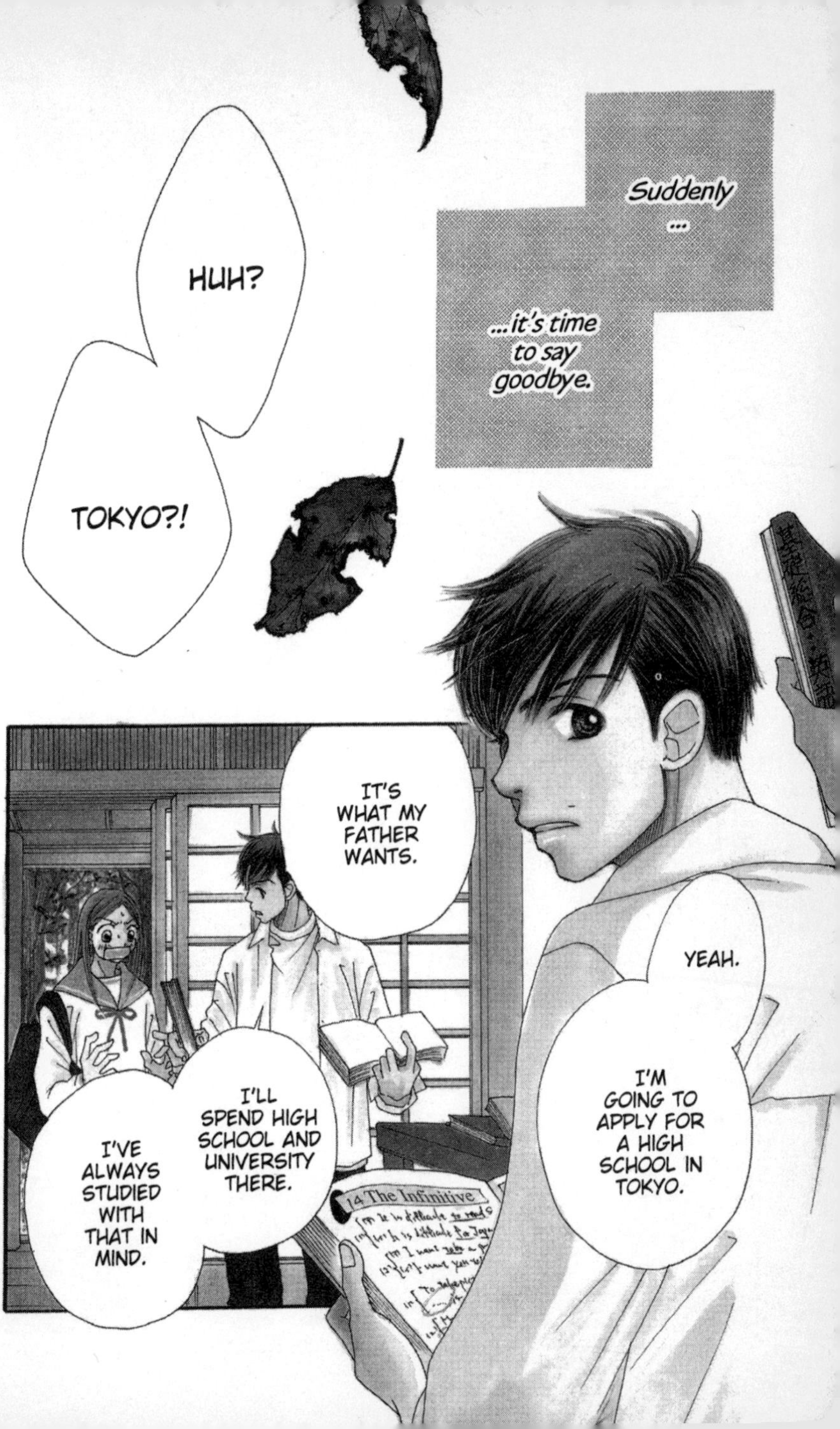
Suddenly ...
...it's time to say goodbye.
HUH?
TOKYO?!
YEAH.
I'M GOING TO APPLY FOR A HIGH SCHOOL IN TOKYO.
IT'S WHAT MY FATHER WANTS.
I'LL SPEND HIGH SCHOOL AND UNIVERSITY THERE.
I'VE ALWAYS STUDIED WITH THAT IN MIND.
14 The Infinitive

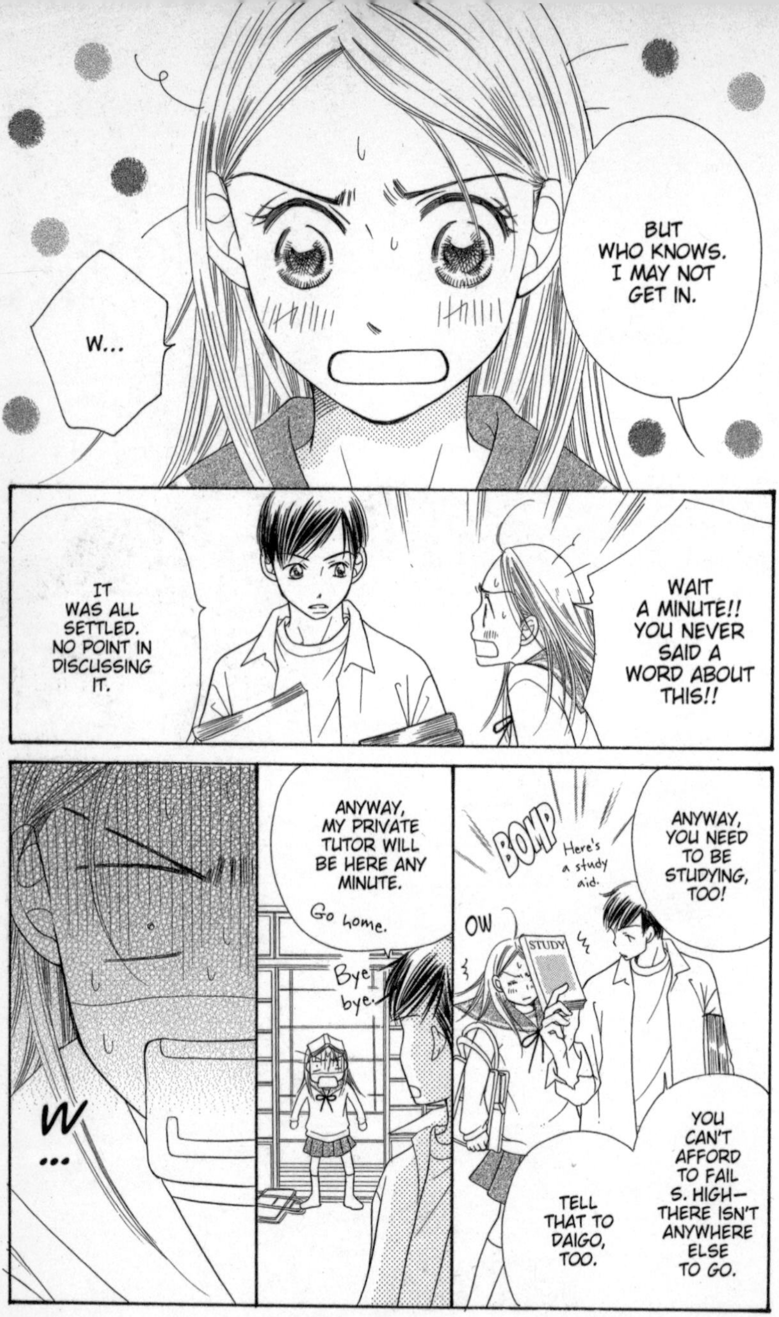
BUT WHO KNOWS. I MAY NOT GET IN.
W...
WAIT A MINUTE!! YOU NEVER SAID A WORD ABOUT THIS!!
IT WAS ALL SETTLED. NO POINT IN DISCUSSING IT.
ANYWAY, YOU NEED TO BE STUDYING, TOO!
BOMP
Here's a study aid.
OW
STUDY
YOU CAN'T AFFORD TO FAIL S. HIGH—THERE ISN'T ANYWHERE ELSE TO GO.
TELL THAT TO DAIGO, TOO.
ANYWAY, MY PRIVATE TUTOR WILL BE HERE ANY MINUTE.
Go home.
Bye bye.
W...

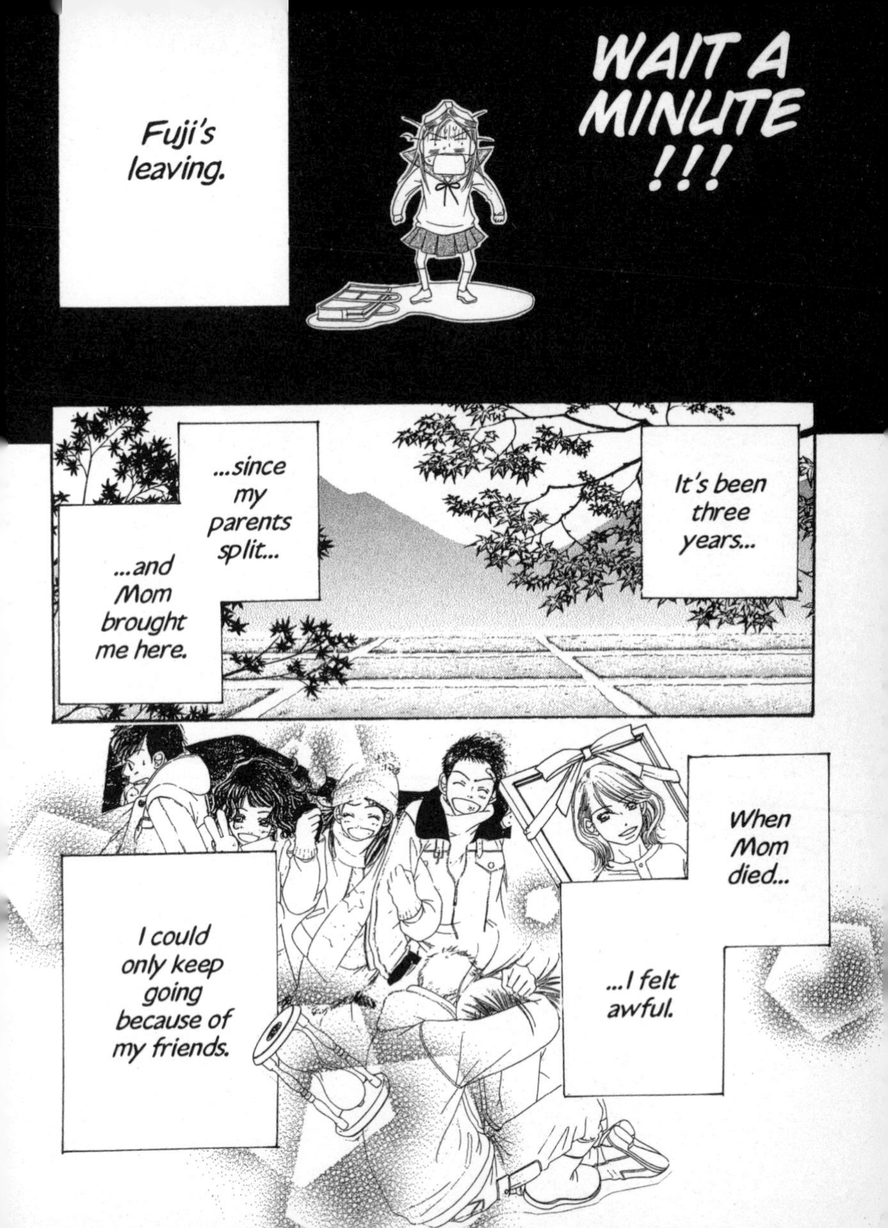
WAIT A MINUTE !!!
Fuji's leaving.
It's been three years...
...since my parents split...
...and Mom brought me here.
When Mom died...
...I felt awful.
I could only keep going because of my friends.

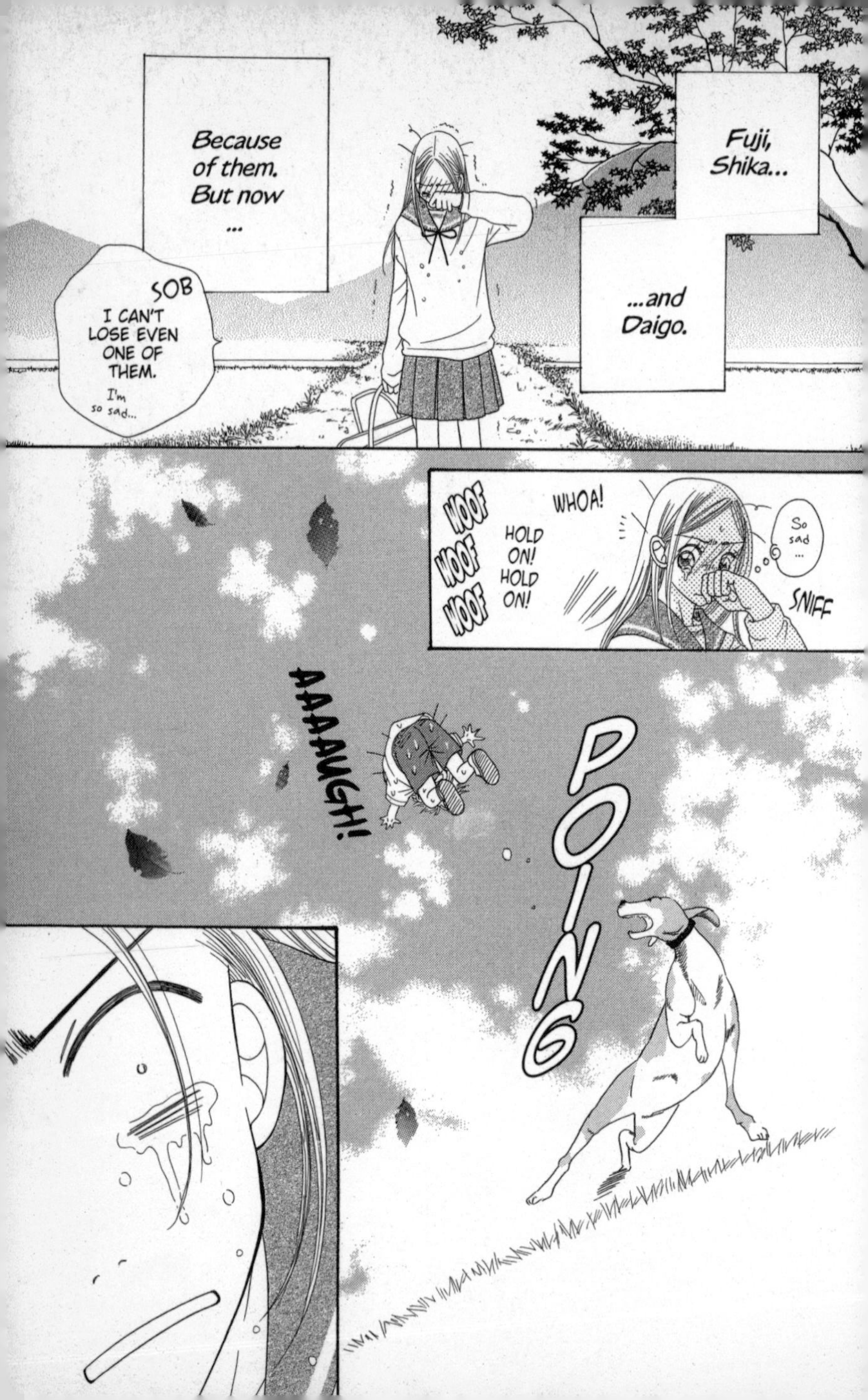

Fuji, Shika...
...and Daigo.
Because of them. But now ...
SOB
I CAN'T LOSE EVEN ONE OF THEM.
I'm so sad...
So sad ...
SNIFF
WHOA!
HOLD ON! HOLD ON!
WOOF WOOF WOOF
POING
AAAAUGH!

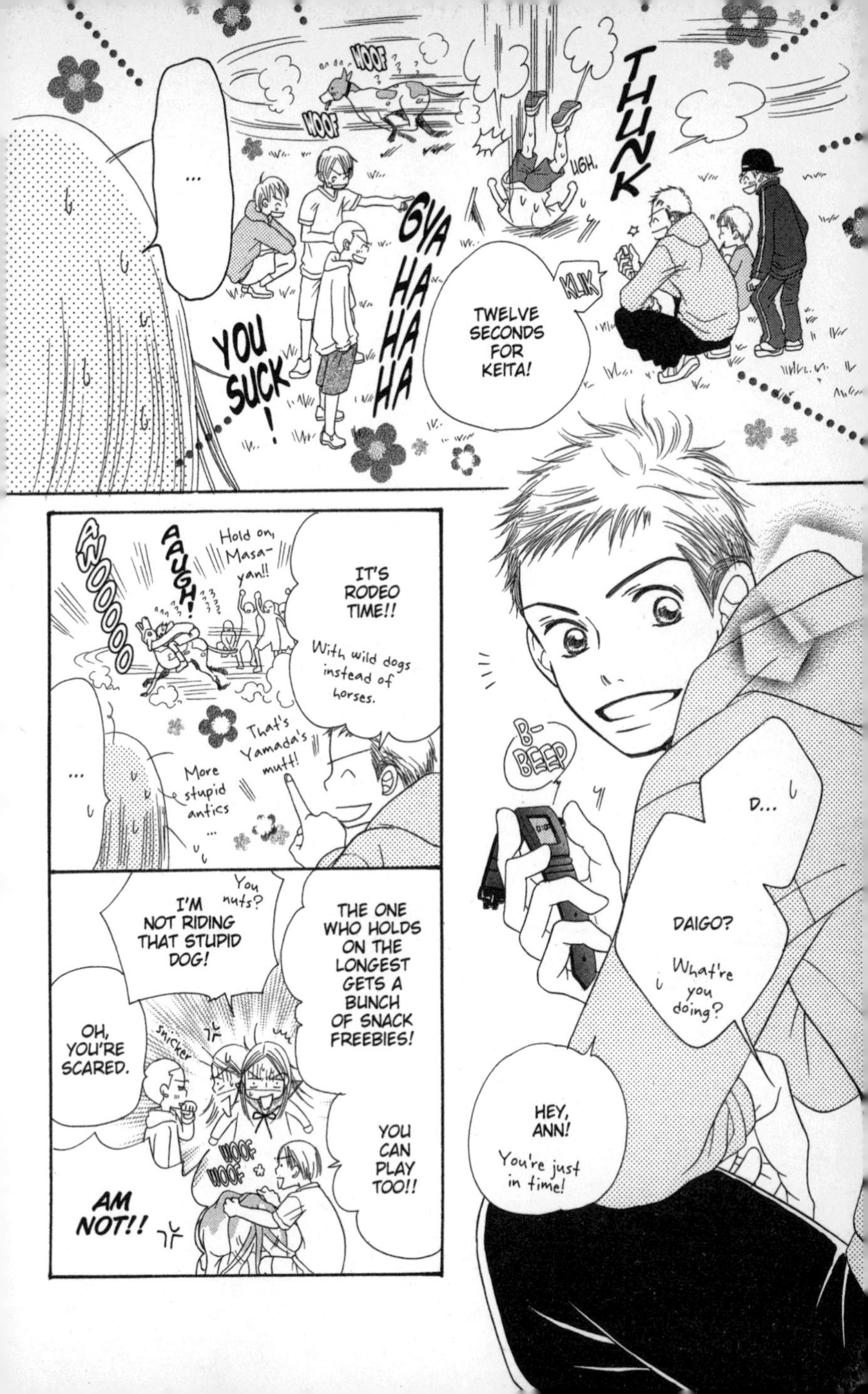
THUNK
UGH.
KLIK
TWELVE SECONDS FOR KEITA!
WOOF
WOOF
GYA HA HA HA HA
YOU SUCK!
...
D...
DAIGO?
What're you doing?
B-BEEP
HEY, ANN!
You're just in time!
IT'S RODEO TIME!!
With wild dogs instead of horses.
Hold on, Masa-yan!!
AAUGH!
AWOOOOO
That's Yamada's mutt!
More stupid antics...
...
THE ONE WHO HOLDS ON THE LONGEST GETS A BUNCH OF SNACK FREEBIES!
You nuts?
I'M NOT RIDING THAT STUPID DOG!
YOU CAN PLAY TOO!!
OH, YOU'RE SCARED.
snicker
WOOF
WOOF
AM NOT!!

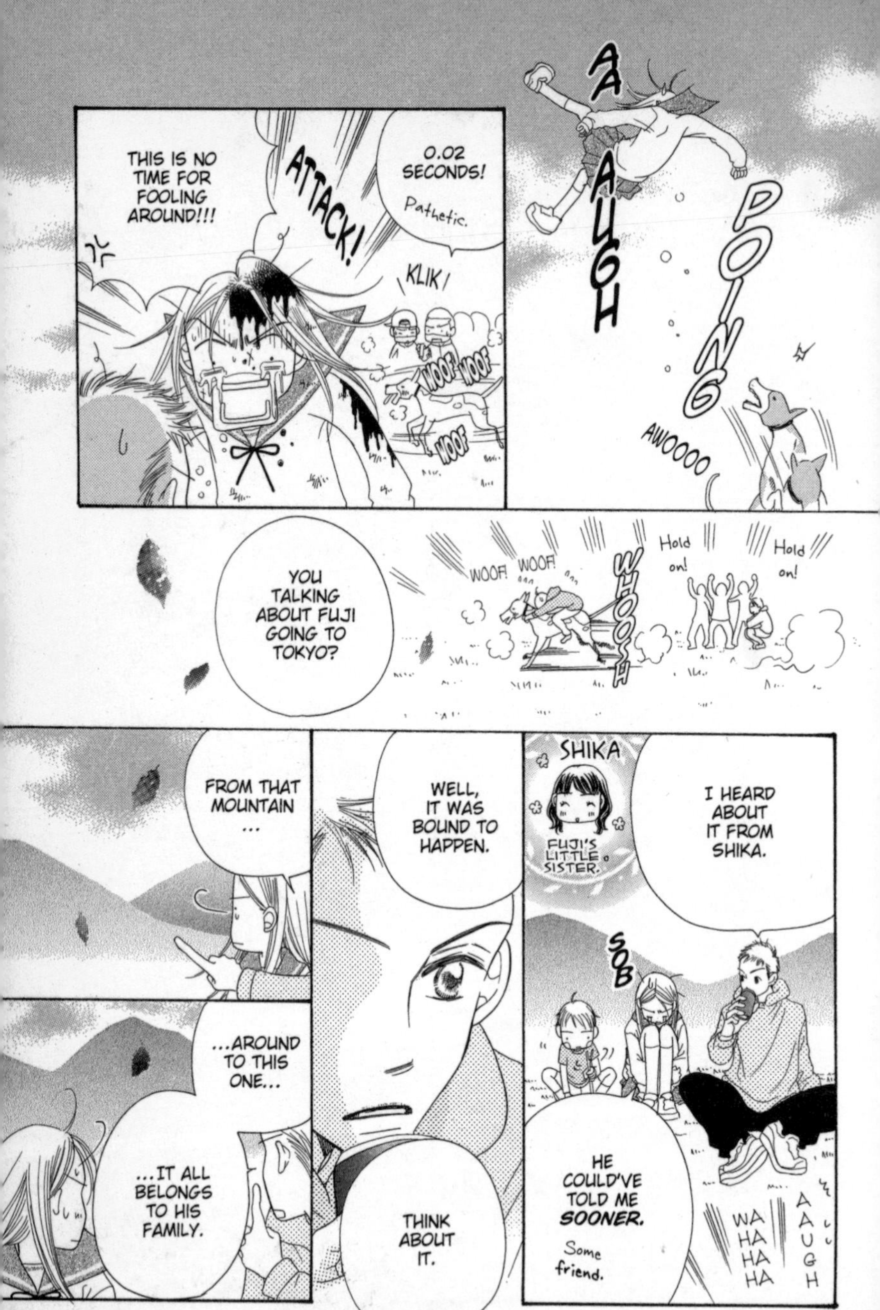
AAAUGH
POING
AWOOOO
0.02 SECONDS!
Pathetic.
ATTACK!
THIS IS NO TIME FOR FOOLING AROUND!!!
KLIK
WOOF WOOF
WOOF
Hold on!
Hold on!
WHOOOSH
WOOF! WOOF!
YOU TALKING ABOUT FUJI GOING TO TOKYO?
I HEARD ABOUT IT FROM SHIKA.
SHIKA
FUJI'S LITTLE SISTER.
SOB
HE COULD'VE TOLD ME SOONER.
Some friend.
AAUGH
WAHAHAHAHA
WELL, IT WAS BOUND TO HAPPEN.
THINK ABOUT IT.
FROM THAT MOUNTAIN...
...AROUND TO THIS ONE...
...IT ALL BELONGS TO HIS FAMILY.

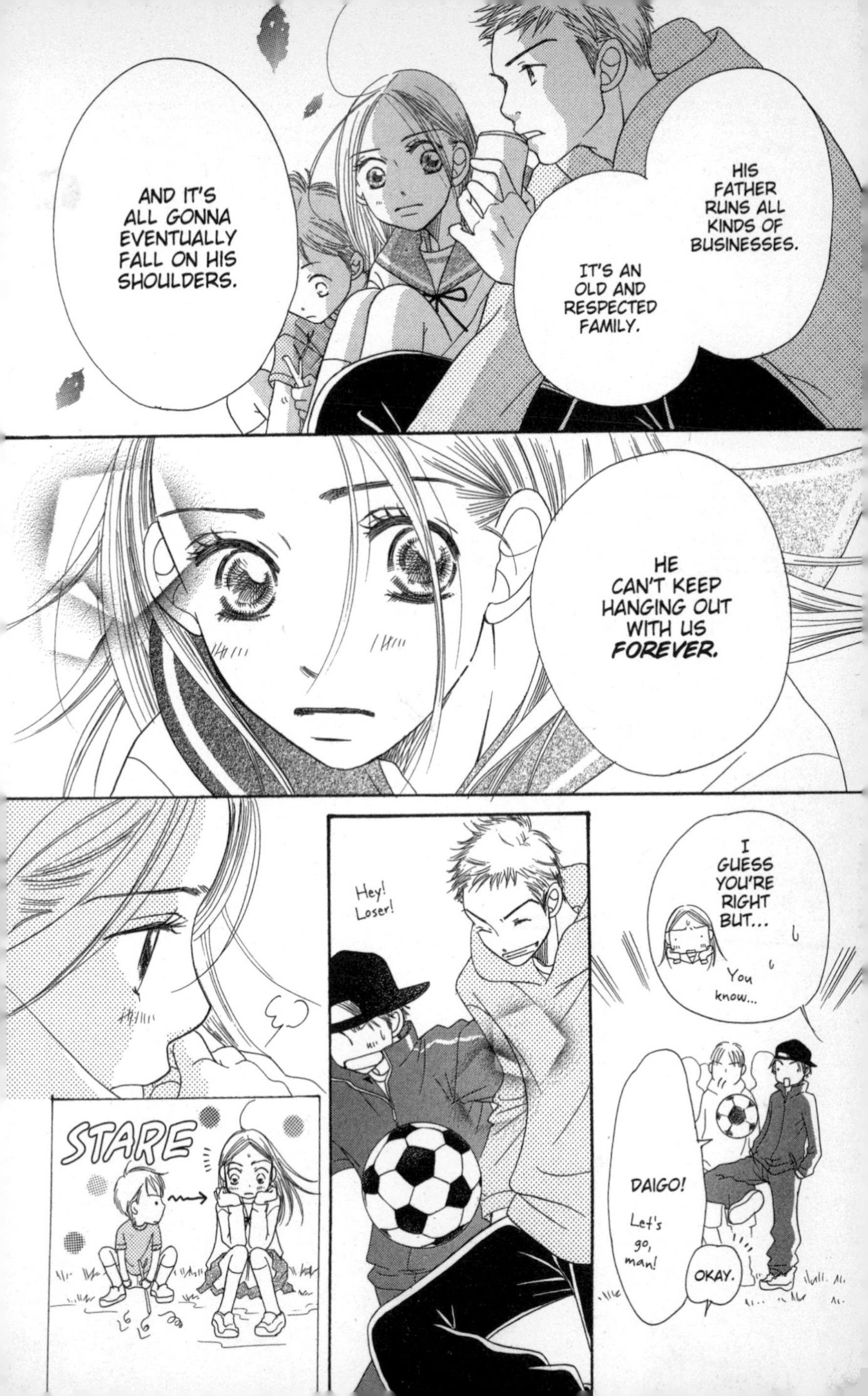
HIS FATHER RUNS ALL KINDS OF BUSINESSES.
IT'S AN OLD AND RESPECTED FAMILY.
AND IT'S ALL GONNA EVENTUALLY FALL ON HIS SHOULDERS.
HE CAN'T KEEP HANGING OUT WITH US *FOREVER.*
I GUESS YOU'RE RIGHT BUT...
You know...
DAIGO!
Let's go, man!
OKAY.
Hey! Loser!
STARE

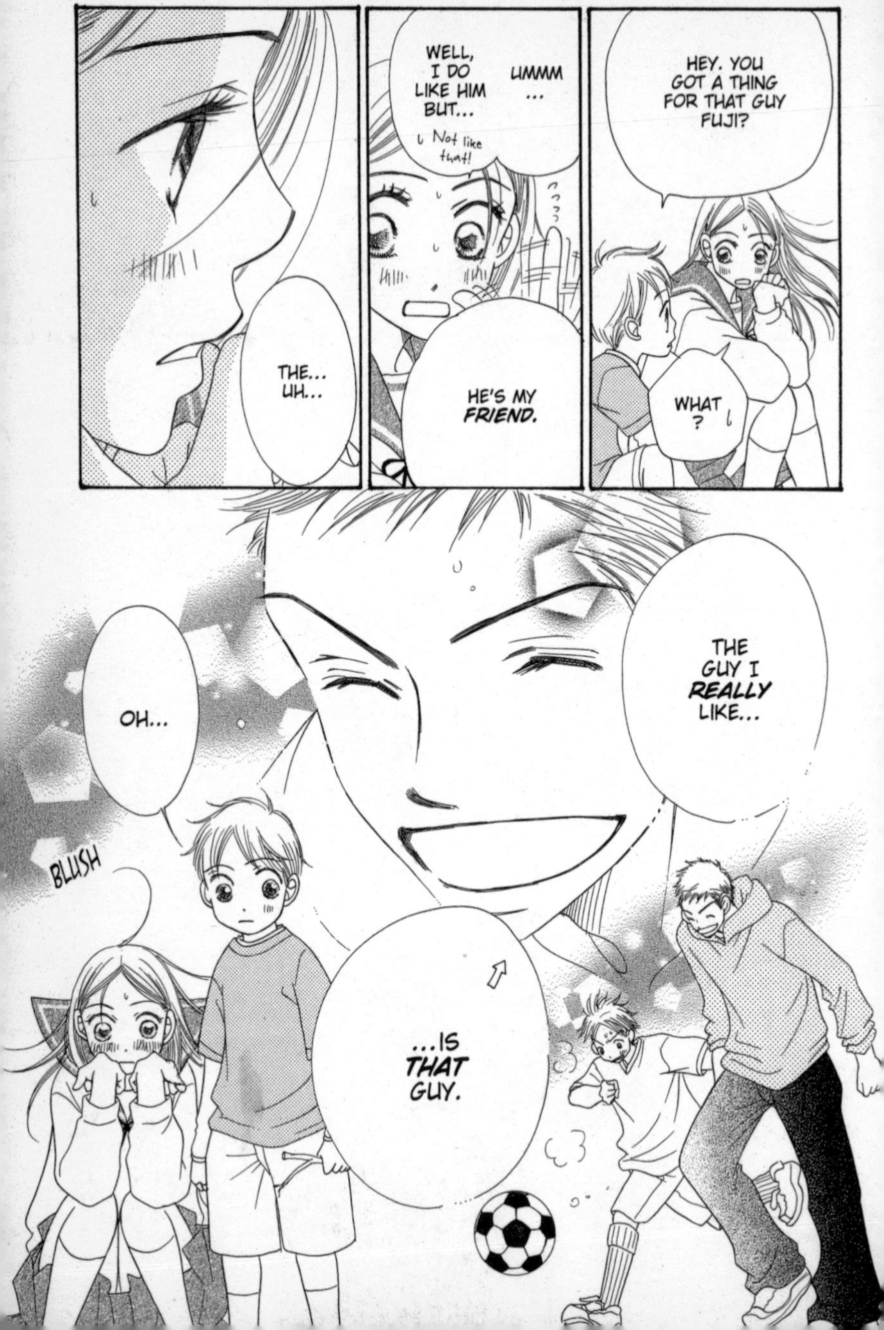
HEY. YOU GOT A THING FOR THAT GUY FUJI?
WHAT ?
UMMM ...
WELL, I DO LIKE HIM BUT...
Not like that!
HE'S MY *FRIEND.*
THE... UH...
THE GUY I *REALLY* LIKE...
...IS *THAT* GUY.
OH...
BLUSH

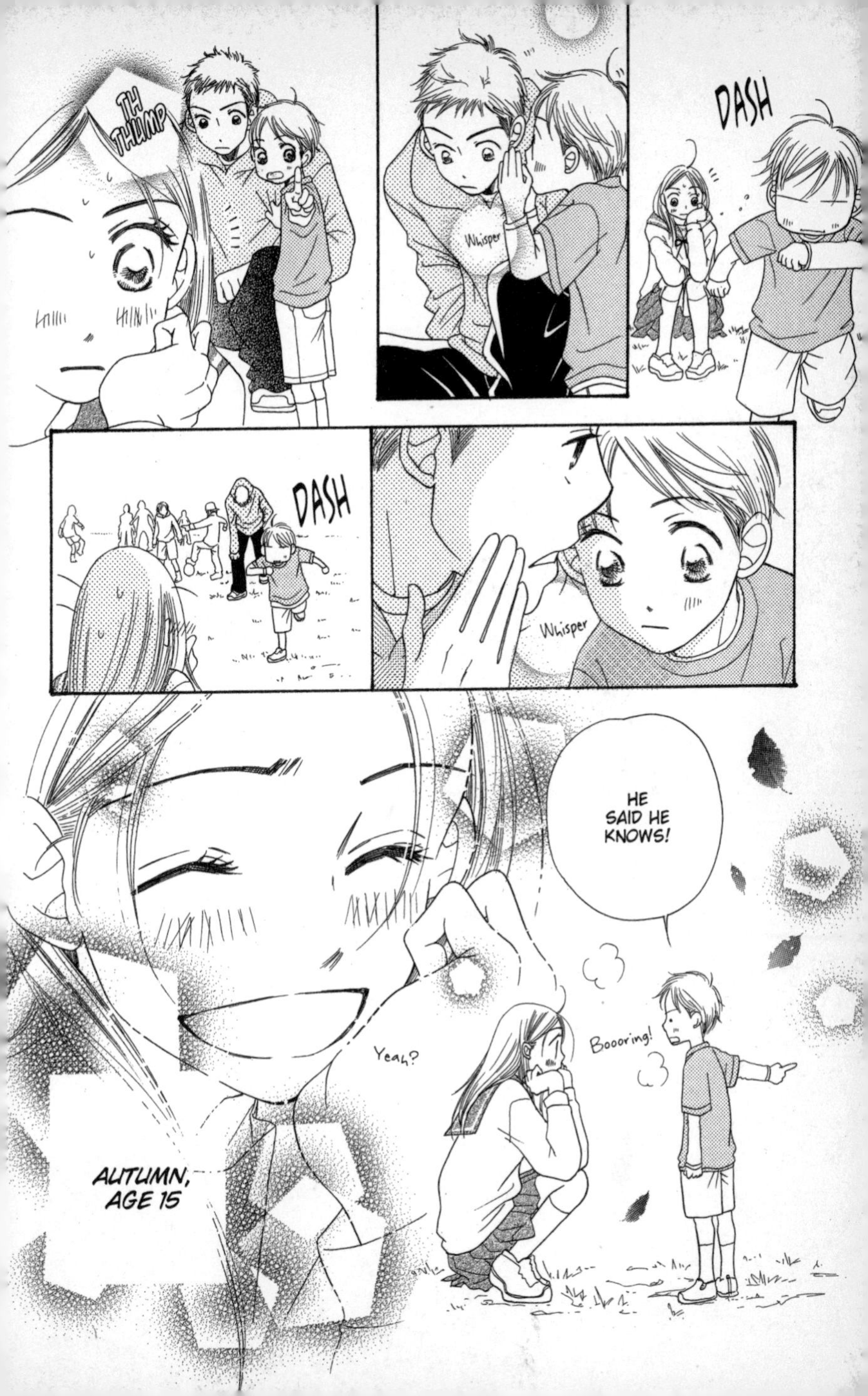
DASH
Whisper
TH THUMP
Whisper
DASH
HE SAID HE KNOWS!
Booooring!
Yeah?
AUTUMN, AGE 15

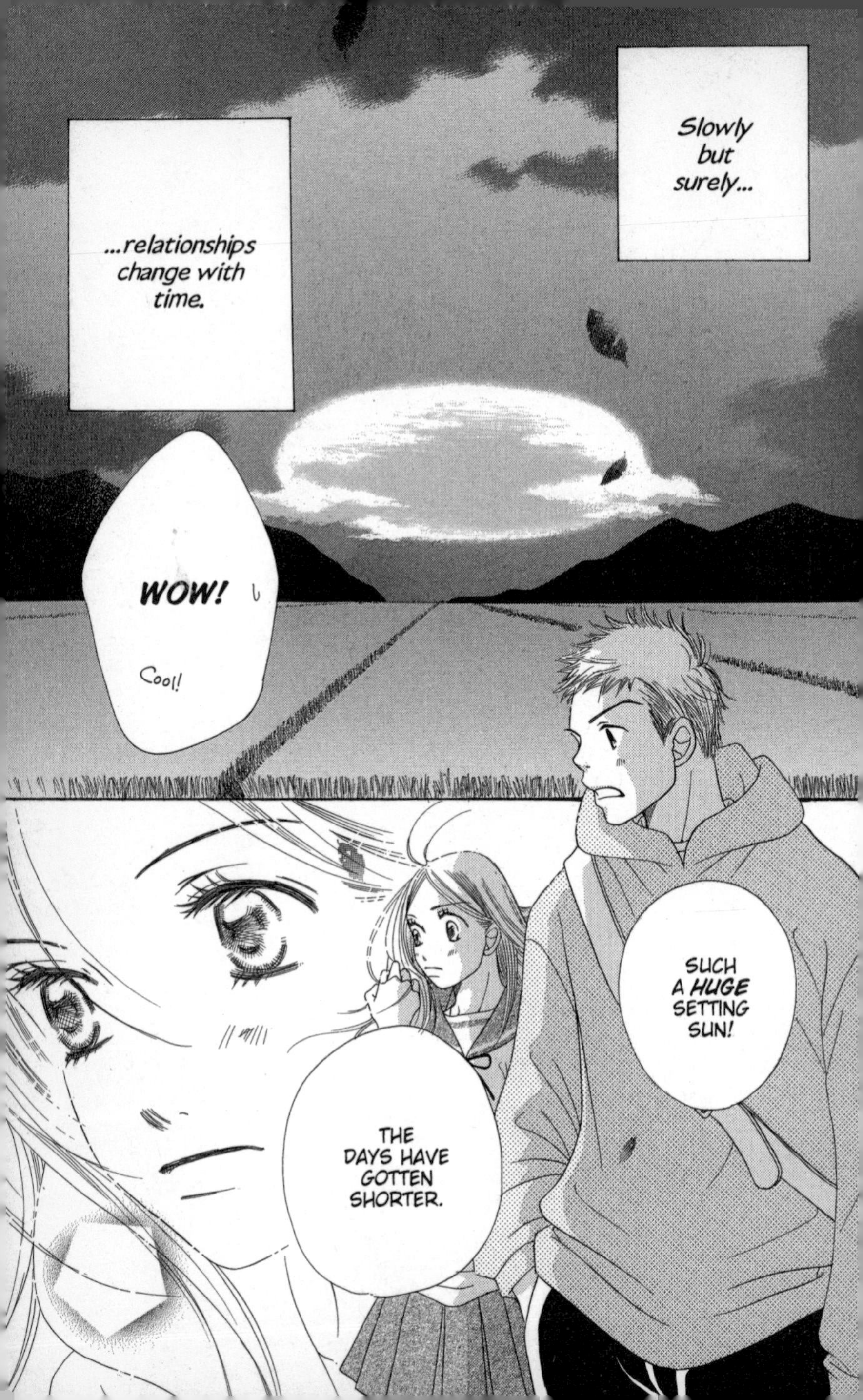

Slowly but surely...
...relationships change with time.
WOW!
Cool!
SUCH A HUGE SETTING SUN!
THE DAYS HAVE GOTTEN SHORTER.

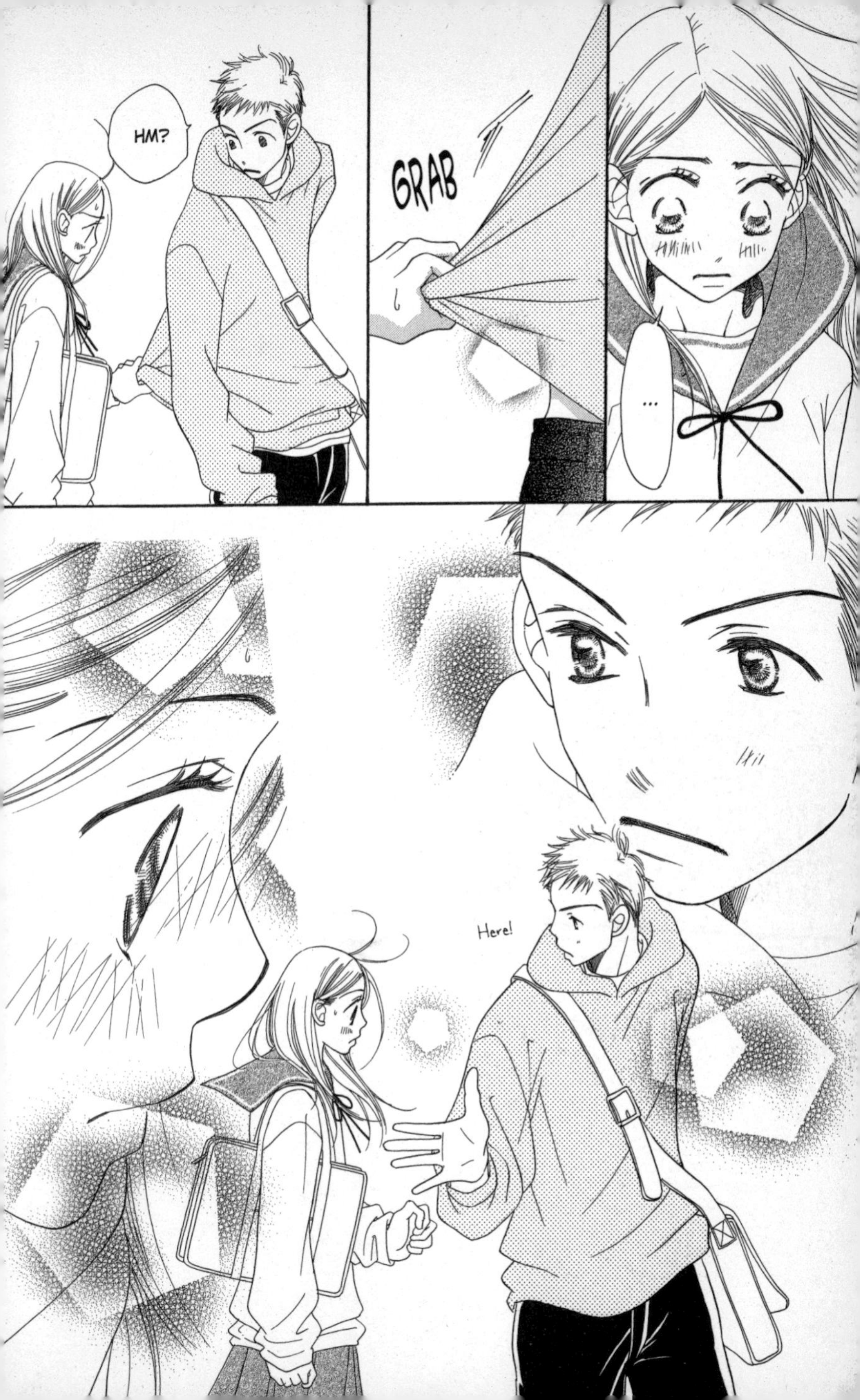
...
GRAB
HM?
Here!

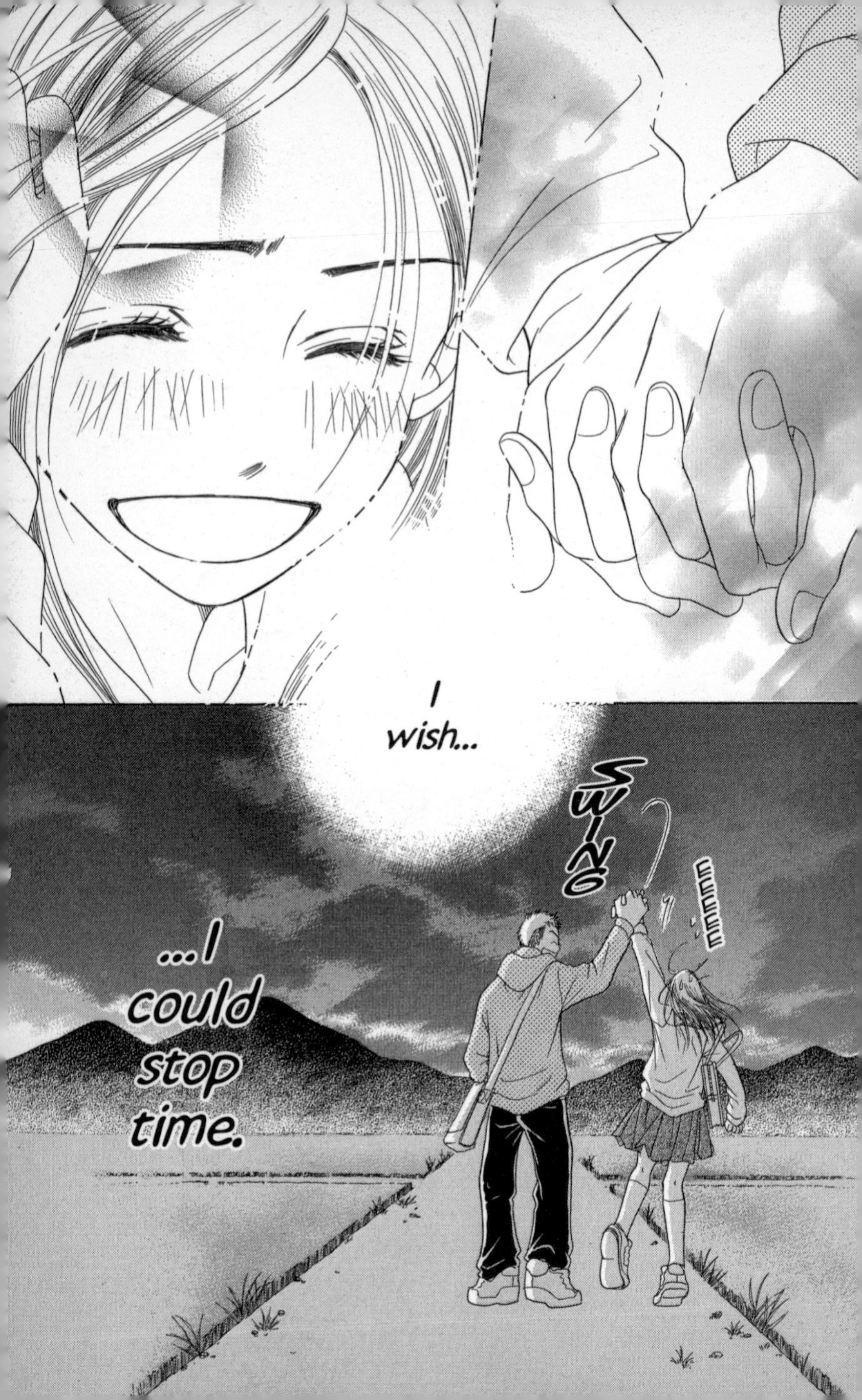

I wish...
SWING
EEEE
...I could stop time.

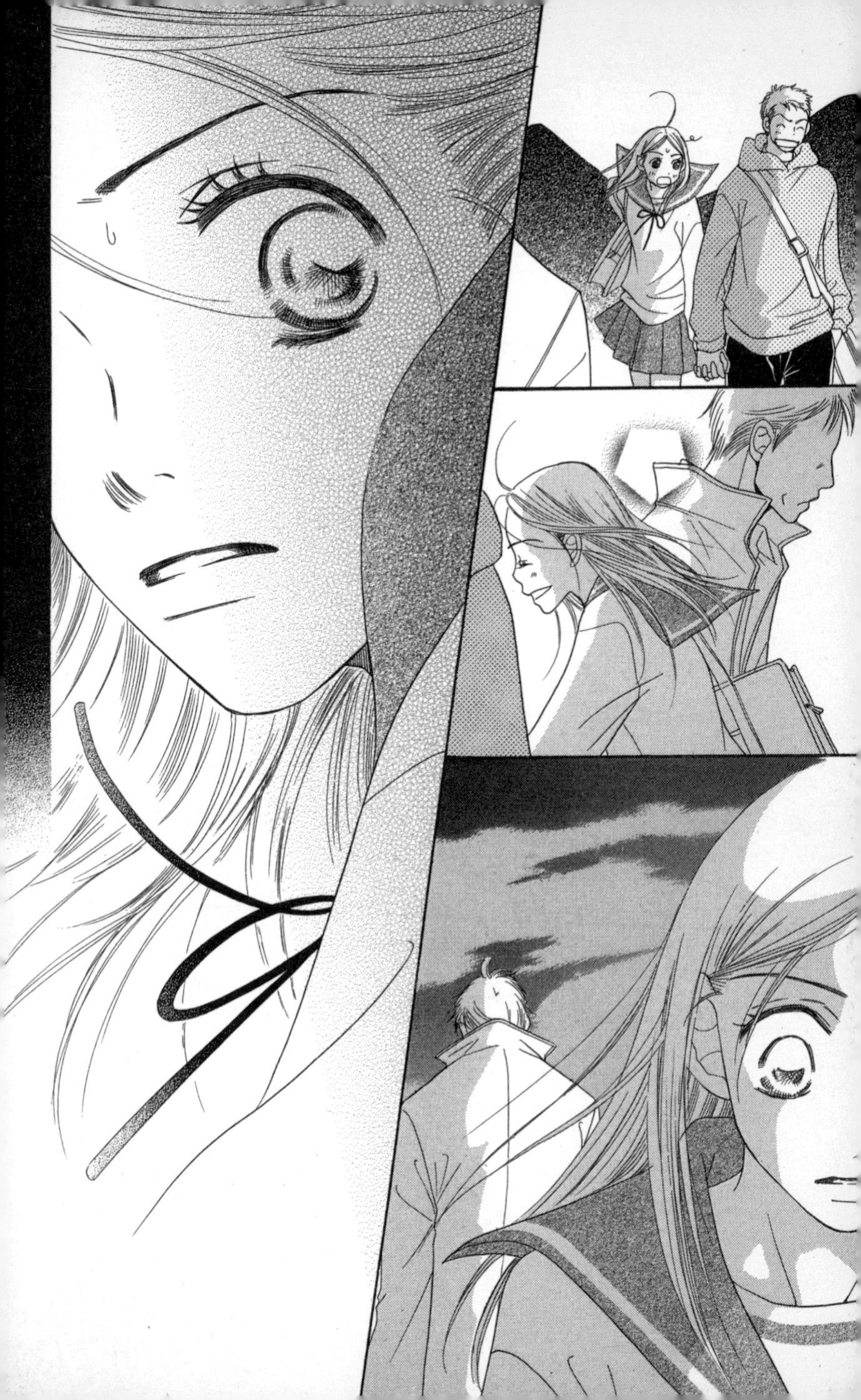

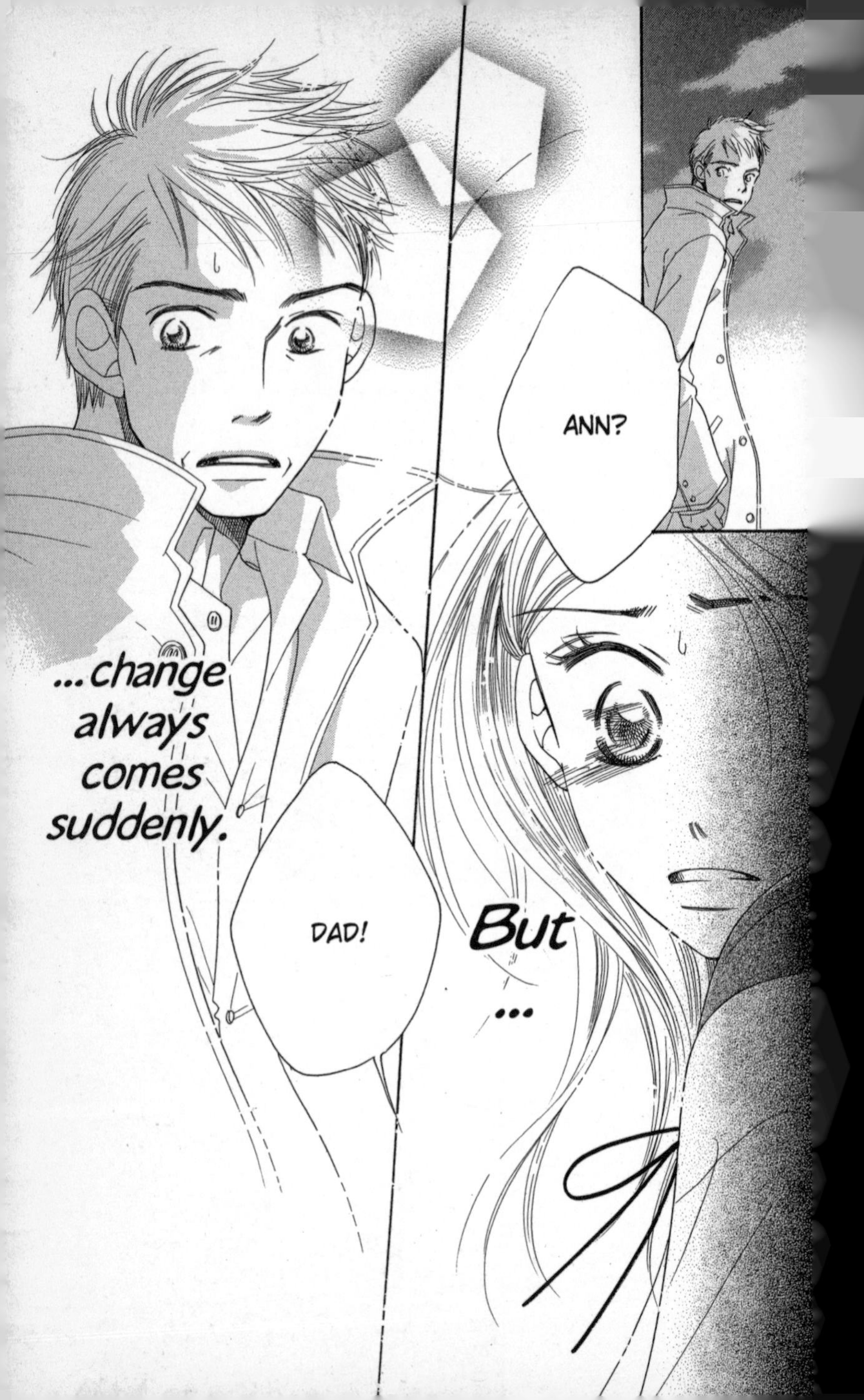
ANN?
But ...
...change always comes suddenly.
DAD!

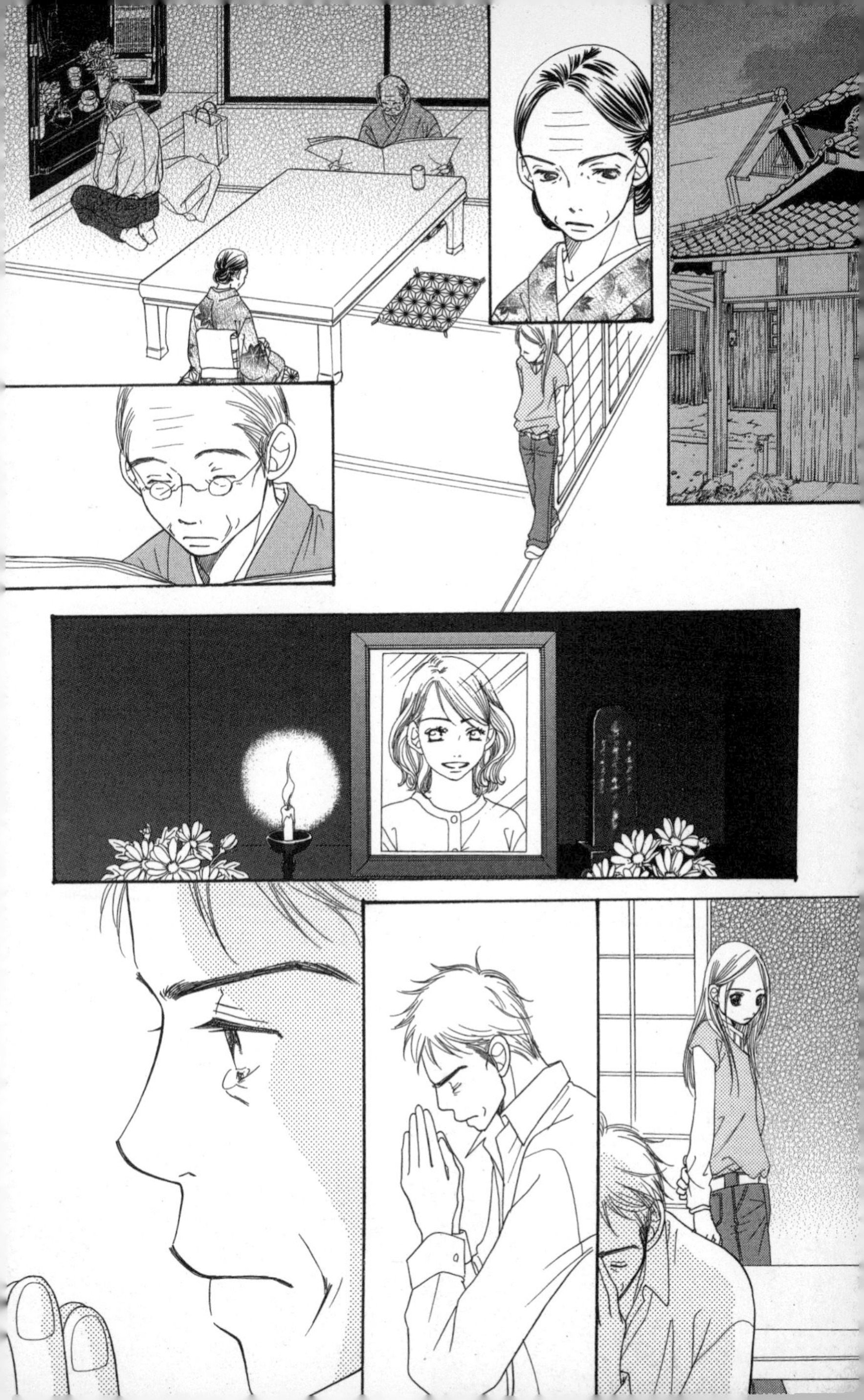

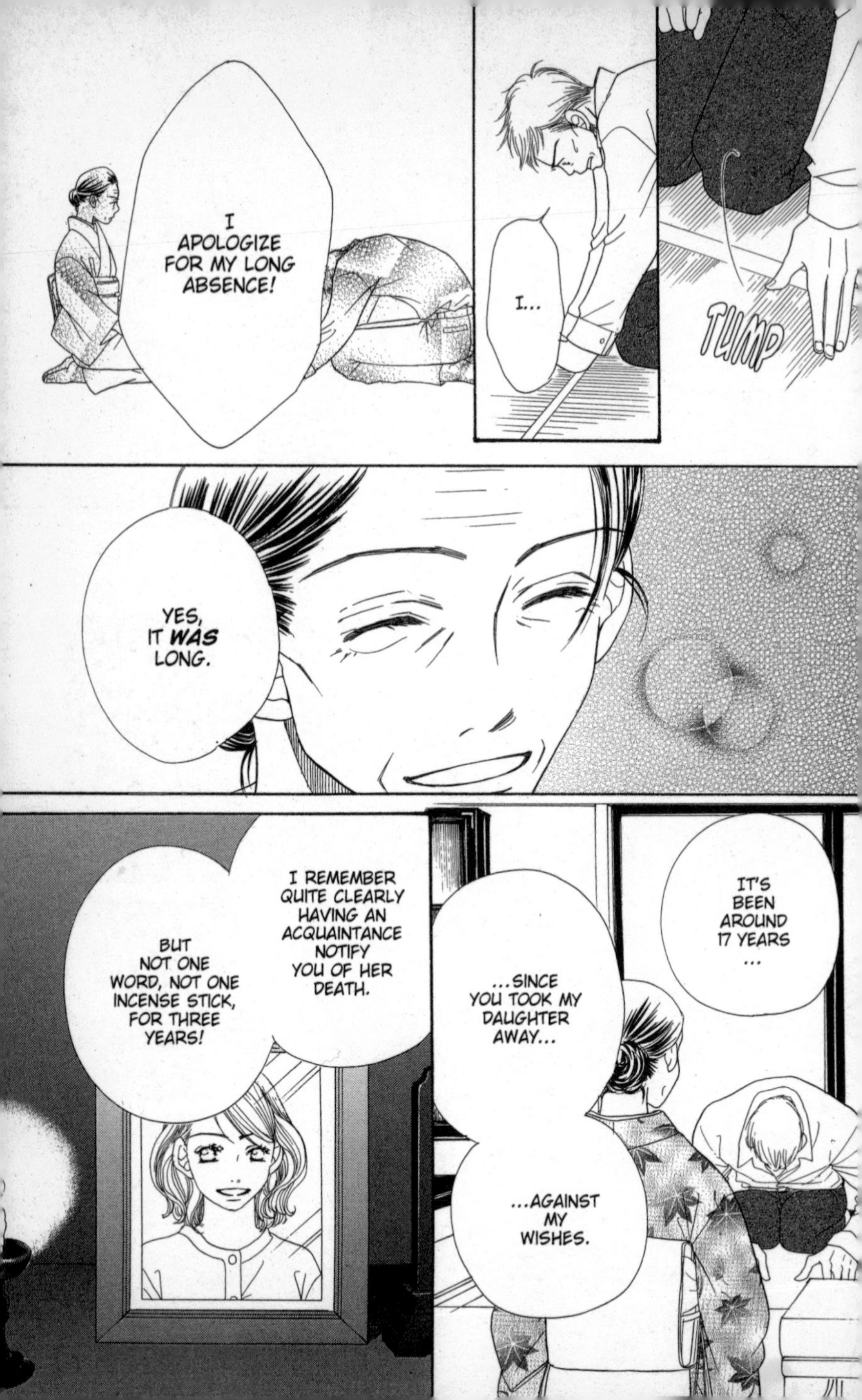
TUMP
I...
I APOLOGIZE FOR MY LONG ABSENCE!
YES, IT WAS LONG.
IT'S BEEN AROUND 17 YEARS...
...SINCE YOU TOOK MY DAUGHTER AWAY...
...AGAINST MY WISHES.
I REMEMBER QUITE CLEARLY HAVING AN ACQUAINTANCE NOTIFY YOU OF HER DEATH.
BUT NOT ONE WORD, NOT ONE INCENSE STICK, FOR THREE YEARS!

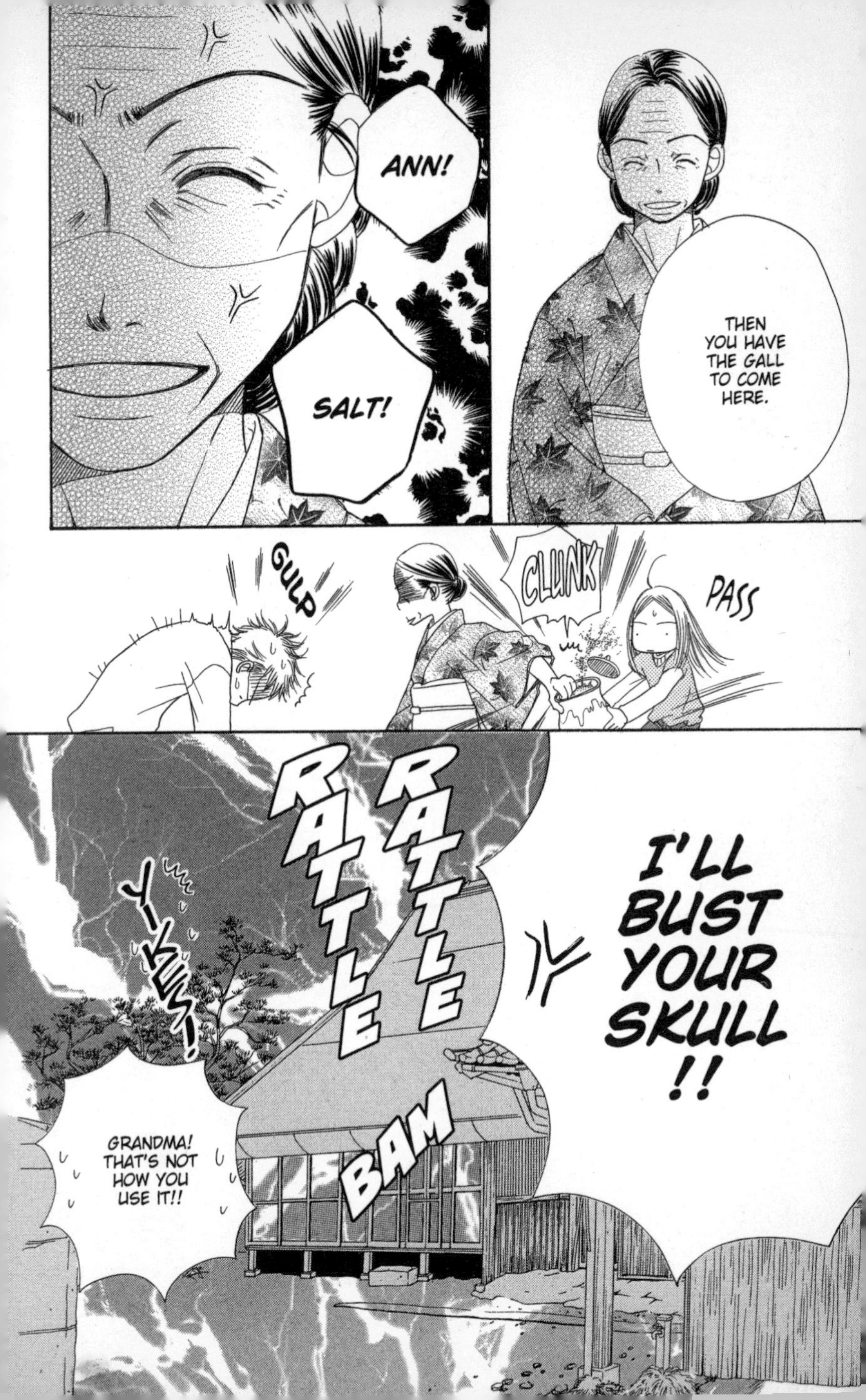
THEN YOU HAVE THE GALL TO COME HERE.
ANN!
SALT!
PASS
CLUNK
GULP
I'LL BUST YOUR SKULL!!
RATTLE
RATTLE
BAM
GRANDMA! THAT'S NOT HOW YOU USE IT!!

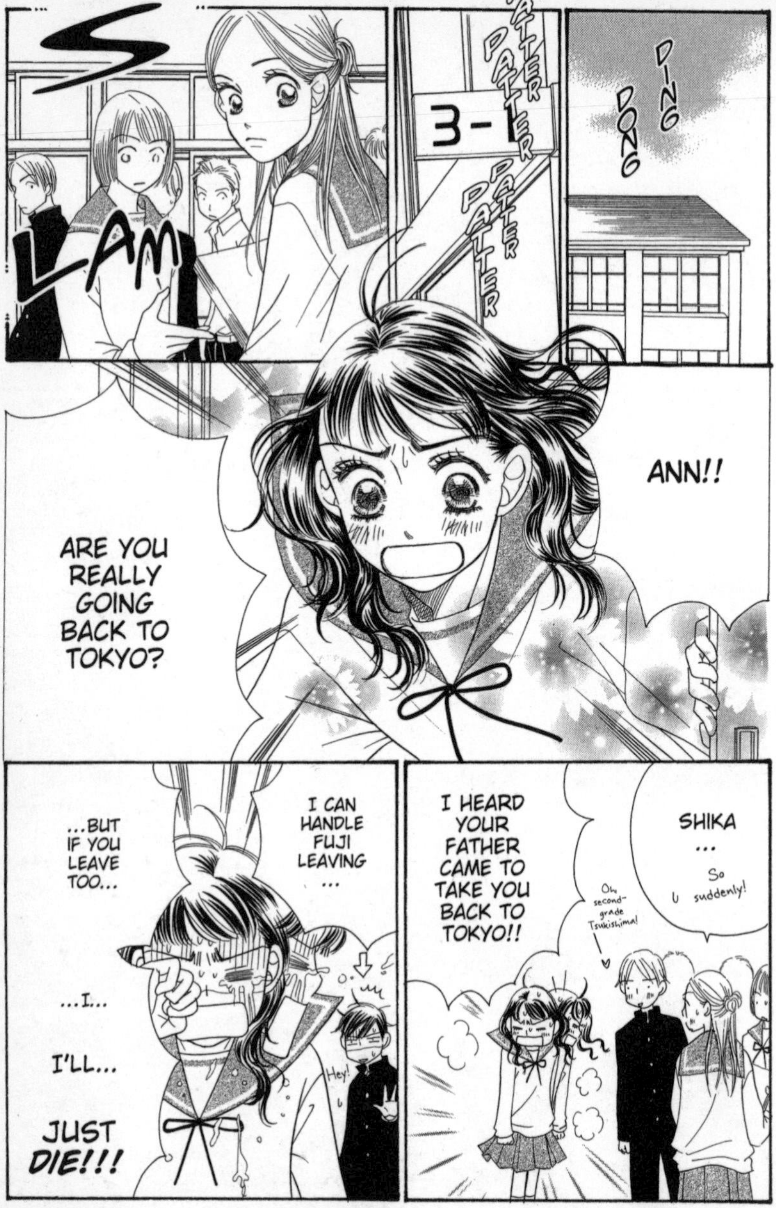
DING DONG
PATTER PATTER
PATTER PATTER
SLAM
ANN!!
ARE YOU REALLY GOING BACK TO TOKYO?
SHIKA...
So suddenly!
Oh second-grade Tsukishima!
I HEARD YOUR FATHER CAME TO TAKE YOU BACK TO TOKYO!!
I CAN HANDLE FUJI LEAVING...
...BUT IF YOU LEAVE TOO...
...I...
I'LL...
JUST DIE!!!
Hey!

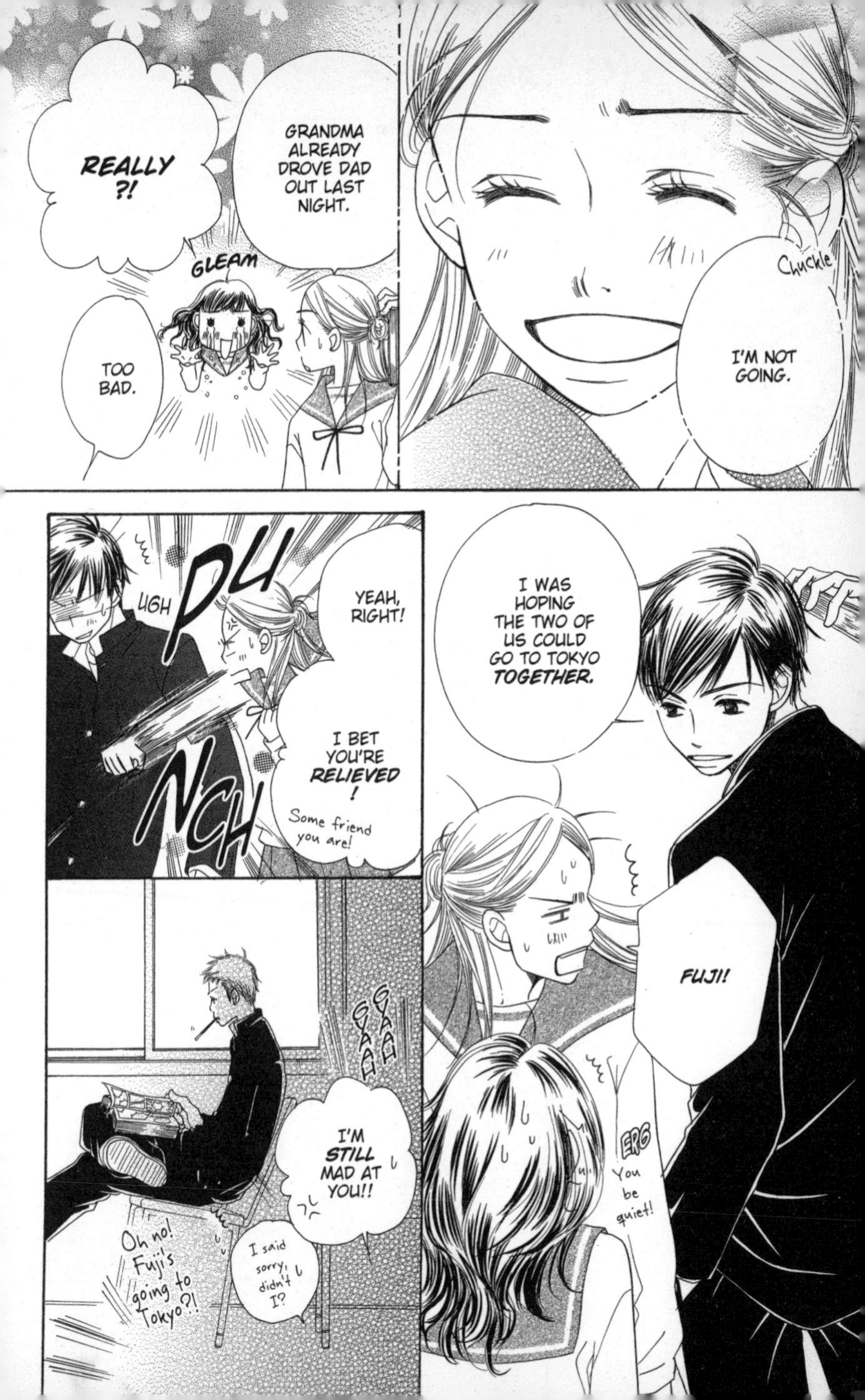
Chuckle
I'M NOT GOING.
GRANDMA ALREADY DROVE DAD OUT LAST NIGHT.
REALLY?!
GLEAM
TOO BAD.
I WAS HOPING THE TWO OF US COULD GO TO TOKYO TOGETHER.
FUJI!
ERG
You be quiet!
YEAH, RIGHT!
PUNCH
UGH
I BET YOU'RE RELIEVED!
Some friend you are!
GYAAH
GYAAH
I'M STILL MAD AT YOU!!
I said sorry, didn't I?
Oh no! Fuji's going to Tokyo?!

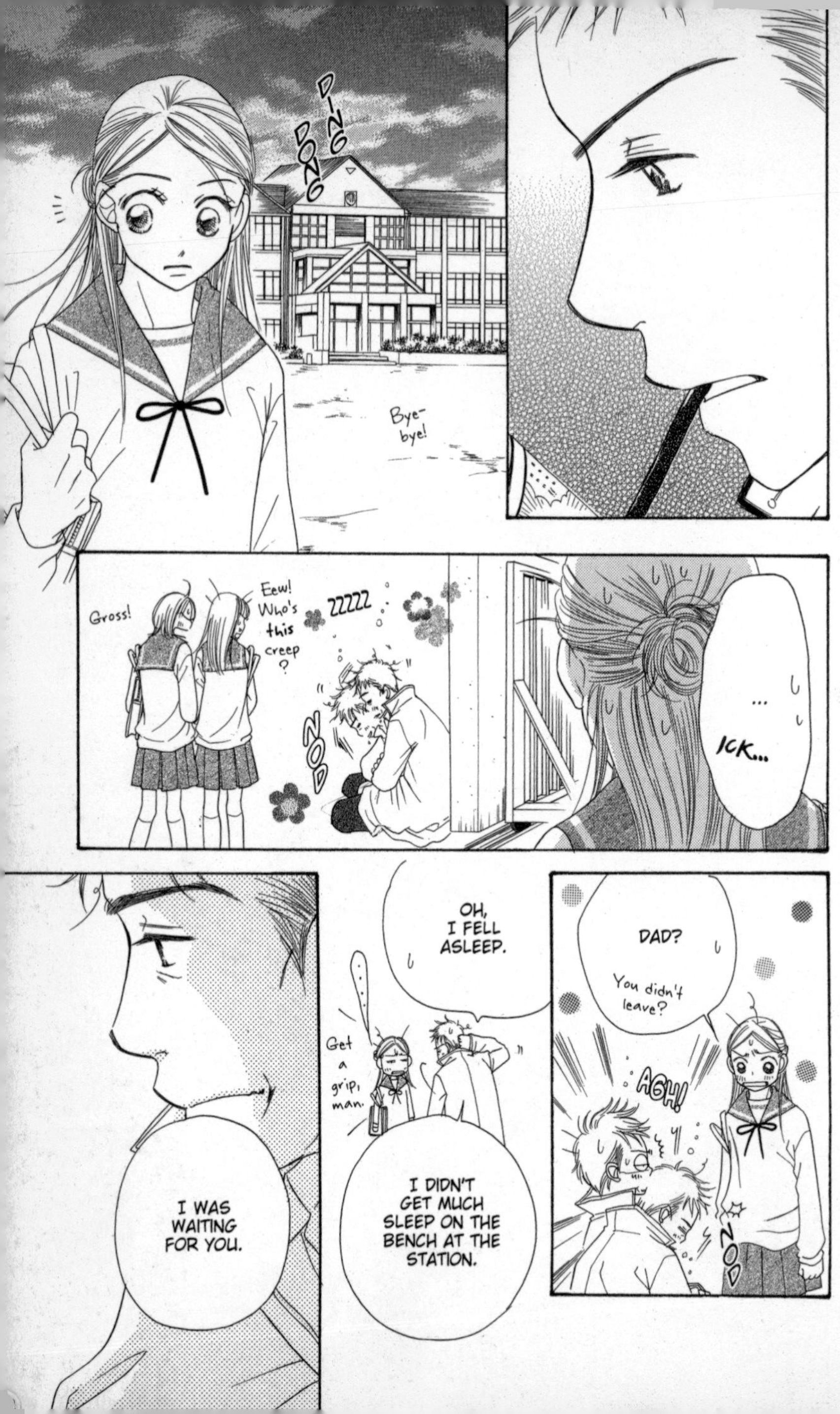
DING
DONG
Bye-bye!
...
ICK...
ZZZZZ
Eew! Who's this creep?
Gross!
NOD
DAD?
You didn't leave?
AGH!
NOD
OH, I FELL ASLEEP.
Get a grip, man.
I DIDN'T GET MUCH SLEEP ON THE BENCH AT THE STATION.
I WAS WAITING FOR YOU.

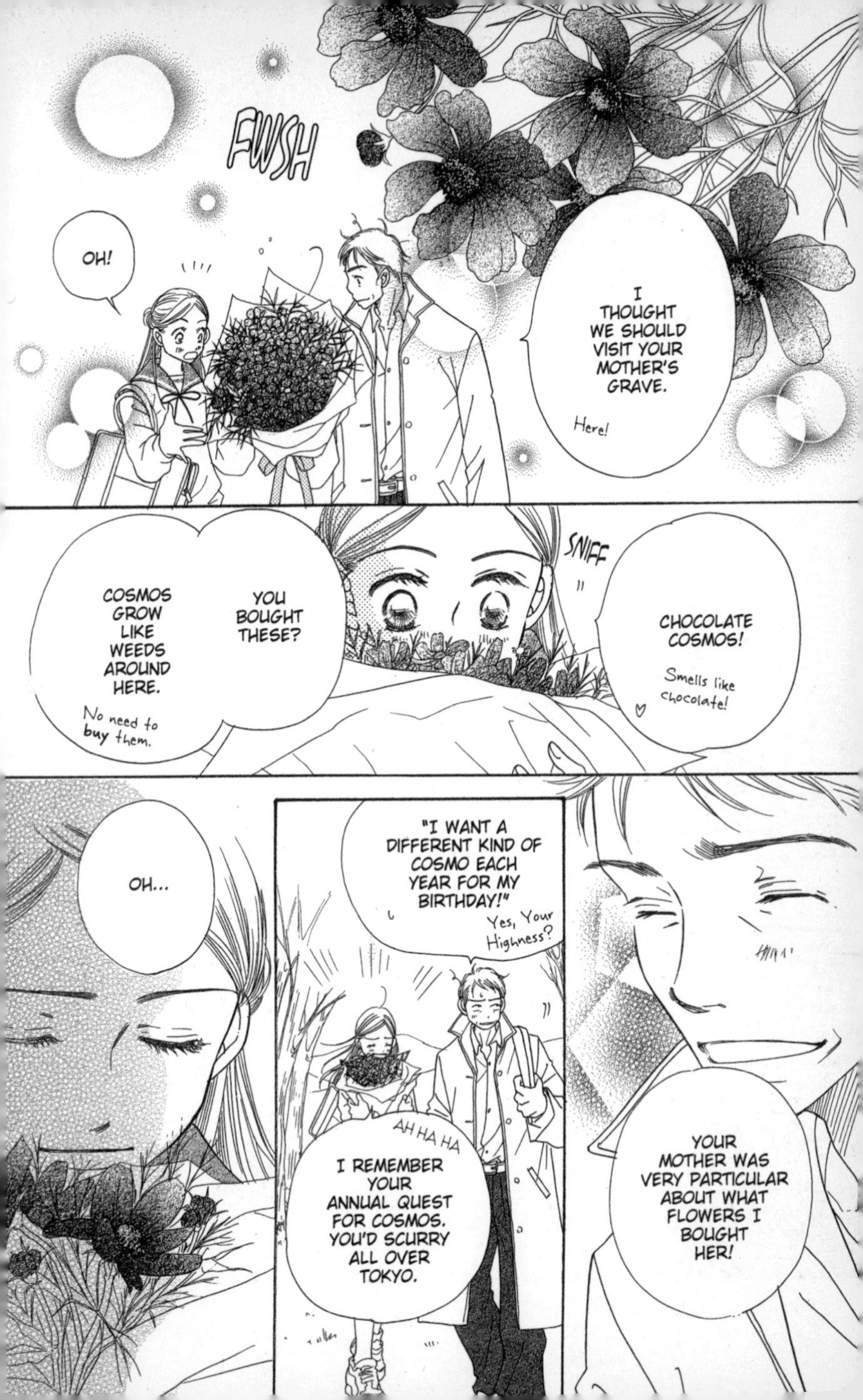
I THOUGHT WE SHOULD VISIT YOUR MOTHER'S GRAVE.
Here!
FWSH
OH!
CHOCOLATE COSMOS!
Smells like chocolate!
SNIFF
YOU BOUGHT THESE?
COSMOS GROW LIKE WEEDS AROUND HERE.
No need to buy them.
YOUR MOTHER WAS VERY PARTICULAR ABOUT WHAT FLOWERS I BOUGHT HER!
"I WANT A DIFFERENT KIND OF COSMO EACH YEAR FOR MY BIRTHDAY!"
Yes, Your Highness?
AH HA HA
I REMEMBER YOUR ANNUAL QUEST FOR COSMOS. YOU'D SCURRY ALL OVER TOKYO.
OH...

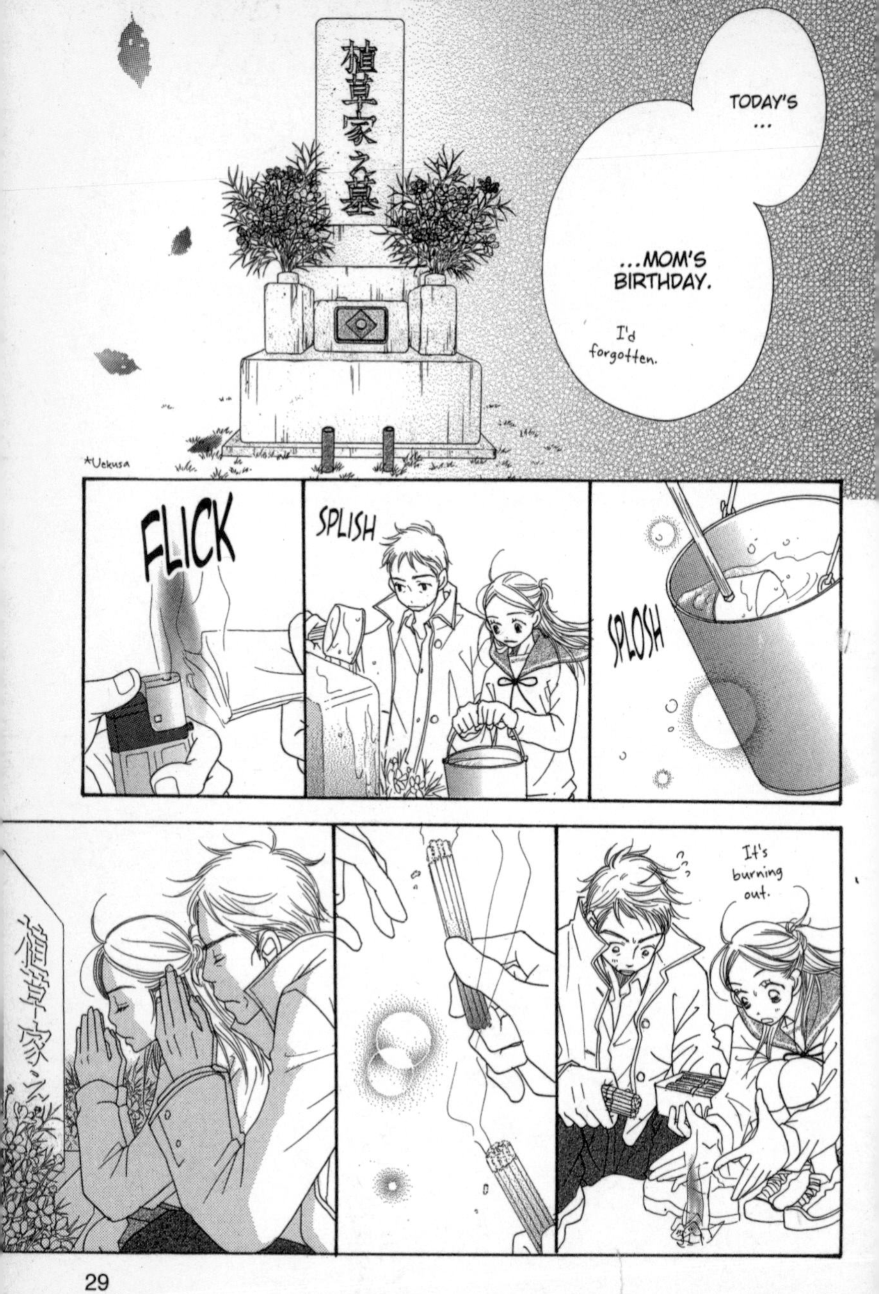

TODAY'S ...
...MOM'S BIRTHDAY.
I'd forgotten.
植草家之墓
*Uekusa
SPLOSH
SPLISH
FLICK
It's burning out.

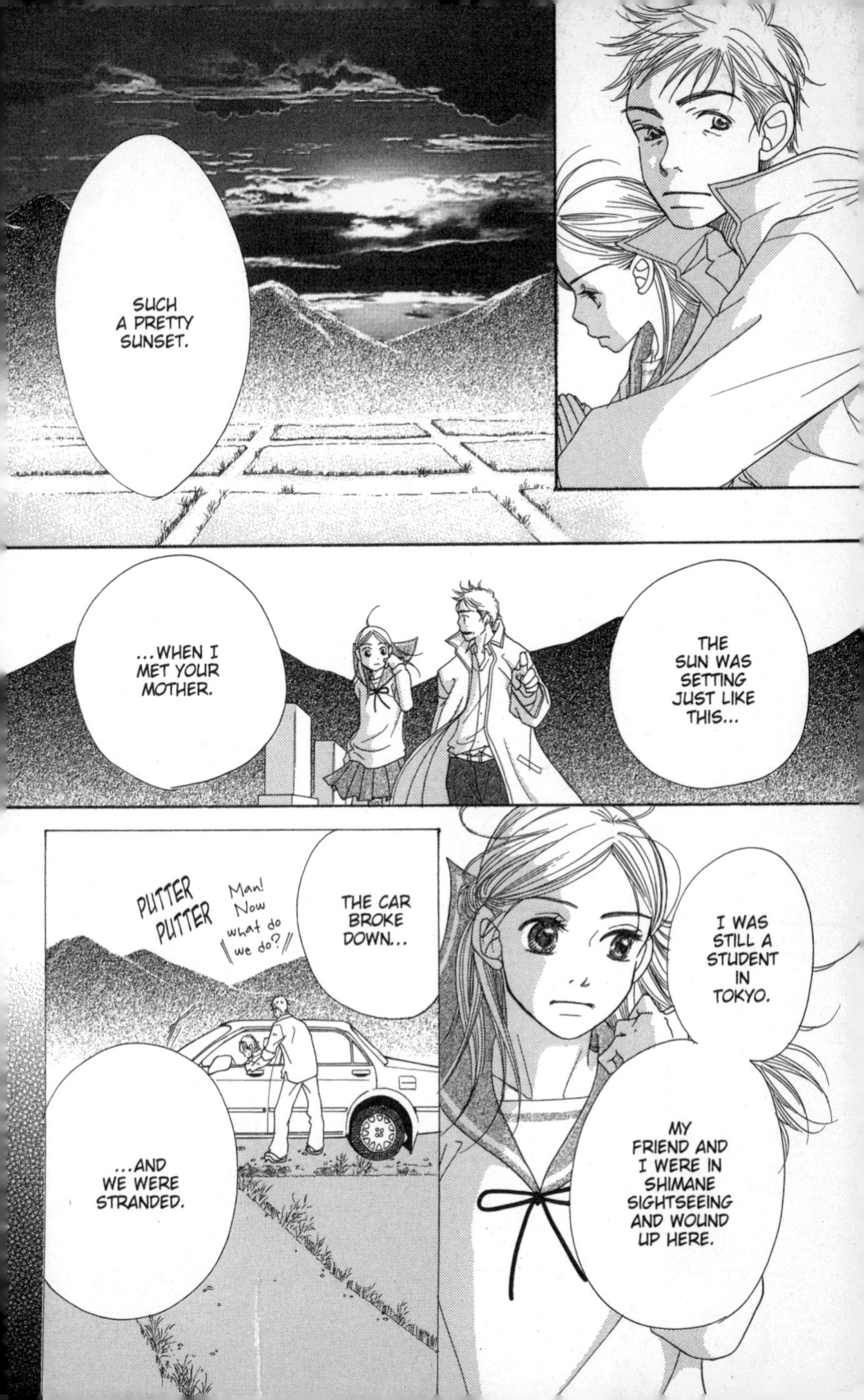
SUCH A PRETTY SUNSET.
THE SUN WAS SETTING JUST LIKE THIS...
...WHEN I MET YOUR MOTHER.
I WAS STILL A STUDENT IN TOKYO.
MY FRIEND AND I WERE IN SHIMANE SIGHTSEEING AND WOUND UP HERE.
THE CAR BROKE DOWN...
Man! Now what do we do?
PUTTER PUTTER
...AND WE WERE STRANDED.

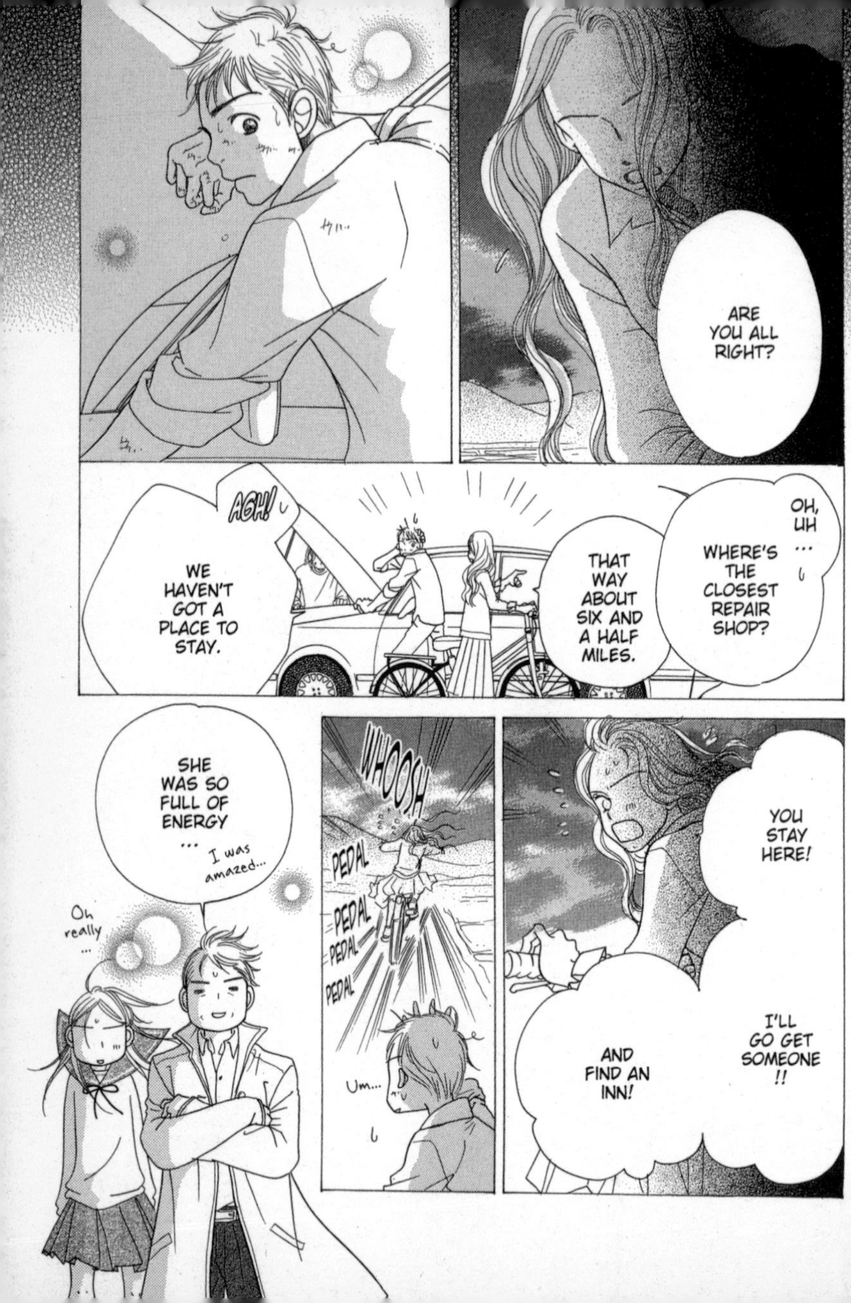
ARE YOU ALL RIGHT?
OH, UH ...
WHERE'S THE CLOSEST REPAIR SHOP?
THAT WAY ABOUT SIX AND A HALF MILES.
AGH!
WE HAVEN'T GOT A PLACE TO STAY.
YOU STAY HERE!
I'LL GO GET SOMEONE !!
AND FIND AN INN!
WHOOSH
PEDAL
PEDAL
PEDAL
PEDAL
Um...
SHE WAS SO FULL OF ENERGY ...
I was amazed...
Oh really ...

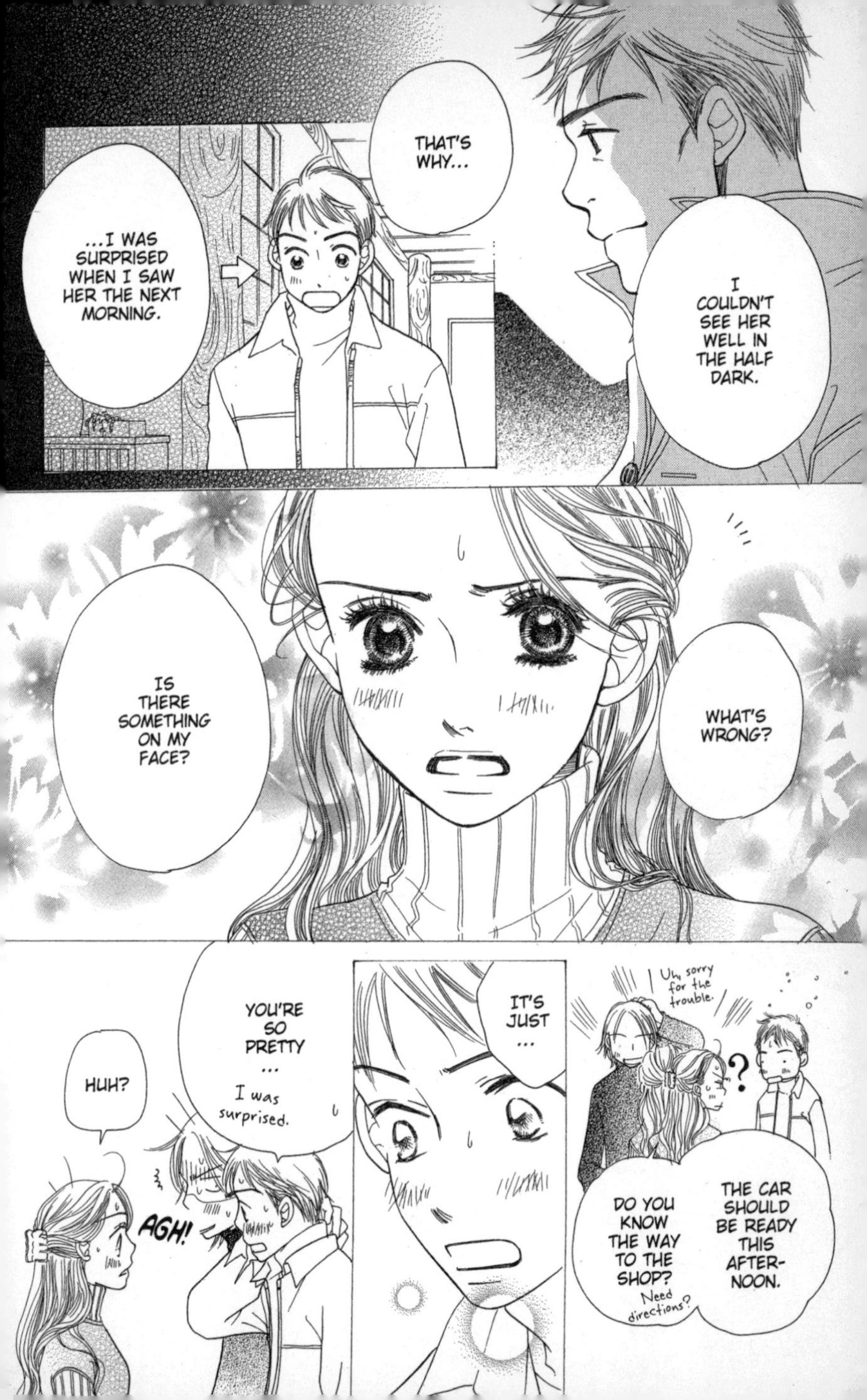
I COULDN'T SEE HER WELL IN THE HALF DARK.
THAT'S WHY...
...I WAS SURPRISED WHEN I SAW HER THE NEXT MORNING.
WHAT'S WRONG?
IS THERE SOMETHING ON MY FACE?
Uh, sorry for the trouble.
THE CAR SHOULD BE READY THIS AFTERNOON.
DO YOU KNOW THE WAY TO THE SHOP?
Need directions?
IT'S JUST ...
YOU'RE SO PRETTY ...
I was surprised.
AGH!
HUH?

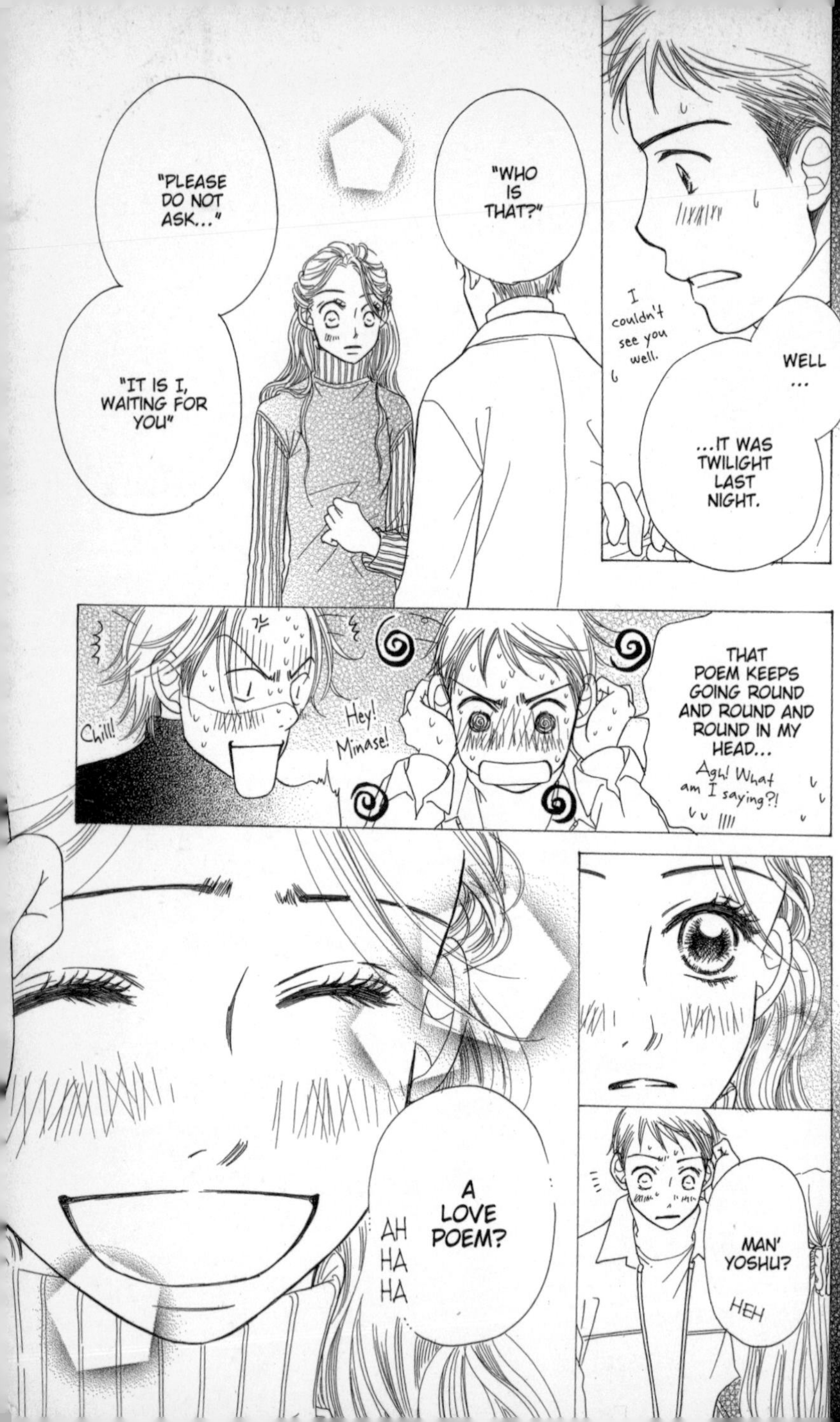
WELL...
...IT WAS TWILIGHT LAST NIGHT.
I couldn't see you well.
"WHO IS THAT?"
"PLEASE DO NOT ASK..."
"IT IS I, WAITING FOR YOU"
THAT POEM KEEPS GOING ROUND AND ROUND AND ROUND IN MY HEAD...
Agh! What am I saying?!
Hey! Minase!
Chill!
MAN' YOSHU?
HEH
A LOVE POEM?
AH HA HA

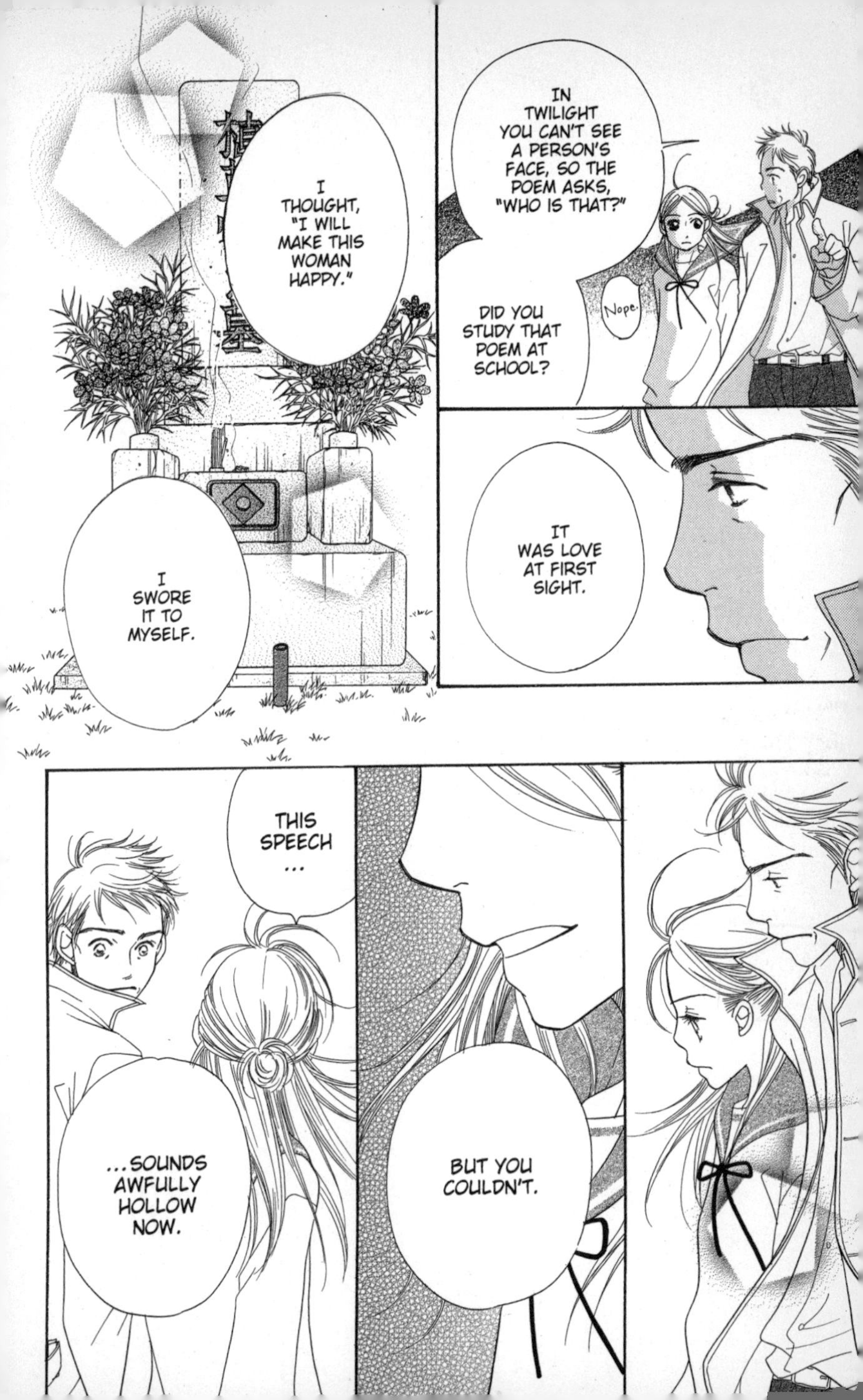
IN TWILIGHT YOU CAN'T SEE A PERSON'S FACE, SO THE POEM ASKS, "WHO IS THAT?"
DID YOU STUDY THAT POEM AT SCHOOL?
Nope.
IT WAS LOVE AT FIRST SIGHT.
I THOUGHT, "I WILL MAKE THIS WOMAN HAPPY."
I SWORE IT TO MYSELF.
BUT YOU COULDN'T.
THIS SPEECH ...
...SOUNDS AWFULLY HOLLOW NOW.

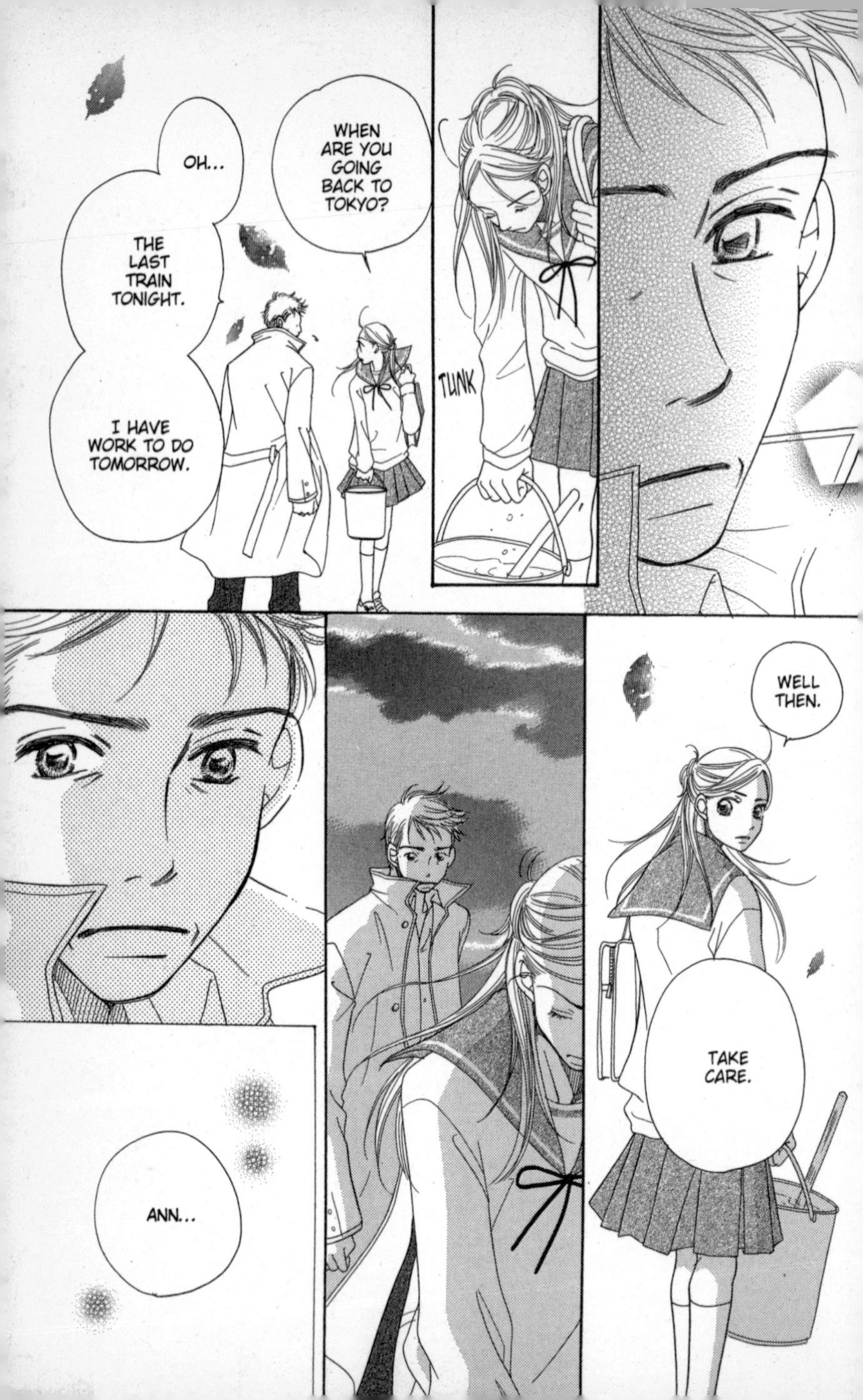
TUNK
WHEN ARE YOU GOING BACK TO TOKYO?
OH...
THE LAST TRAIN TONIGHT.
I HAVE WORK TO DO TOMORROW.
WELL THEN.
TAKE CARE.
ANN...

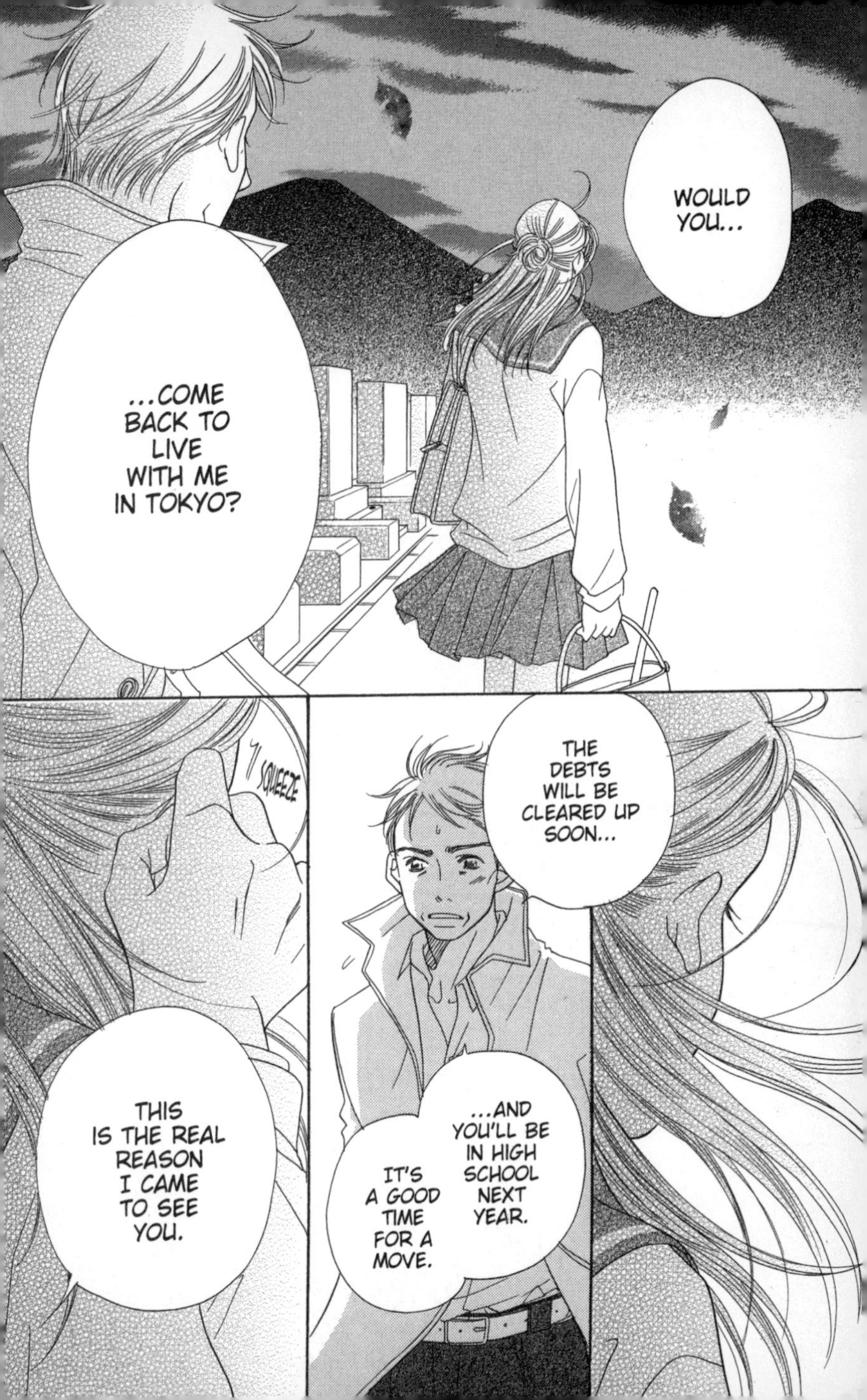
WOULD YOU...
...COME BACK TO LIVE WITH ME IN TOKYO?
THE DEBTS WILL BE CLEARED UP SOON...
...AND YOU'LL BE IN HIGH SCHOOL NEXT YEAR.
IT'S A GOOD TIME FOR A MOVE.
SQUEEZE
THIS IS THE REAL REASON I CAME TO SEE YOU.

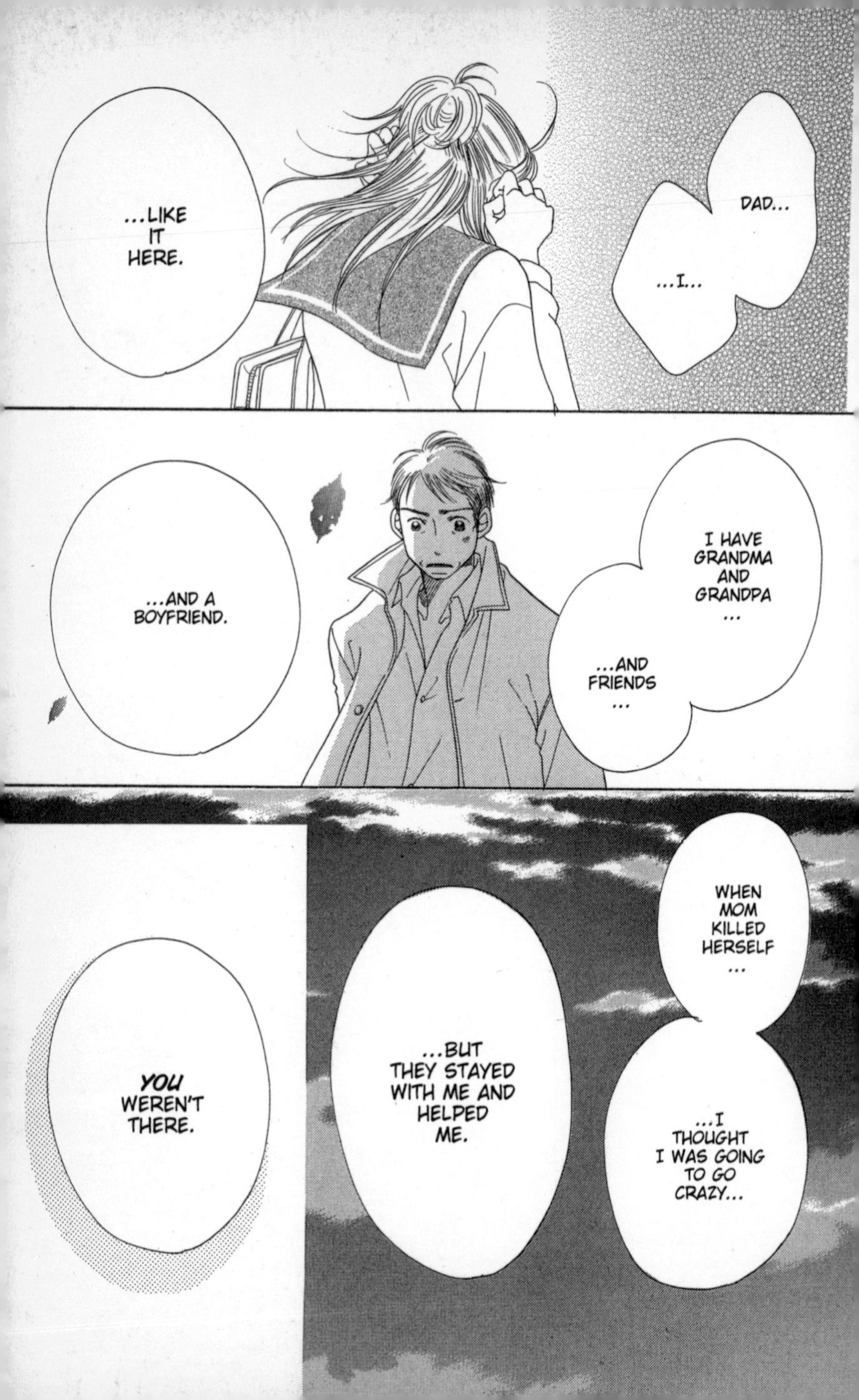

DAD...
...I...
...LIKE IT HERE.
I HAVE GRANDMA AND GRANDPA ...
...AND FRIENDS ...
...AND A BOYFRIEND.
WHEN MOM KILLED HERSELF ...
...I THOUGHT I WAS GOING TO GO CRAZY...
...BUT THEY STAYED WITH ME AND HELPED ME.
YOU WEREN'T THERE.

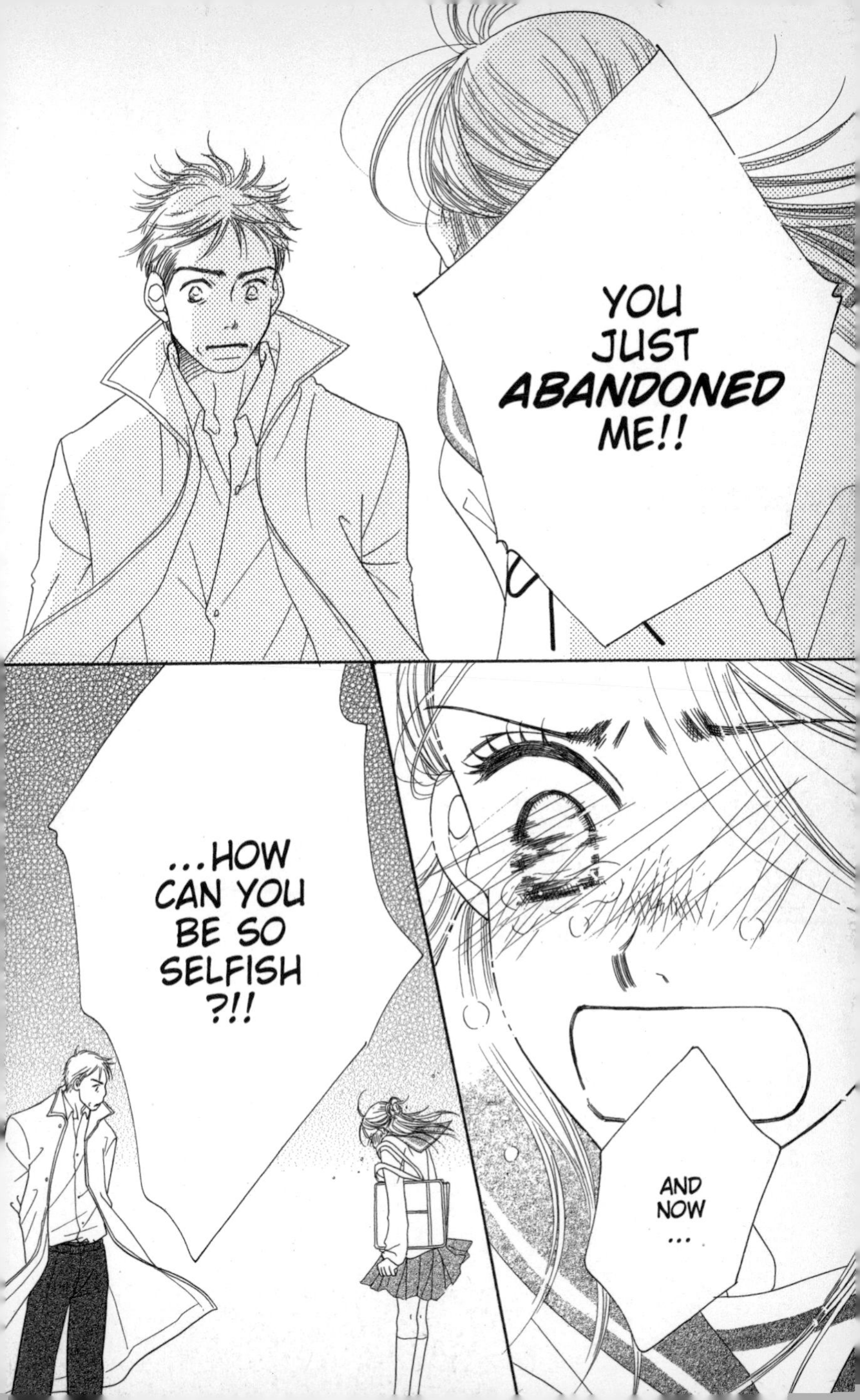
YOU JUST ABANDONED ME!!
AND NOW ...
...HOW CAN YOU BE SO SELFISH ?!!

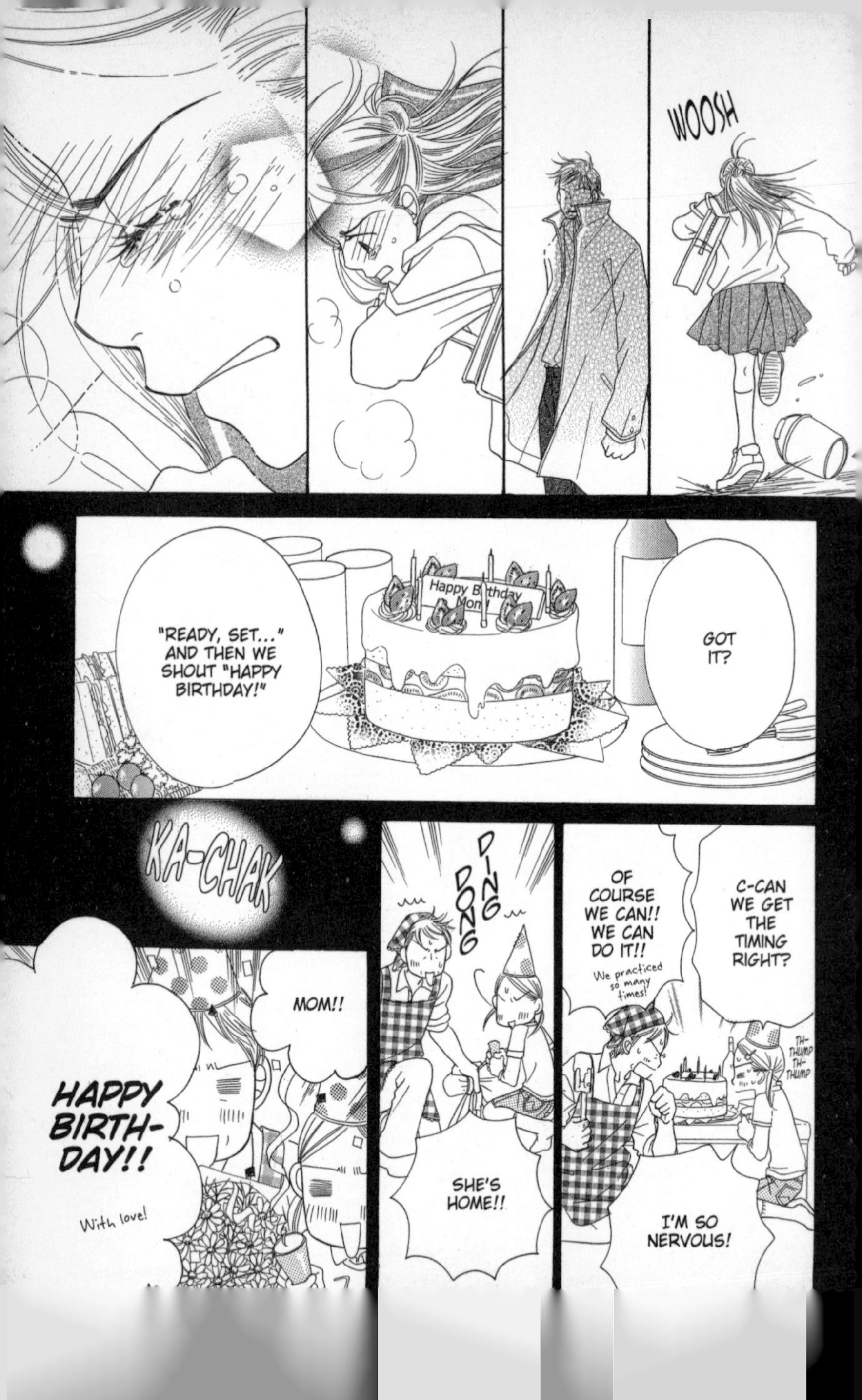
WOOSH
GOT IT?
"READY, SET..." AND THEN WE SHOUT "HAPPY BIRTHDAY!"
C-CAN WE GET THE TIMING RIGHT?
TH-THUMP TH-THUMP
OF COURSE WE CAN!! WE CAN DO IT!!
We practiced so many times!
I'M SO NERVOUS!
DING DONG
SHE'S HOME!!
KA-CHAK
MOM!!
HAPPY BIRTH-DAY!!
With love!

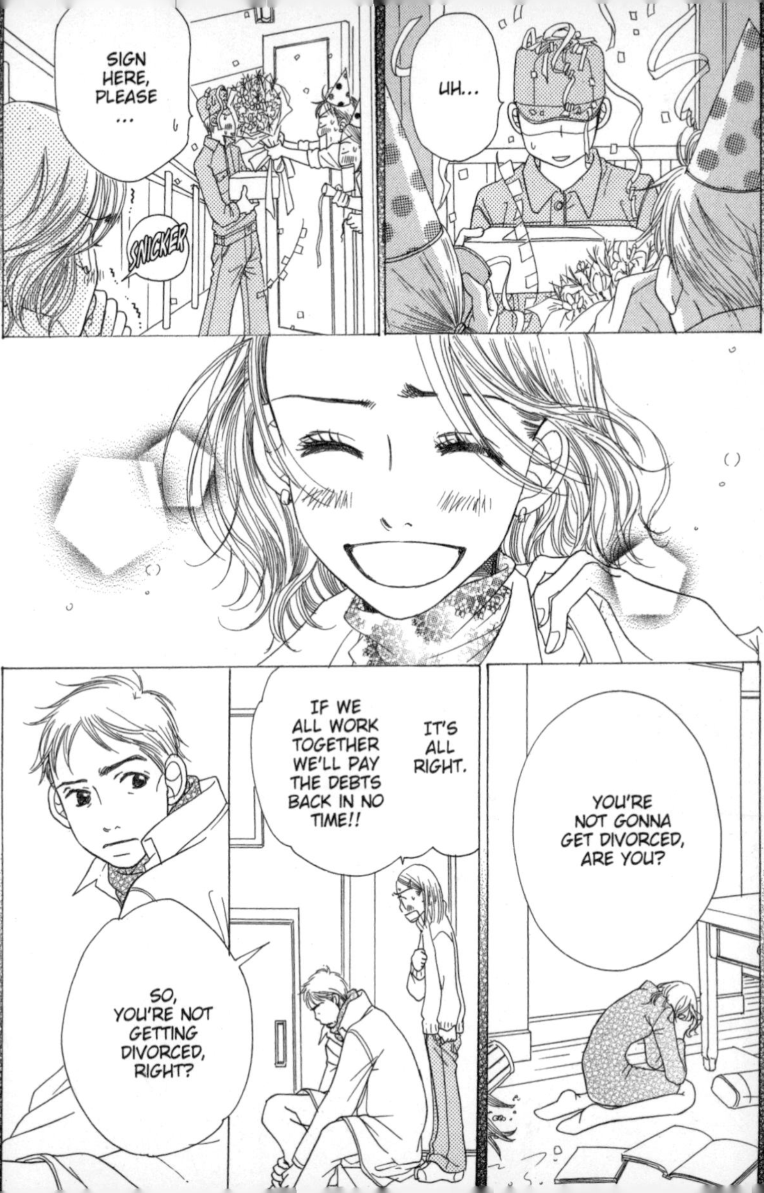
UH...
SIGN HERE, PLEASE ...
SNICKER
YOU'RE NOT GONNA GET DIVORCED, ARE YOU?
IT'S ALL RIGHT.
IF WE ALL WORK TOGETHER WE'LL PAY THE DEBTS BACK IN NO TIME!!
SO, YOU'RE NOT GETTING DIVORCED, RIGHT?

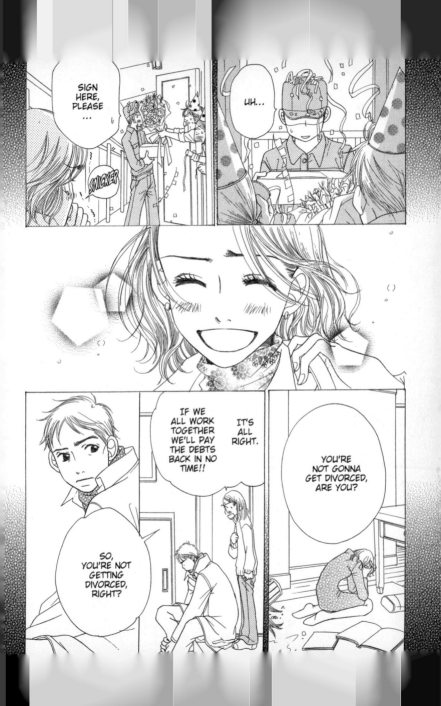

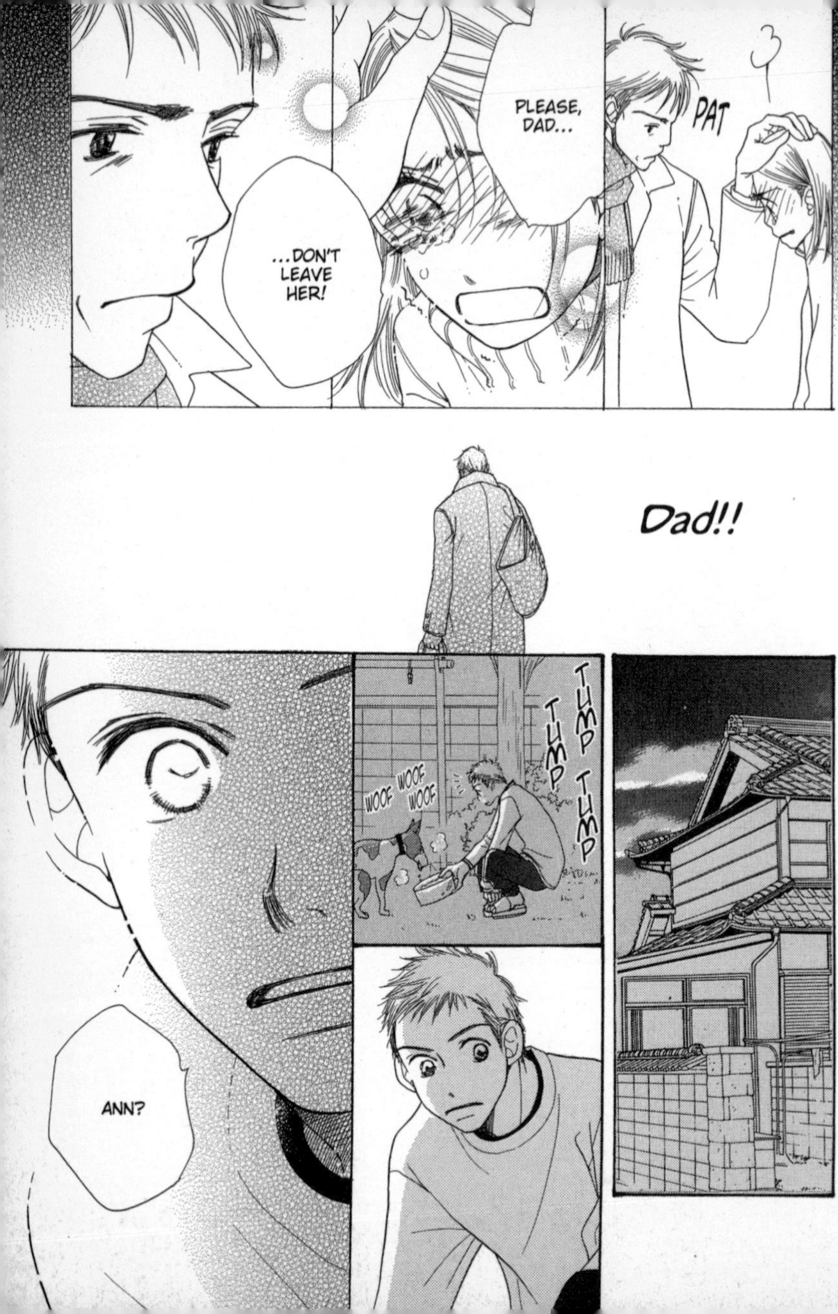
PAT
PLEASE, DAD...
...DON'T LEAVE HER!
Dad!!
TUMP TUMP TUMP
TUMP
WOOF WOOF WOOF
ANN?

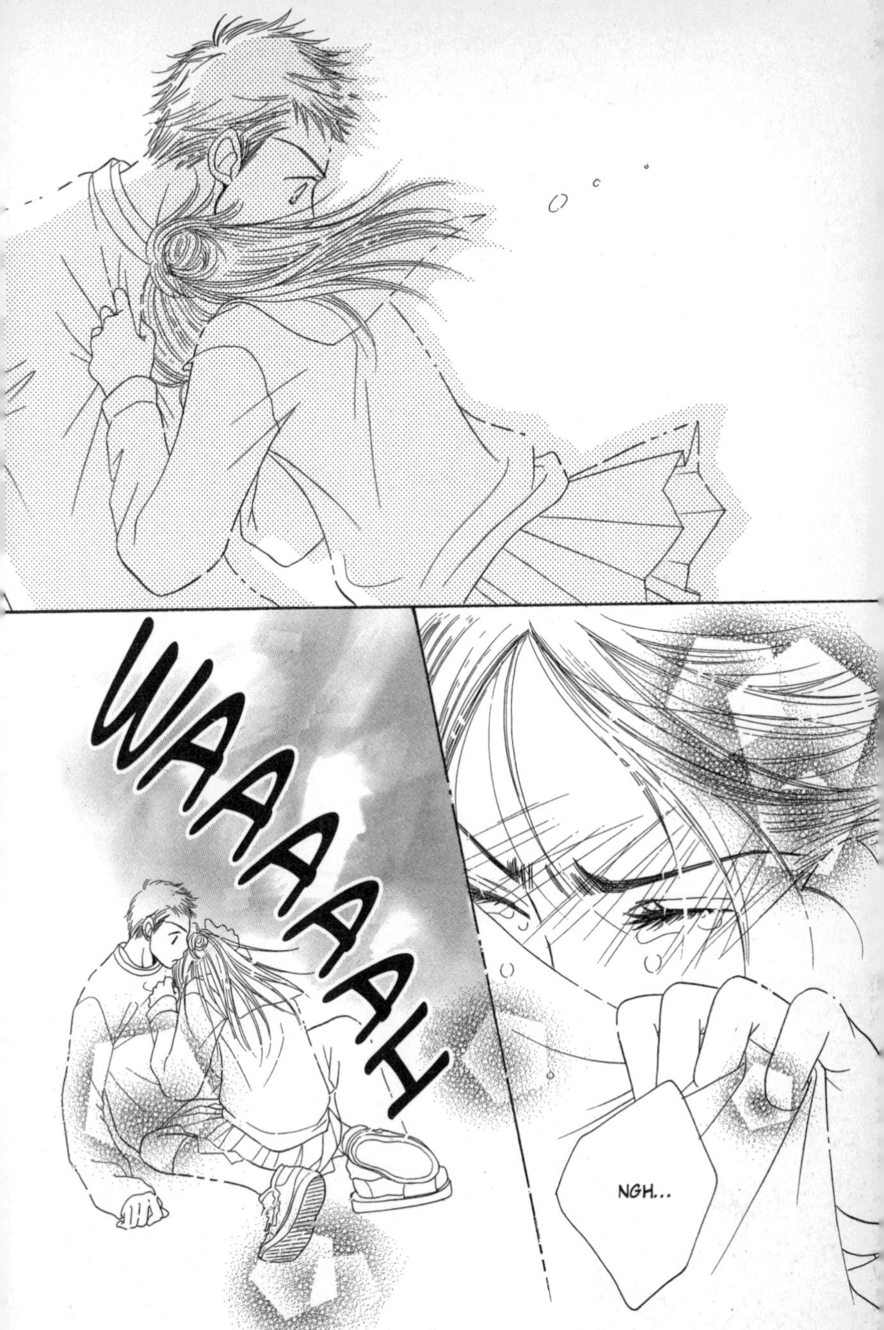
NGH...
WAAAAAAH

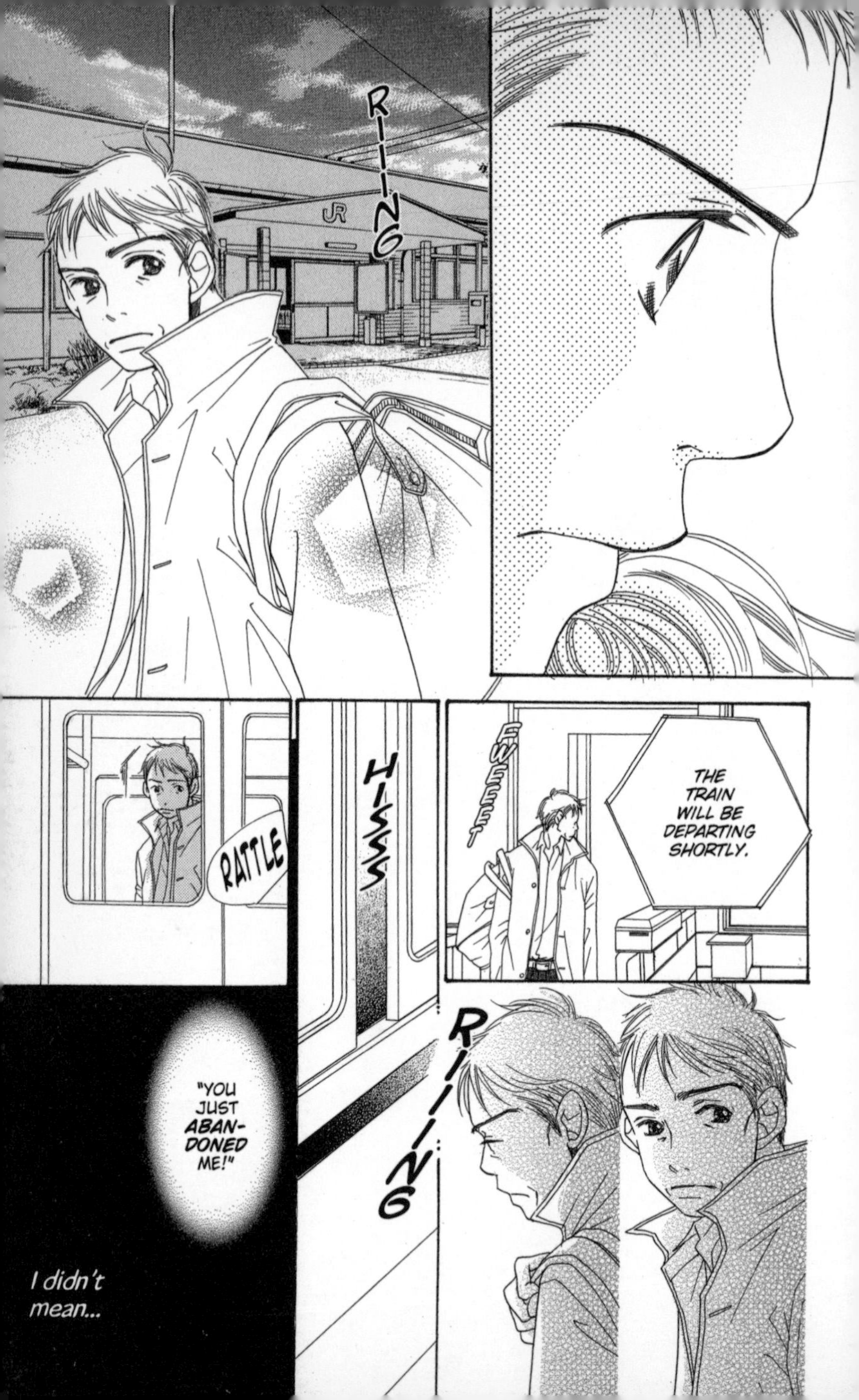
RIIING
FWEEET
THE TRAIN WILL BE DEPARTING SHORTLY.
HISSS
RATTLE
RIIING
"YOU JUST ABAN-DONED ME!"
I didn't mean...

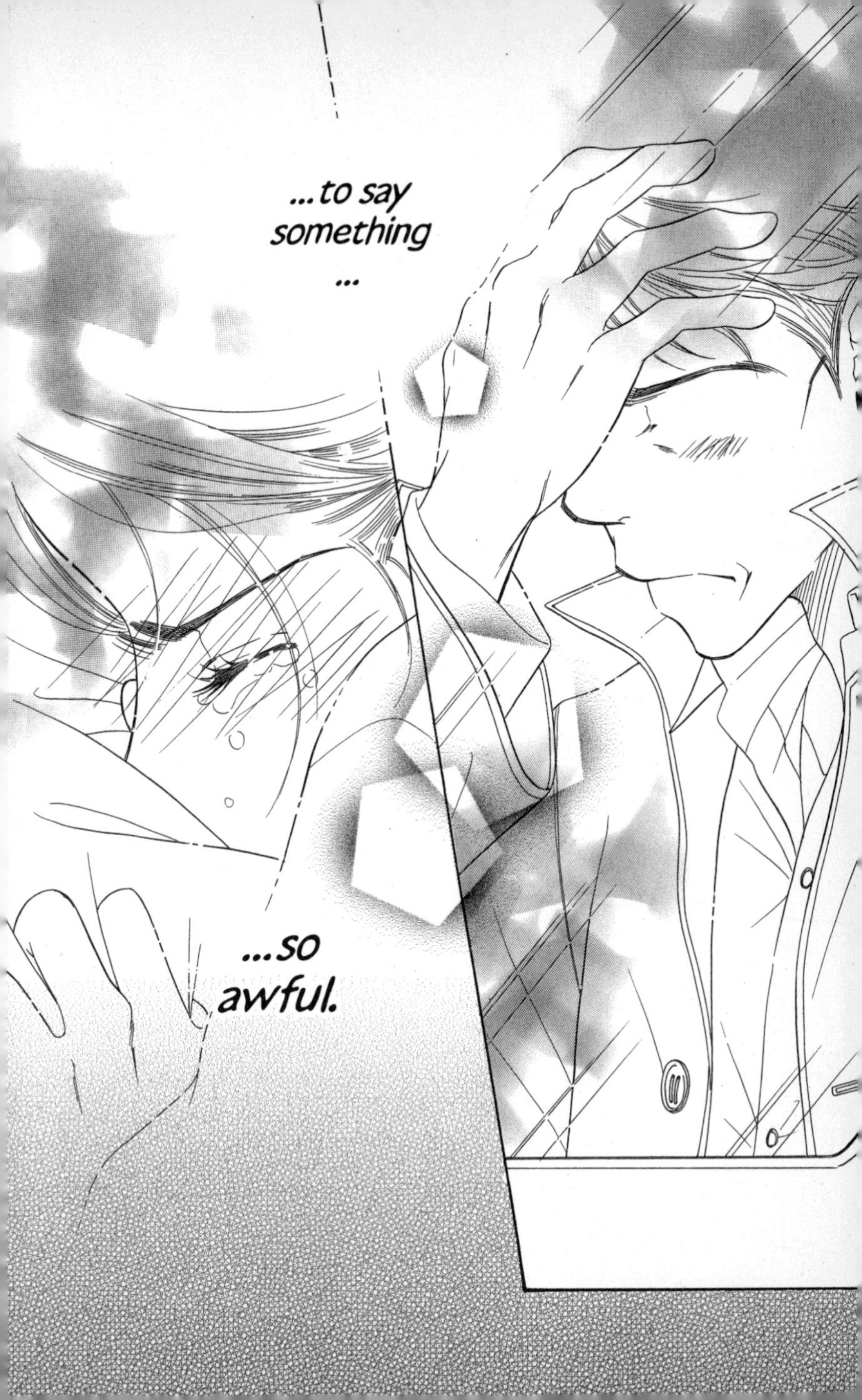
...to say something ...
...so awful.

This is volume 2. Thank you for reading. When this comes out, 2003 will almost be over. As always, the year went by so fast...

A little note on the "Wild Dog Rodeo" in this chapter. I actually did this when I was a kid...with a big dog I had at home. It threw me off right away. It was a frightening and painful experience, even though I had imagined myself looking really cool. What an idiot!

Tasokare (Who is that?) Tasogare (twilight). What a neat expression! These days I've been realizing what a beautiful language Japanese is. Dusk, twilight... there's a touch of loneliness to these words. And add autumn as the season to that and you've got heaps of lonely. Anyway, I like it all...twilight, fall and everything else.

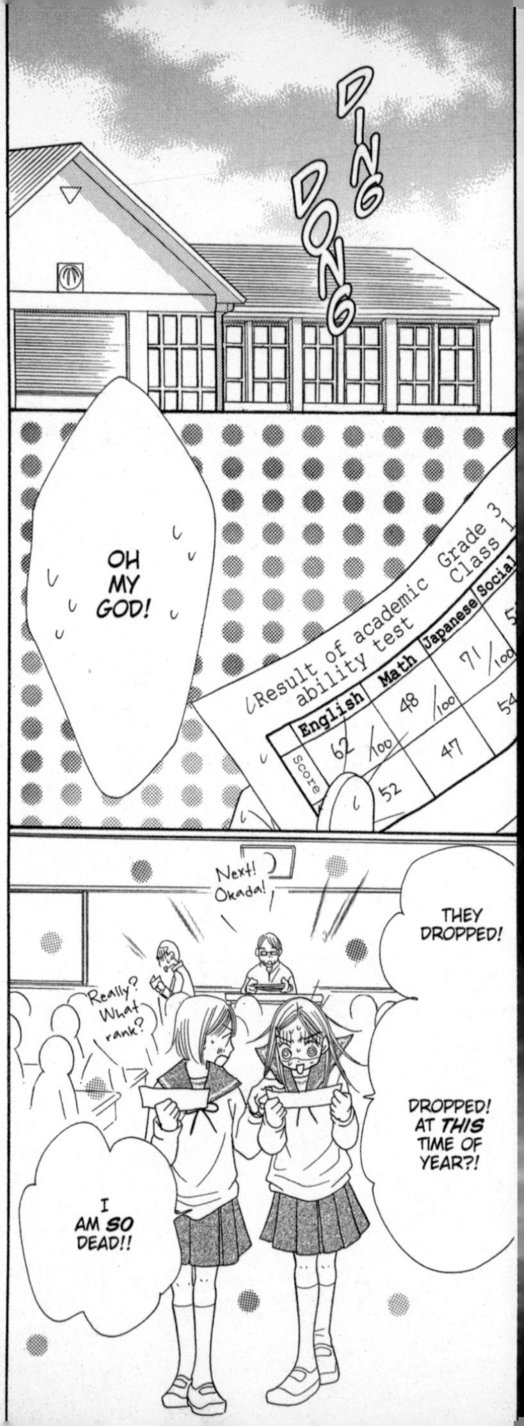
DING DONG
OH MY GOD!
Result of academic ability test
Grade 3 Class 1
English
Math
Japanese
Social
Score
62/100
48/100
71/100
THEY DROPPED!
Next! Okada!
Really? What rank?
DROPPED! AT THIS TIME OF YEAR?!
I AM SO DEAD!!

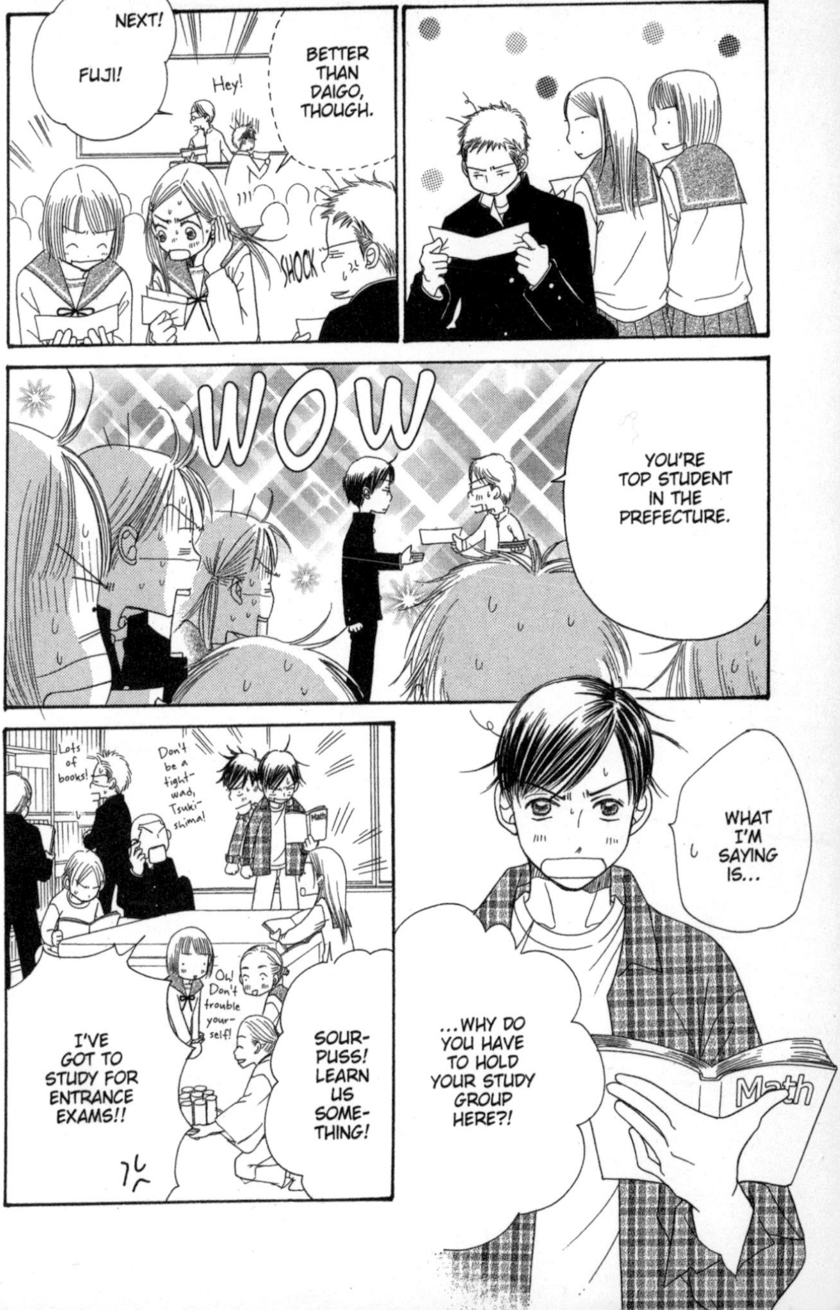
BETTER THAN DAIGO, THOUGH.
NEXT!
FUJI!
Hey!
SHOCK
WOW
YOU'RE TOP STUDENT IN THE PREFECTURE.
WHAT I'M SAYING IS...
...WHY DO YOU HAVE TO HOLD YOUR STUDY GROUP HERE?!
Math
Don't be a tight-wad, Tsuki-shima!
Lots of books!
Math
Oh! Don't trouble your-self!
SOUR-PUSS! LEARN US SOME-THING!
I'VE GOT TO STUDY FOR ENTRANCE EXAMS!!

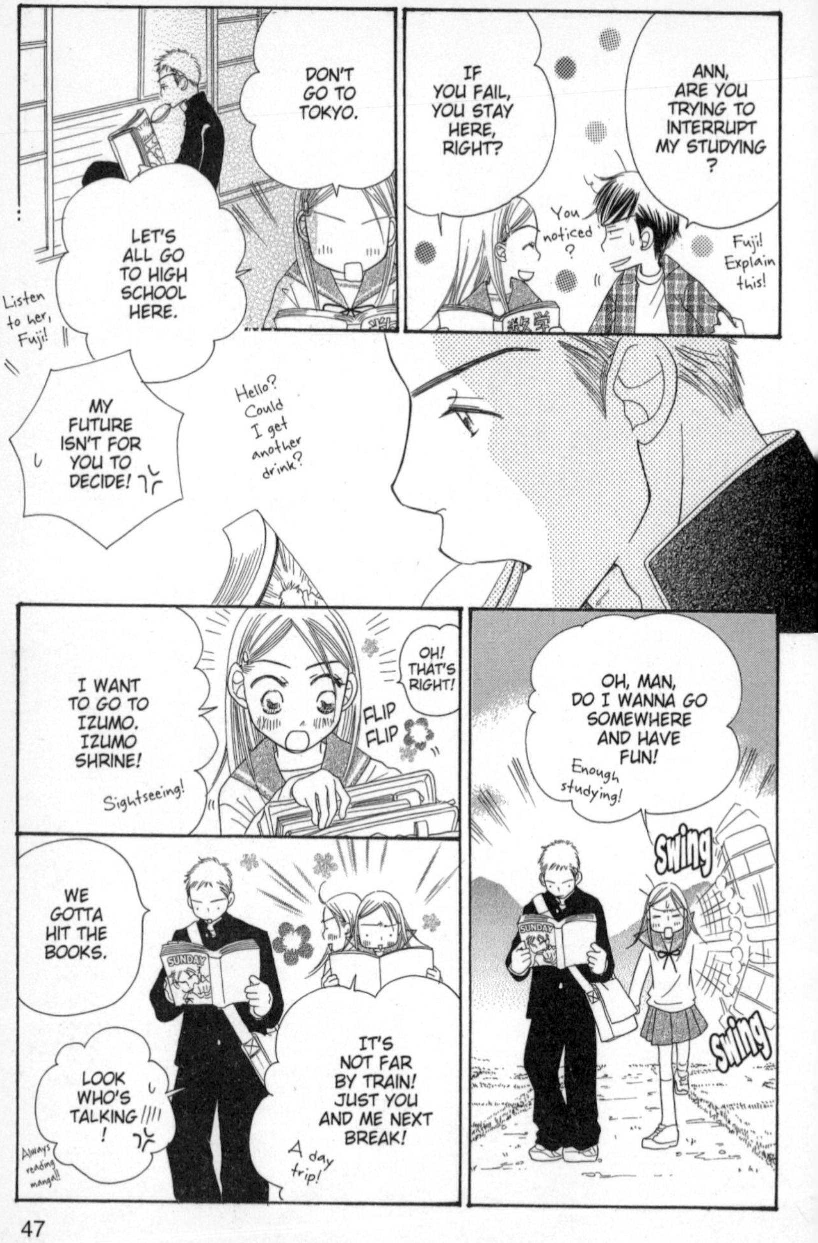
ANN, ARE YOU TRYING TO INTERRUPT MY STUDYING?
Fuji! Explain this!
IF YOU FAIL, YOU STAY HERE, RIGHT?
You noticed?
DON'T GO TO TOKYO.
LET'S ALL GO TO HIGH SCHOOL HERE.
Listen to her, Fuji!
Hello? Could I get another drink?
MY FUTURE ISN'T FOR YOU TO DECIDE!
OH, MAN, DO I WANNA GO SOMEWHERE AND HAVE FUN!
Enough studying!
SWING
SWING
OH! THAT'S RIGHT!
FLIP FLIP
I WANT TO GO TO IZUMO. IZUMO SHRINE!
Sightseeing!
IT'S NOT FAR BY TRAIN! JUST YOU AND ME NEXT BREAK!
A day trip!
WE GOTTA HIT THE BOOKS.
LOOK WHO'S TALKING!
Always reading manga!!

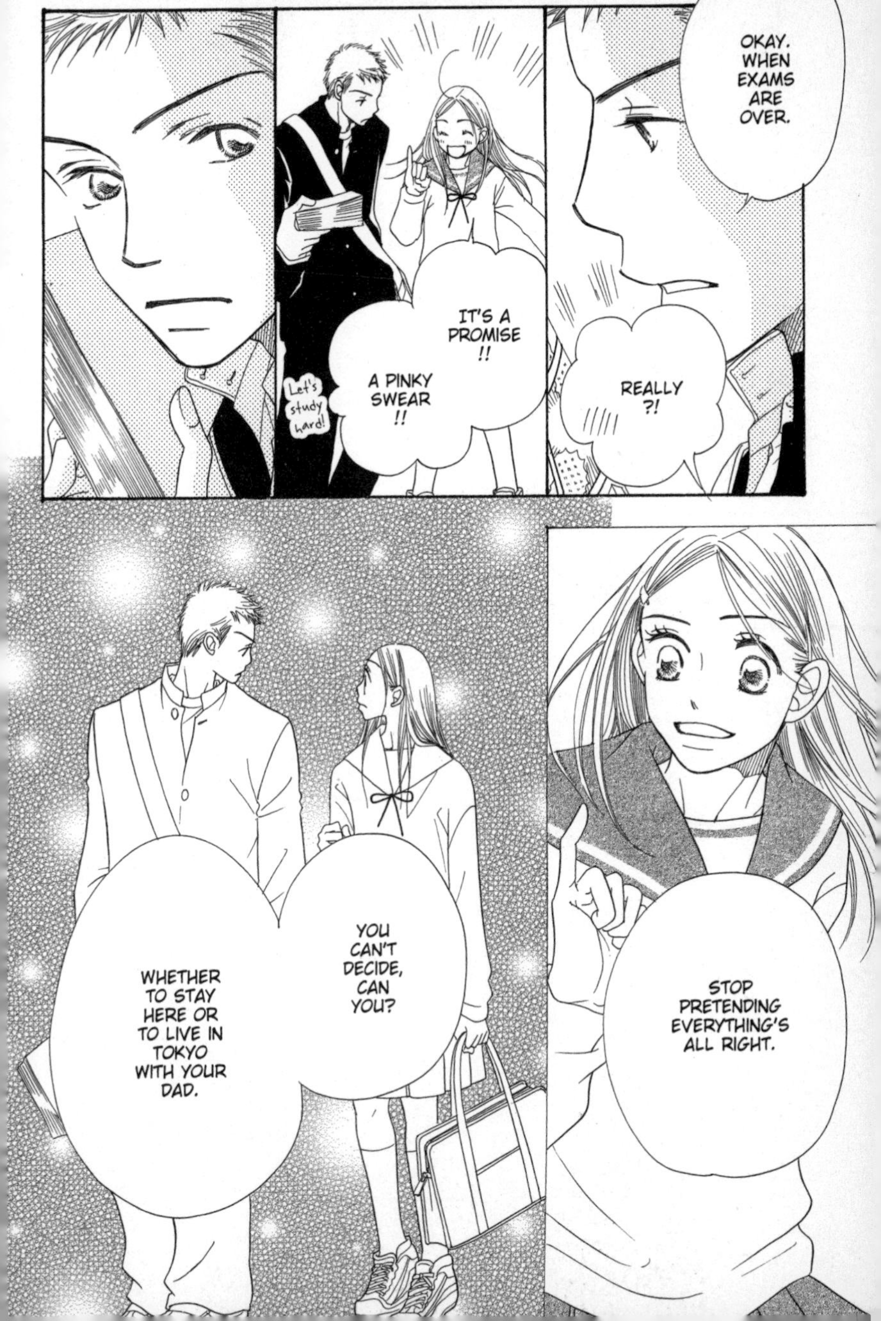
OKAY. WHEN EXAMS ARE OVER.
REALLY ?!
IT'S A PROMISE !!
A PINKY SWEAR !!
Let's study hard!
STOP PRETENDING EVERYTHING'S ALL RIGHT.
YOU CAN'T DECIDE, CAN YOU?
WHETHER TO STAY HERE OR TO LIVE IN TOKYO WITH YOUR DAD.

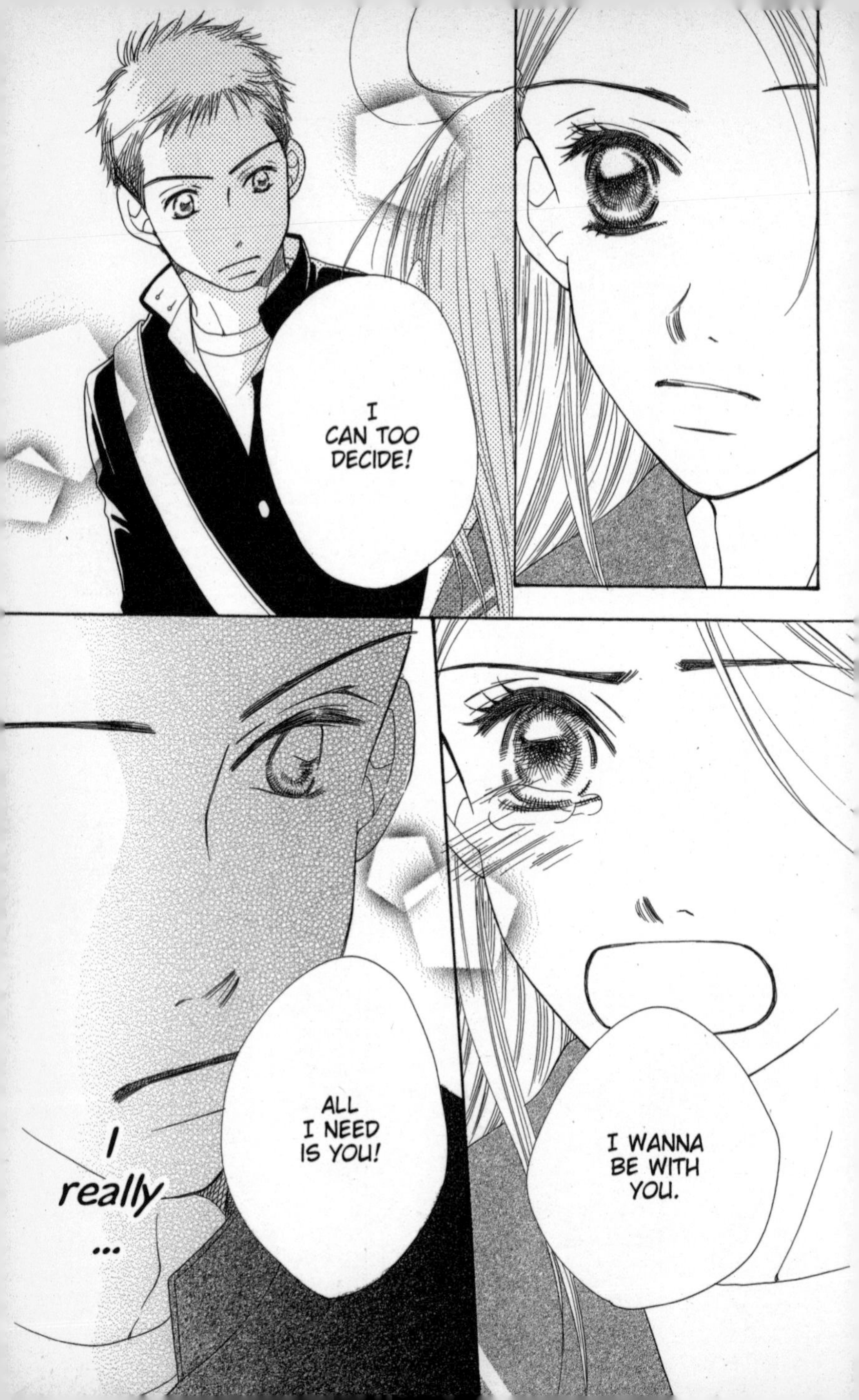
I CAN TOO DECIDE!
I WANNA BE WITH YOU.
ALL I NEED IS YOU!
I really ...

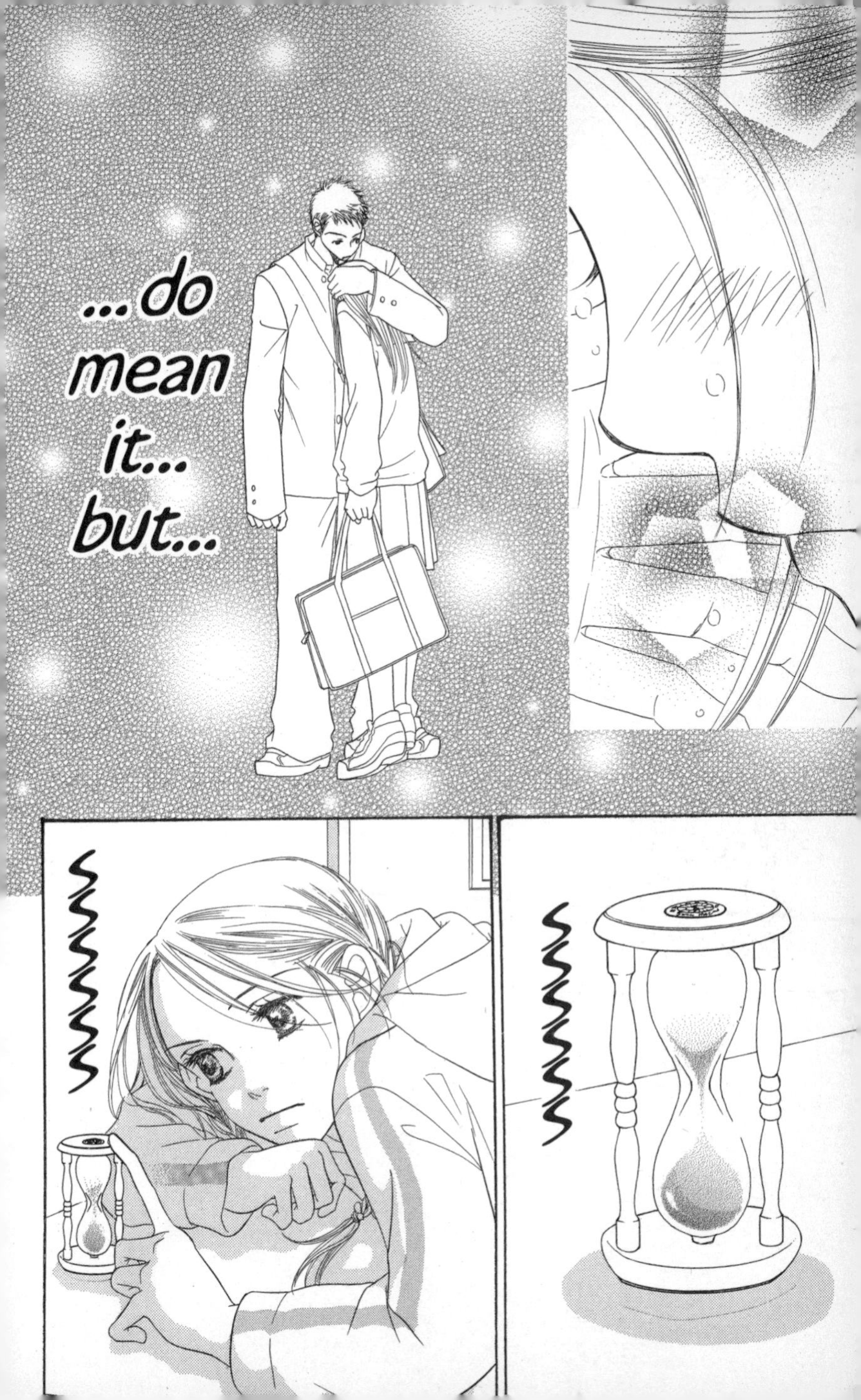
...do mean it... but...
SSSSSSS
SSSSSSS

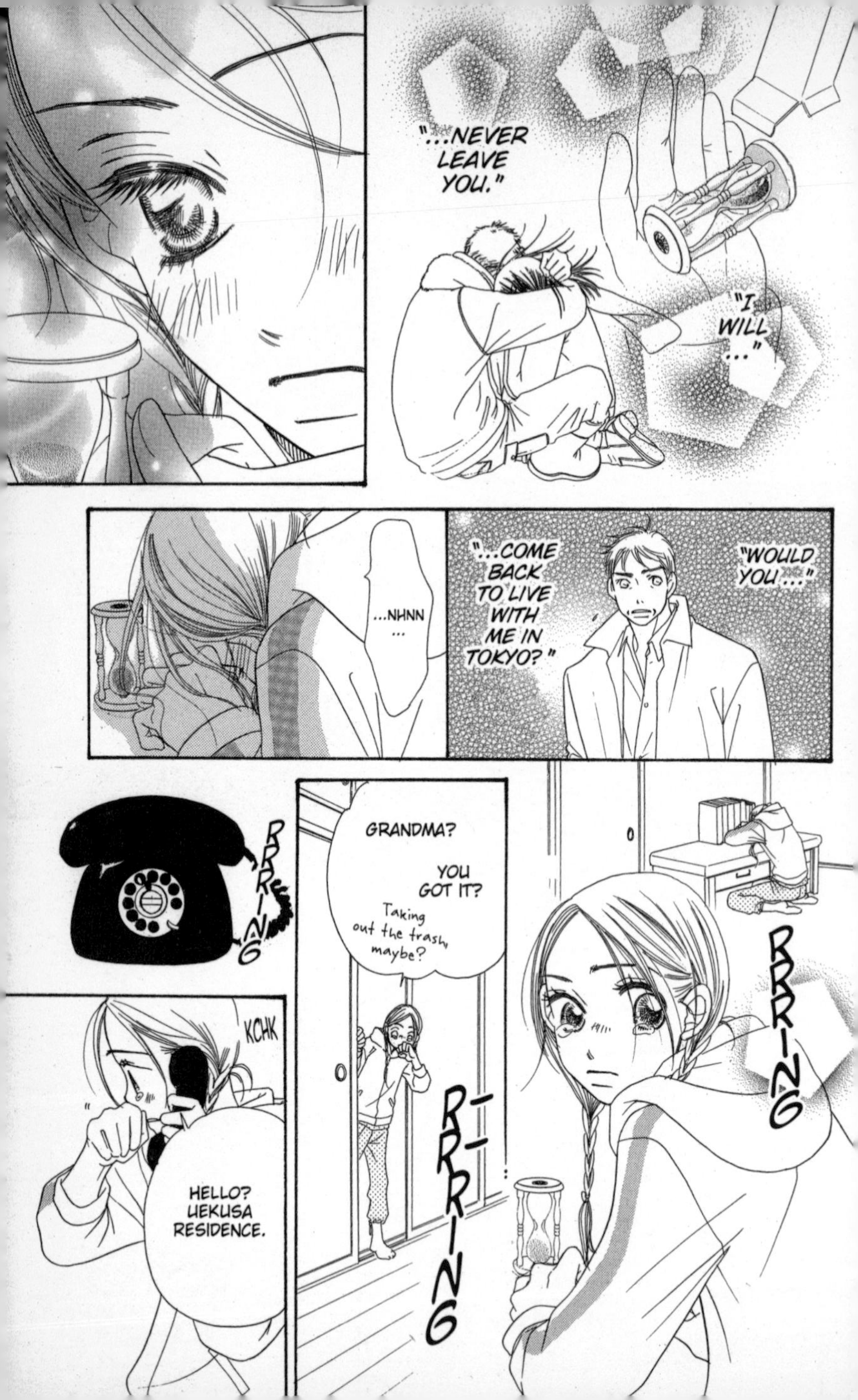
"I WILL ..."
"...NEVER LEAVE YOU."
"WOULD YOU..."
"...COME BACK TO LIVE WITH ME IN TOKYO?"
...NHNN ...
RRRING
GRANDMA?
YOU GOT IT?
Taking out the trash, maybe?
R-R-RRRING
RRRING
KCHK
HELLO? UEKUSA RESIDENCE.

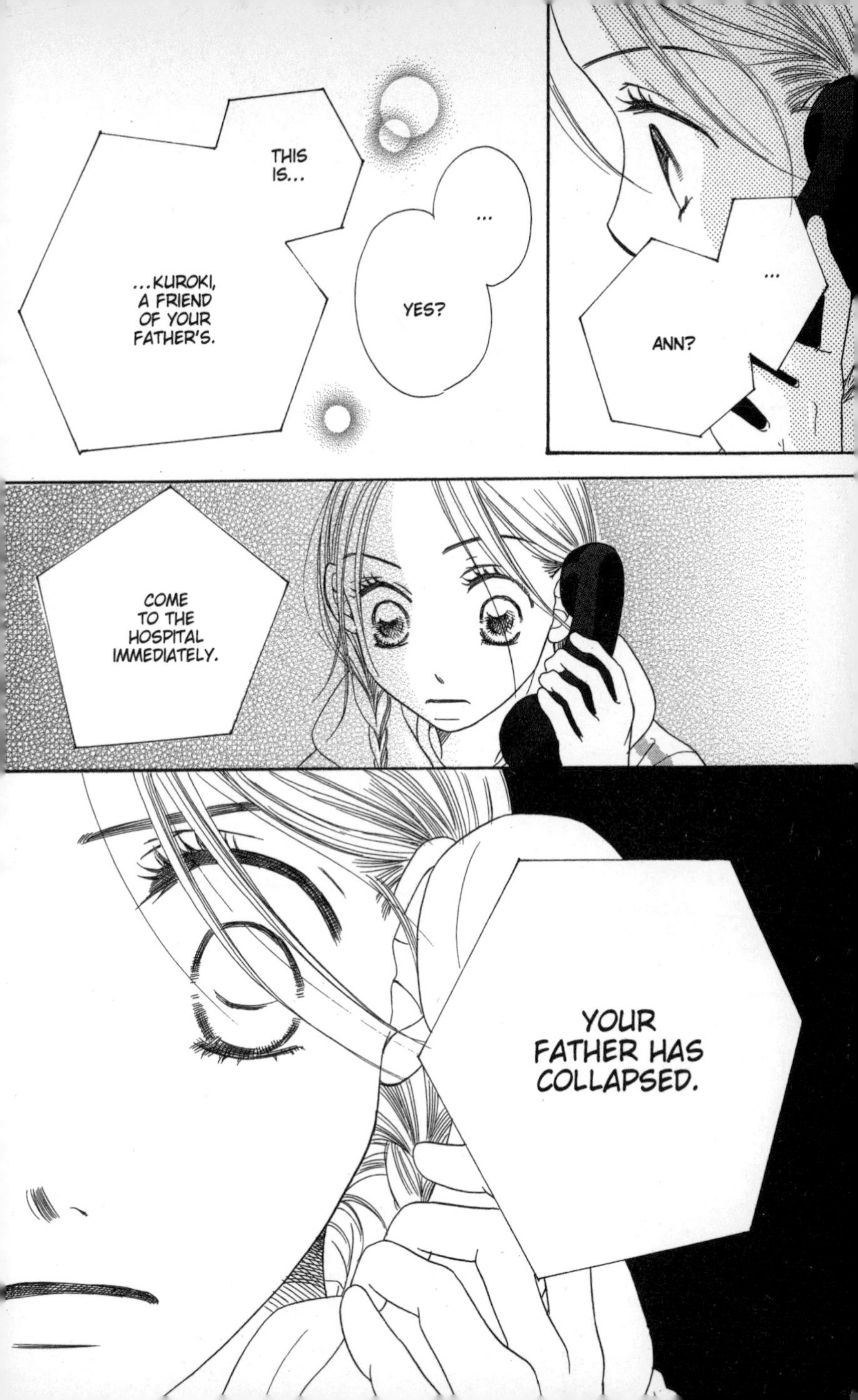
... ANN?
... YES?
THIS IS...
...KUROKI, A FRIEND OF YOUR FATHER'S.
COME TO THE HOSPITAL IMMEDIATELY.
YOUR FATHER HAS COLLAPSED.

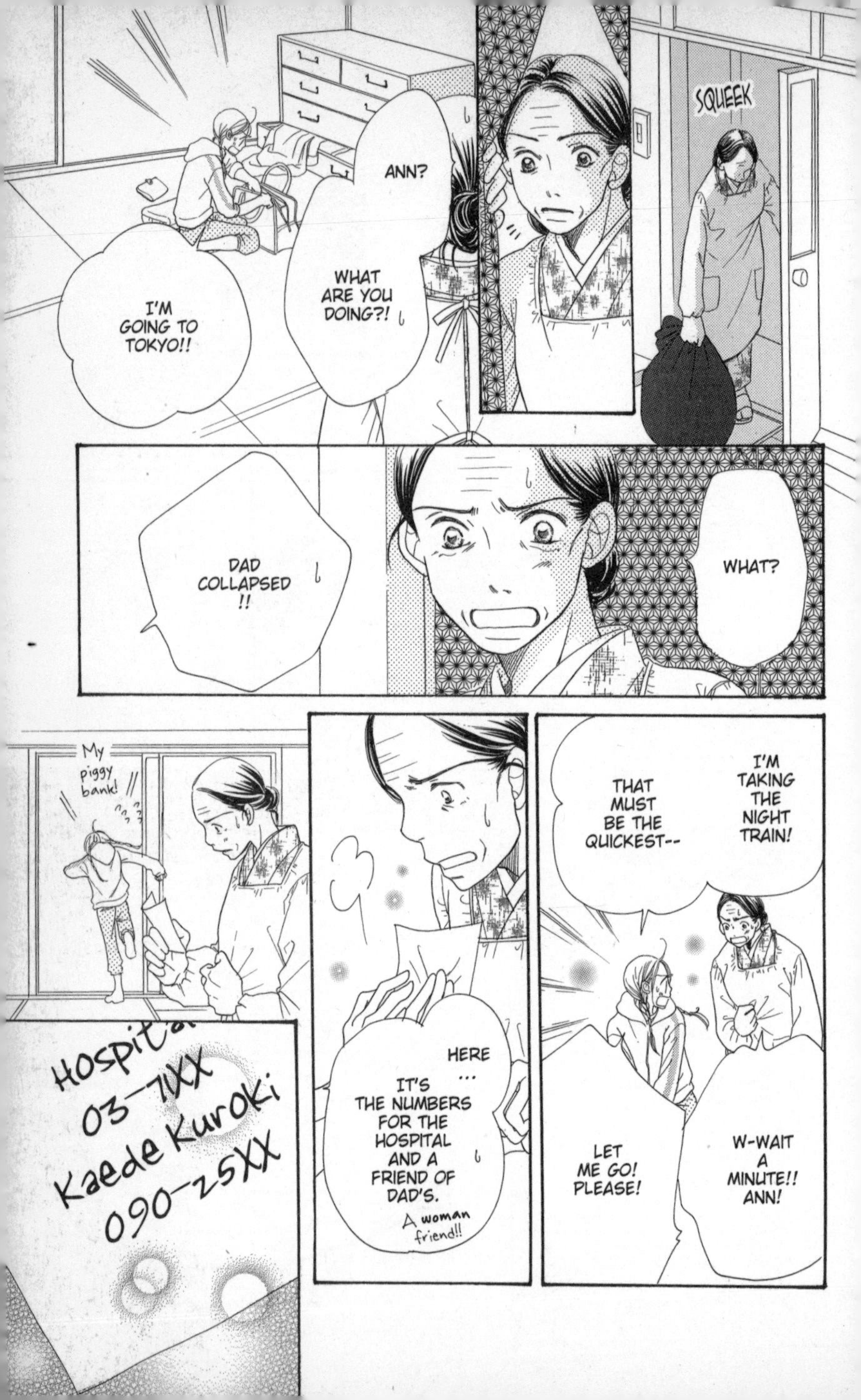
SQUEEK
ANN?
WHAT ARE YOU DOING?!
I'M GOING TO TOKYO!!
WHAT?
DAD COLLAPSED !!
I'M TAKING THE NIGHT TRAIN!
THAT MUST BE THE QUICKEST--
W-WAIT A MINUTE!! ANN!
LET ME GO! PLEASE!
HERE...
IT'S THE NUMBERS FOR THE HOSPITAL AND A FRIEND OF DAD'S.
A woman friend!!
My piggy bank!
Hospital
03-7XX
Kaede Kuroki
090-25XX

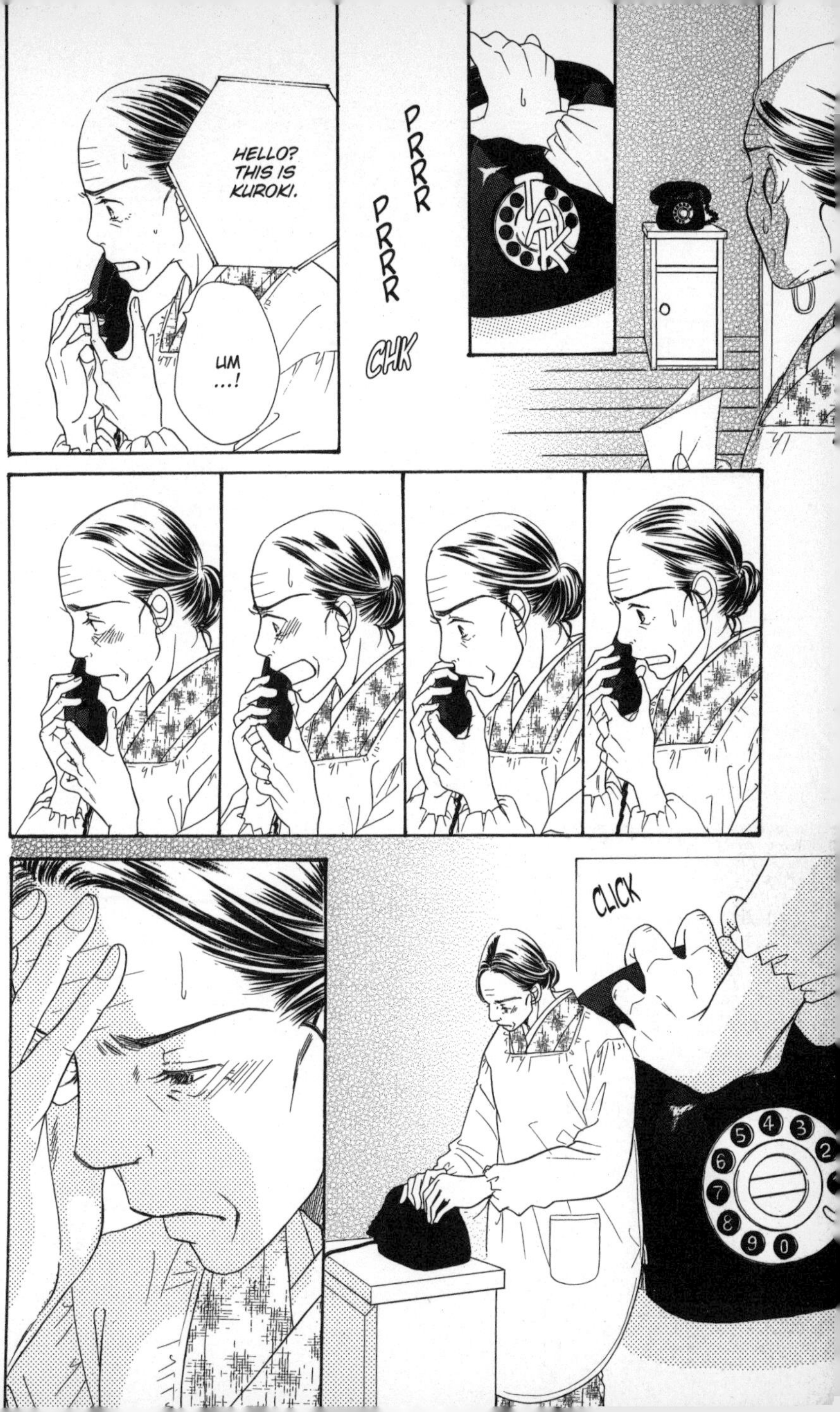
TAK
PRRR
PRRR
CHK
HELLO? THIS IS KUROKI.
UM ...!
CLICK

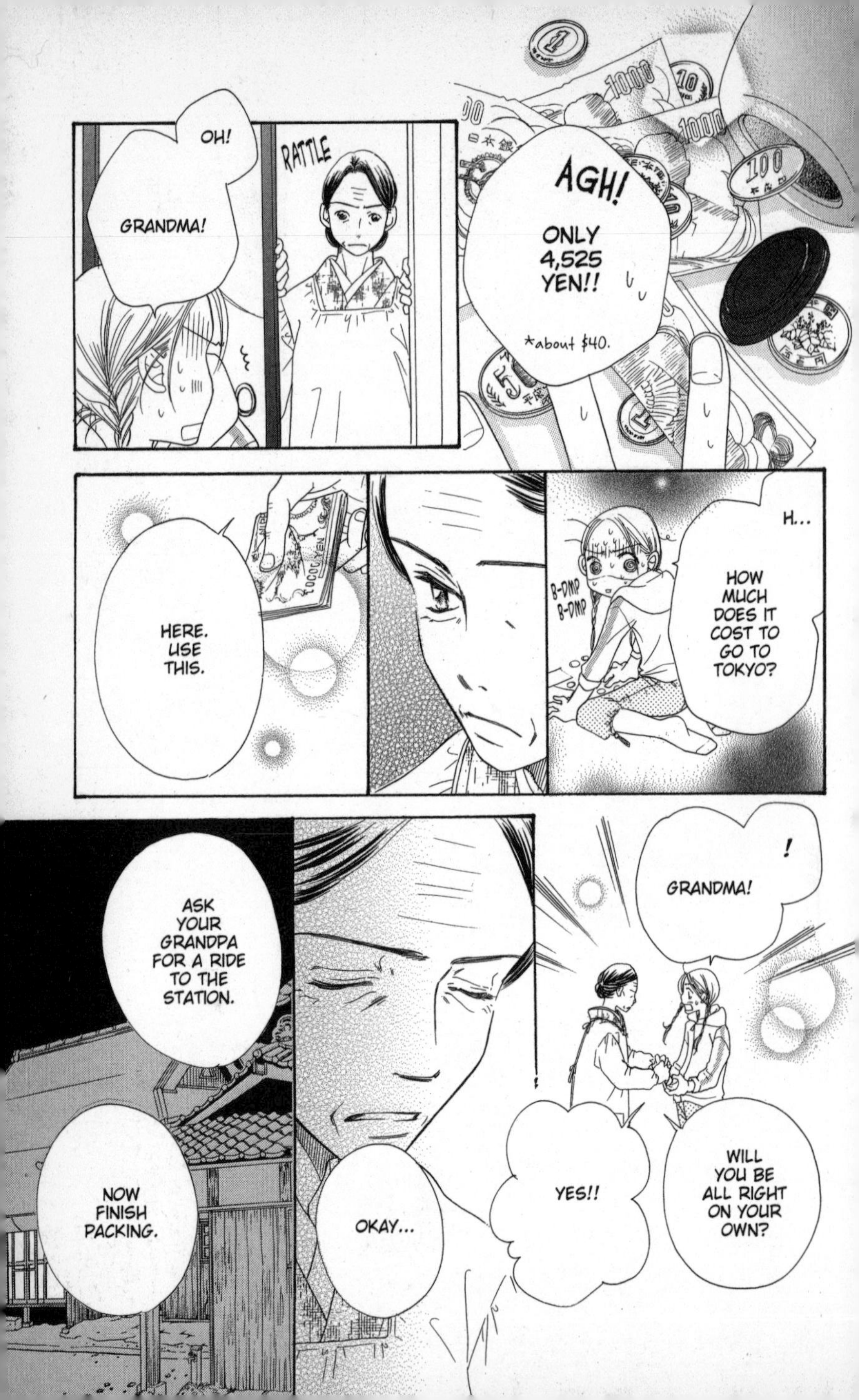
AGH!
ONLY 4,525 YEN!!
*about $40.
RATTLE
OH!
GRANDMA!
H...
HOW MUCH DOES IT COST TO GO TO TOKYO?
B-DMP B-DMP
HERE. USE THIS.
!
GRANDMA!
WILL YOU BE ALL RIGHT ON YOUR OWN?
YES!!
OKAY...
ASK YOUR GRANDPA FOR A RIDE TO THE STATION.
NOW FINISH PACKING.

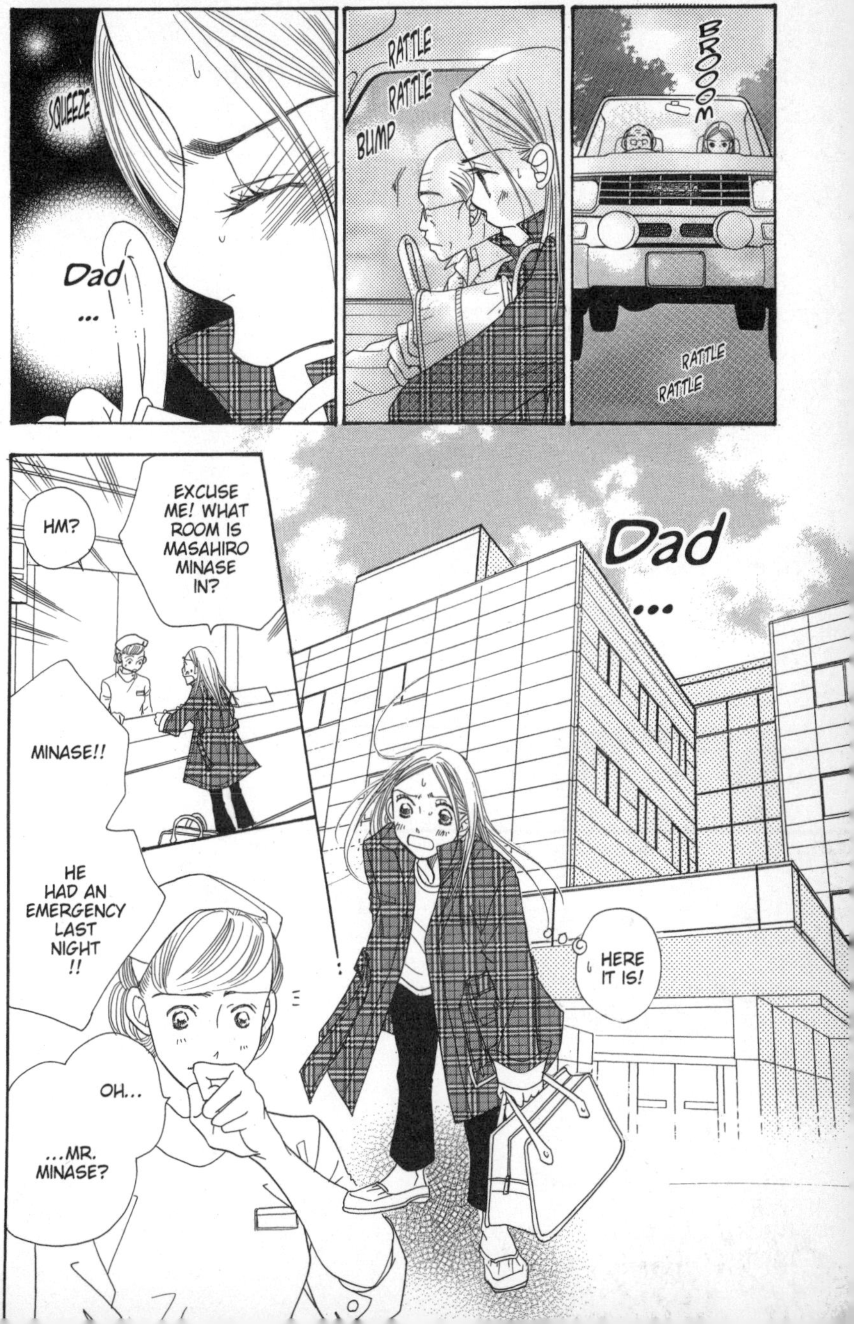
BROOOM
RATTLE RATTLE
RATTLE RATTLE
BUMP
SQUEEZE
Dad...
Dad...
HERE IT IS!
EXCUSE ME! WHAT ROOM IS MASAHIRO MINASE IN?
HM?
MINASE!!
HE HAD AN EMERGENCY LAST NIGHT!!
OH...
...MR. MINASE?

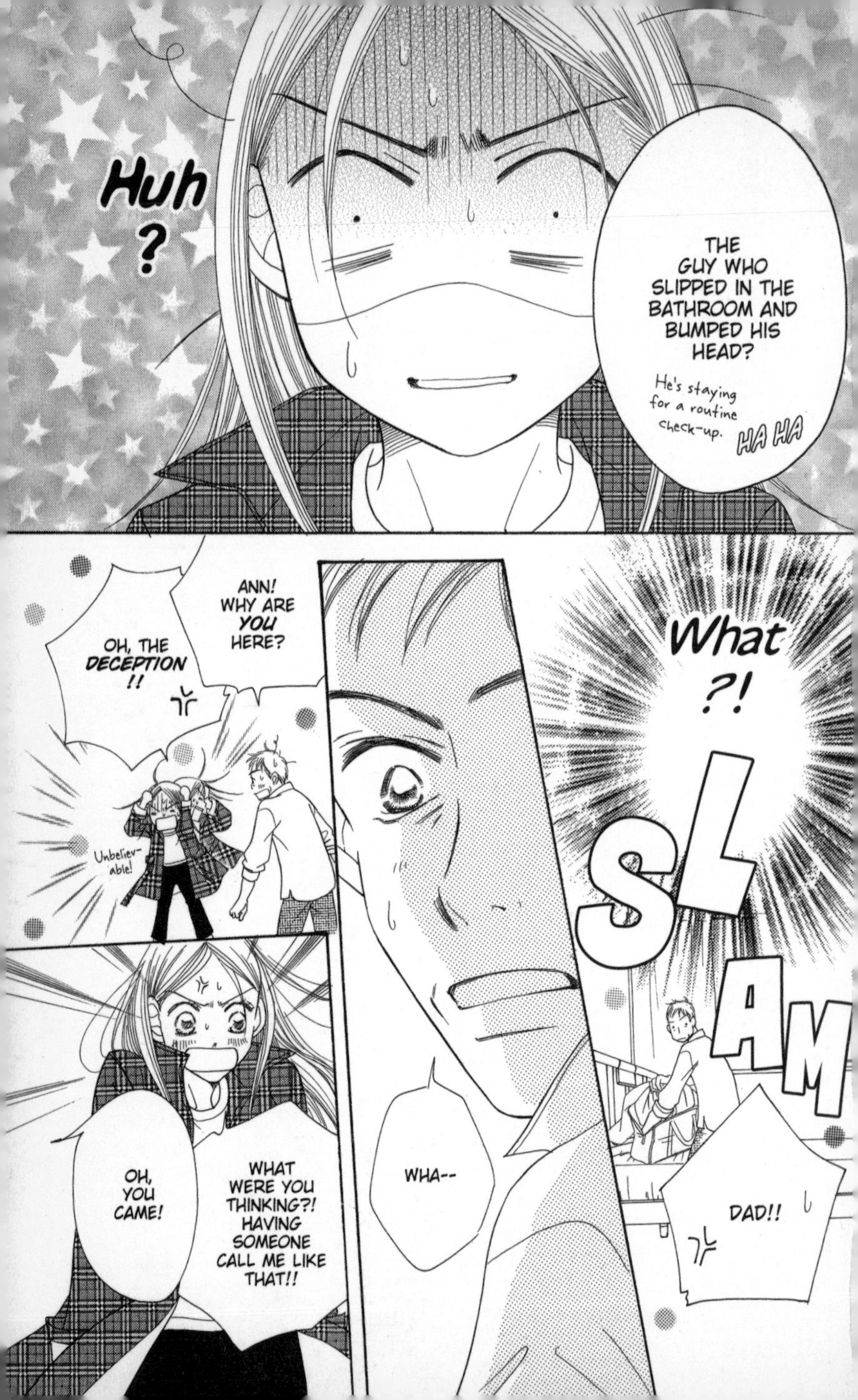
THE GUY WHO SLIPPED IN THE BATHROOM AND BUMPED HIS HEAD?
He's staying for a routine check-up.
HA HA
Huh ?
What ?!
SLAM
DAD!!
WHA--
ANN! WHY ARE YOU HERE?
OH, THE DECEPTION !!
Unbeliev-able!
WHAT WERE YOU THINKING?! HAVING SOMEONE CALL ME LIKE THAT!!
OH, YOU CAME!

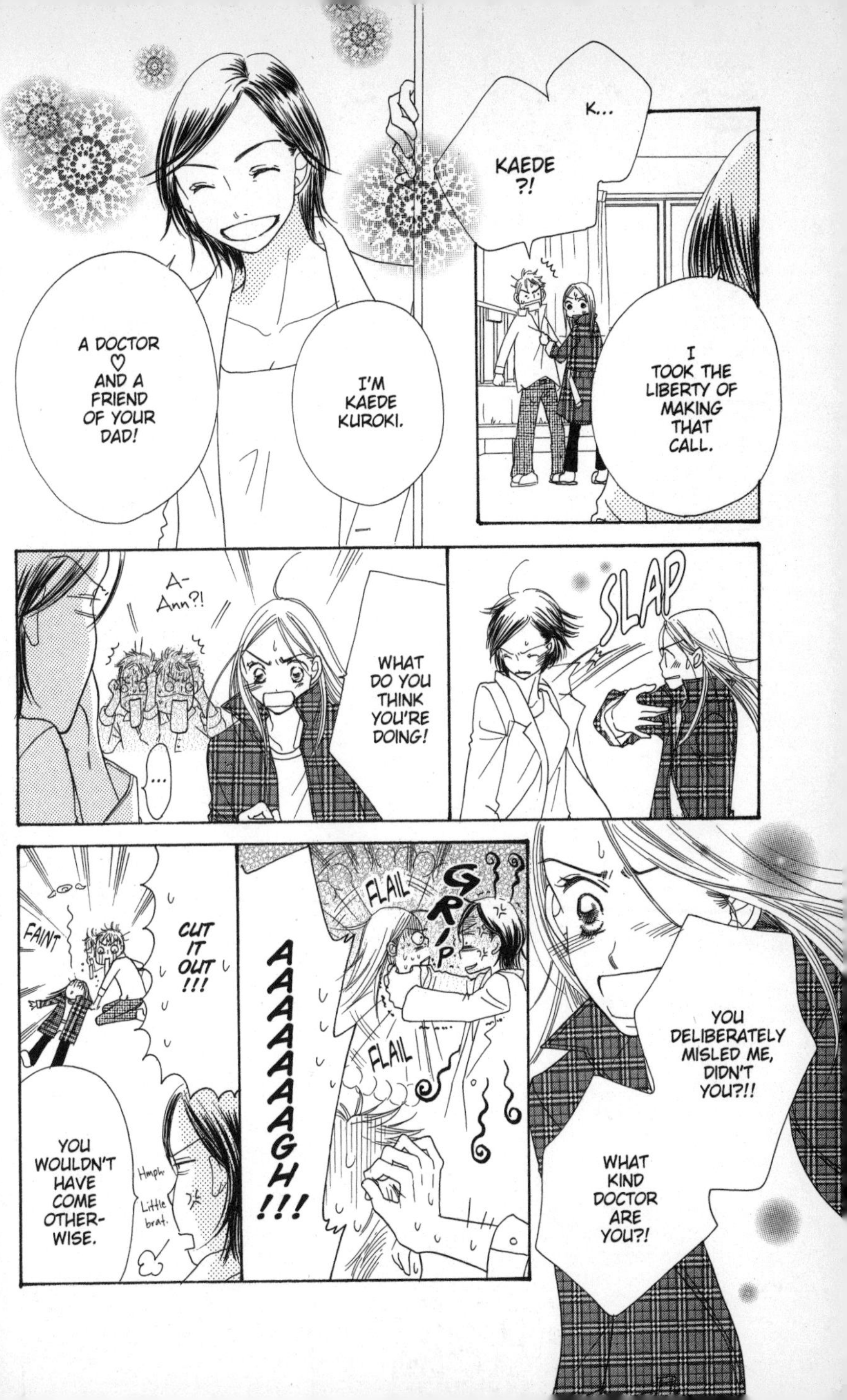
K...
KAEDE ?!
I TOOK THE LIBERTY OF MAKING THAT CALL.
I'M KAEDE KUROKI.
A DOCTOR ♡ AND A FRIEND OF YOUR DAD!
SLAP
WHAT DO YOU THINK YOU'RE DOING!
A- Ann?!
...
YOU DELIBERATELY MISLED ME, DIDN'T YOU?!!
WHAT KIND DOCTOR ARE YOU?!
GRIP
FLAIL
AAAAAAAAGH!!!
FLAIL
CUT IT OUT!!!
FAINT
YOU WOULDN'T HAVE COME OTHER-WISE.
Hmph
Little brat.

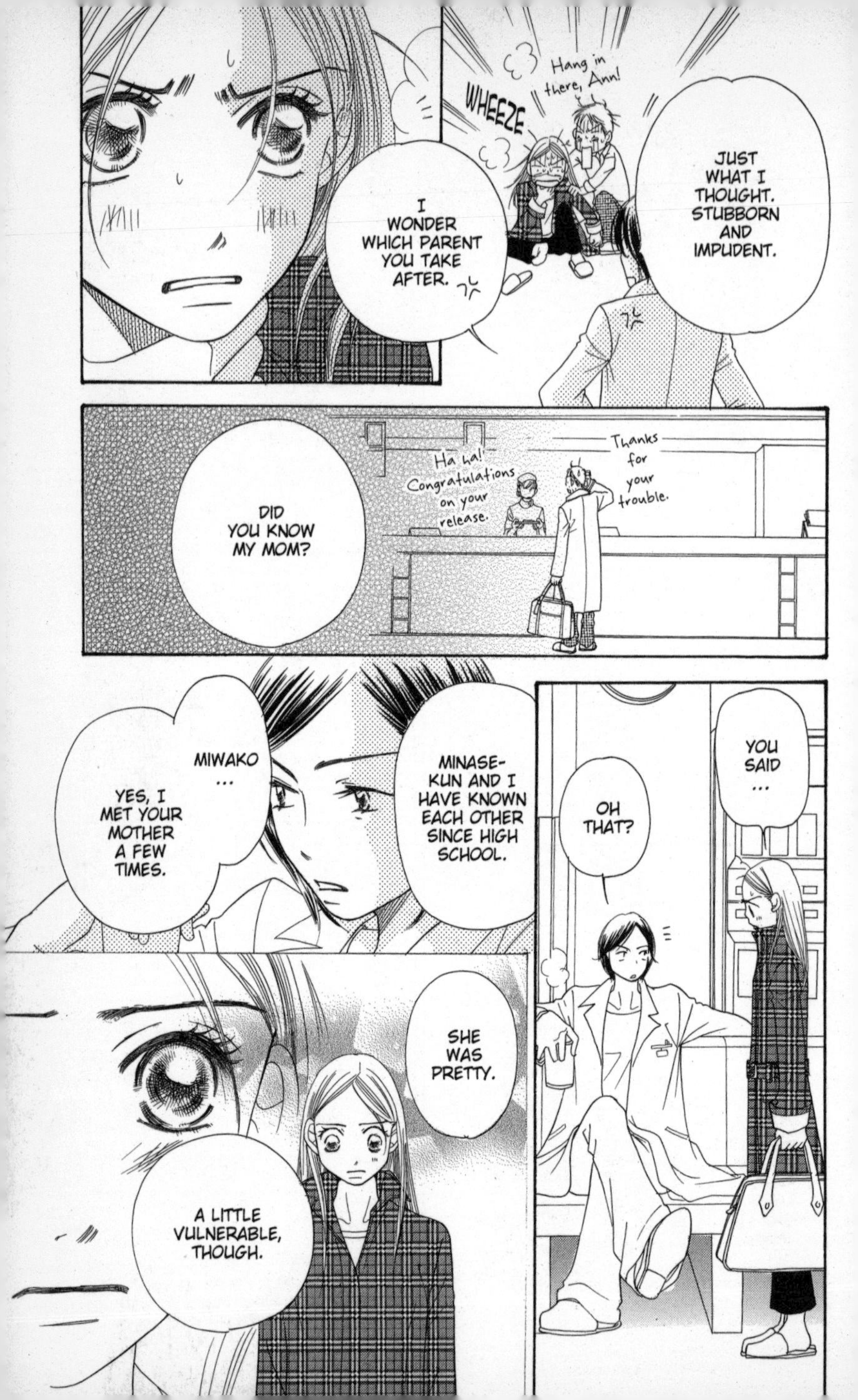
JUST WHAT I THOUGHT. STUBBORN AND IMPUDENT.
Hang in there, Ann!
WHEEZE
I WONDER WHICH PARENT YOU TAKE AFTER.
Thanks for your trouble.
Ha ha! Congratulations on your release.
DID YOU KNOW MY MOM?
YOU SAID ...
OH THAT?
MINASE-KUN AND I HAVE KNOWN EACH OTHER SINCE HIGH SCHOOL.
MIWAKO ...
YES, I MET YOUR MOTHER A FEW TIMES.
SHE WAS PRETTY.
A LITTLE VULNERABLE, THOUGH.

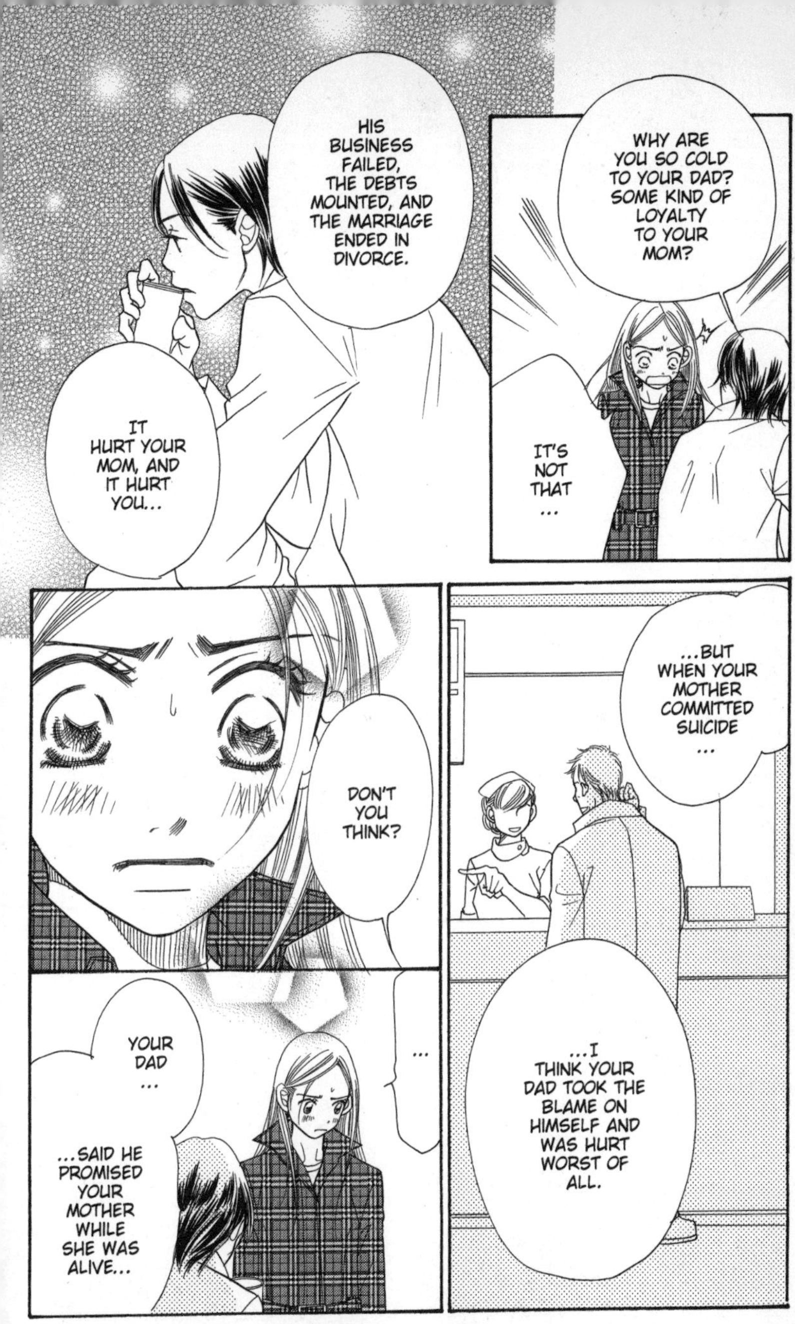
WHY ARE YOU SO COLD TO YOUR DAD? SOME KIND OF LOYALTY TO YOUR MOM?
IT'S NOT THAT ...
HIS BUSINESS FAILED, THE DEBTS MOUNTED, AND THE MARRIAGE ENDED IN DIVORCE.
IT HURT YOUR MOM, AND IT HURT YOU...
...BUT WHEN YOUR MOTHER COMMITTED SUICIDE ...
...I THINK YOUR DAD TOOK THE BLAME ON HIMSELF AND WAS HURT WORST OF ALL.
DON'T YOU THINK?
...
YOUR DAD ...
...SAID HE PROMISED YOUR MOTHER WHILE SHE WAS ALIVE...

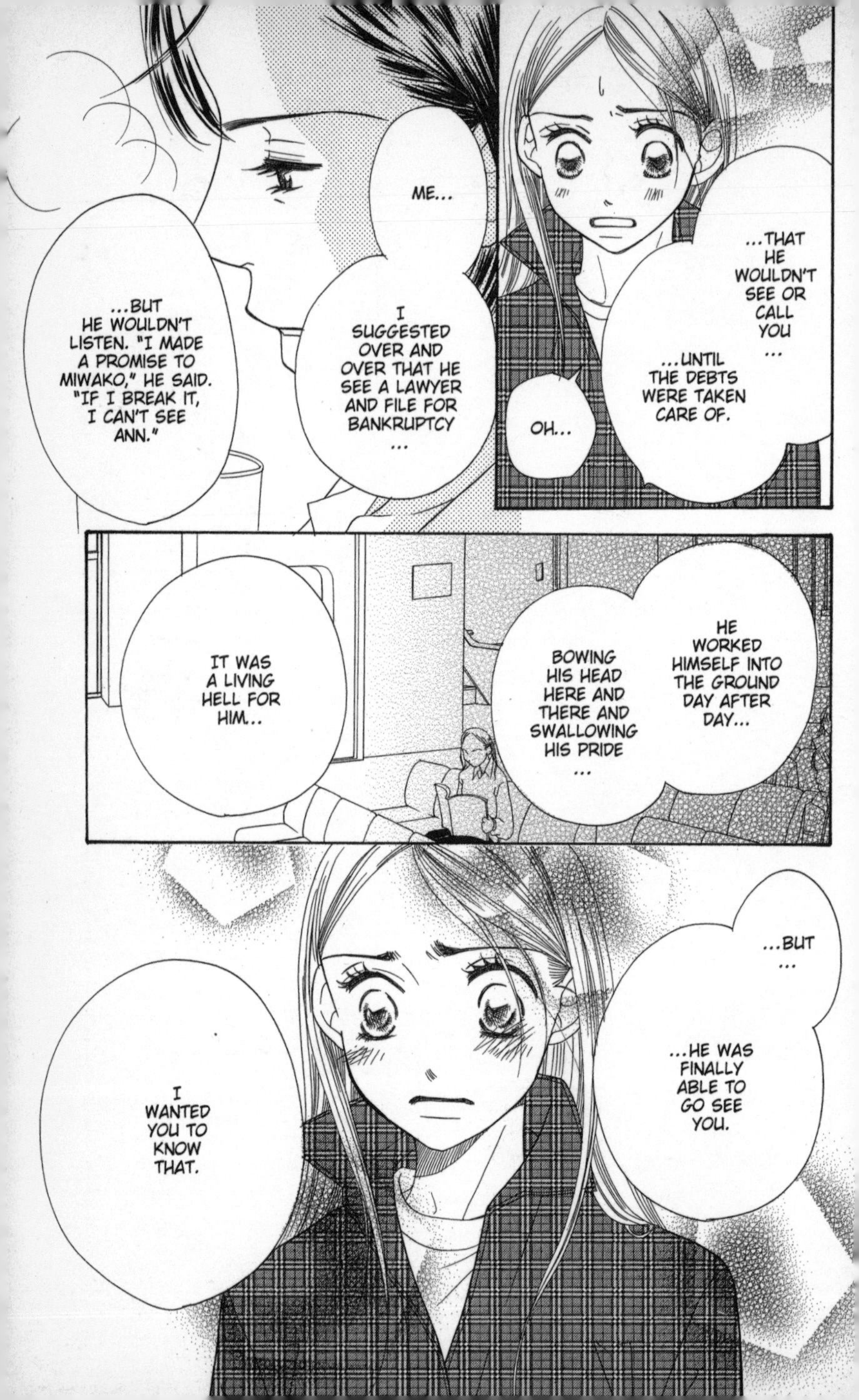
...THAT HE WOULDN'T SEE OR CALL YOU ...
...UNTIL THE DEBTS WERE TAKEN CARE OF.
OH...
ME...
I SUGGESTED OVER AND OVER THAT HE SEE A LAWYER AND FILE FOR BANKRUPTCY ...
...BUT HE WOULDN'T LISTEN. "I MADE A PROMISE TO MIWAKO," HE SAID. "IF I BREAK IT, I CAN'T SEE ANN."
HE WORKED HIMSELF INTO THE GROUND DAY AFTER DAY...
BOWING HIS HEAD HERE AND THERE AND SWALLOWING HIS PRIDE ...
IT WAS A LIVING HELL FOR HIM...
...BUT ...
...HE WAS FINALLY ABLE TO GO SEE YOU.
I WANTED YOU TO KNOW THAT.

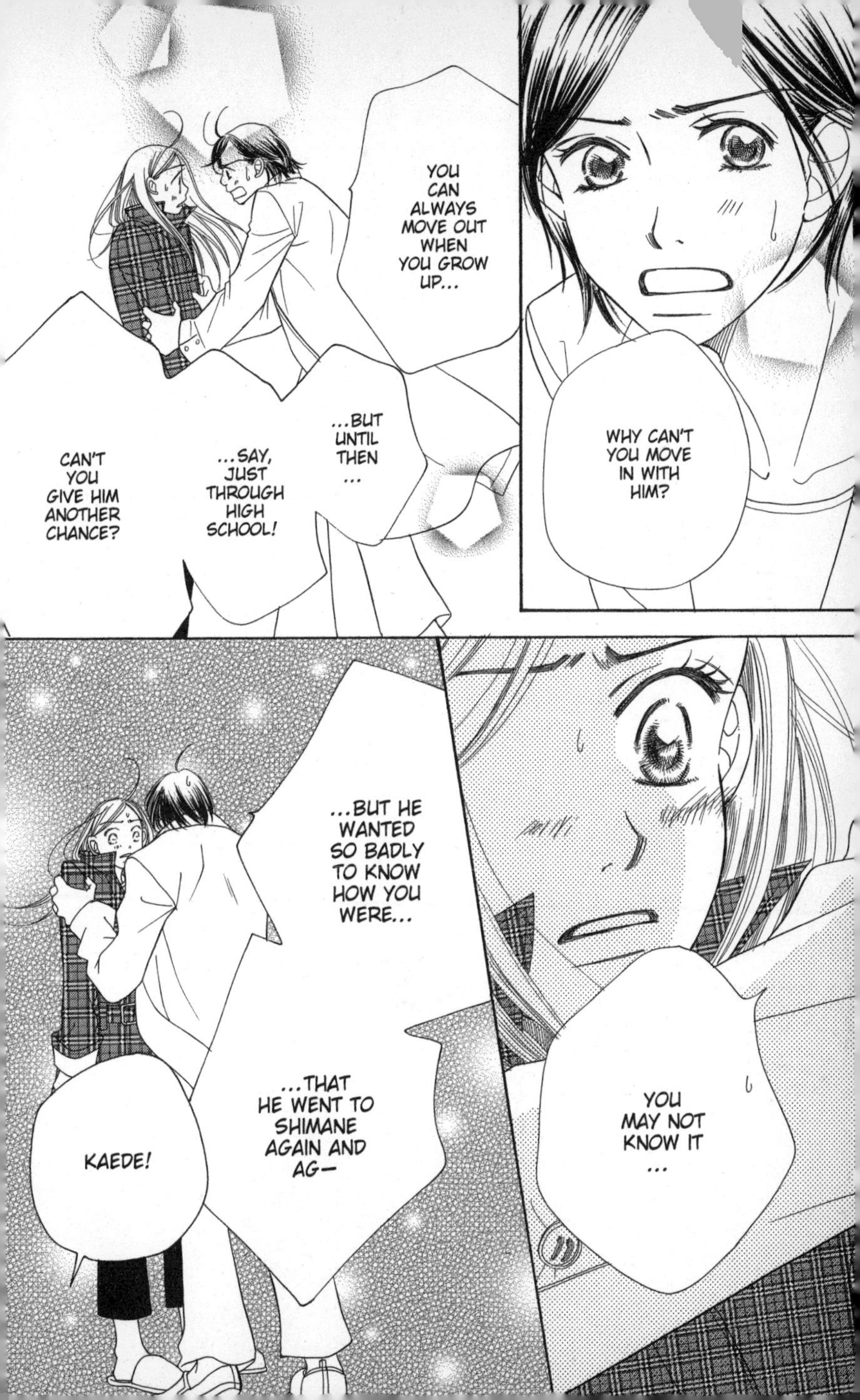
WHY CAN'T YOU MOVE IN WITH HIM?
YOU CAN ALWAYS MOVE OUT WHEN YOU GROW UP...
...BUT UNTIL THEN ...
...SAY, JUST THROUGH HIGH SCHOOL!
CAN'T YOU GIVE HIM ANOTHER CHANCE?
YOU MAY NOT KNOW IT ...
...BUT HE WANTED SO BADLY TO KNOW HOW YOU WERE...
...THAT HE WENT TO SHIMANE AGAIN AND AG—
KAEDE!

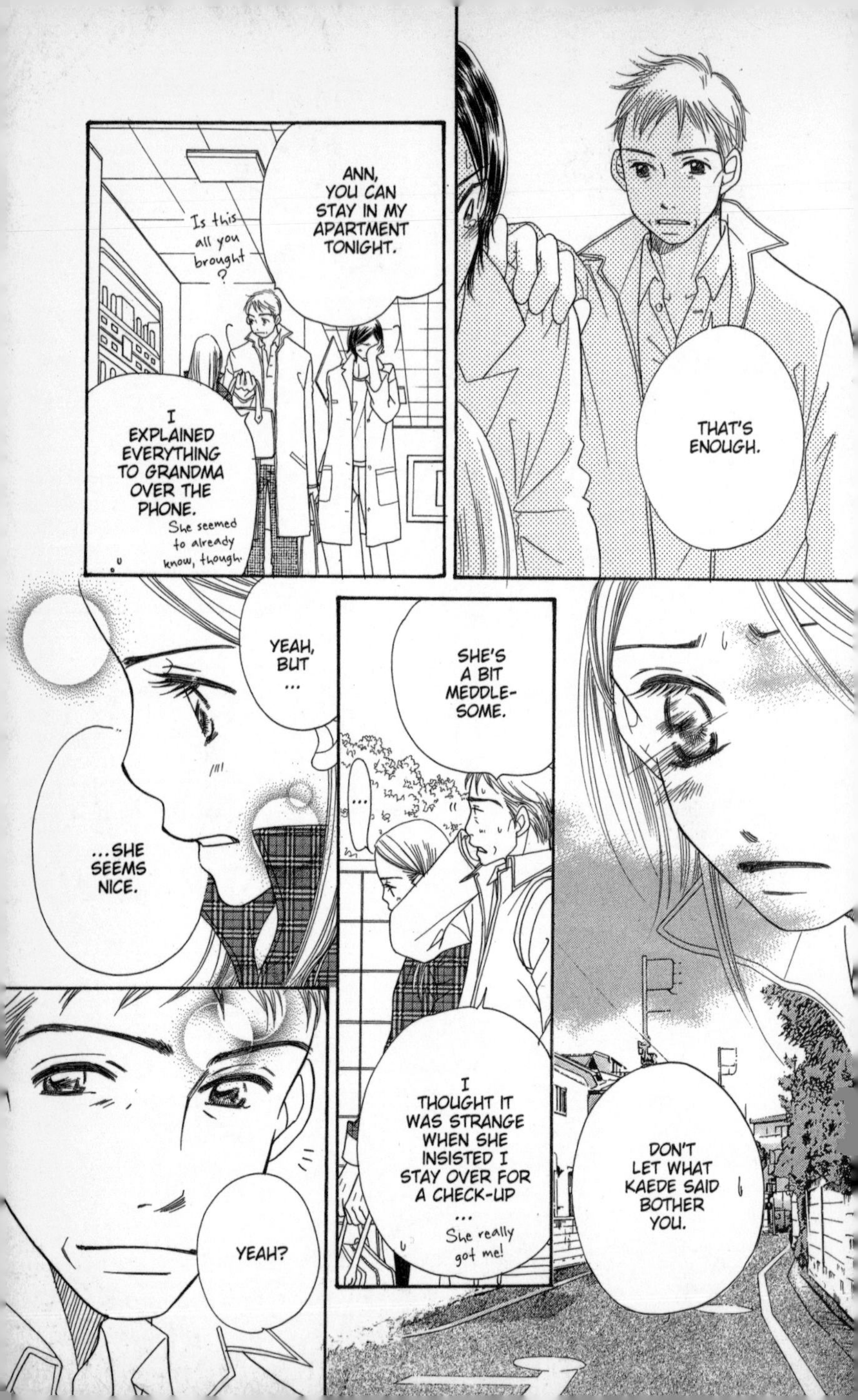
THAT'S ENOUGH.
ANN, YOU CAN STAY IN MY APARTMENT TONIGHT.
Is this all you brought?
I EXPLAINED EVERYTHING TO GRANDMA OVER THE PHONE.
She seemed to already know, though.
DON'T LET WHAT KAEDE SAID BOTHER YOU.
SHE'S A BIT MEDDLE-SOME.
...
I THOUGHT IT WAS STRANGE WHEN SHE INSISTED I STAY OVER FOR A CHECK-UP...
She really got me!
YEAH, BUT...
...SHE SEEMS NICE.
YEAH?

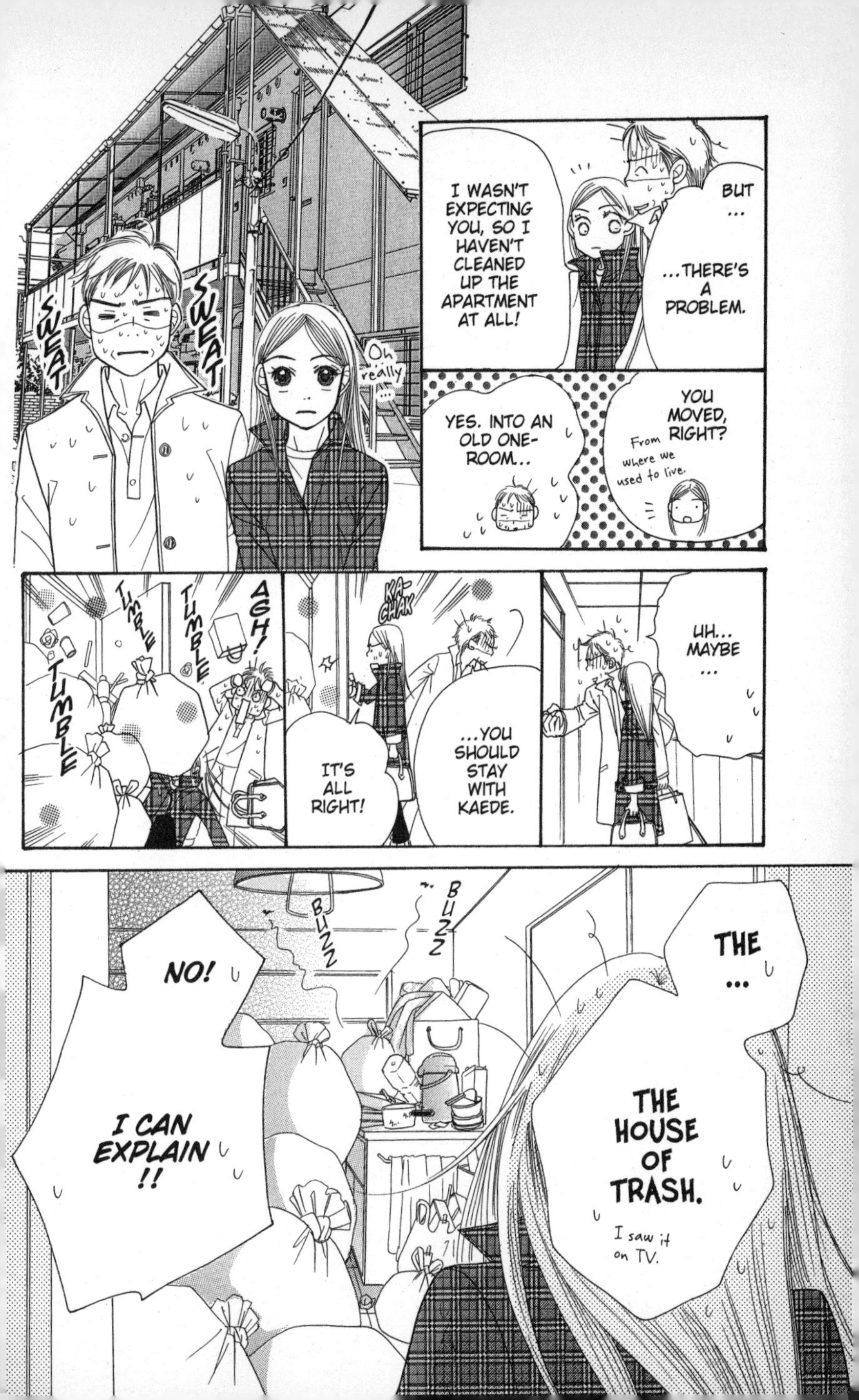

BUT...
...THERE'S A PROBLEM.
I WASN'T EXPECTING YOU, SO I HAVEN'T CLEANED UP THE APARTMENT AT ALL!
YOU MOVED, RIGHT?
From where we used to live.
YES. INTO AN OLD ONE-ROOM...
SWEAT
SWEAT
Oh really...
UH... MAYBE...
KA-CHAK
...YOU SHOULD STAY WITH KAEDE.
IT'S ALL RIGHT!
AGH!
TUMBLE
TUMBLE
TUMBLE
THE...
THE HOUSE OF TRASH.
I saw it on TV.
BUZZ
BUZZ
NO!
I CAN EXPLAIN!!

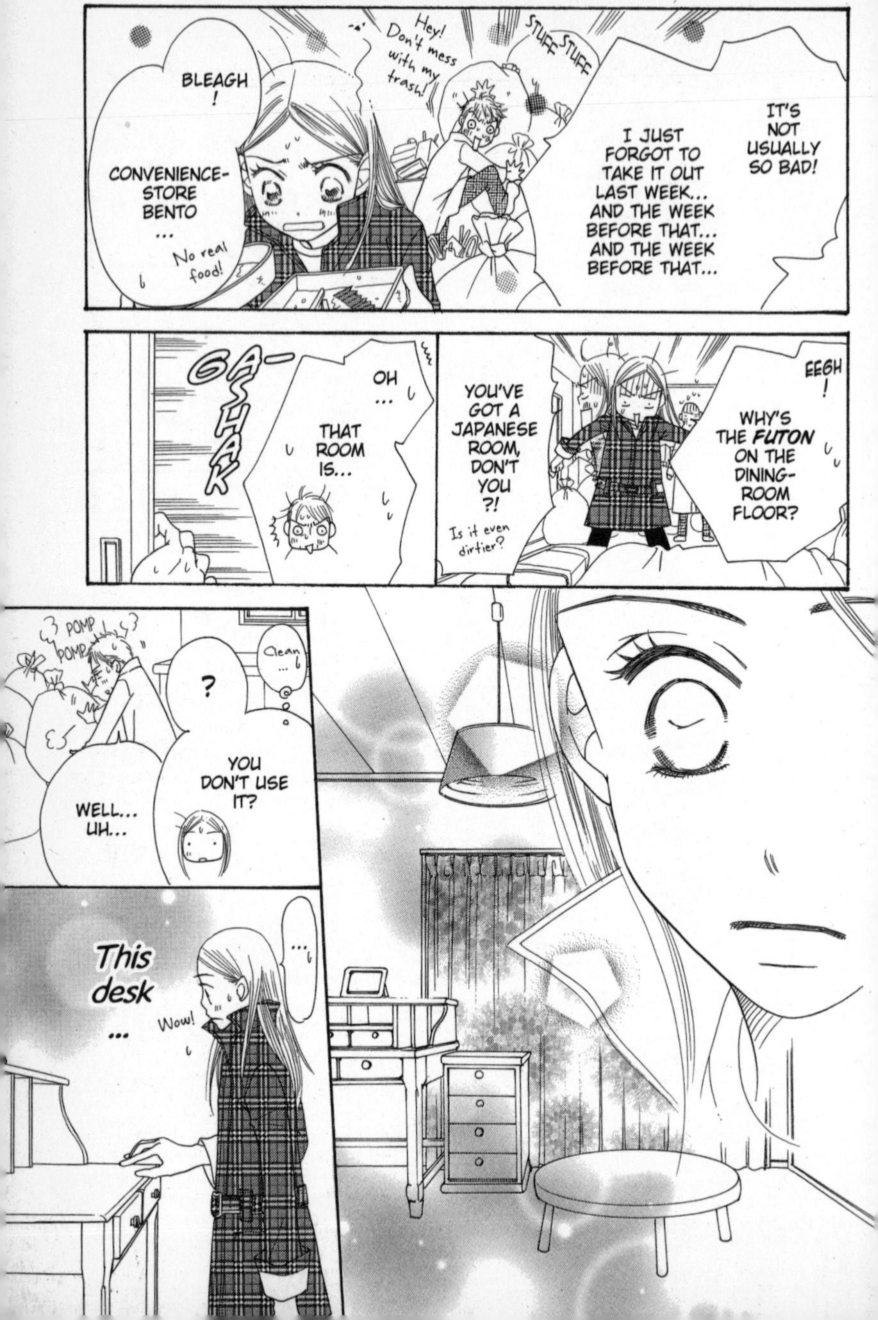
IT'S NOT USUALLY SO BAD!
I JUST FORGOT TO TAKE IT OUT LAST WEEK... AND THE WEEK BEFORE THAT... AND THE WEEK BEFORE THAT...
STUFF STUFF
Hey! Don't mess with my trash!
BLEAGH!
CONVENIENCE-STORE BENTO...
No real food!
EEGH!
WHY'S THE *FUTON* ON THE DINING-ROOM FLOOR?
YOU'VE GOT A JAPANESE ROOM, DON'T YOU?!
Is it even dirtier?
OH...
THAT ROOM IS...
GA-SHAK
Clean...
?
YOU DON'T USE IT?
WELL... UH...
POMP POMP
...
This desk...
Wow!

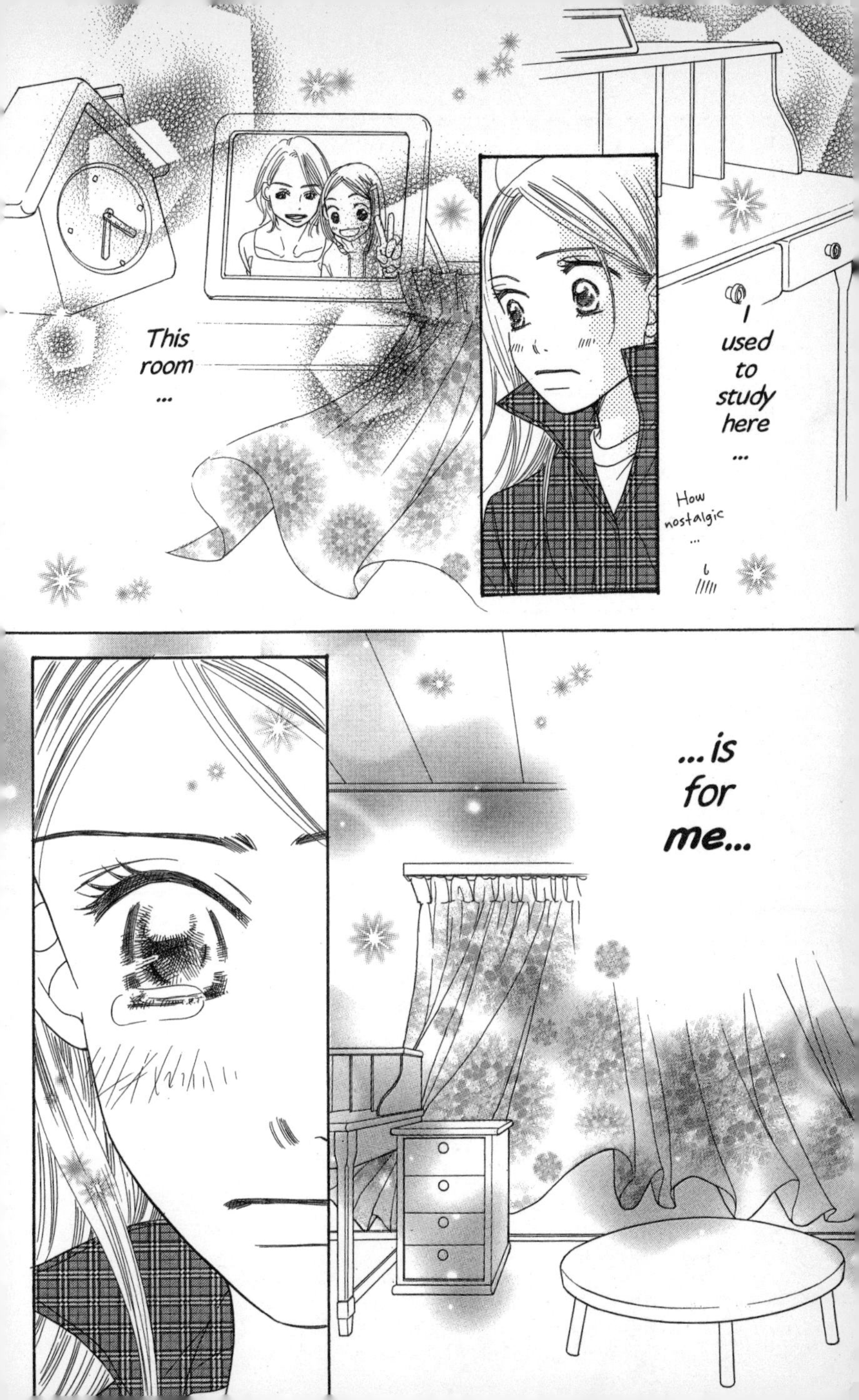
I used to study here...
How nostalgic...
This room...
...is for me...

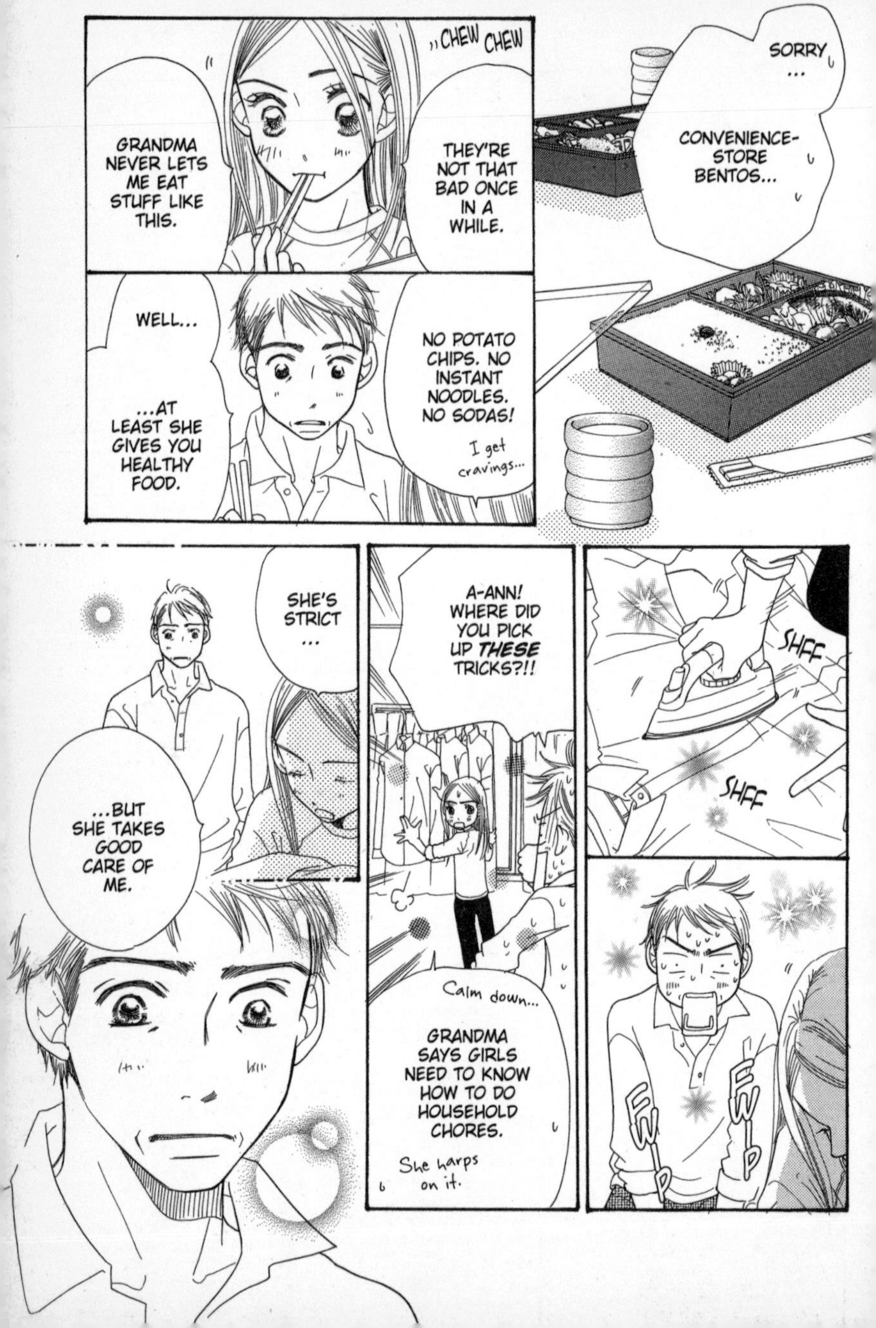
SORRY...
CONVENIENCE-STORE BENTOS...
CHEW CHEW
THEY'RE NOT THAT BAD ONCE IN A WHILE.
GRANDMA NEVER LETS ME EAT STUFF LIKE THIS.
NO POTATO CHIPS. NO INSTANT NOODLES. NO SODAS!
I get cravings...
WELL...
...AT LEAST SHE GIVES YOU HEALTHY FOOD.
SHFF
SHFF
FWIP
FWIP
A-ANN! WHERE DID YOU PICK UP THESE TRICKS?!!
Calm down...
GRANDMA SAYS GIRLS NEED TO KNOW HOW TO DO HOUSEHOLD CHORES.
She harps on it.
SHE'S STRICT...
...BUT SHE TAKES GOOD CARE OF ME.

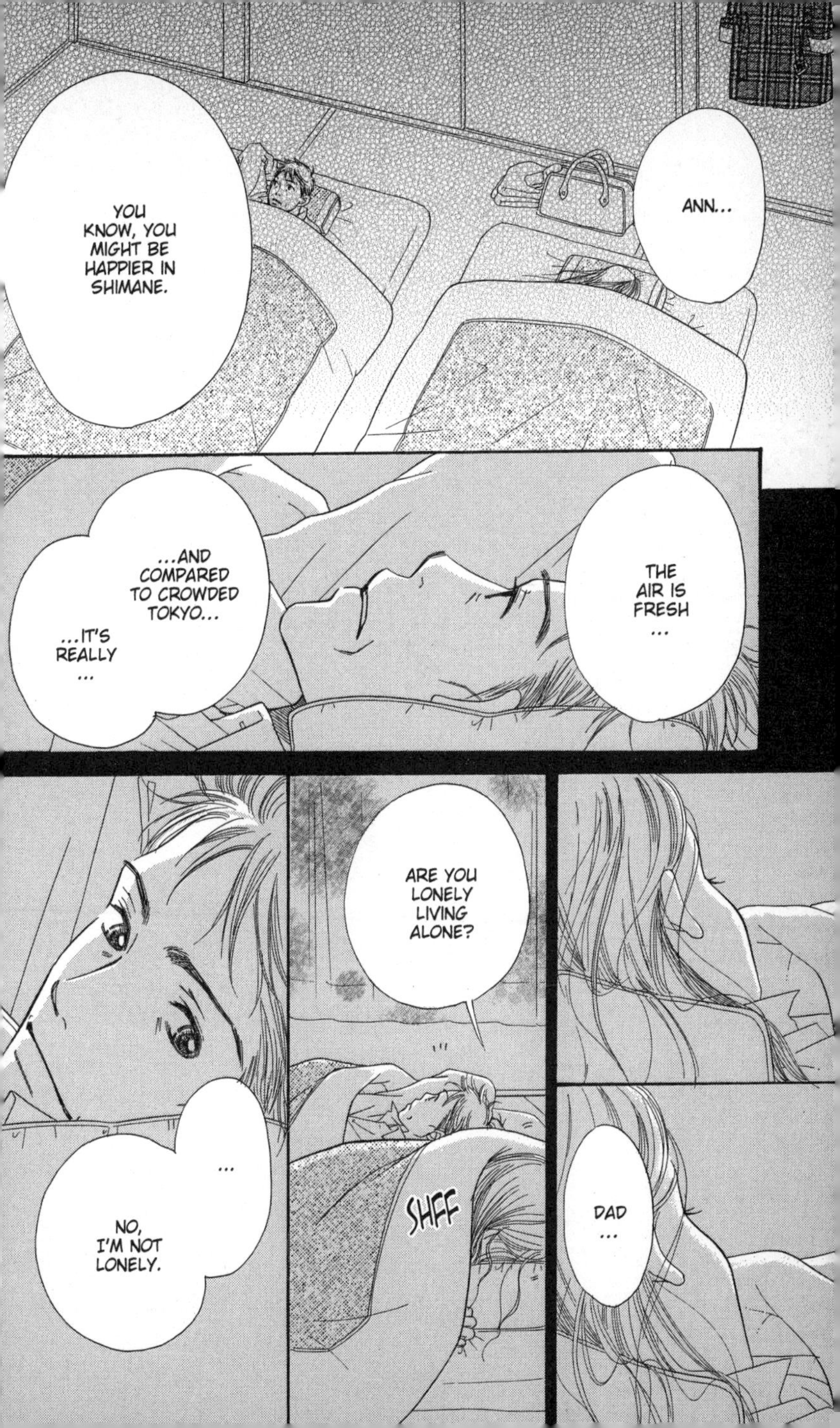
ANN...
YOU KNOW, YOU MIGHT BE HAPPIER IN SHIMANE.
THE AIR IS FRESH ...
...AND COMPARED TO CROWDED TOKYO...
...IT'S REALLY ...
DAD ...
ARE YOU LONELY LIVING ALONE?
SHFF
...
NO, I'M NOT LONELY.

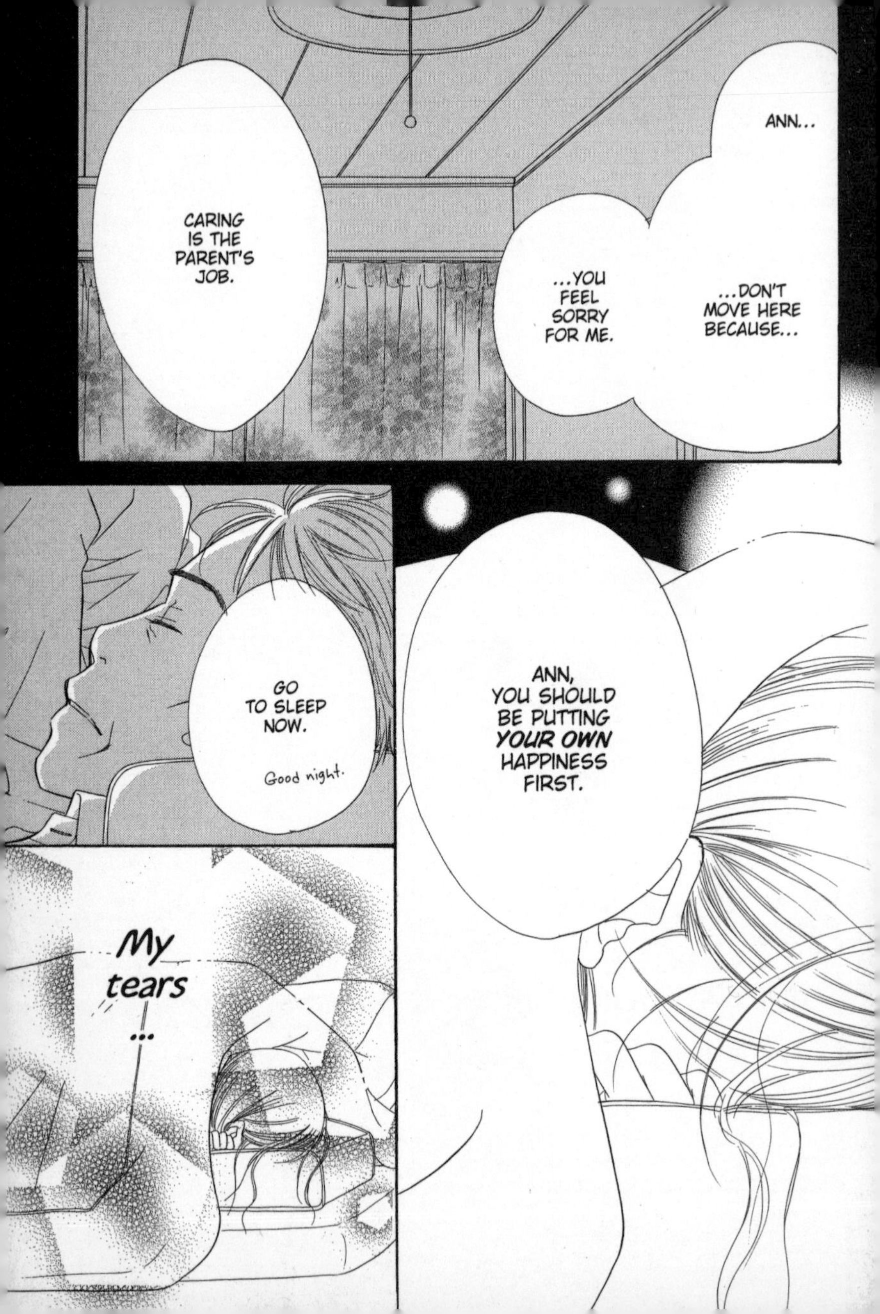
ANN...
...DON'T MOVE HERE BECAUSE...
...YOU FEEL SORRY FOR ME.
CARING IS THE PARENT'S JOB.
ANN, YOU SHOULD BE PUTTING YOUR OWN HAPPINESS FIRST.
GO TO SLEEP NOW.
Good night.
My tears...

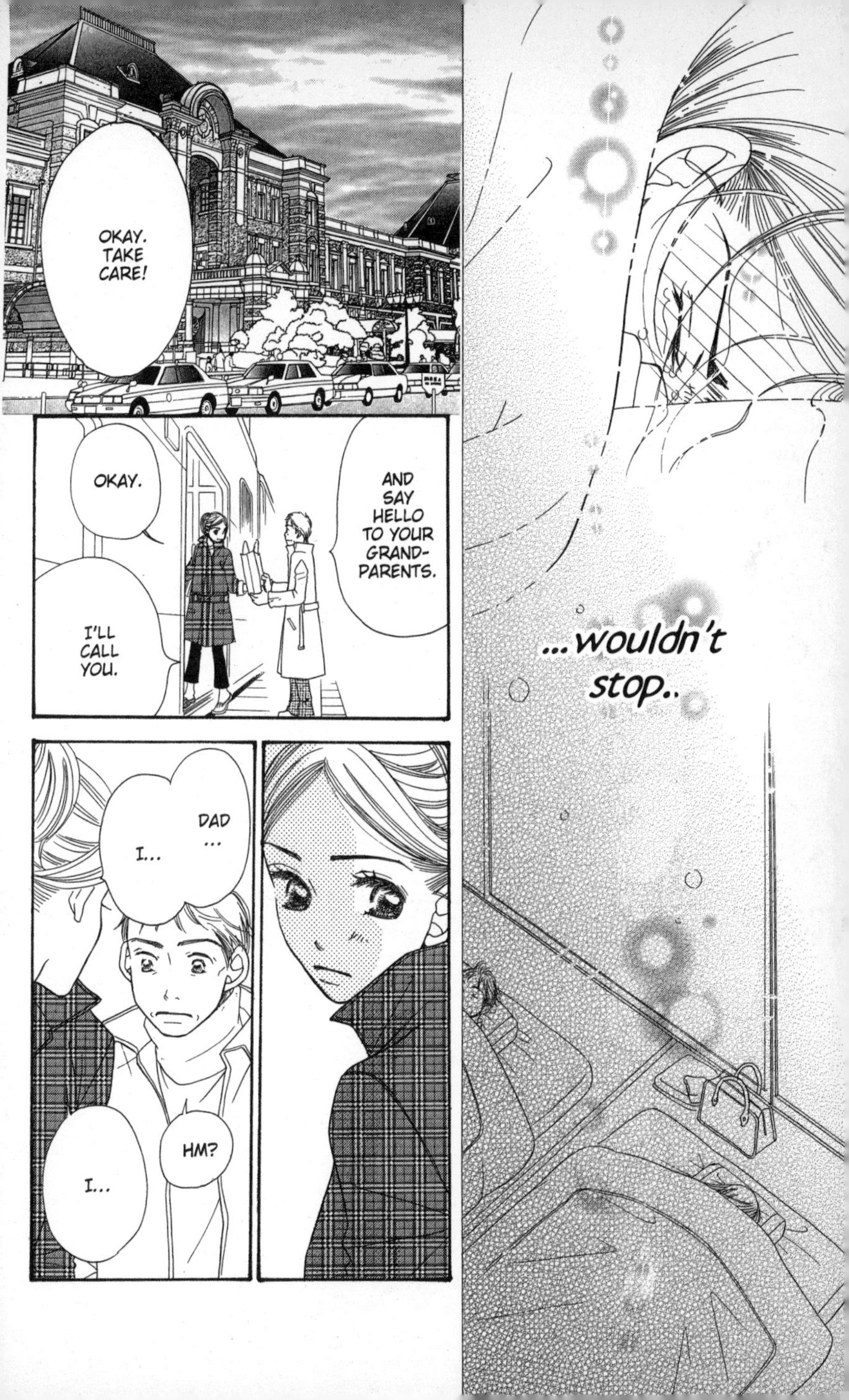
...wouldn't stop..
OKAY. TAKE CARE!
AND SAY HELLO TO YOUR GRAND-PARENTS.
OKAY.
I'LL CALL YOU.
DAD... I...
HM?
I...

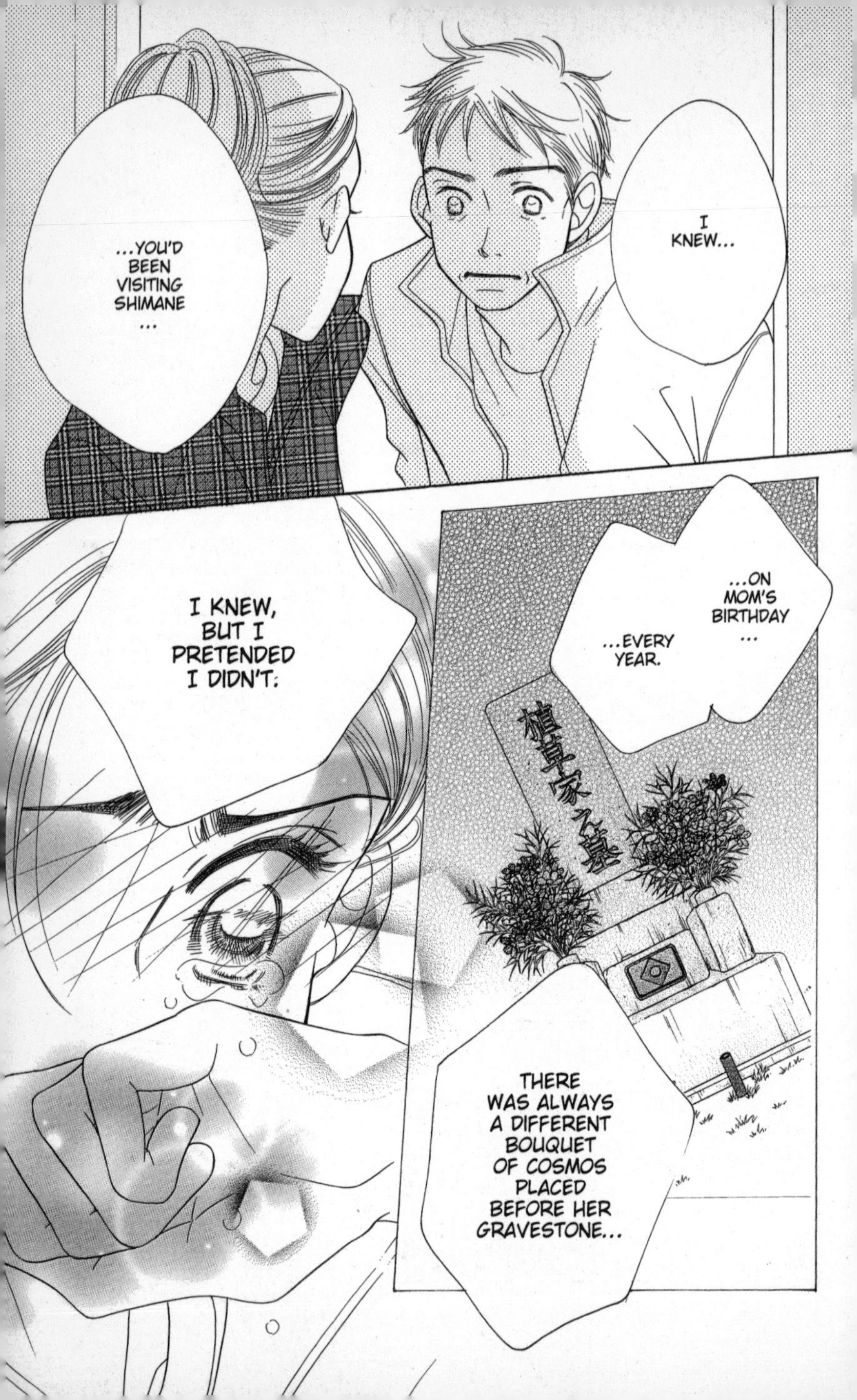

I KNEW...
...YOU'D BEEN VISITING SHIMANE ...
...ON MOM'S BIRTHDAY ...
...EVERY YEAR.
植草家之墓
THERE WAS ALWAYS A DIFFERENT BOUQUET OF COSMOS PLACED BEFORE HER GRAVESTONE...
I KNEW, BUT I PRETENDED I DIDN'T.

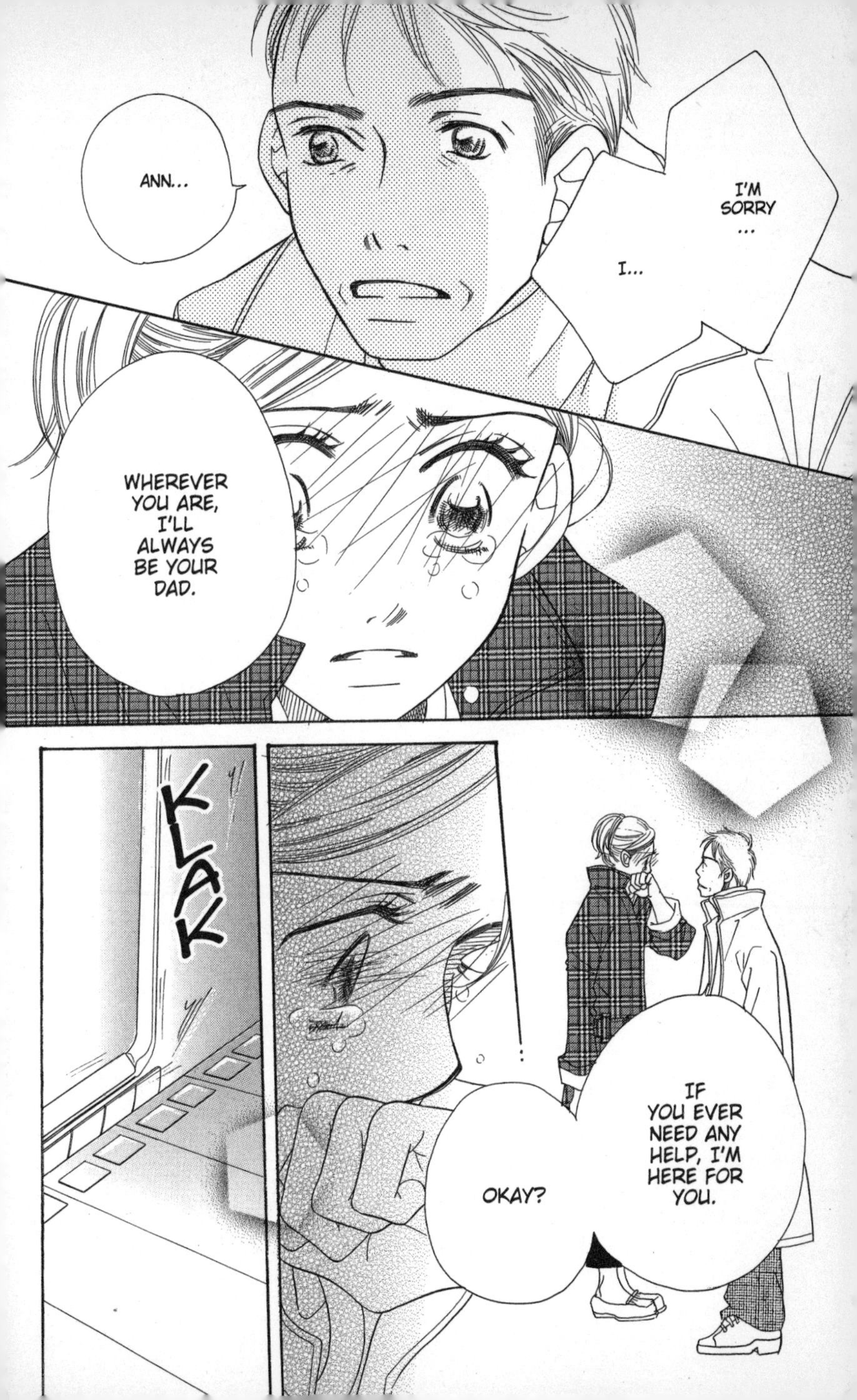
I'M SORRY ...
I...
ANN...
WHEREVER YOU ARE, I'LL ALWAYS BE YOUR DAD.
IF YOU EVER NEED ANY HELP, I'M HERE FOR YOU.
OKAY?
KLAK

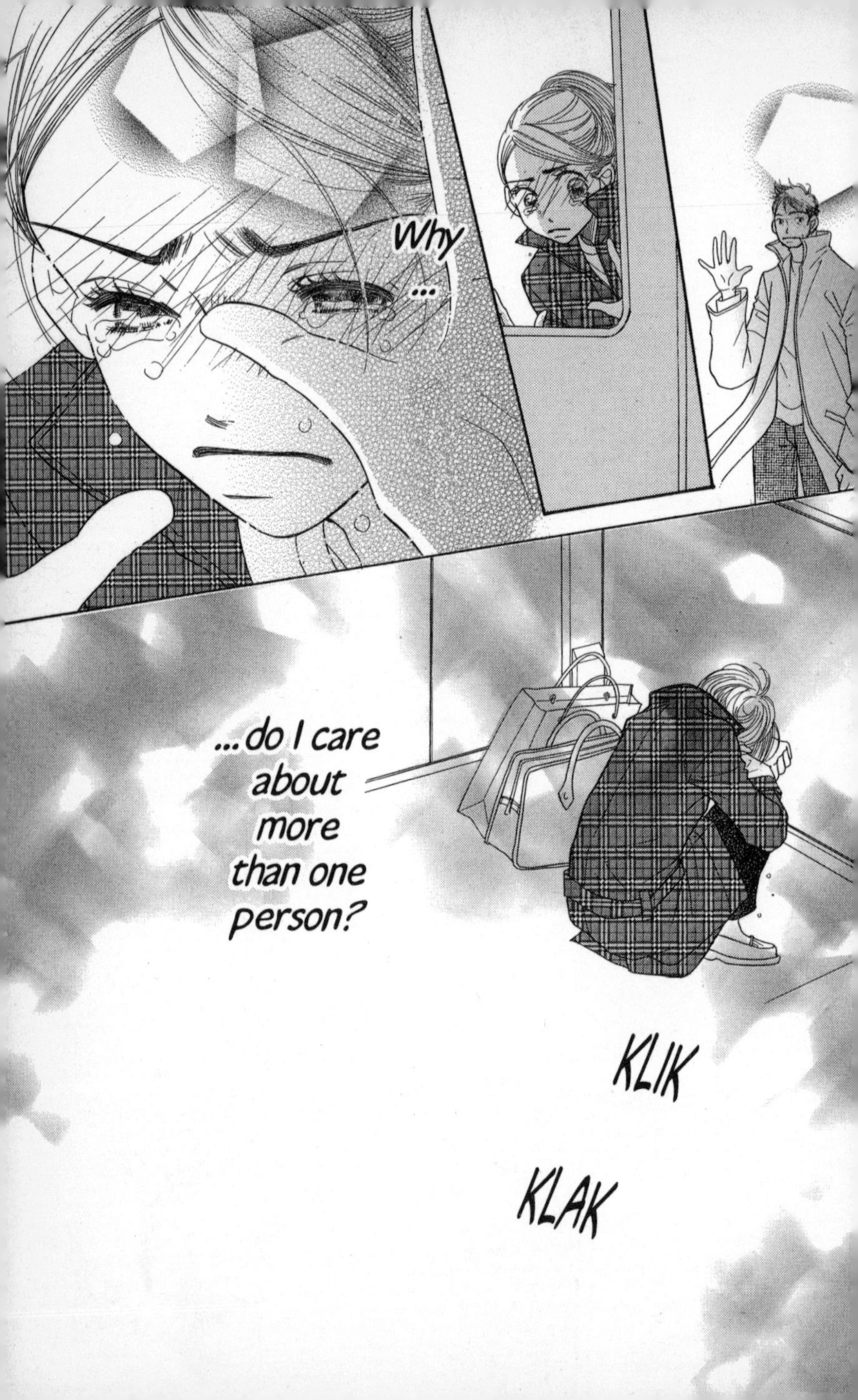
Why ...
...do I care about more than one person?
KLIK
KLAK

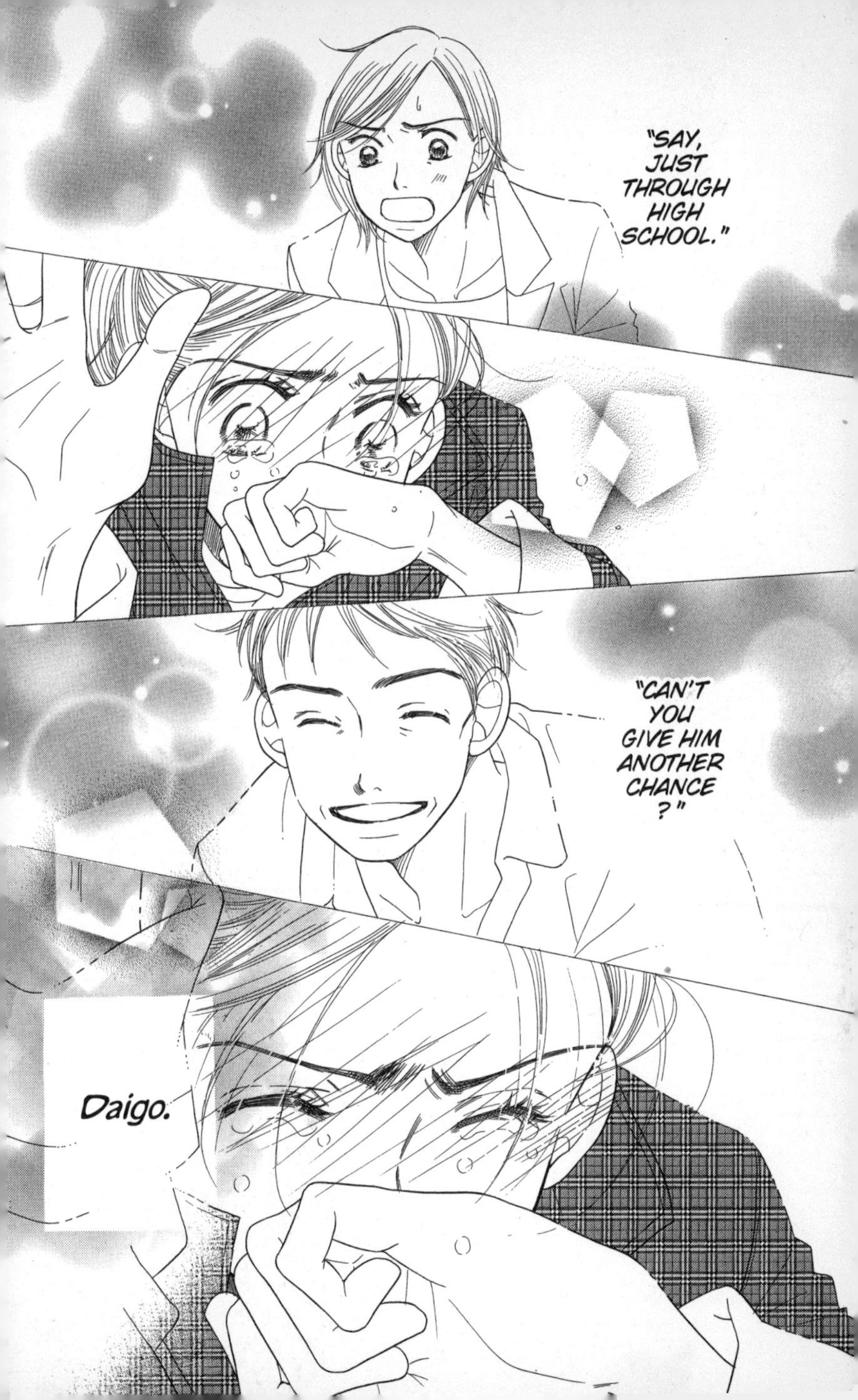
"SAY, JUST THROUGH HIGH SCHOOL."
"CAN'T YOU GIVE HIM ANOTHER CHANCE?"
Daigo.

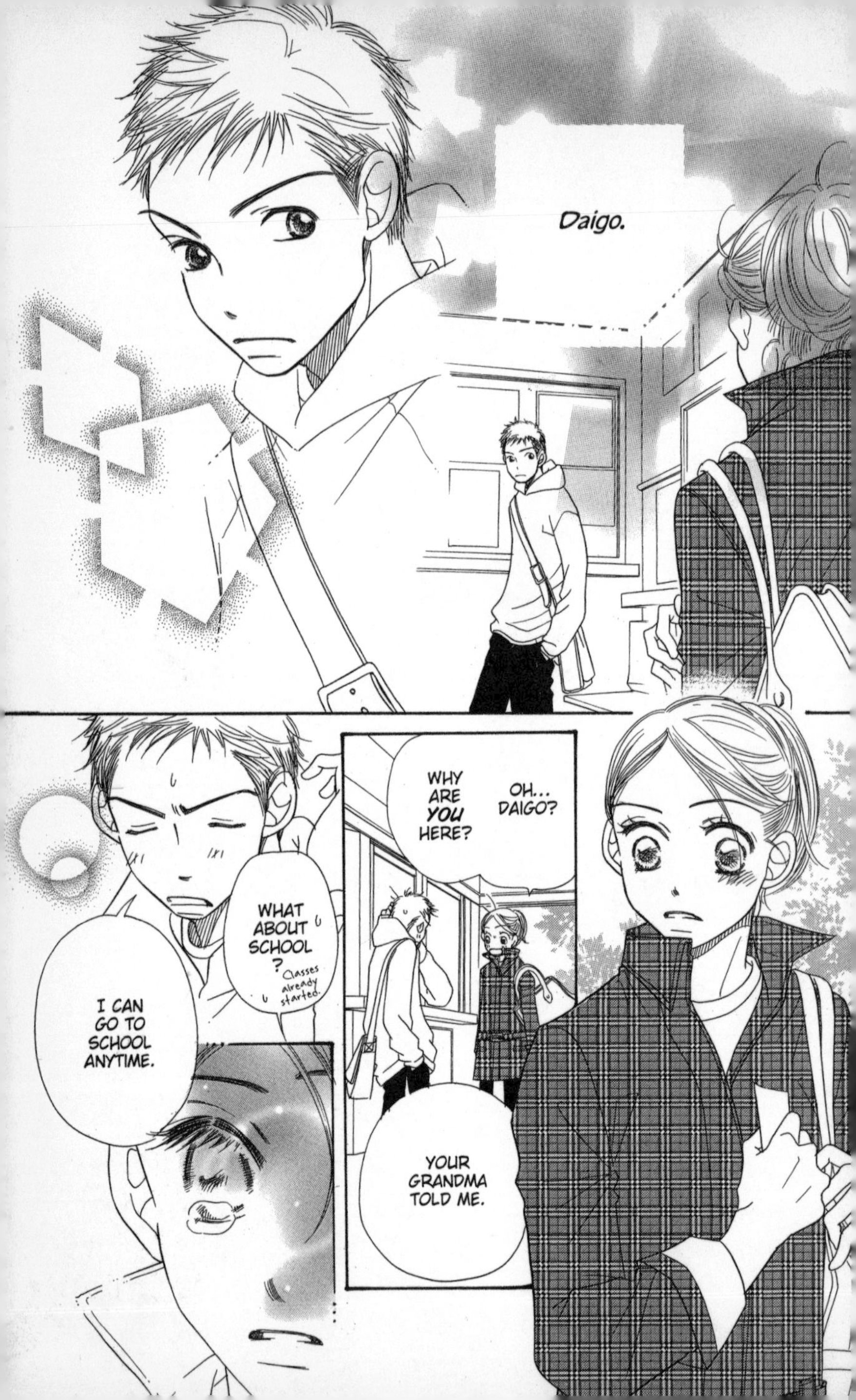
Daigo.
OH... DAIGO?
WHY ARE YOU HERE?
YOUR GRANDMA TOLD ME.
WHAT ABOUT SCHOOL?
Classes already started.
I CAN GO TO SCHOOL ANYTIME.

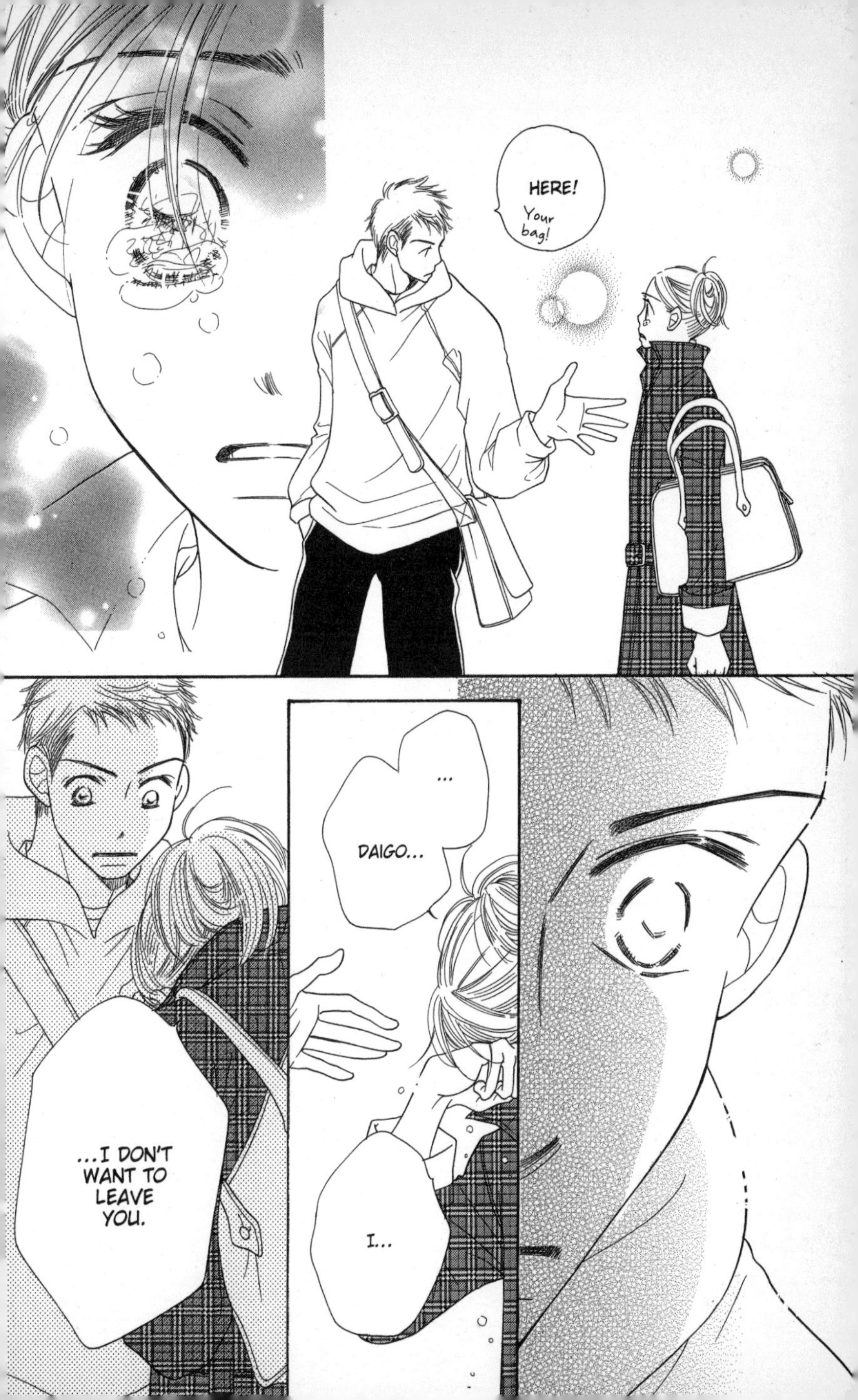
HERE! Your bag!
...
DAIGO...
I...
...I DON'T WANT TO LEAVE YOU.

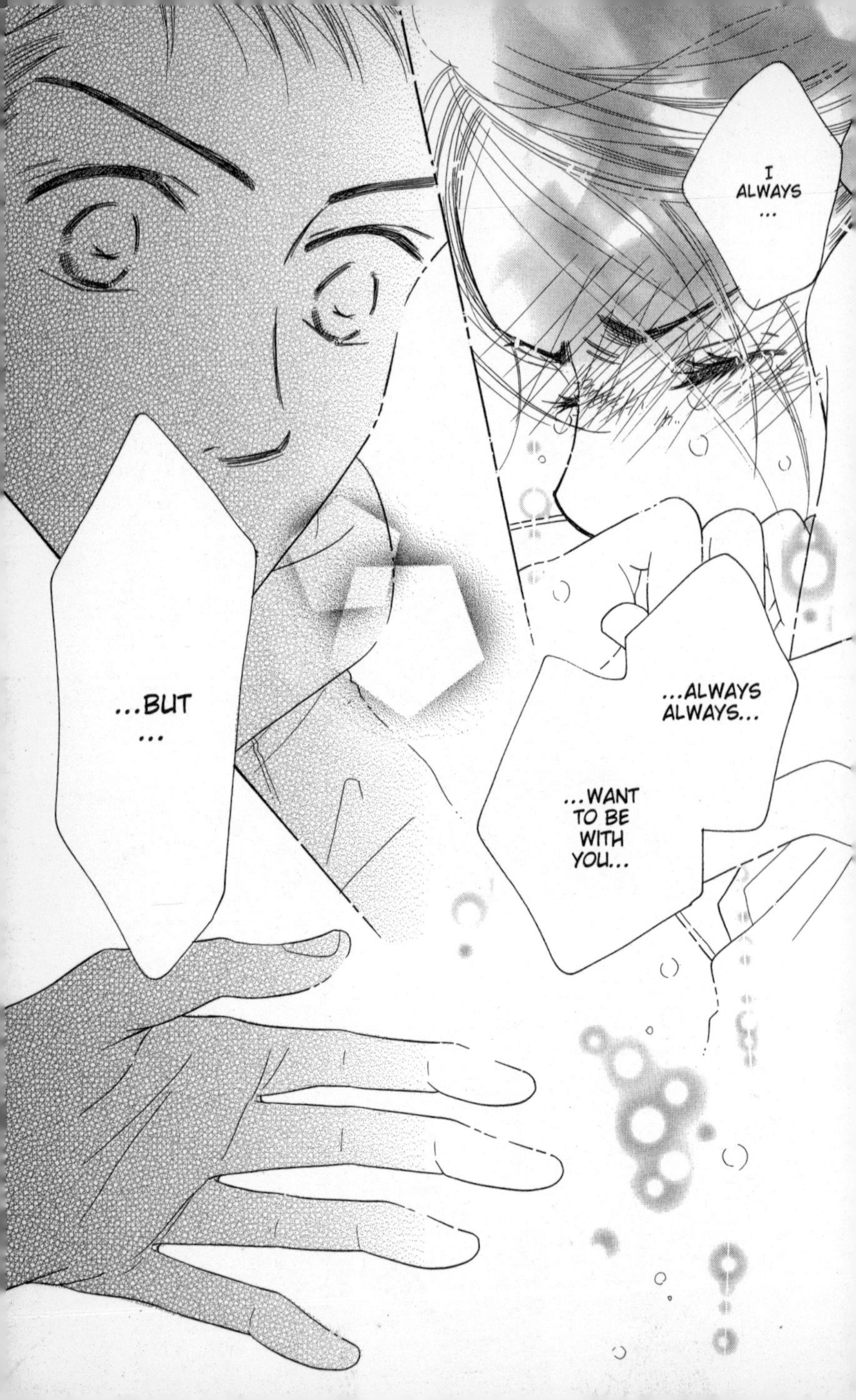
I ALWAYS ...
...ALWAYS ALWAYS...
...WANT TO BE WITH YOU...
...BUT ...

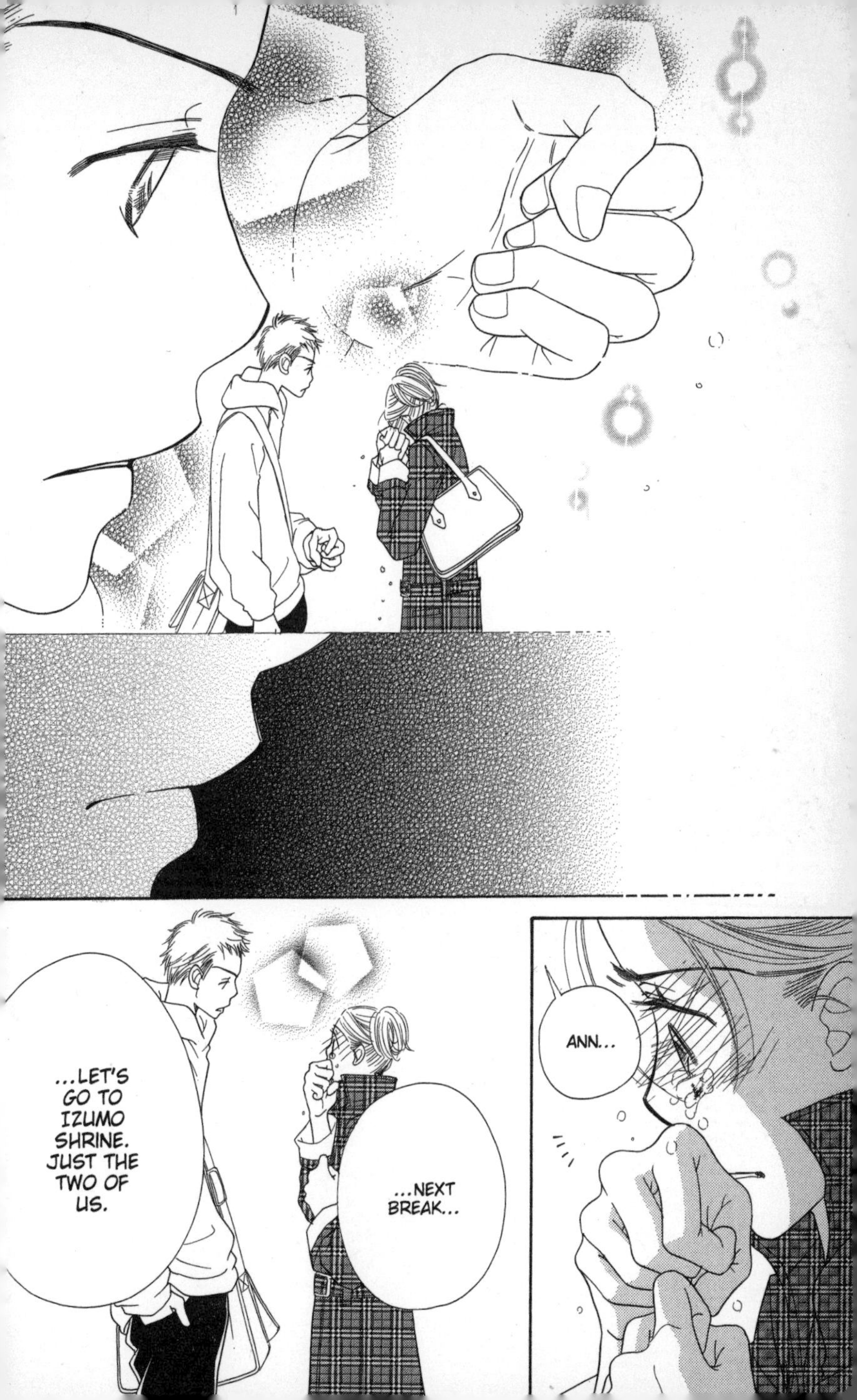
ANN...
...NEXT BREAK...
...LET'S GO TO IZUMO SHRINE. JUST THE TWO OF US.

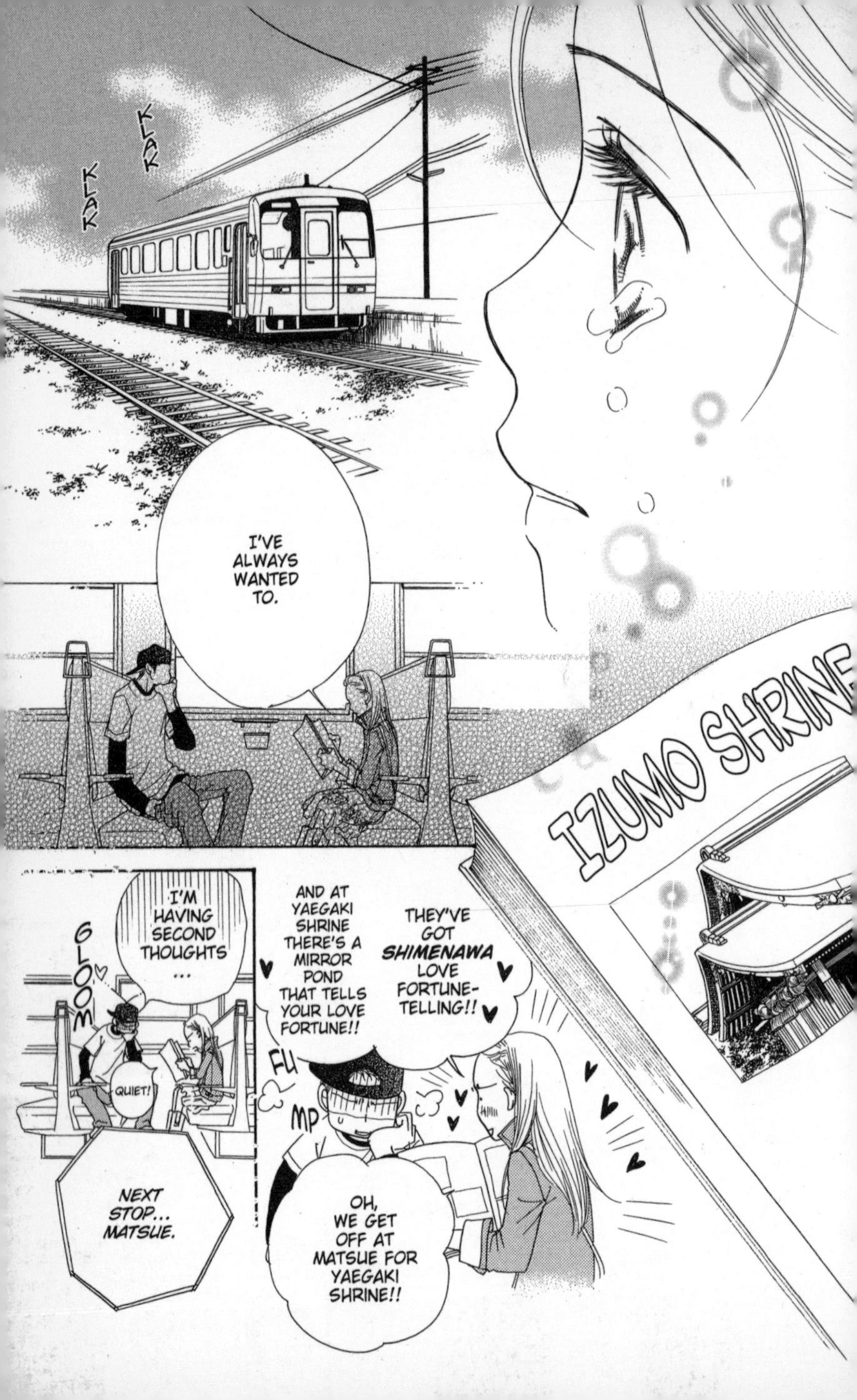
KLAK
KLAK
I'VE ALWAYS WANTED TO.
IZUMO SHRINE
THEY'VE GOT **SHIMENAWA** LOVE FORTUNE-TELLING!!
AND AT YAEGAKI SHRINE THERE'S A MIRROR POND THAT TELLS YOUR LOVE FORTUNE!!
FU
MP
OH, WE GET OFF AT MATSUE FOR YAEGAKI SHRINE!!
I'M HAVING SECOND THOUGHTS...
GLOOM
QUIET!
NEXT STOP... MATSUE.

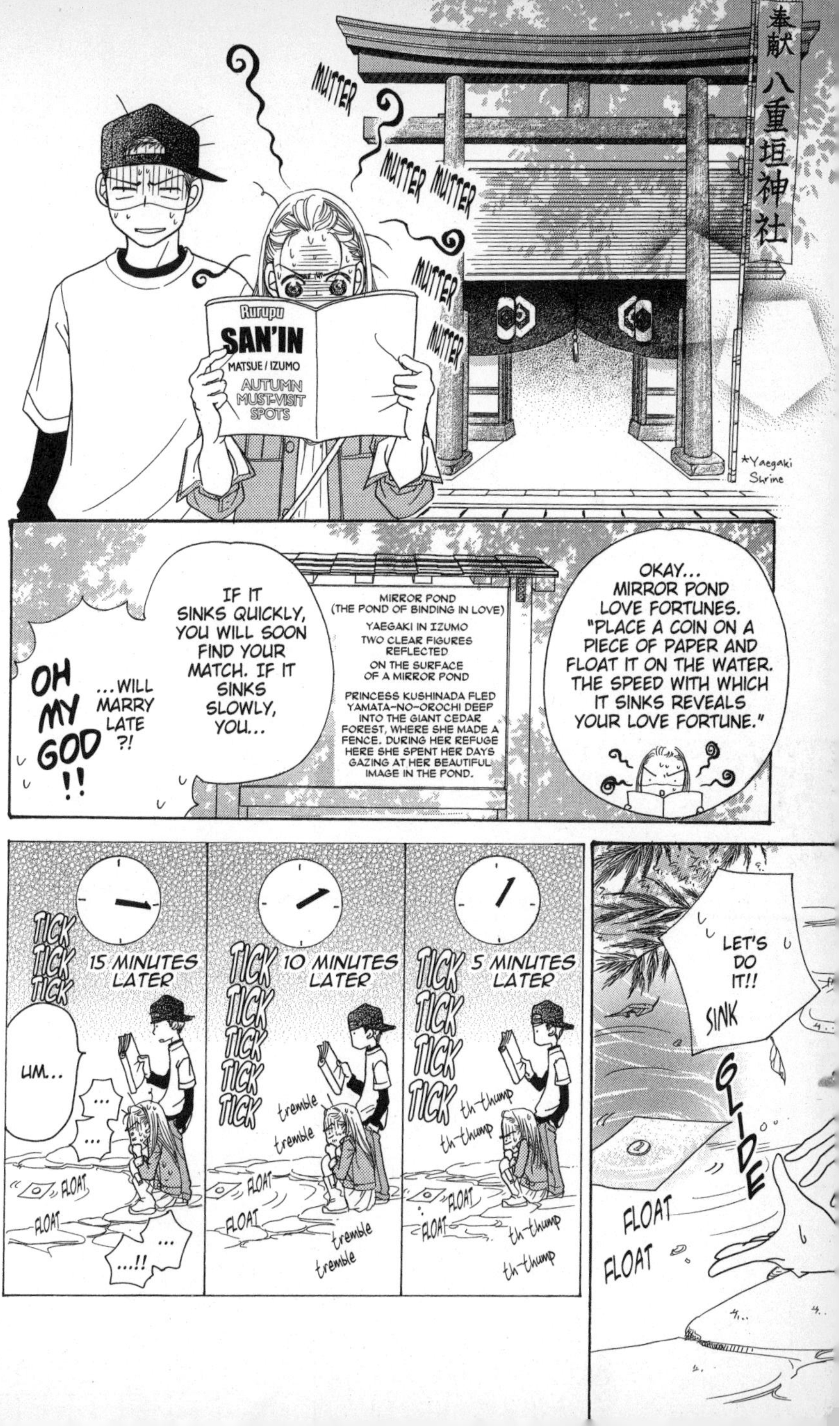
奉献 八重垣神社
*Yaegaki Shrine
MUTTER
MUTTER MUTTER
MUTTER
MUTTER
Rurupu
SAN'IN
MATSUE / IZUMO
AUTUMN MUST-VISIT SPOTS
OKAY... MIRROR POND LOVE FORTUNES. "PLACE A COIN ON A PIECE OF PAPER AND FLOAT IT ON THE WATER. THE SPEED WITH WHICH IT SINKS REVEALS YOUR LOVE FORTUNE."
MIRROR POND (THE POND OF BINDING IN LOVE)
YAEGAKI IN IZUMO
TWO CLEAR FIGURES REFLECTED
ON THE SURFACE OF A MIRROR POND
PRINCESS KUSHINADA FLED YAMATA-NO-OROCHI DEEP INTO THE GIANT CEDAR FOREST, WHERE SHE MADE A FENCE. DURING HER REFUGE HERE SHE SPENT HER DAYS GAZING AT HER BEAUTIFUL IMAGE IN THE POND.
IF IT SINKS QUICKLY, YOU WILL SOON FIND YOUR MATCH. IF IT SINKS SLOWLY, YOU...
...WILL MARRY LATE?!
OH MY GOD!!
LET'S DO IT!!
SINK
GLIDE
FLOAT
FLOAT
5 MINUTES LATER
TICK TICK TICK TICK
th-thump
th-thump
FLOAT
FLOAT
th-thump
th-thump
10 MINUTES LATER
TICK TICK TICK TICK TICK
tremble
tremble
FLOAT
FLOAT
tremble
tremble
15 MINUTES LATER
TICK TICK TICK
UM...
...
...
FLOAT
FLOAT
...
...!!

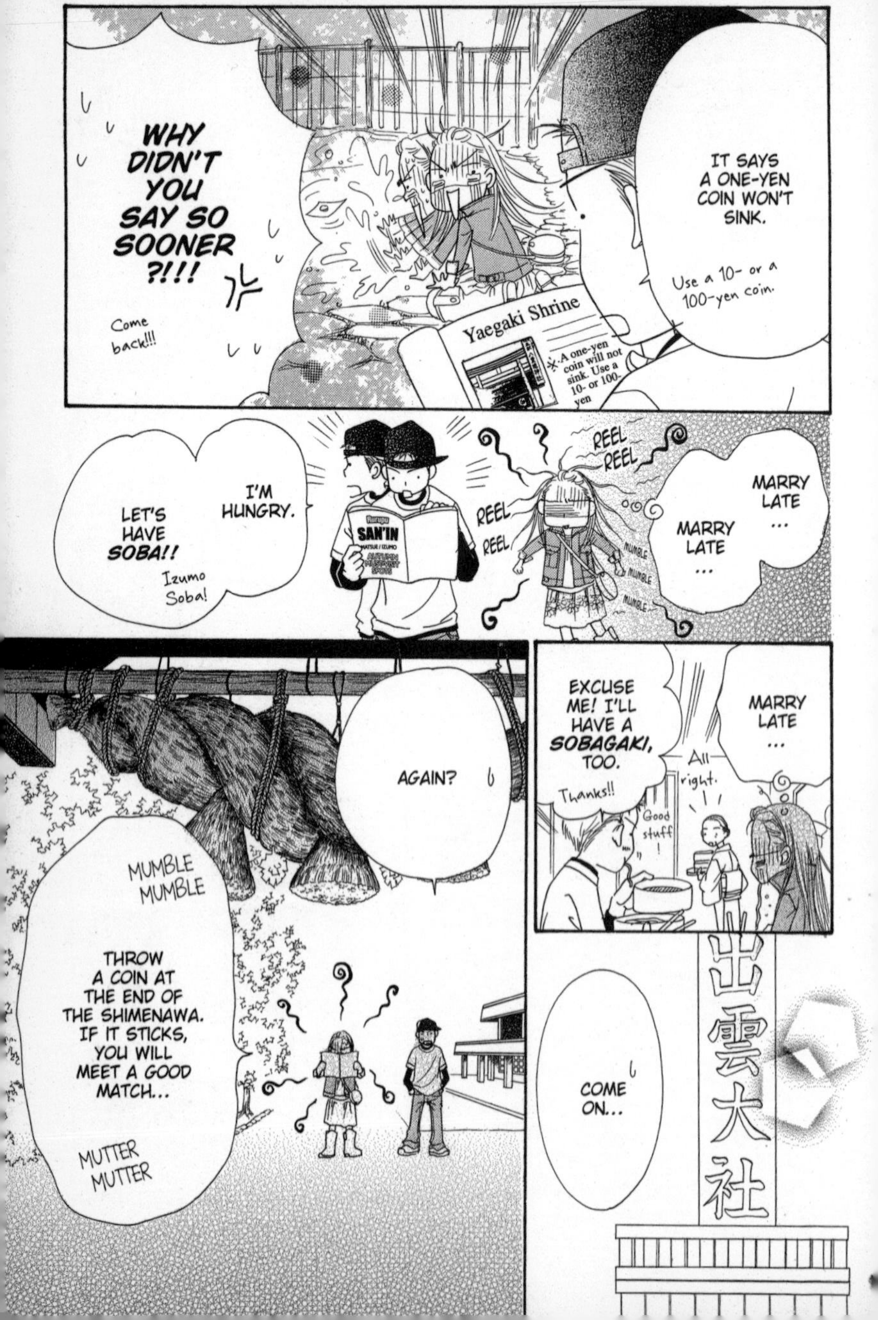
IT SAYS A ONE-YEN COIN WON'T SINK.
Use a 10- or a 100-yen coin.
Yaegaki Shrine
※A one-yen coin will not sink. Use a 10- or 100-yen
WHY DIDN'T YOU SAY SO SOONER?!!!
Come back!!!
MARRY LATE...
MARRY LATE...
REEL REEL
REEL REEL
MUMBLE MUMBLE MUMBLE
Rurubu SAN'IN MATSUE / IZUMO AUTUMN MUST-VISIT SPOTS
I'M HUNGRY.
LET'S HAVE SOBA!!
Izumo Soba!
MARRY LATE...
EXCUSE ME! I'LL HAVE A SOBAGAKI, TOO.
Thanks!!
All right.
Good stuff!
出雲大社
COME ON...
AGAIN?
MUMBLE MUMBLE
THROW A COIN AT THE END OF THE SHIMENAWA. IF IT STICKS, YOU WILL MEET A GOOD MATCH...
MUTTER MUTTER

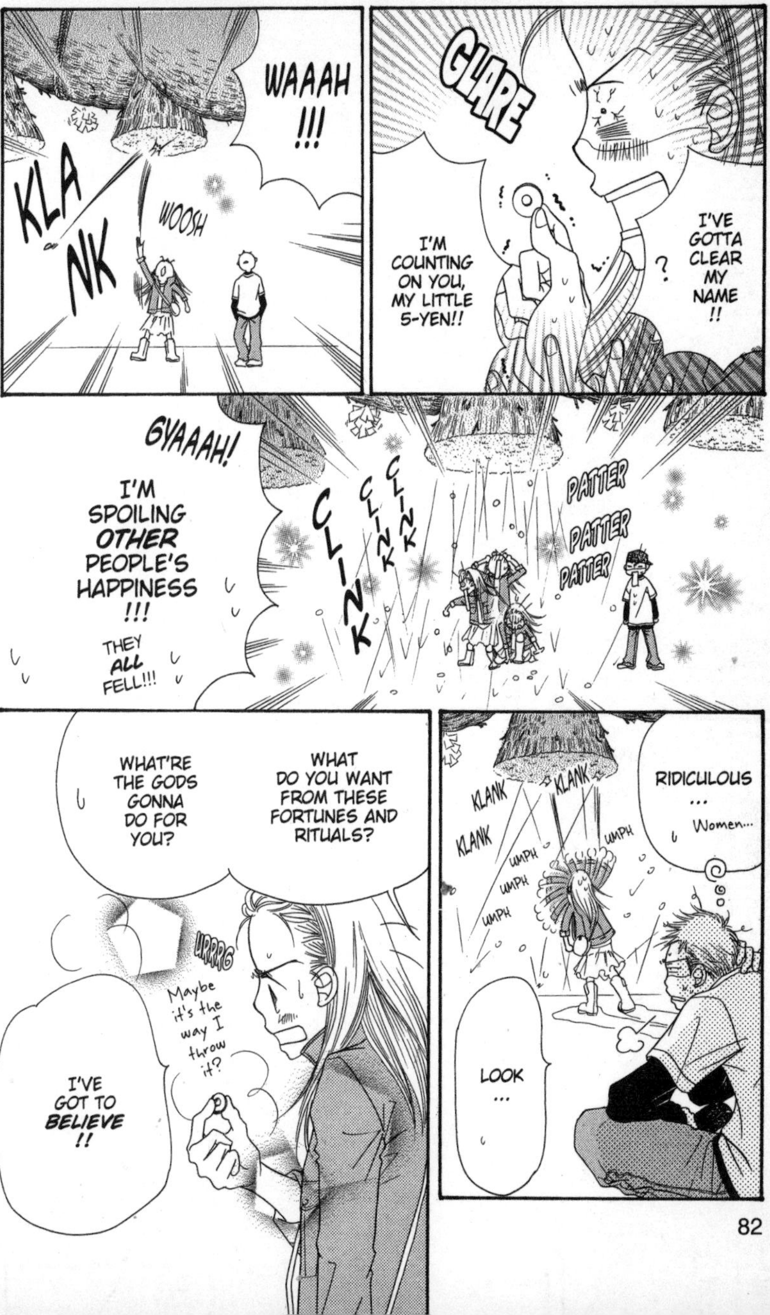
GLARE
I'VE GOTTA CLEAR MY NAME!!
I'M COUNTING ON YOU, MY LITTLE 5-YEN!!
WAAAH!!!
KLANK
WOOSH
PATTER
PATTER
PATTER
CLINK
CLINK
CLINK
GYAAAH!
I'M SPOILING OTHER PEOPLE'S HAPPINESS!!!
THEY ALL FELL!!!
RIDICULOUS...
Women...
KLANK
KLANK
KLANK
UMPH
UMPH
UMPH
UMPH
LOOK...
WHAT DO YOU WANT FROM THESE FORTUNES AND RITUALS?
WHAT'RE THE GODS GONNA DO FOR YOU?
URRRG
Maybe it's the way I throw it?
I'VE GOT TO BELIEVE!!

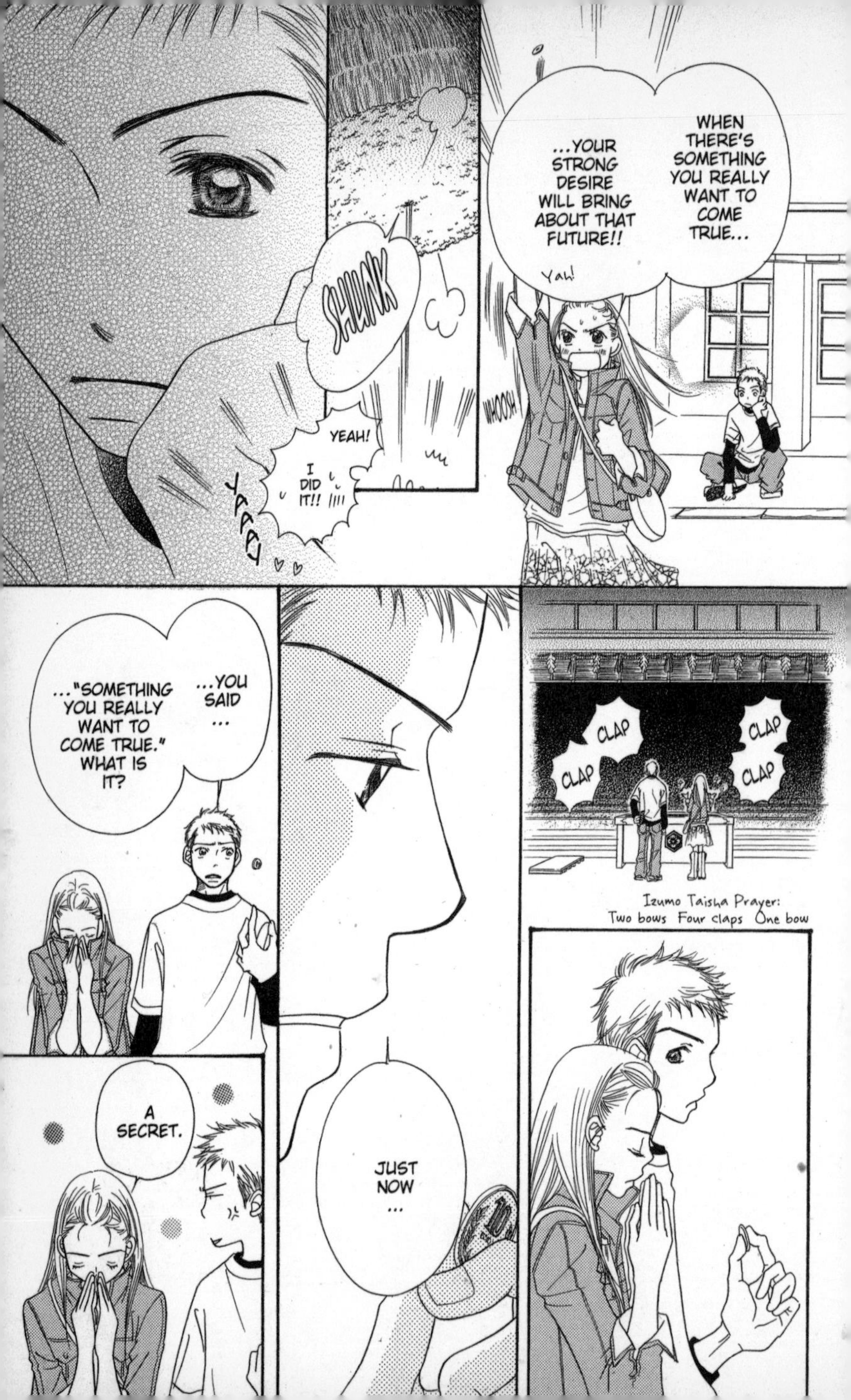
WHEN THERE'S SOMETHING YOU REALLY WANT TO COME TRUE...
...YOUR STRONG DESIRE WILL BRING ABOUT THAT FUTURE!!
Yah!
WHOOSH
SHUNK
YEAH!
I DID IT!!
YAAAY
CLAP
CLAP
CLAP
CLAP
Izumo Taisha Prayer: Two bows Four claps One bow
JUST NOW...
...YOU SAID...
..."SOMETHING YOU REALLY WANT TO COME TRUE." WHAT IS IT?
A SECRET.

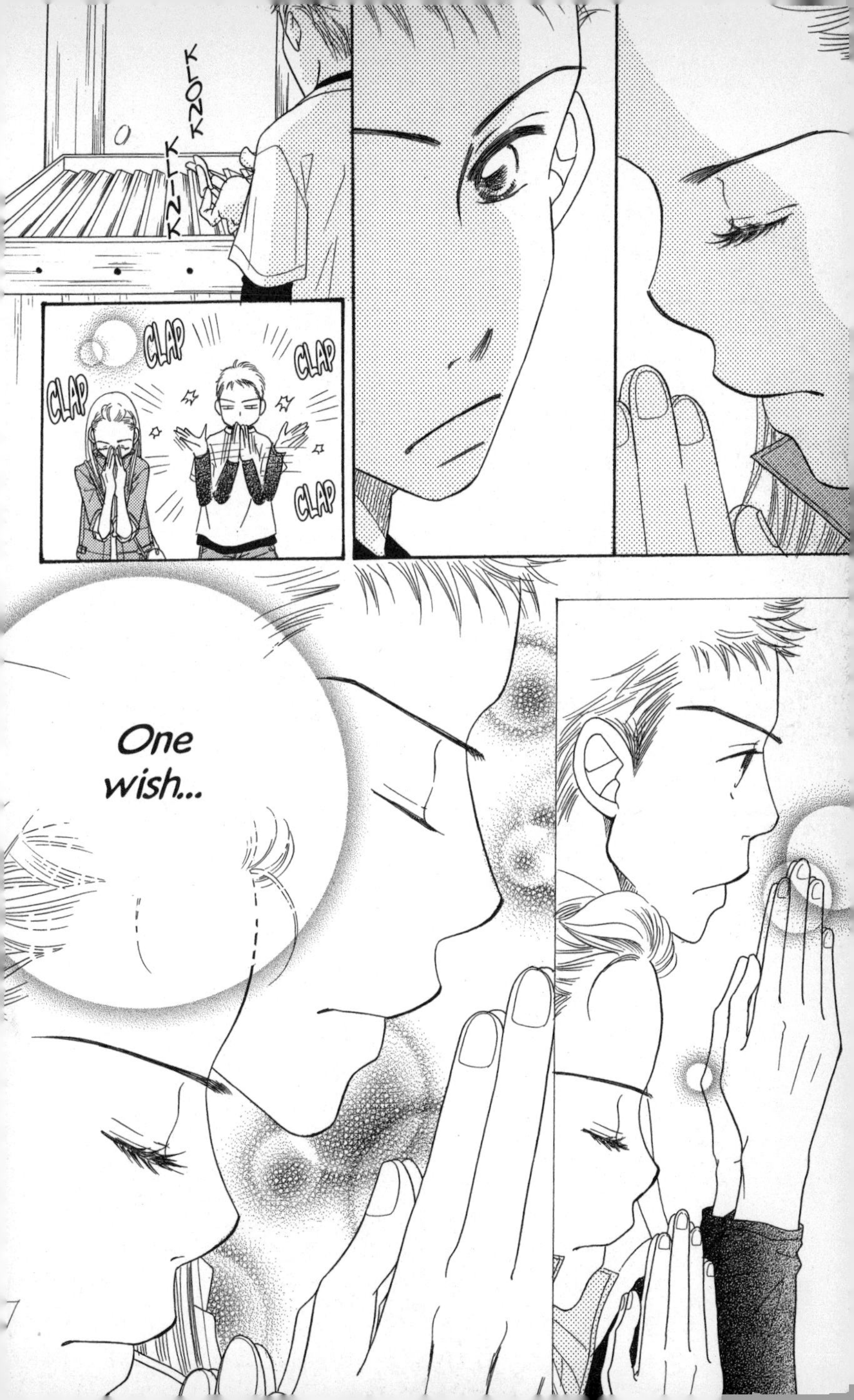
KLONK
KLINK
CLAP
CLAP
CLAP
CLAP
One wish...

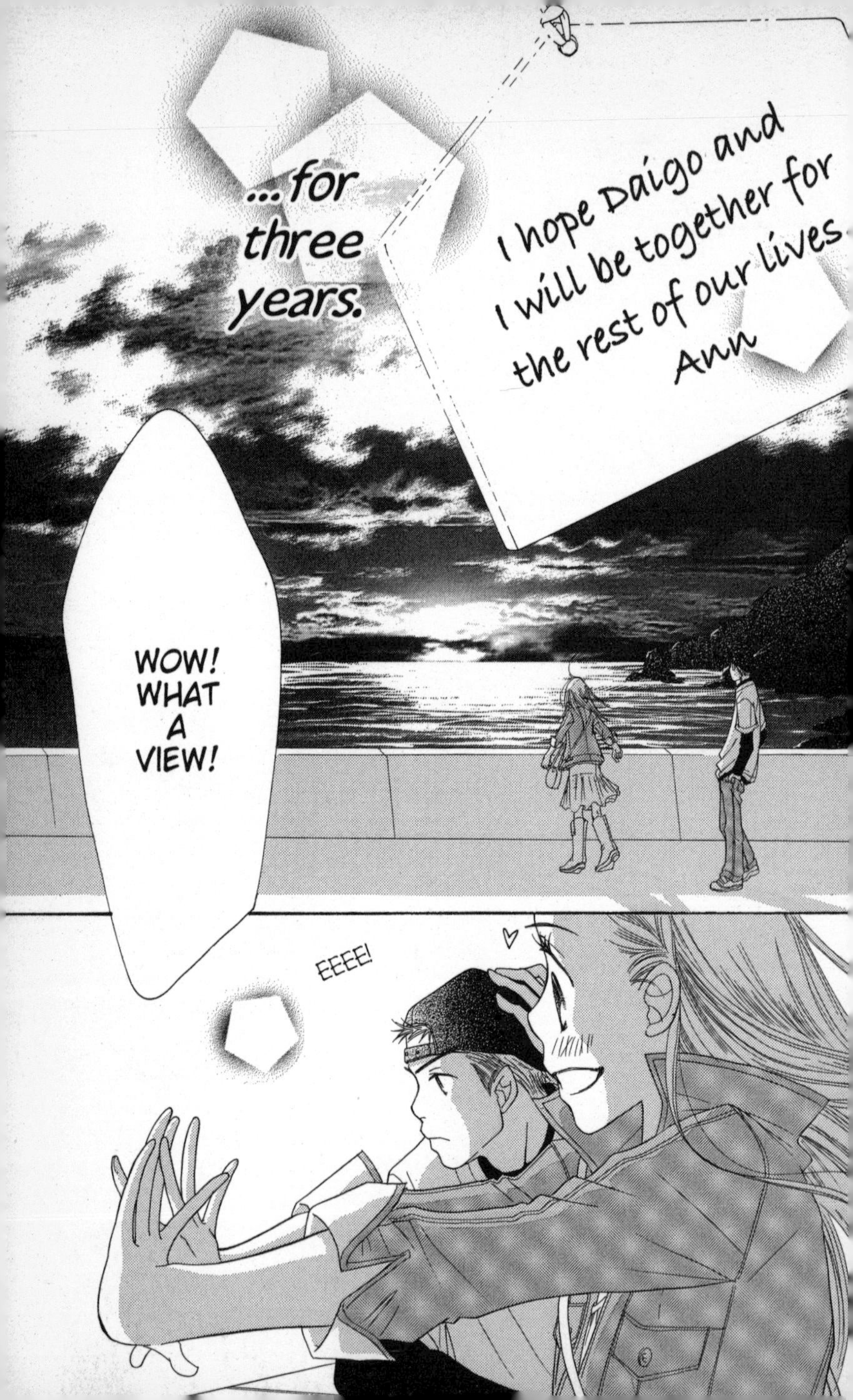
I hope Daigo and I will be together for the rest of our lives
Ann
...for three years.
WOW! WHAT A VIEW!
EEEE!

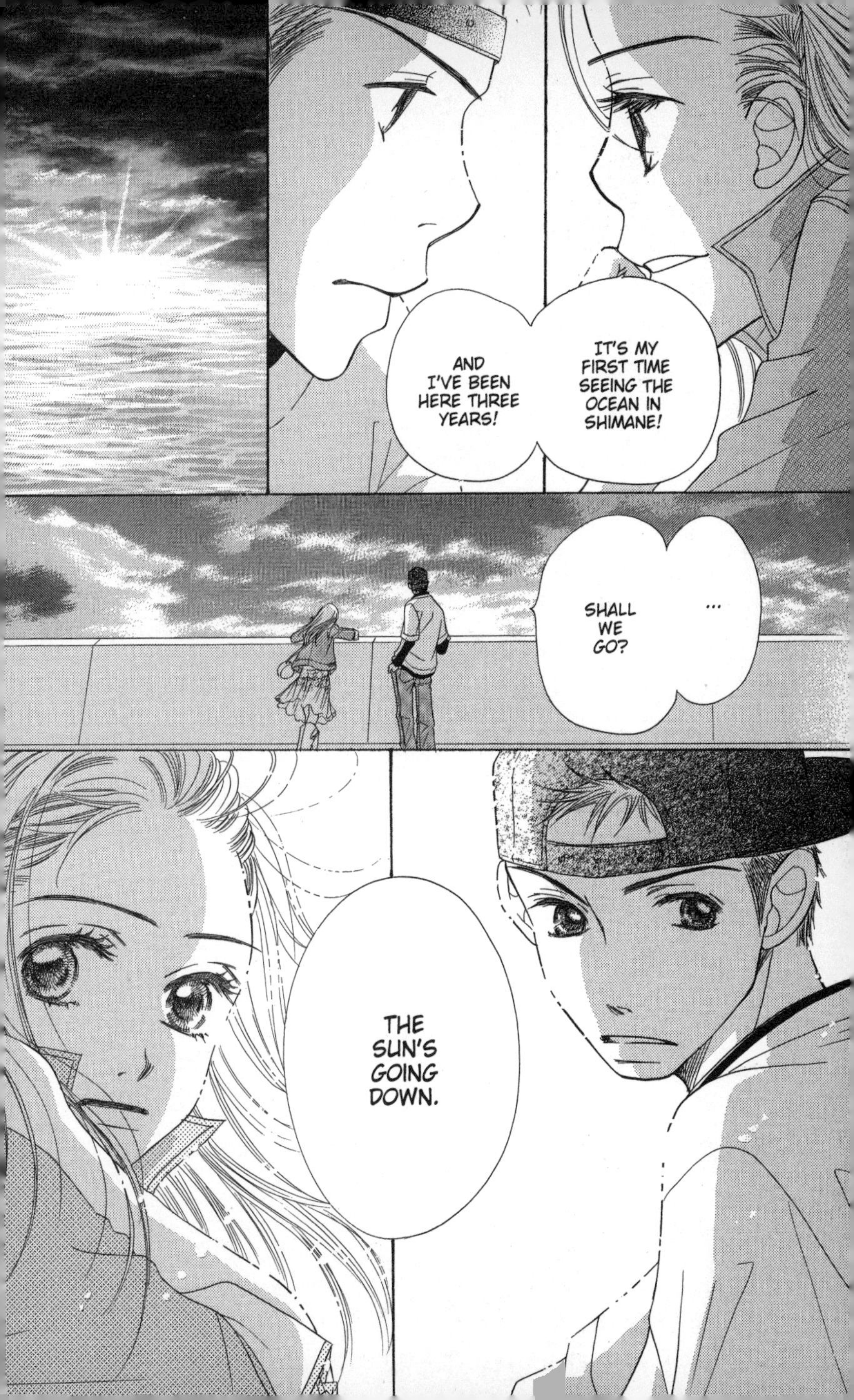
IT'S MY FIRST TIME SEEING THE OCEAN IN SHIMANE!
AND I'VE BEEN HERE THREE YEARS!
...
SHALL WE GO?
THE SUN'S GOING DOWN.

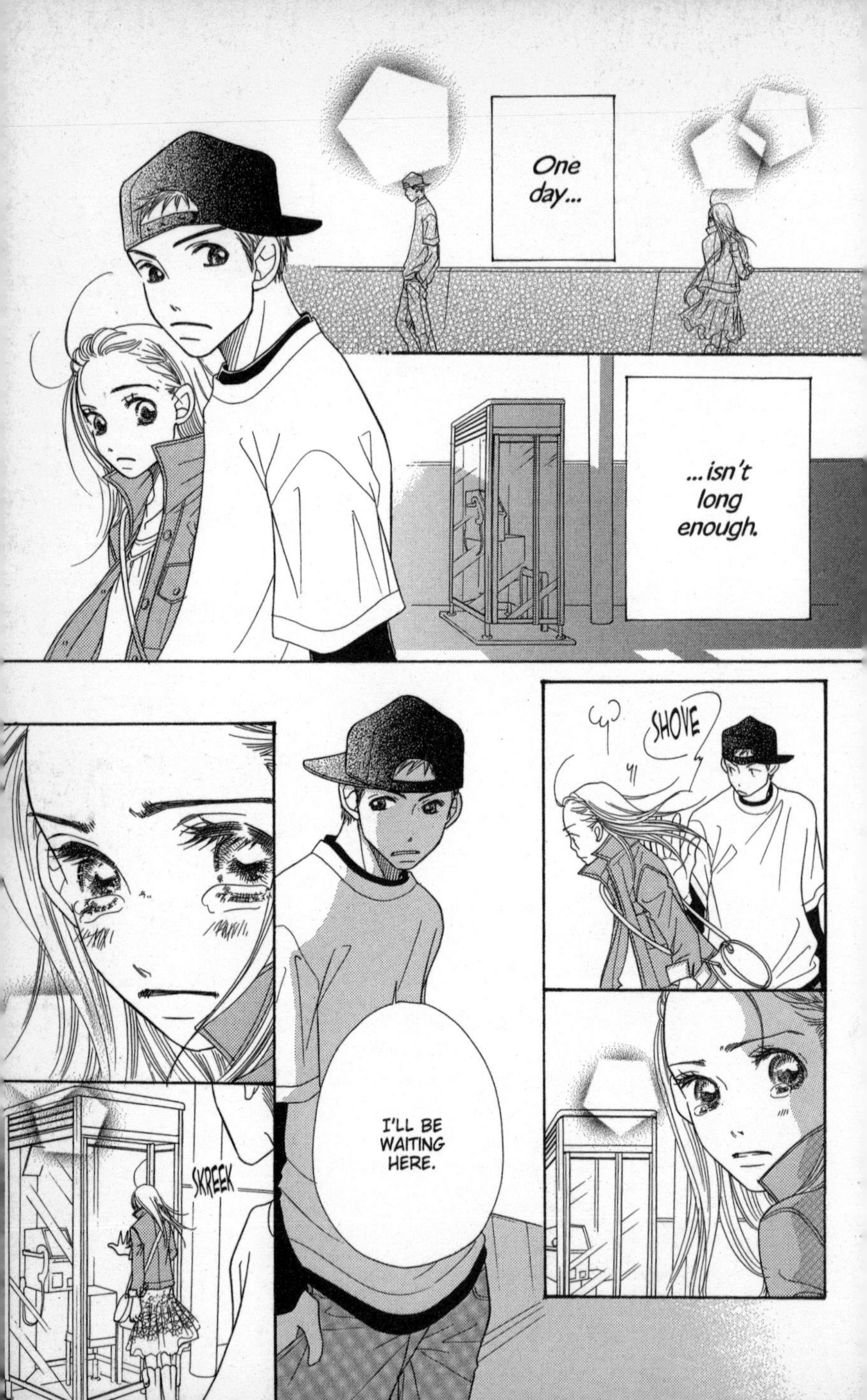
One day...
...isn't long enough.
SHOVE
I'LL BE WAITING HERE.
SKREEK

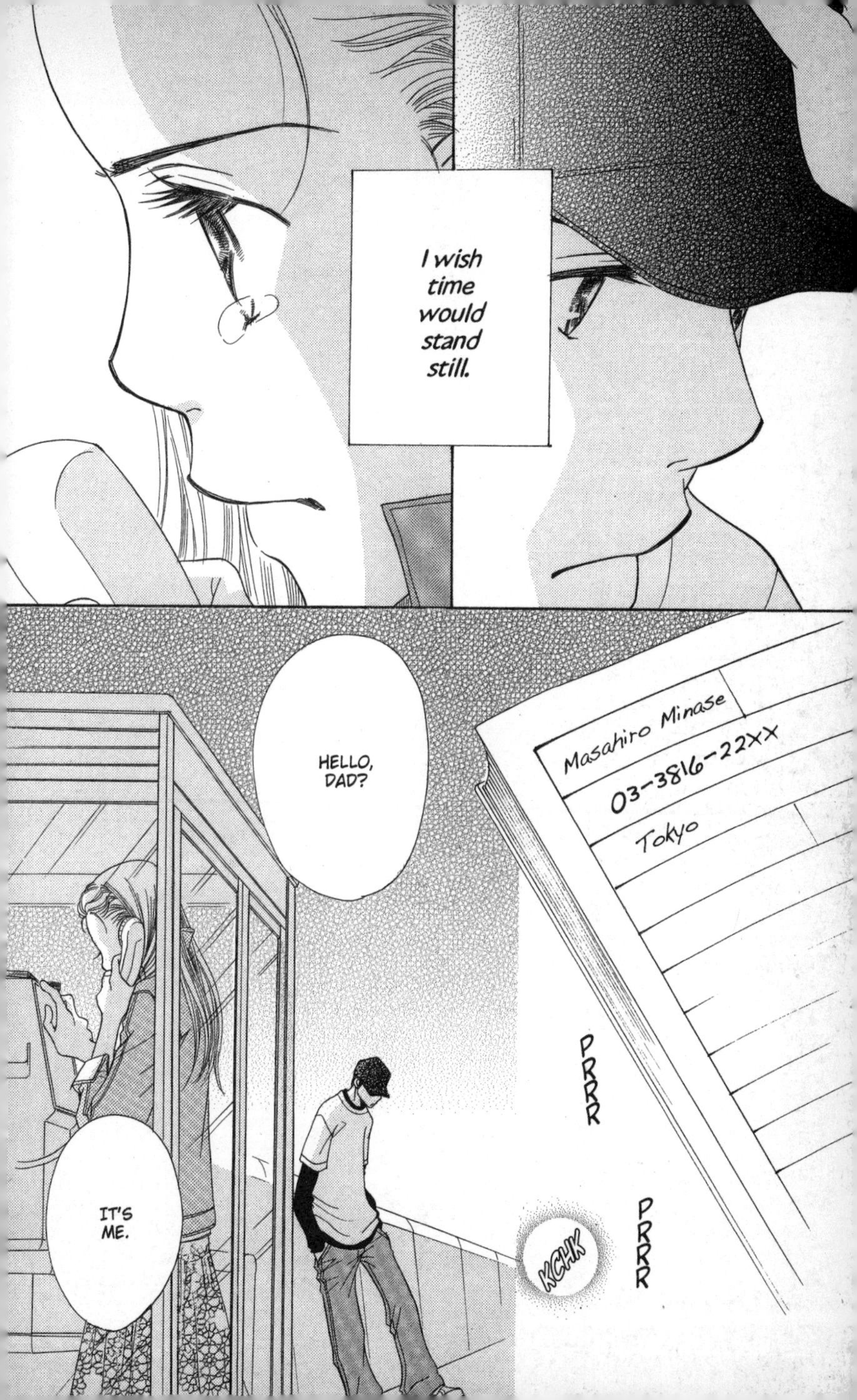
I wish time would stand still.
Masahiro Minase
03-3816-22XX
Tokyo
PRRR
PRRR
KCHK
HELLO, DAD?
IT'S ME.

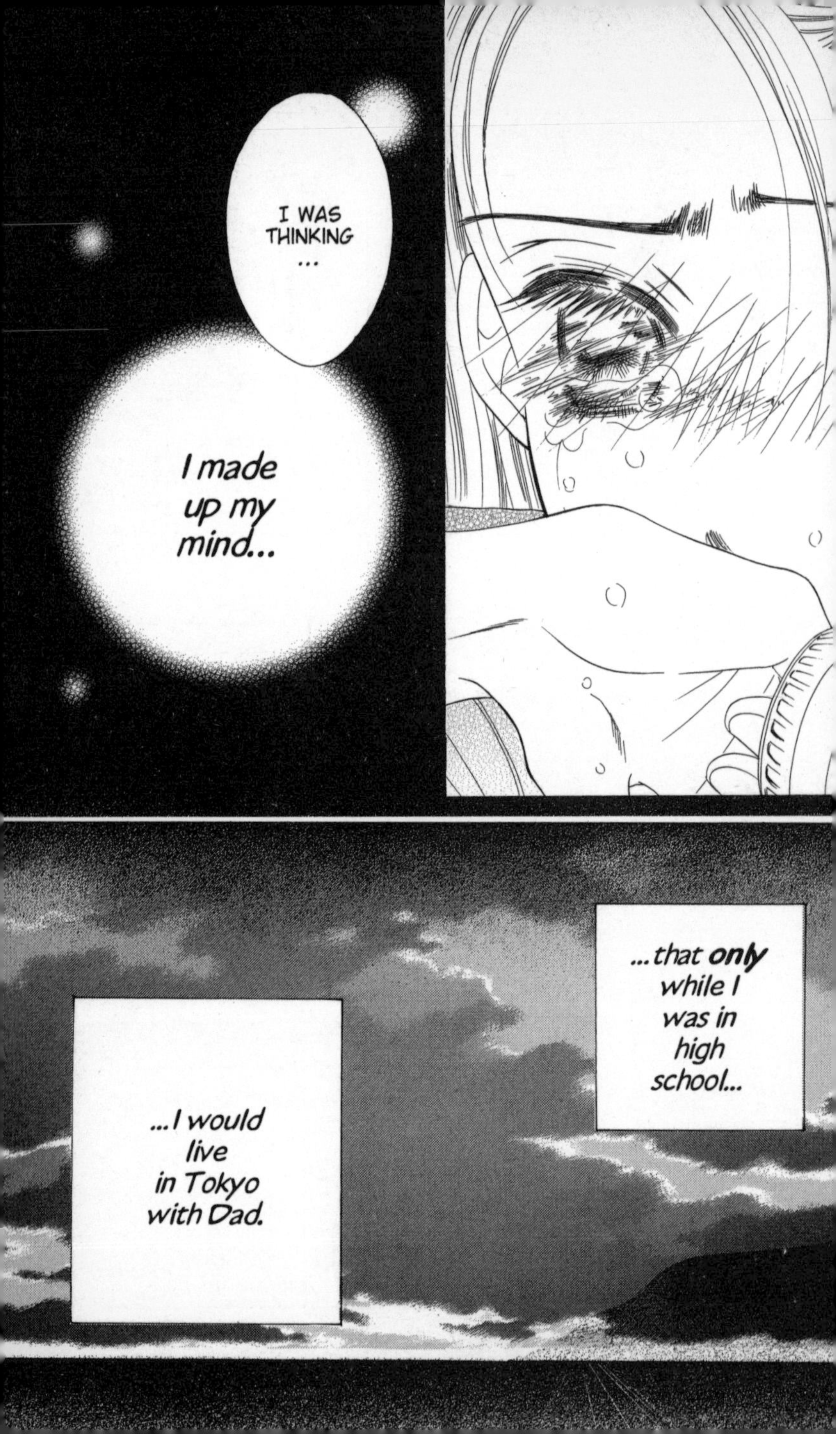
I WAS THINKING ...
I made up my mind...
...that **only** while I was in high school...
...I would live in Tokyo with Dad.

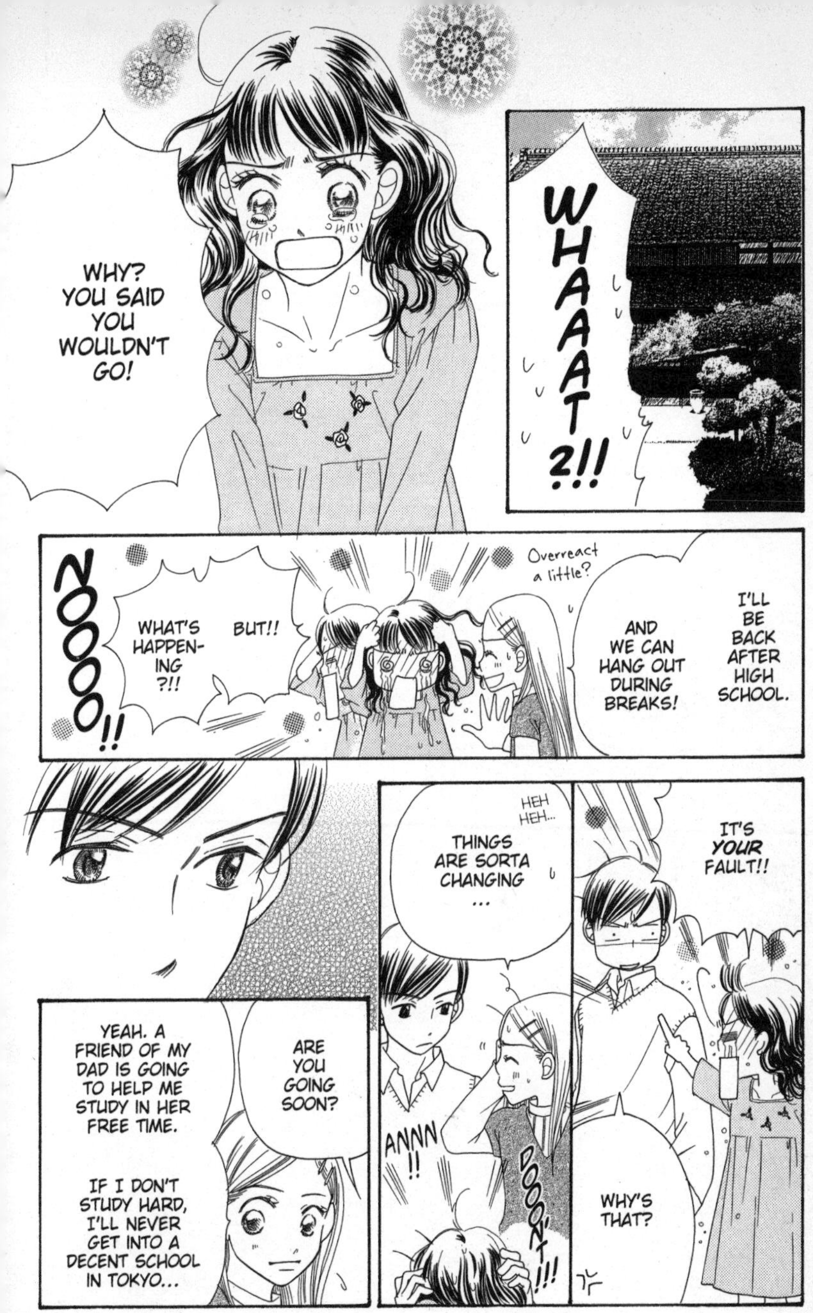
WHAAAT?!!
WHY? YOU SAID YOU WOULDN'T GO!
I'LL BE BACK AFTER HIGH SCHOOL.
AND WE CAN HANG OUT DURING BREAKS!
Overreact a little?
BUT!!
WHAT'S HAPPEN-ING?!!
NOOOOO!!
IT'S *YOUR* FAULT!!
WHY'S THAT?
HEH HEH...
THINGS ARE SORTA CHANGING...
ANNN!!
DOOON'T!!!
ARE YOU GOING SOON?
YEAH. A FRIEND OF MY DAD IS GOING TO HELP ME STUDY IN HER FREE TIME.
IF I DON'T STUDY HARD, I'LL NEVER GET INTO A DECENT SCHOOL IN TOKYO...

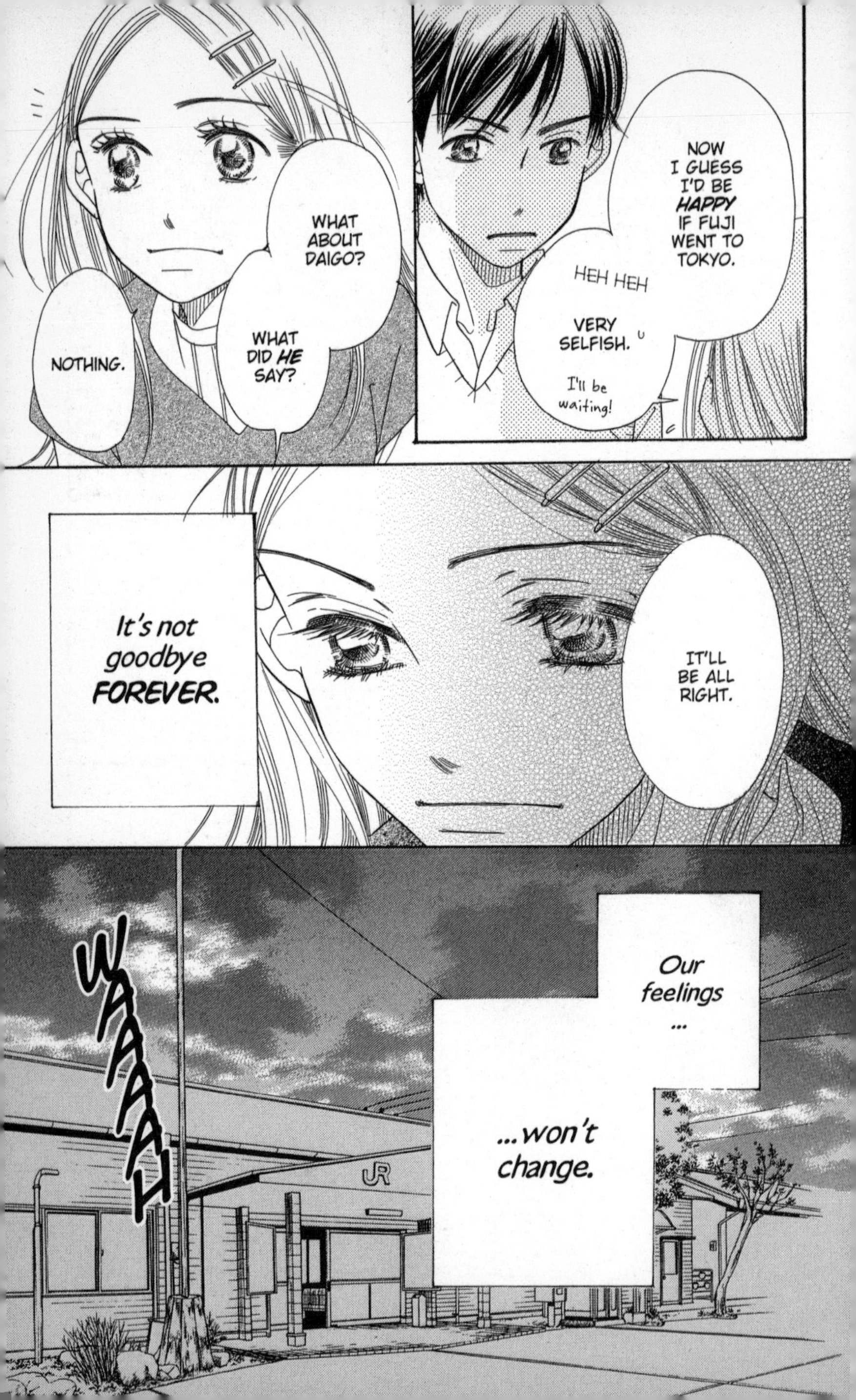
NOW I GUESS I'D BE *HAPPY* IF FUJI WENT TO TOKYO.
HEH HEH
VERY SELFISH.
I'll be waiting!
WHAT ABOUT DAIGO?
WHAT DID *HE* SAY?
NOTHING.
IT'LL BE ALL RIGHT.
It's not goodbye **FOREVER.**
WAAAAAH
Our feelings ...
...won't change.

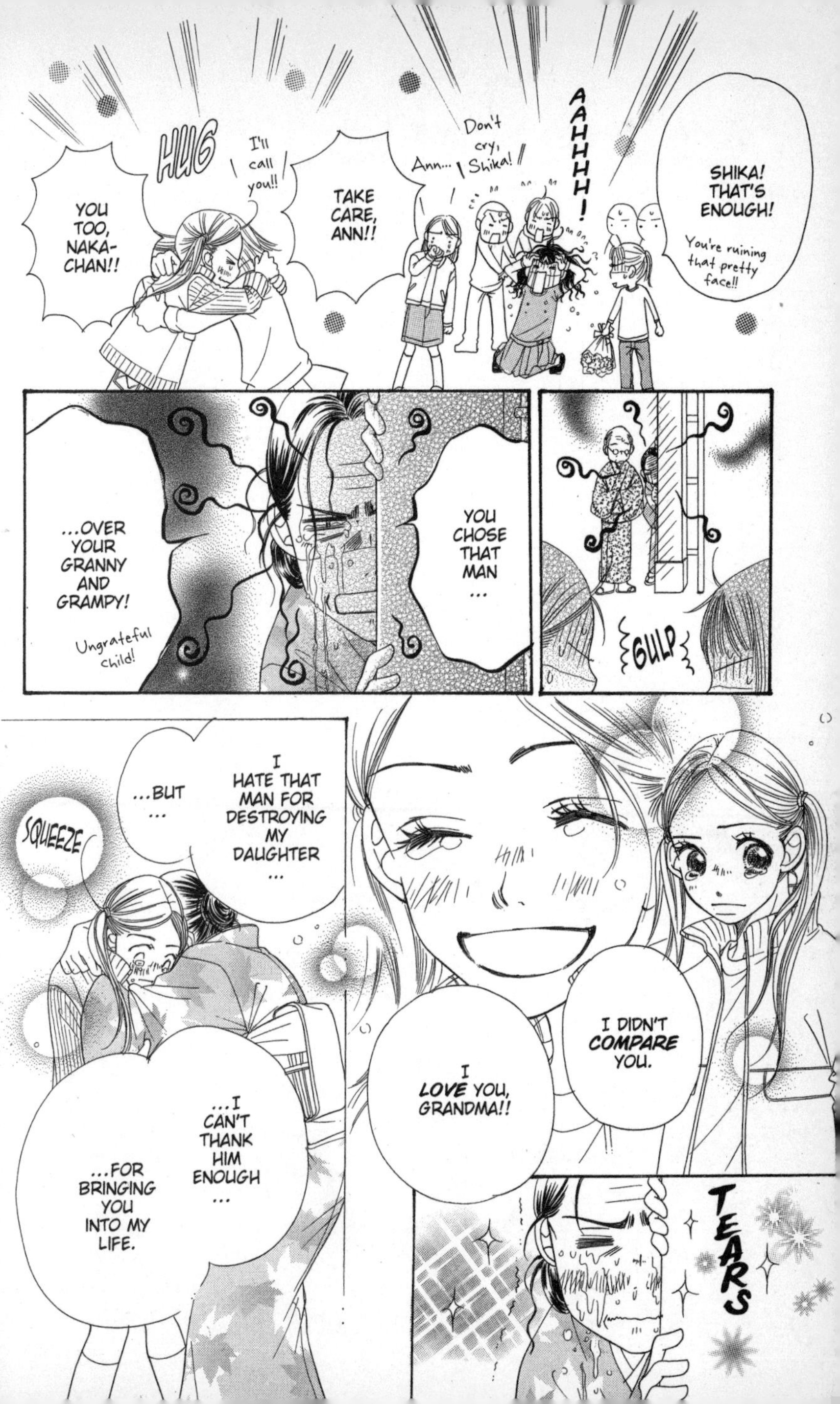

SHIKA! THAT'S ENOUGH!
You're ruining that pretty face!!
AAHHHH!
Don't cry, Shika!
Ann...
TAKE CARE, ANN!!
I'll call you!!
HUG
YOU TOO, NAKA-CHAN!!
GULP
YOU CHOSE THAT MAN...
...OVER YOUR GRANNY AND GRAMPY!
Ungrateful child!
I DIDN'T COMPARE YOU.
I LOVE YOU, GRANDMA!!
TEARS
I HATE THAT MAN FOR DESTROYING MY DAUGHTER...
...BUT...
SQUEEZE
...I CAN'T THANK HIM ENOUGH...
...FOR BRINGING YOU INTO MY LIFE.

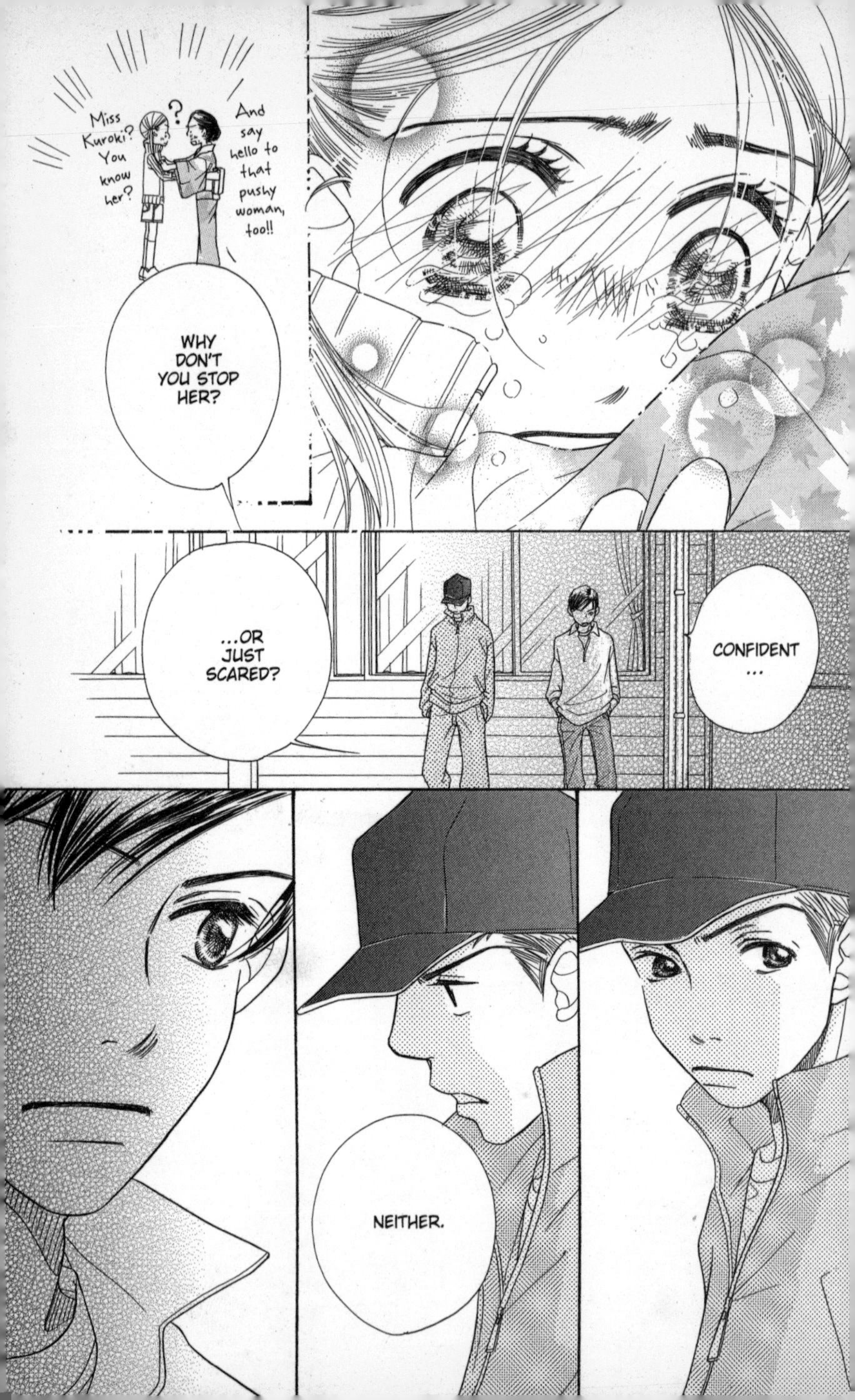
And say hello to that pushy woman, too!!
Miss Kuroki? You know her?
?
WHY DON'T YOU STOP HER?
CONFIDENT...
...OR JUST SCARED?
NEITHER.

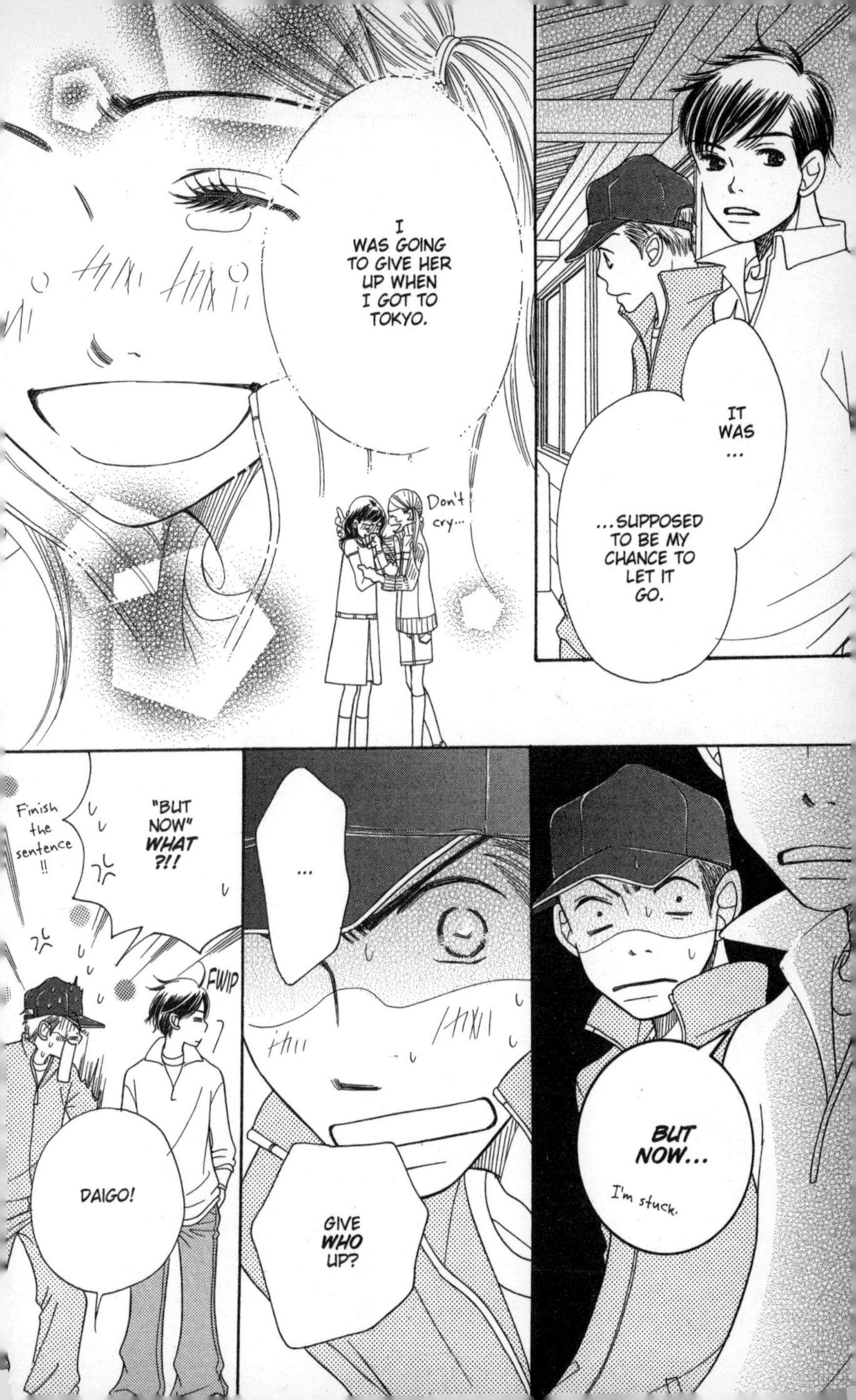
IT WAS...
...SUPPOSED TO BE MY CHANCE TO LET IT GO.
I WAS GOING TO GIVE HER UP WHEN I GOT TO TOKYO.
Don't cry...
BUT NOW...
I'm stuck.
...
GIVE WHO UP?
"BUT NOW" WHAT?!!
Finish the sentence !!
FWIP
DAIGO!

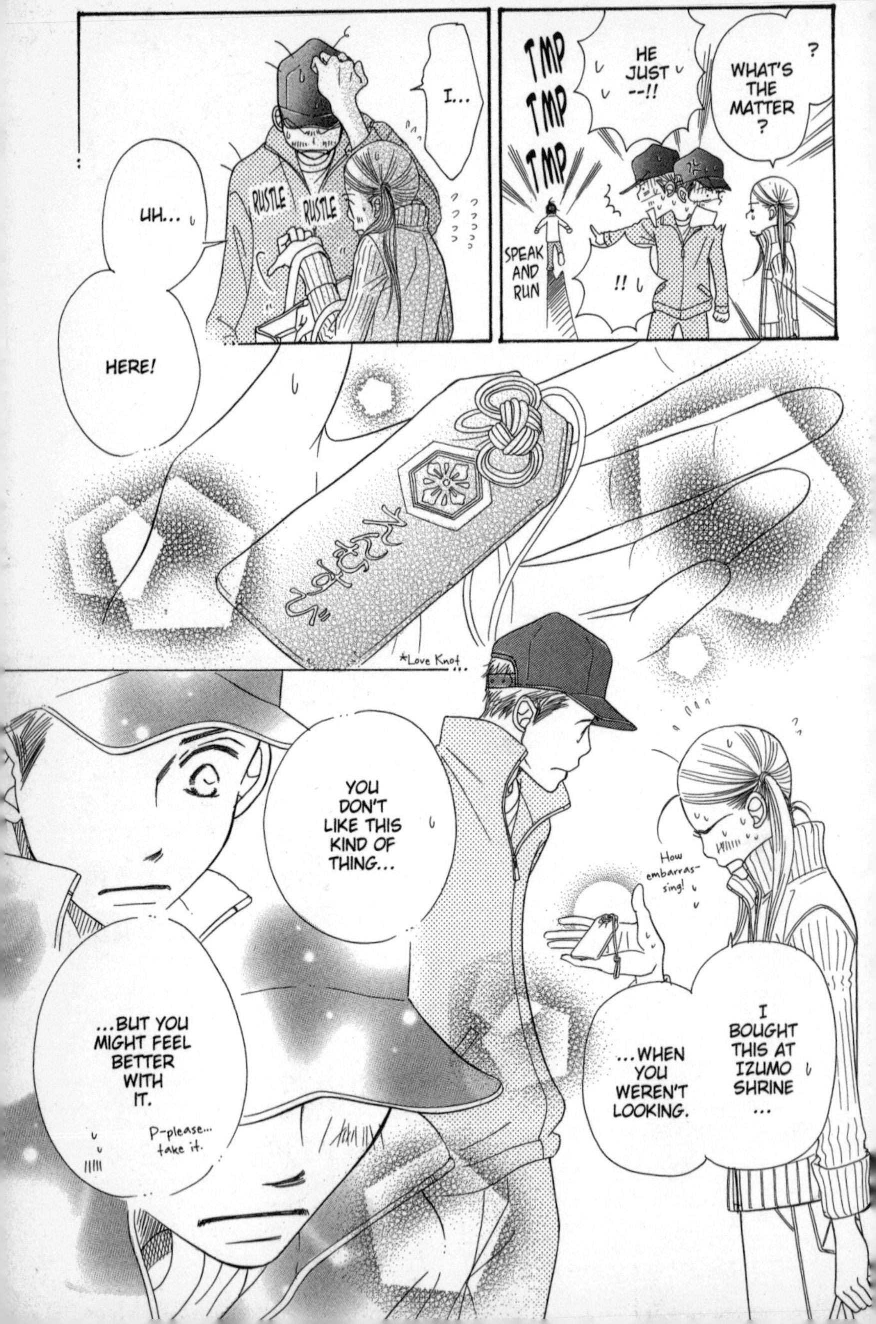
?
WHAT'S THE MATTER ?
HE JUST --!!
TMP TMP TMP
SPEAK AND RUN
!!
I...
RUSTLE
RUSTLE
UH...
HERE!
*Love Knot
I BOUGHT THIS AT IZUMO SHRINE ...
...WHEN YOU WEREN'T LOOKING.
How embarras-sing!
YOU DON'T LIKE THIS KIND OF THING...
...BUT YOU MIGHT FEEL BETTER WITH IT.
P-please... take it.

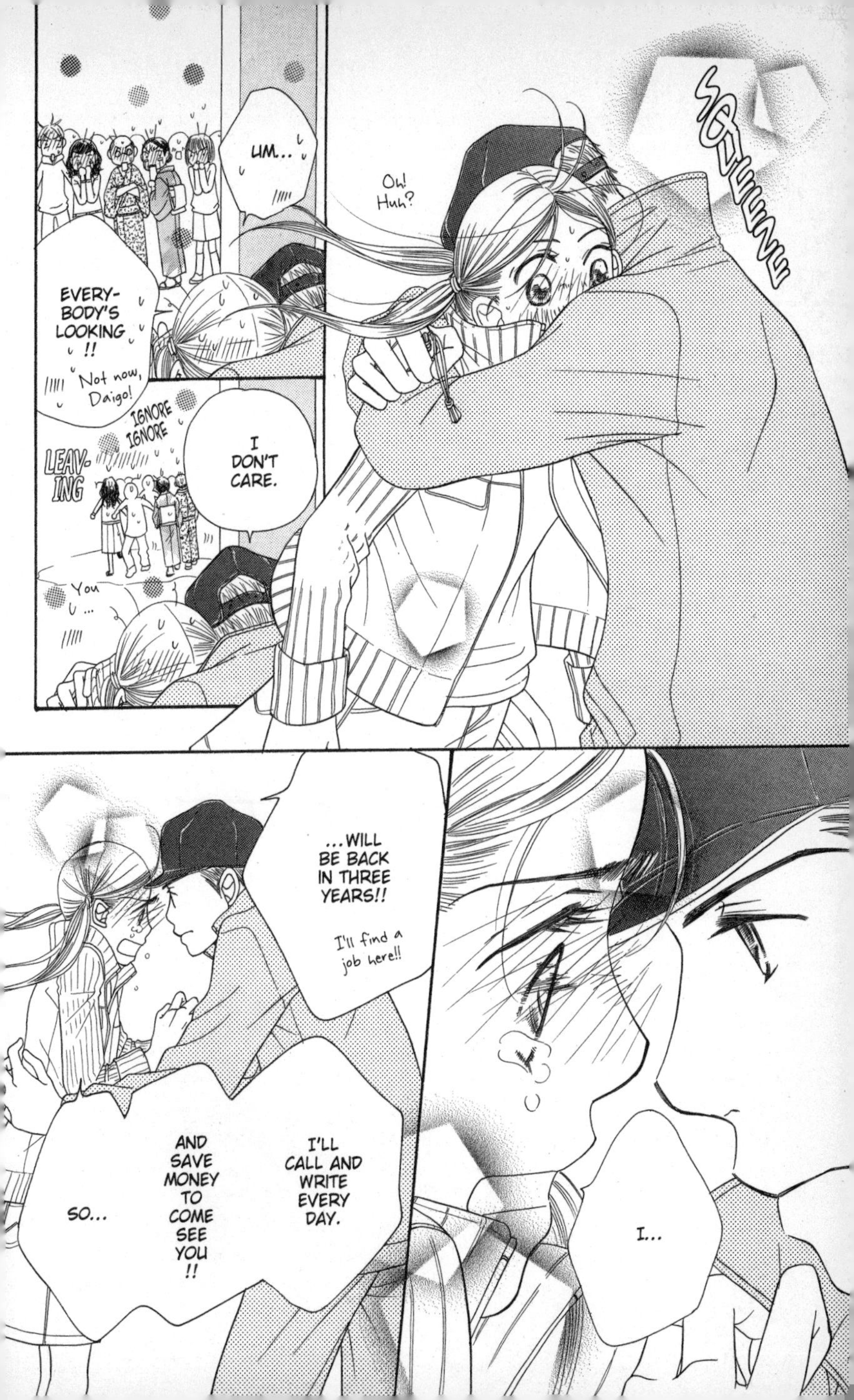
SQUEEZE
Oh! Huh?
UM...
EVERY-BODY'S LOOKING!!
Not now, Daigo!
I DON'T CARE.
IGNORE IGNORE
LEAVING
You...
I...
...WILL BE BACK IN THREE YEARS!!
I'll find a job here!!
I'LL CALL AND WRITE EVERY DAY.
AND SAVE MONEY TO COME SEE YOU!!
SO...

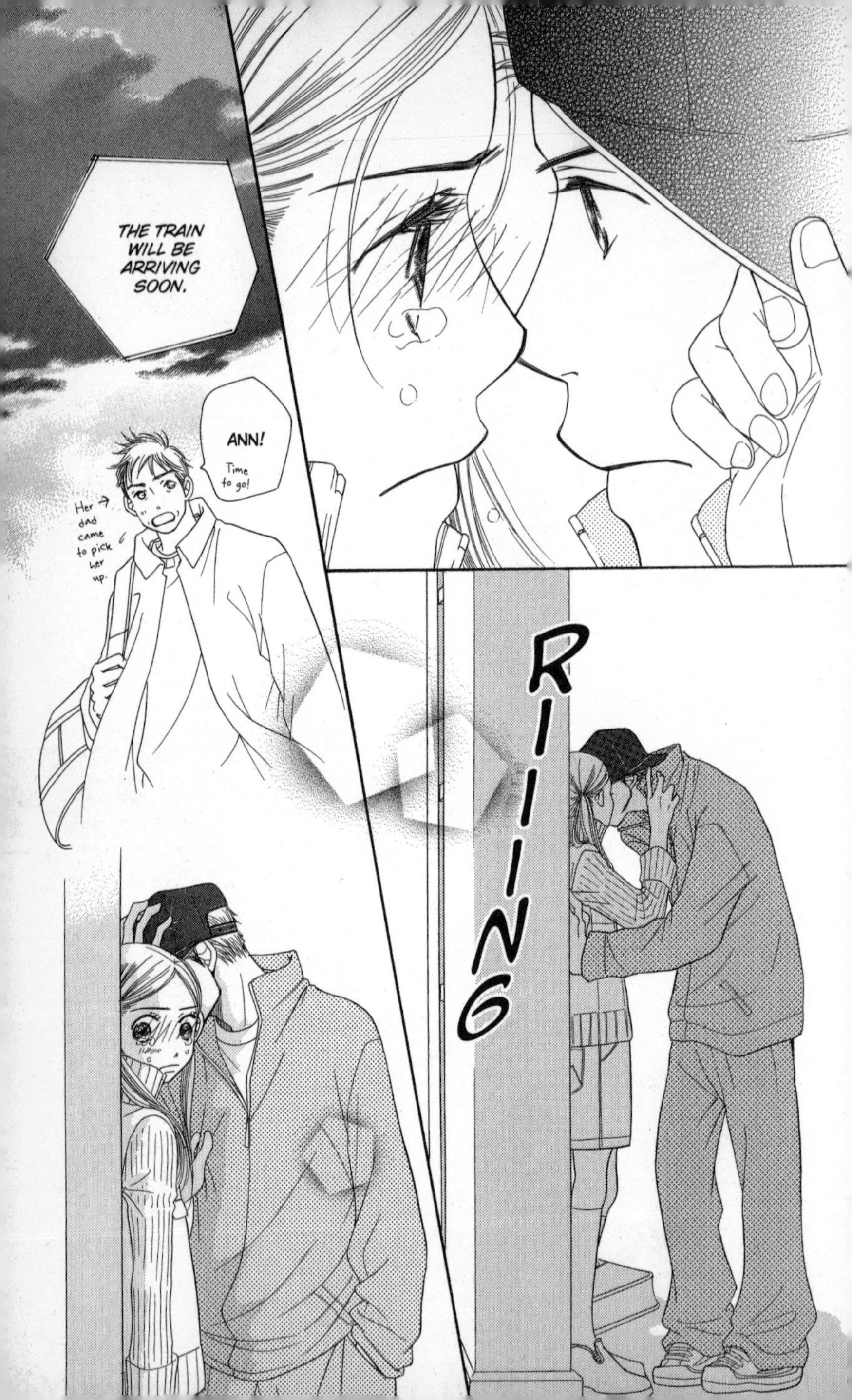
THE TRAIN WILL BE ARRIVING SOON.
ANN!
Time to go!
Her dad came to pick her up.
RIIING

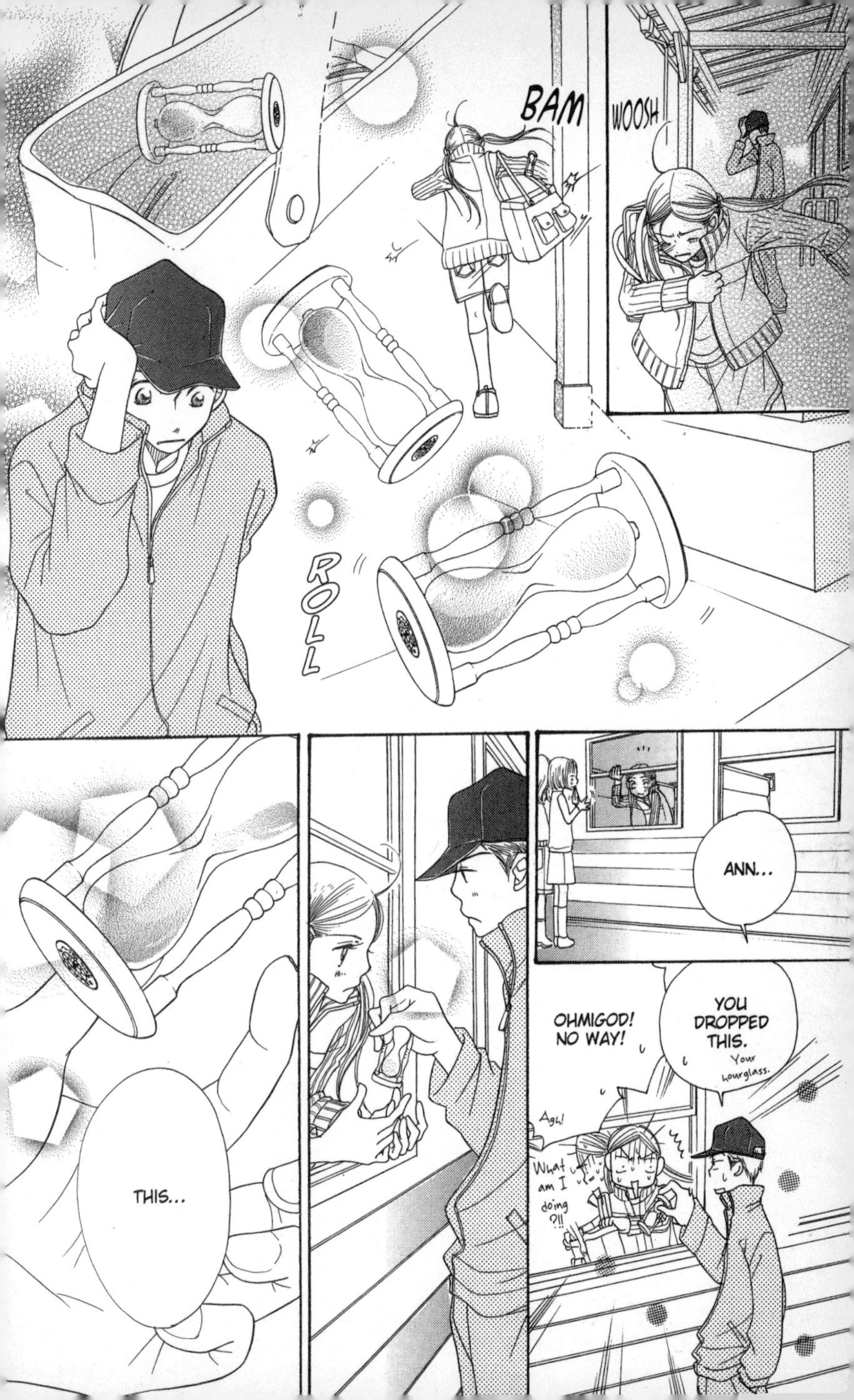
WOOSH
BAM
ROLL
ANN...
YOU DROPPED THIS.
Your hourglass.
OHMIGOD! NO WAY!
Agh!
What am I doing ?!!
THIS...

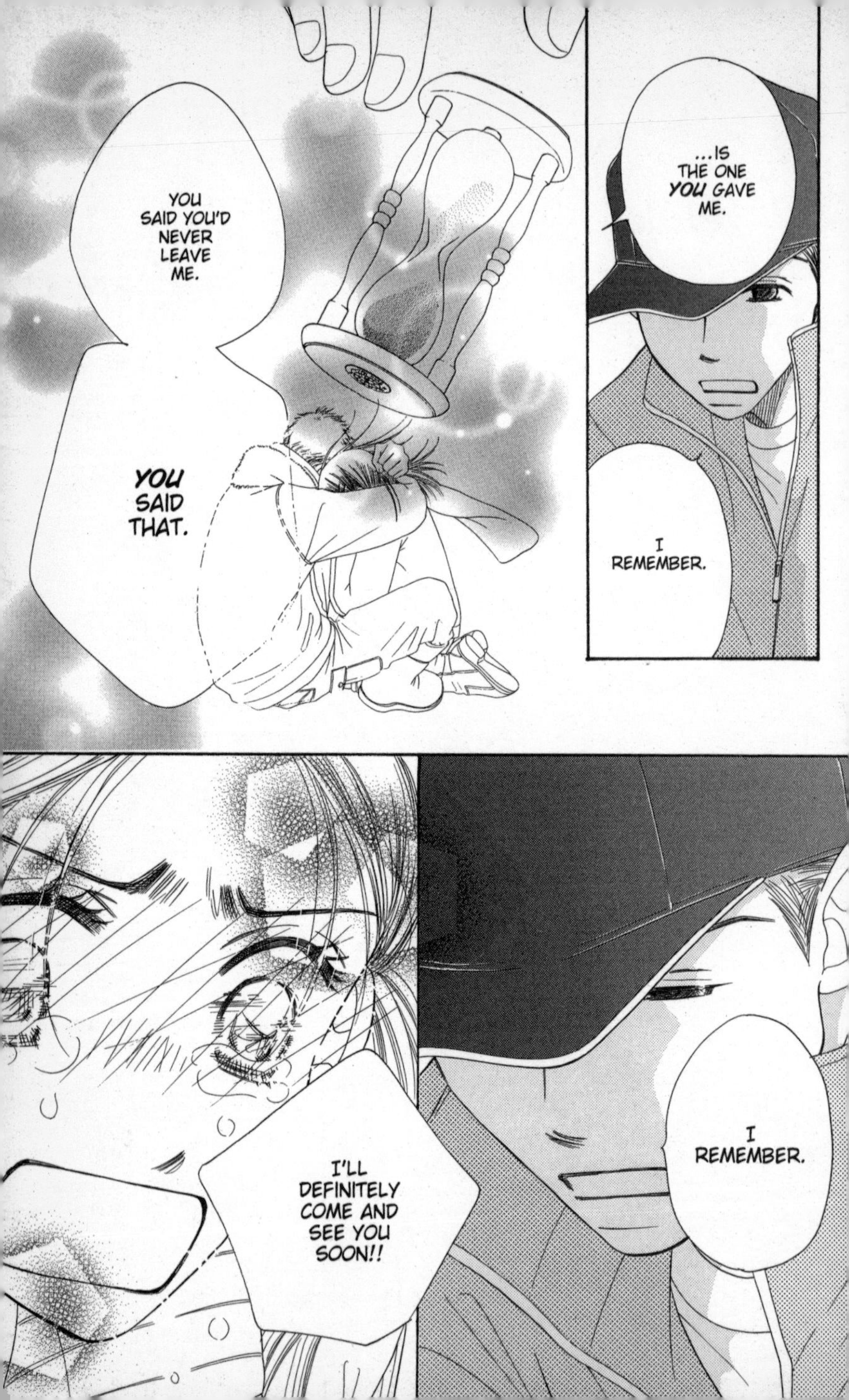
...IS THE ONE YOU GAVE ME.
I REMEMBER.
YOU SAID YOU'D NEVER LEAVE ME.
YOU SAID THAT.
I REMEMBER.
I'LL DEFINITELY COME AND SEE YOU SOON!!

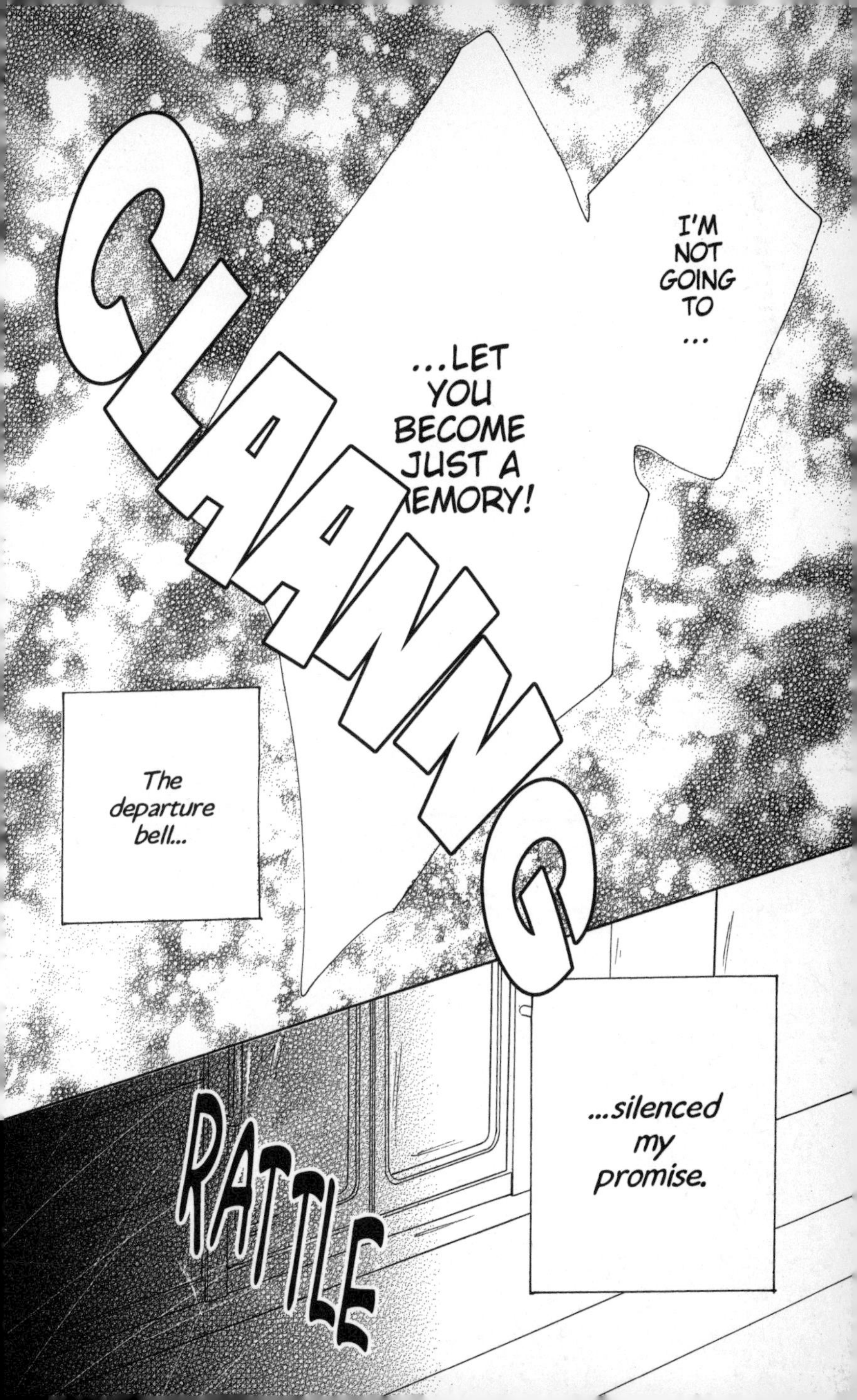
I'M NOT GOING TO ...
...LET YOU BECOME JUST A MEMORY!
CLAANNG
The departure bell...
...silenced my promise.
RATTLE

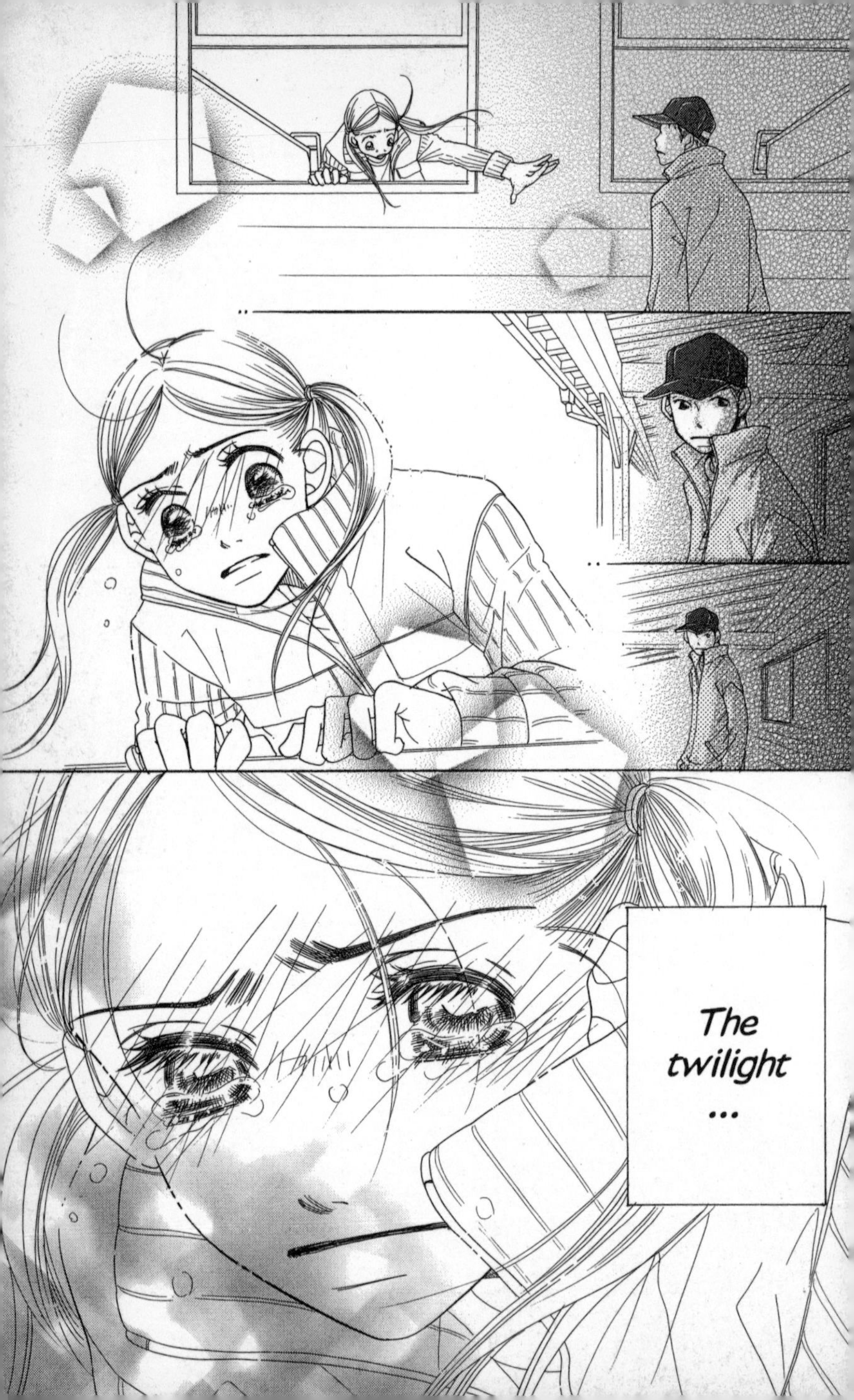
The twilight ...

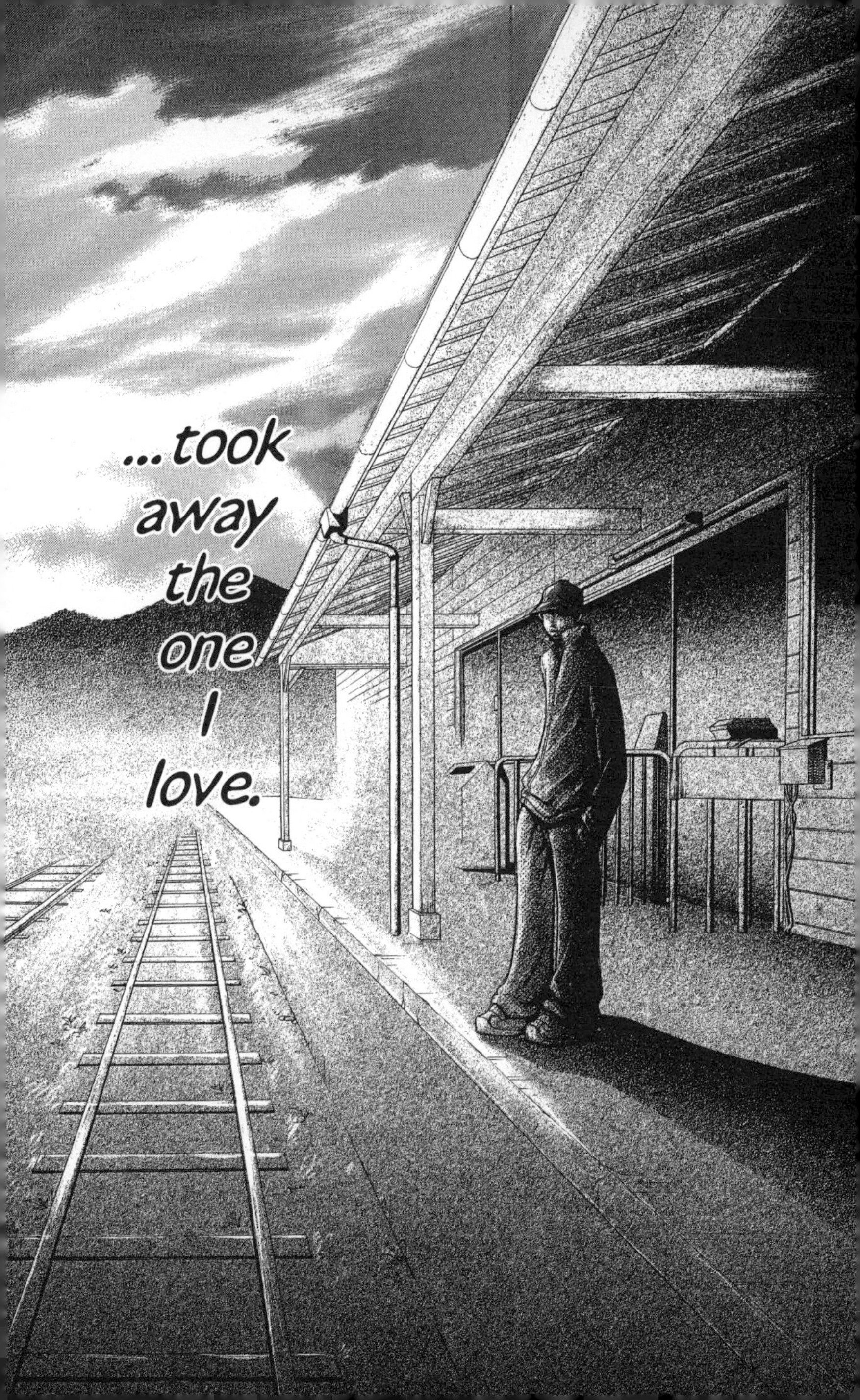
...took away the one I love.

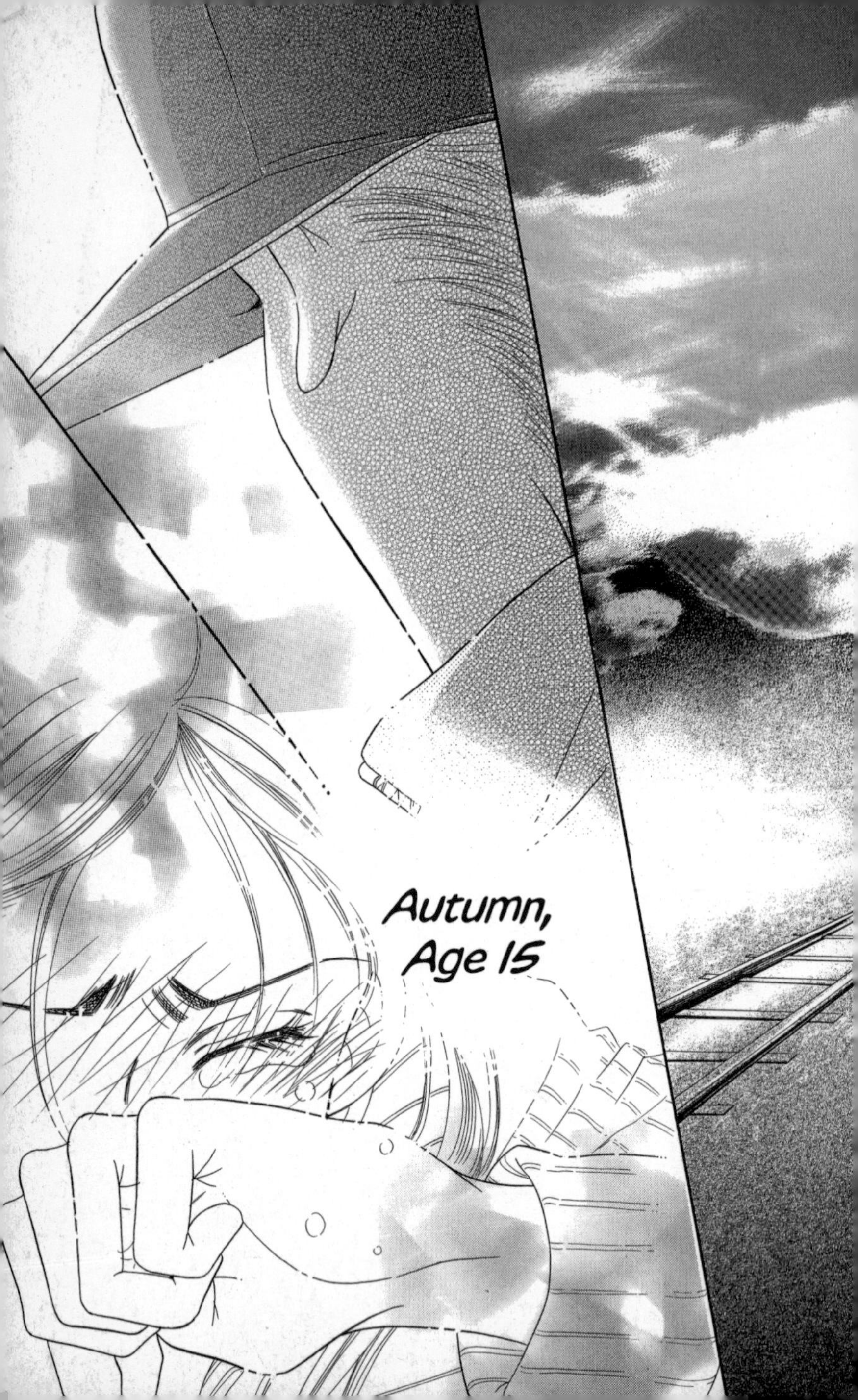
Autumn, Age 15

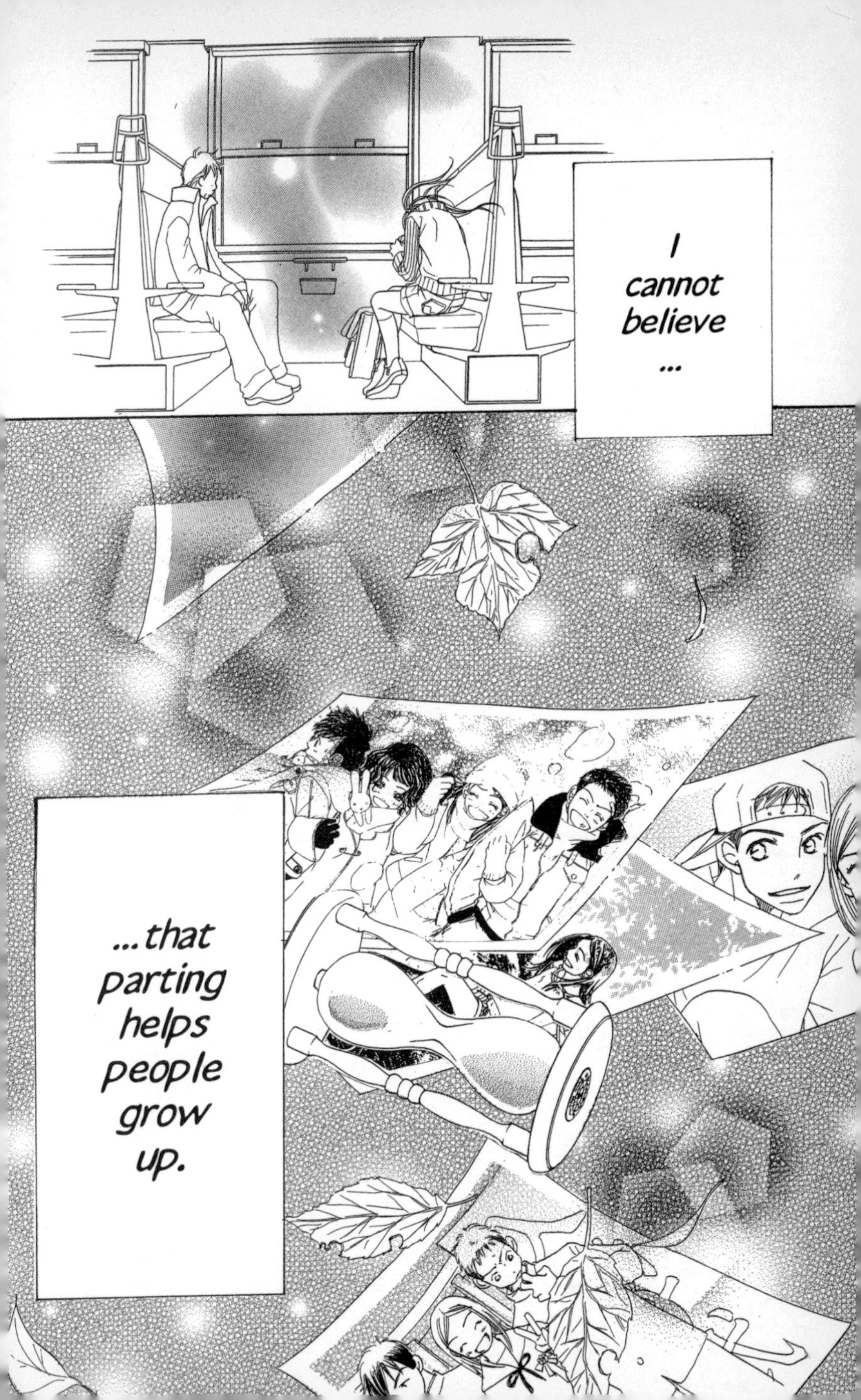
I cannot believe ...
...that parting helps people grow up.

Fuji Tsukishima, Age 15

"I hope things will work out fine between Daigo and Ann, but I like Fuji better." I get a lot of messages like this. So...is that what you think? He's an awkward and complicated person. He's the type not to act until he sees what others are doing first.

Sand Chronicles

Sand Chronicles

Shika Tsukishima, Age 14

A cute, good girl
from a good family.
Inside, though, she's
as complex as
the next person...
I'll follow up
on that later.

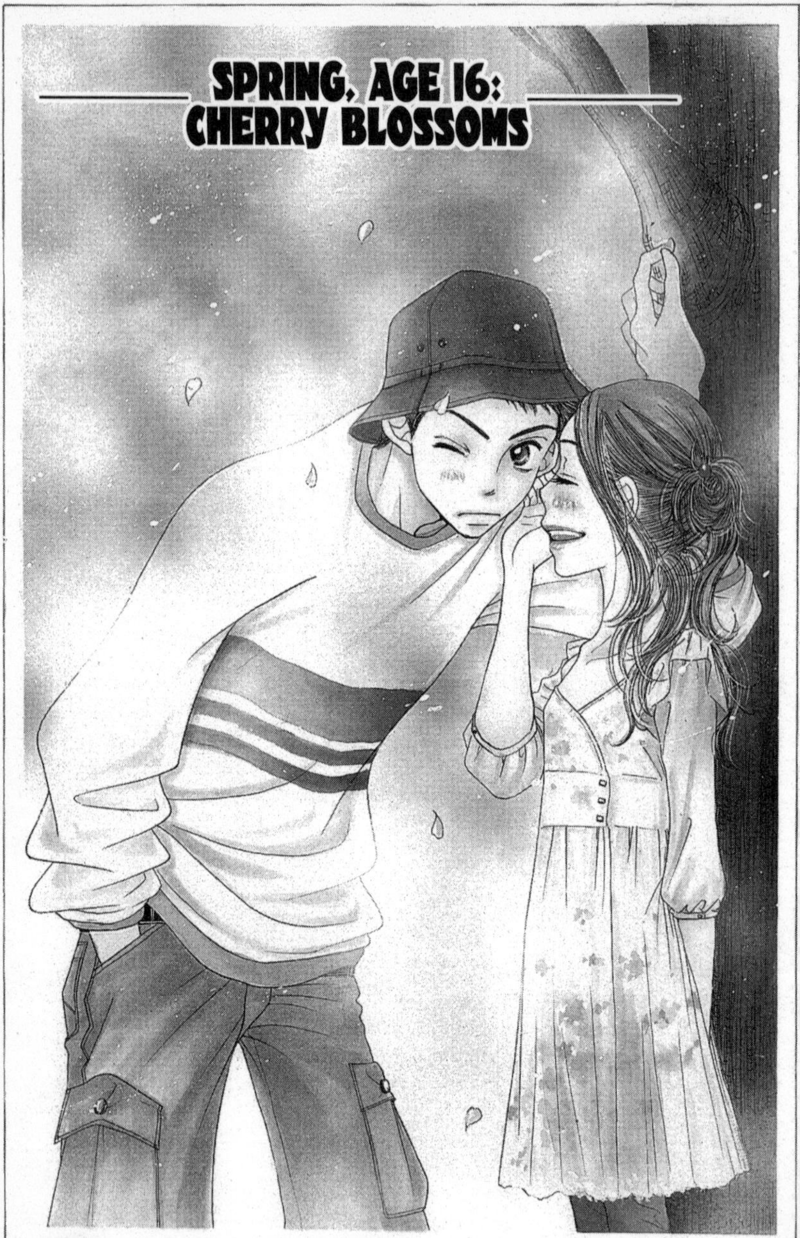
SPRING, AGE 16:
CHERRY BLOSSOMS

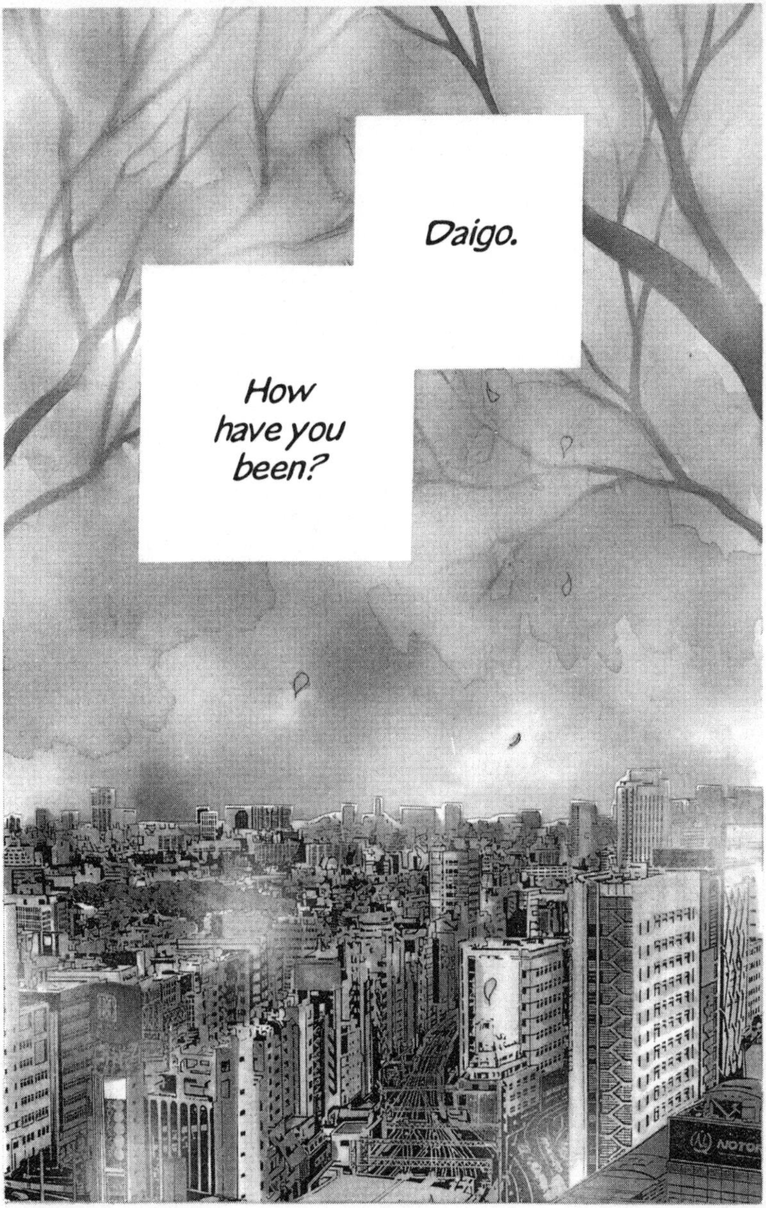
Daigo.
How have you been?
NOTO

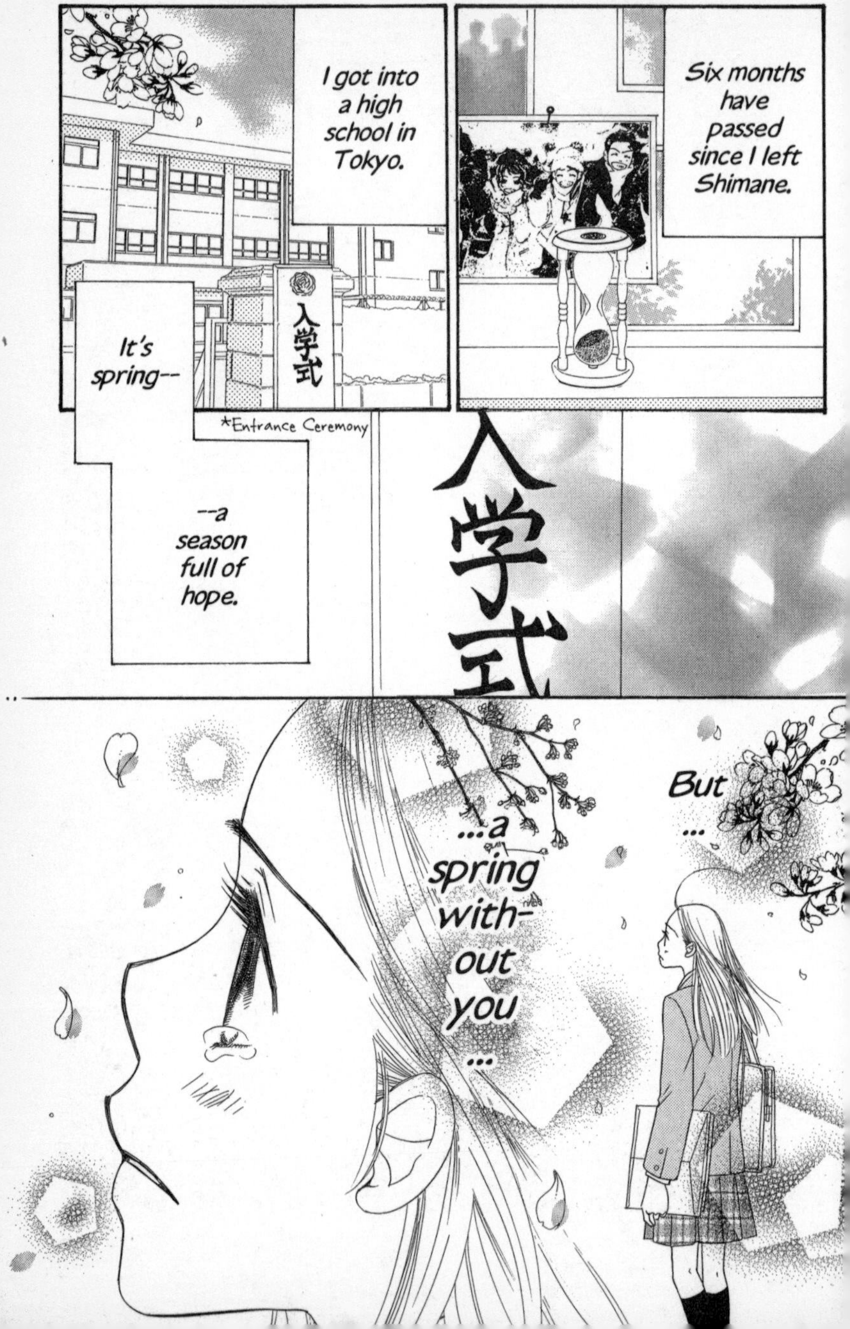
Six months have passed since I left Shimane.
I got into a high school in Tokyo.
入学式
It's spring--
*Entrance Ceremony
入学式
--a season full of hope.
But ...
...a spring with-out you ...

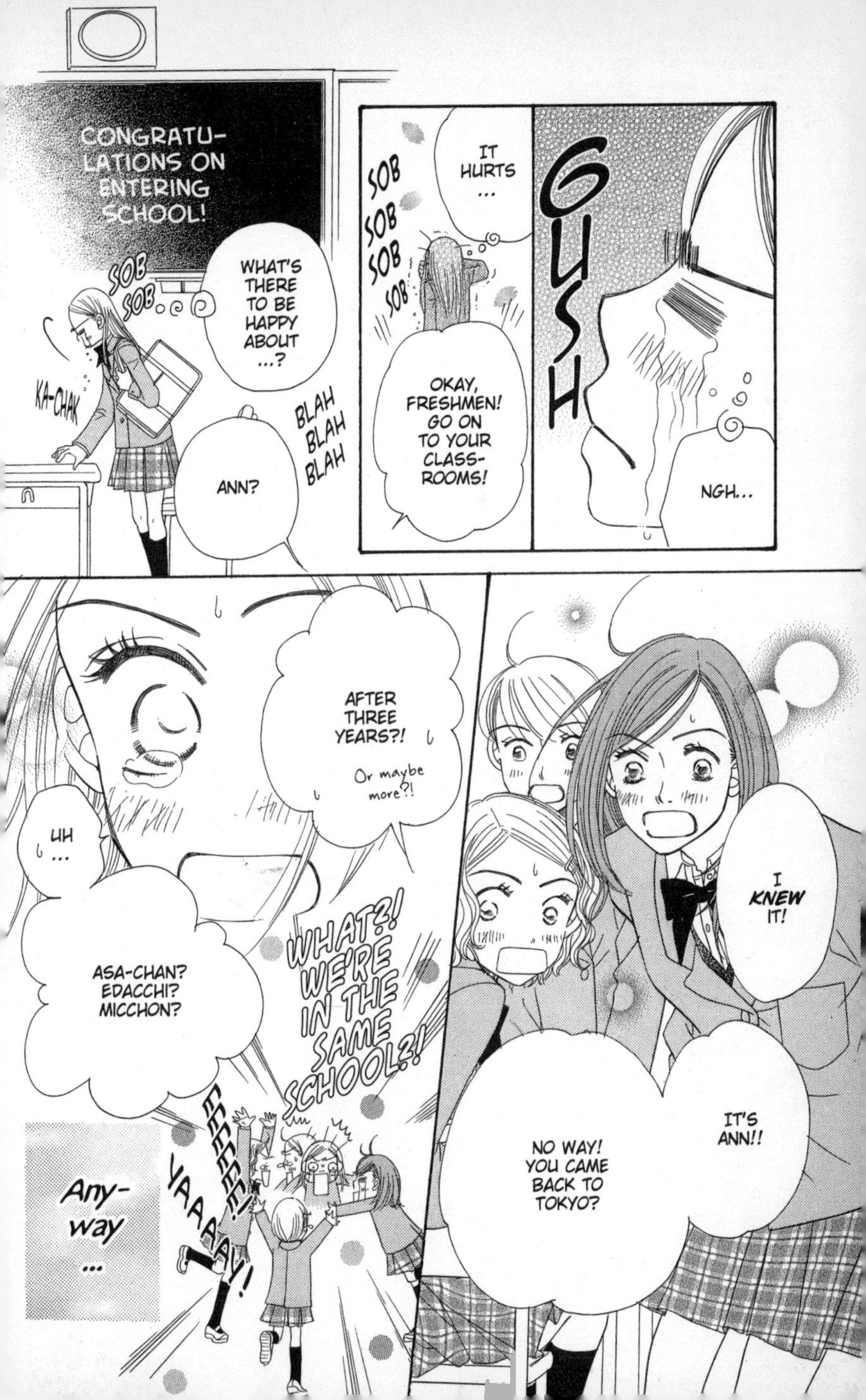
GUSH
NGH...
IT HURTS ...
SOB SOB SOB SOB
OKAY, FRESHMEN! GO ON TO YOUR CLASSROOMS!
CONGRATULATIONS ON ENTERING SCHOOL!
SOB SOB
WHAT'S THERE TO BE HAPPY ABOUT ...?
KA-CHAK
BLAH BLAH BLAH
ANN?
I KNEW IT!
IT'S ANN!!
NO WAY! YOU CAME BACK TO TOKYO?
AFTER THREE YEARS?!
Or maybe more?!
UH ...
ASA-CHAN? EDACCHI? MICCHON?
WHAT?! WE'RE IN THE SAME SCHOOL?!
EEEEEE!
YAAAAAY!
Any-way ...

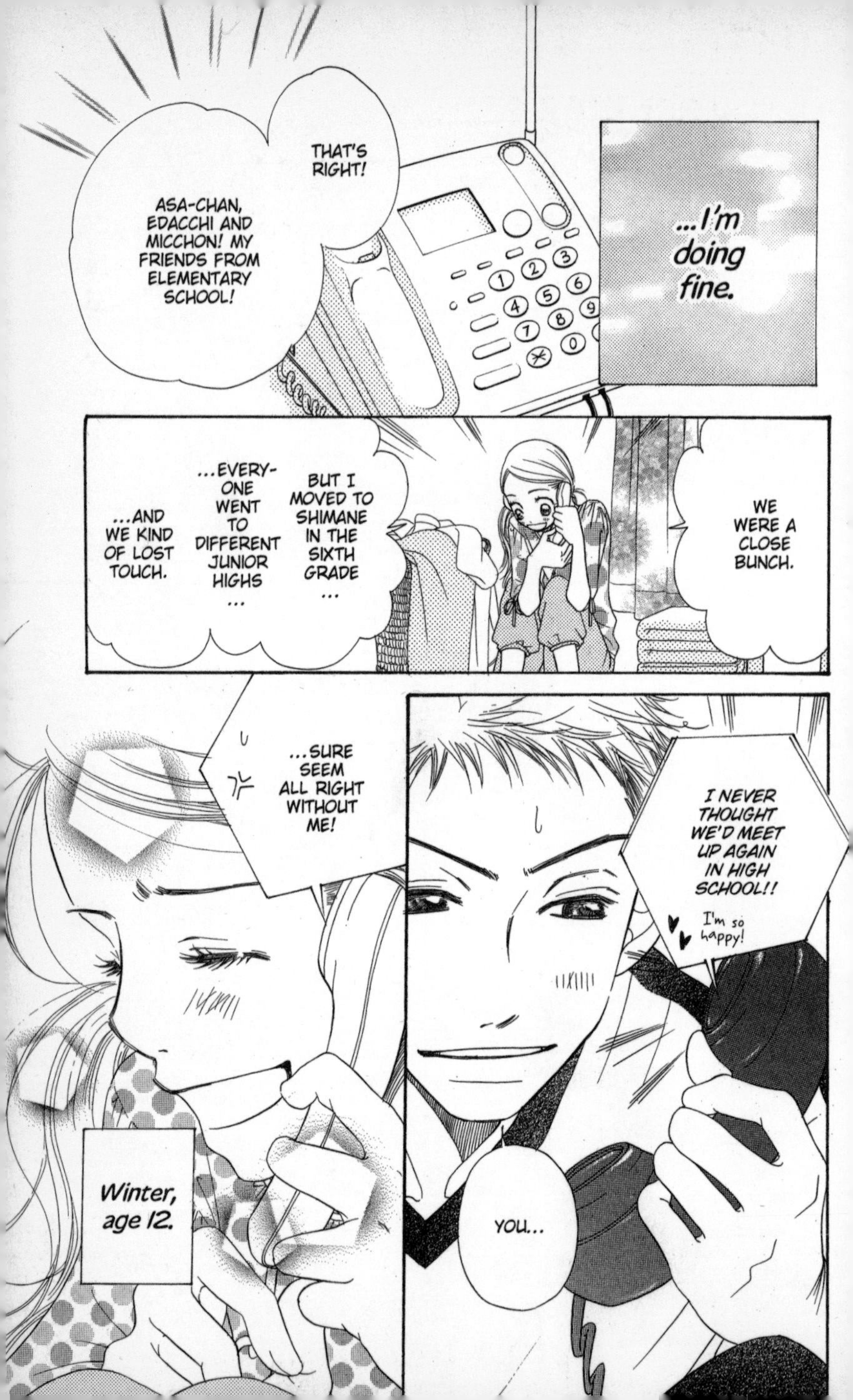
...I'm doing fine.
THAT'S RIGHT!
ASA-CHAN, EDACCHI AND MICCHON! MY FRIENDS FROM ELEMENTARY SCHOOL!
WE WERE A CLOSE BUNCH.
BUT I MOVED TO SHIMANE IN THE SIXTH GRADE...
...EVERY-ONE WENT TO DIFFERENT JUNIOR HIGHS...
...AND WE KIND OF LOST TOUCH.
I NEVER THOUGHT WE'D MEET UP AGAIN IN HIGH SCHOOL!!
I'm so happy!
YOU...
...SURE SEEM ALL RIGHT WITHOUT ME!
Winter, age 12.

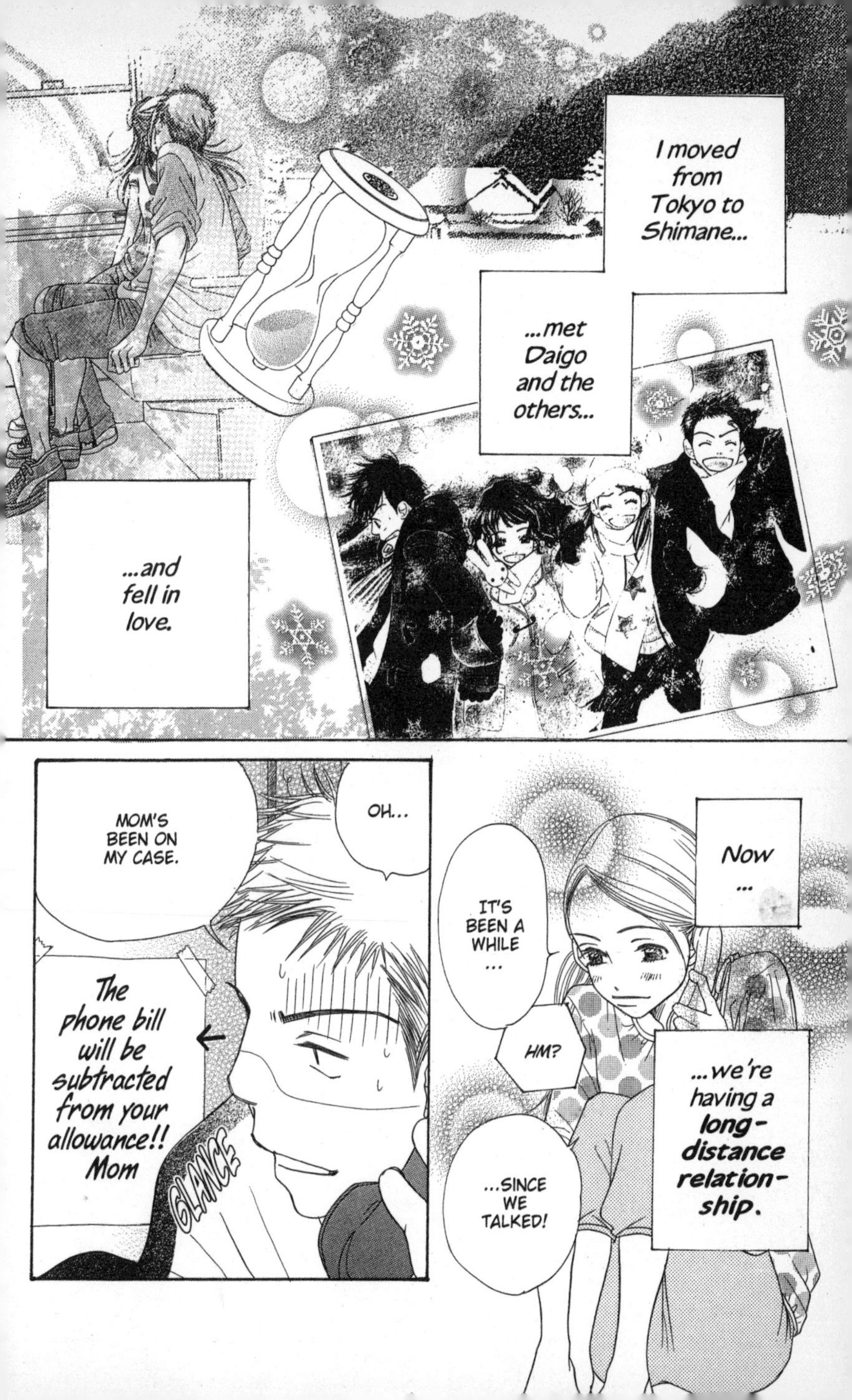
I moved from Tokyo to Shimane...
...met Daigo and the others...
...and fell in love.
Now ...
IT'S BEEN A WHILE ...
...we're having a long-distance relationship.
HM?
...SINCE WE TALKED!
OH...
MOM'S BEEN ON MY CASE.
The phone bill will be subtracted from your allowance!! Mom
GLANCE

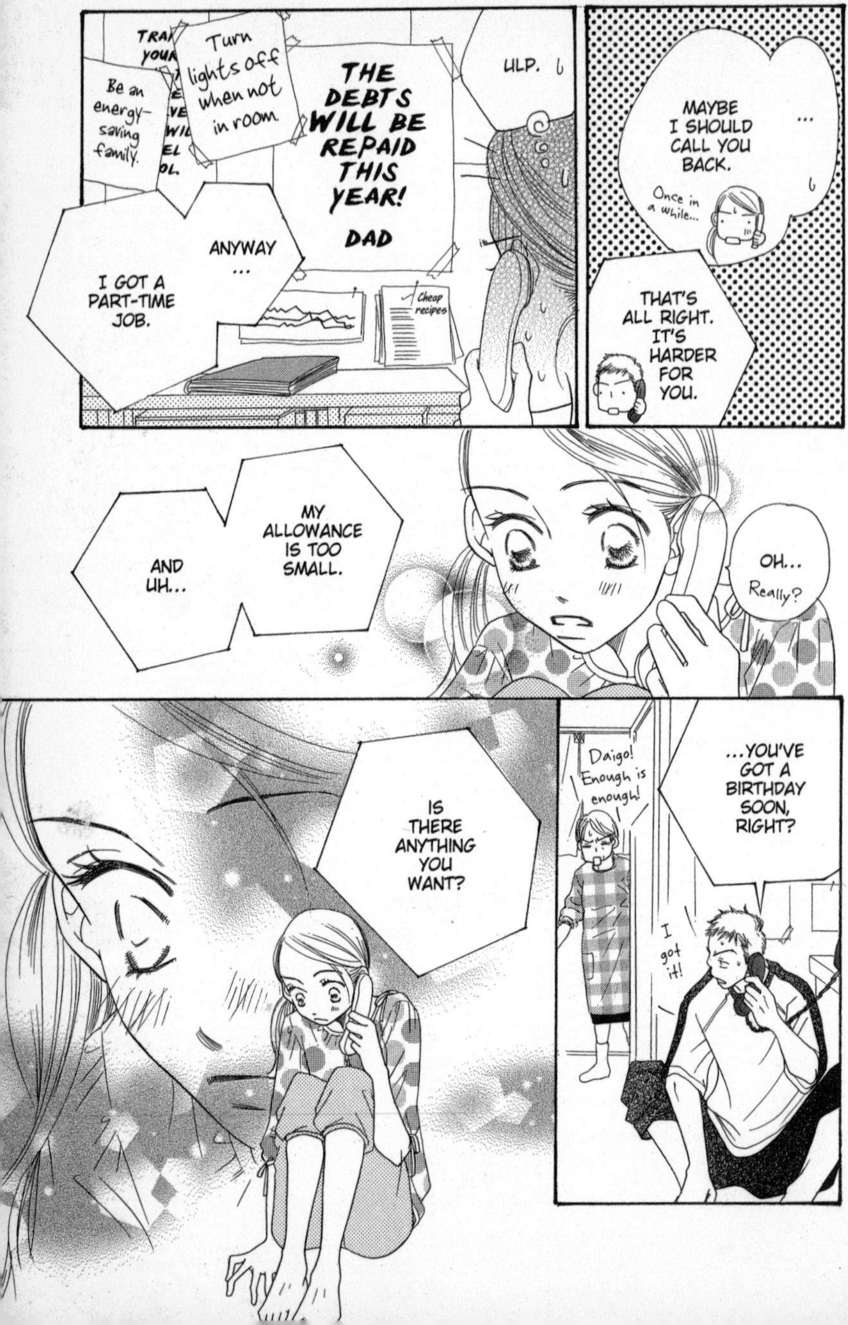
MAYBE I SHOULD CALL YOU BACK.
...
Once in a while...
THAT'S ALL RIGHT. IT'S HARDER FOR YOU.
ULP.
THE DEBTS WILL BE REPAID THIS YEAR! DAD
Turn lights off when not in room.
Be an energy-saving family.
ANYWAY...
I GOT A PART-TIME JOB.
Cheap recipes
OH...
Really?
AND UH...
MY ALLOWANCE IS TOO SMALL.
...YOU'VE GOT A BIRTHDAY SOON, RIGHT?
Daigo! Enough is enough!
I got it!
IS THERE ANYTHING YOU WANT?

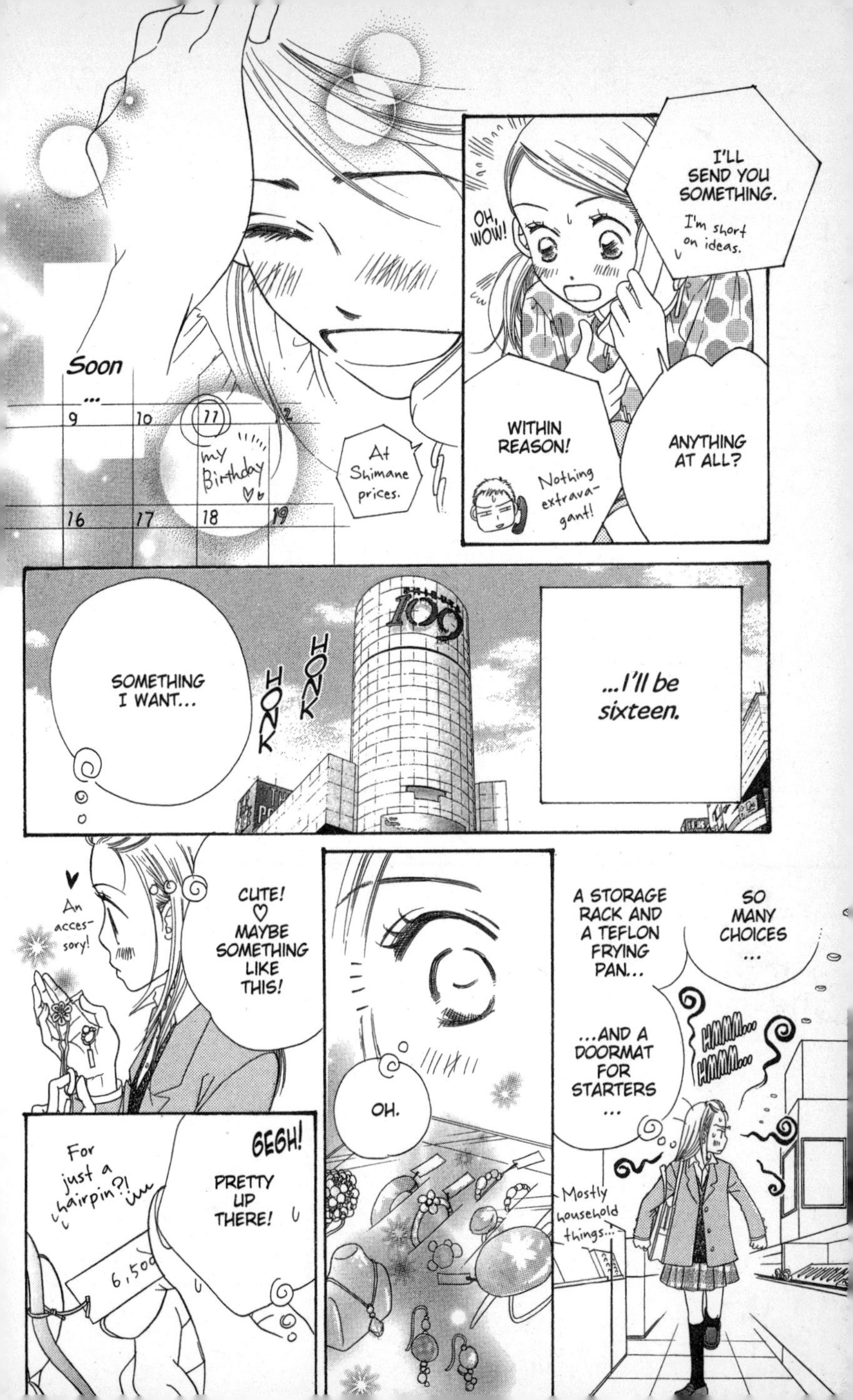
I'LL SEND YOU SOMETHING.
I'm short on ideas.
OH, WOW!
ANYTHING AT ALL?
WITHIN REASON!
Nothing extravagant!
At Shimane prices.
Soon...
9
10
11
12
my Birthday
16
17
18
19
...I'll be sixteen.
HONK HONK
SOMETHING I WANT...
SO MANY CHOICES...
A STORAGE RACK AND A TEFLON FRYING PAN...
...AND A DOORMAT FOR STARTERS...
HMMM... HMMM...
Mostly household things...
OH.
CUTE! ♡ MAYBE SOMETHING LIKE THIS!
An accessory!
GEGH!
PRETTY UP THERE!
For just a hairpin?!
6,500

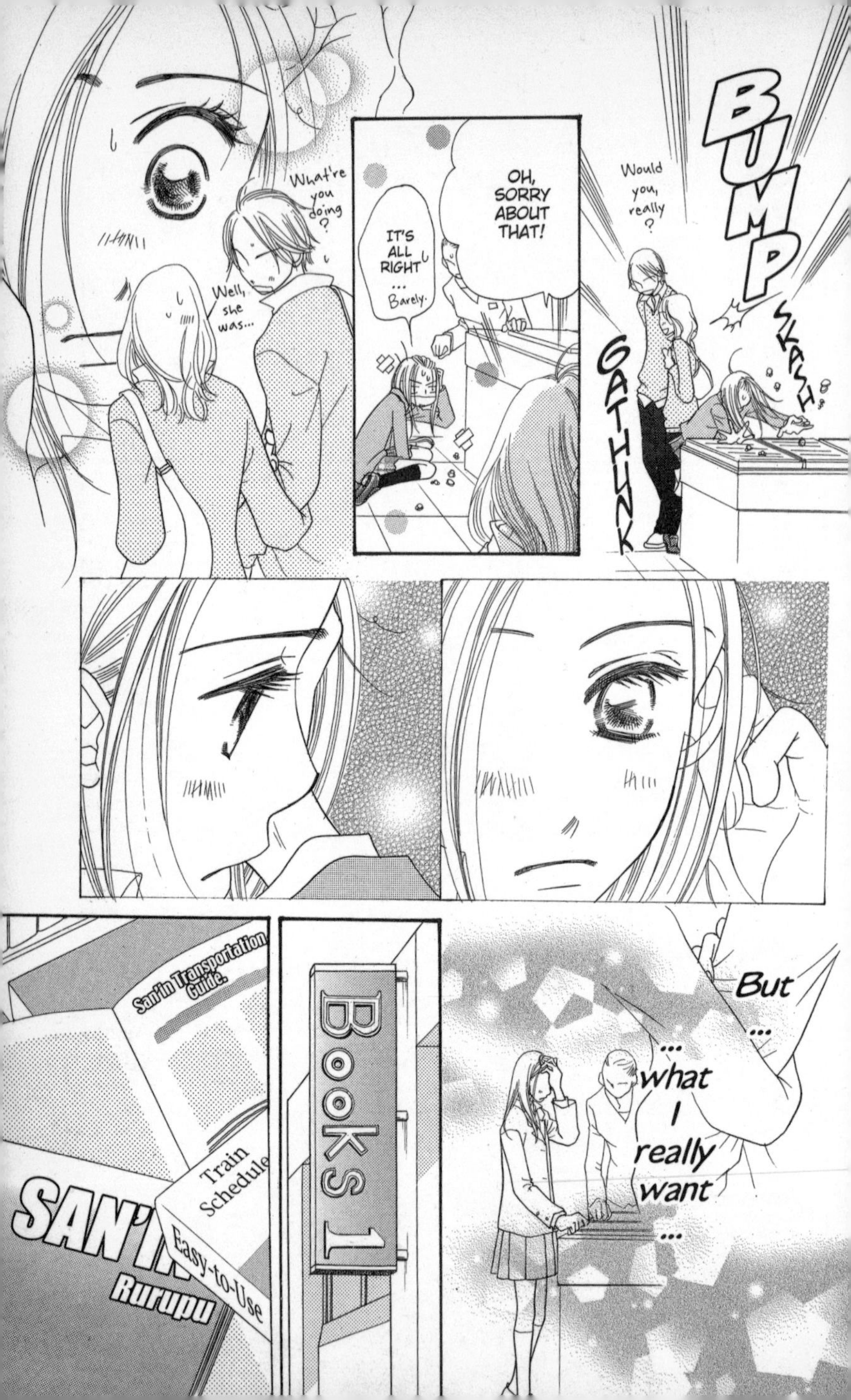
BUMP
SKASH
GATHUNK
Would you, really?
OH, SORRY ABOUT THAT!
IT'S ALL RIGHT... Barely.
What're you doing?
Well, she was...
But...
...what I really want...
BOOKS 1
San'in Transportation Guide.
Train Schedule
Easy-to-Use
SAN'IN
Rurupu

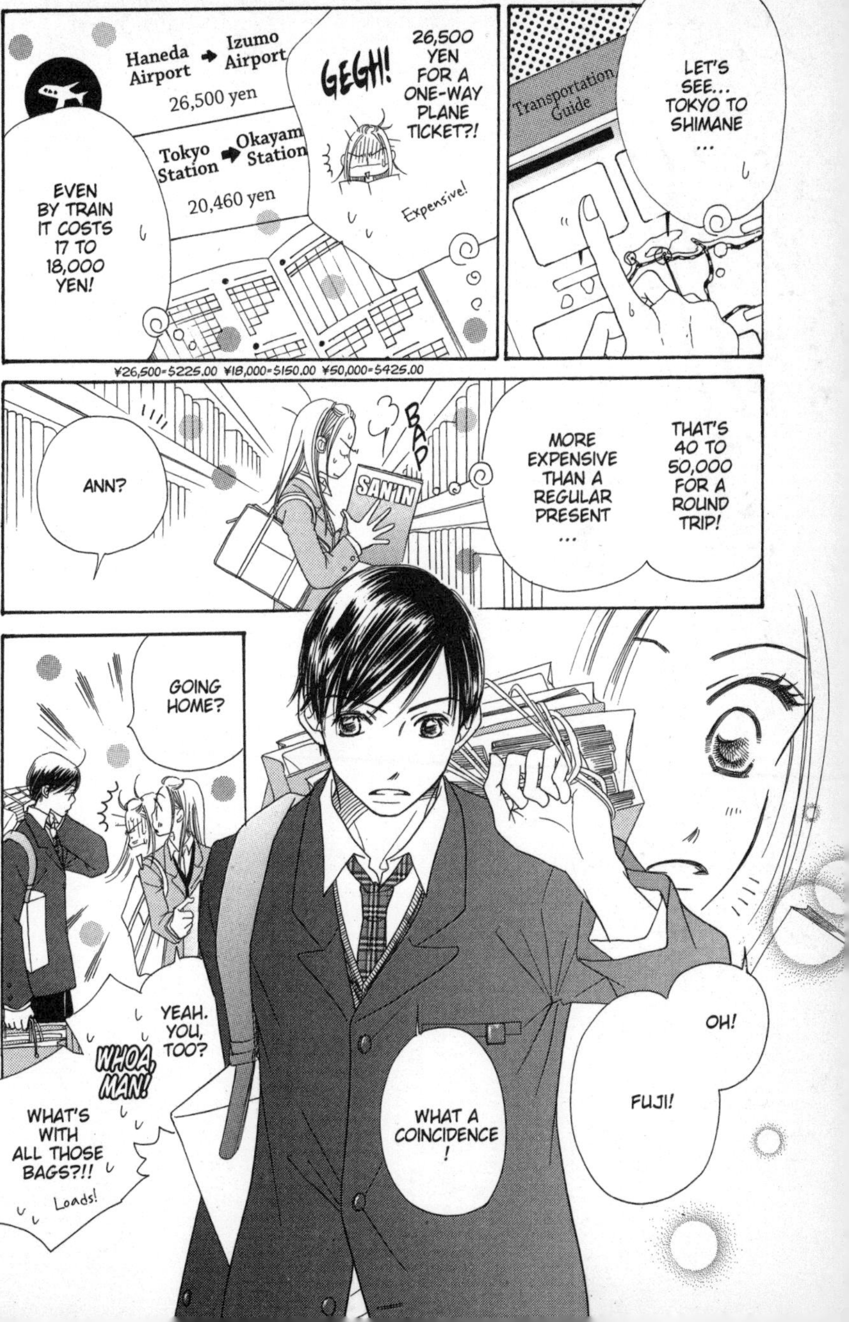
Transportation Guide
LET'S SEE... TOKYO TO SHIMANE ...
26,500 YEN FOR A ONE-WAY PLANE TICKET?!
GEGH!
Expensive!
Haneda Airport ➔ Izumo Airport
26,500 yen
Tokyo Station ➔ Okayama Station
20,460 yen
EVEN BY TRAIN IT COSTS 17 TO 18,000 YEN!
THAT'S 40 TO 50,000 FOR A ROUND TRIP!
MORE EXPENSIVE THAN A REGULAR PRESENT ...
BAP
SAN'IN
ANN?
OH!
FUJI!
WHAT A COINCIDENCE!
GOING HOME?
YEAH. YOU, TOO?
WHOA, MAN!
WHAT'S WITH ALL THOSE BAGS?!!
Loads!

¥26,500=$225.00 ¥18,000=$150.00 ¥50,000=$425.00

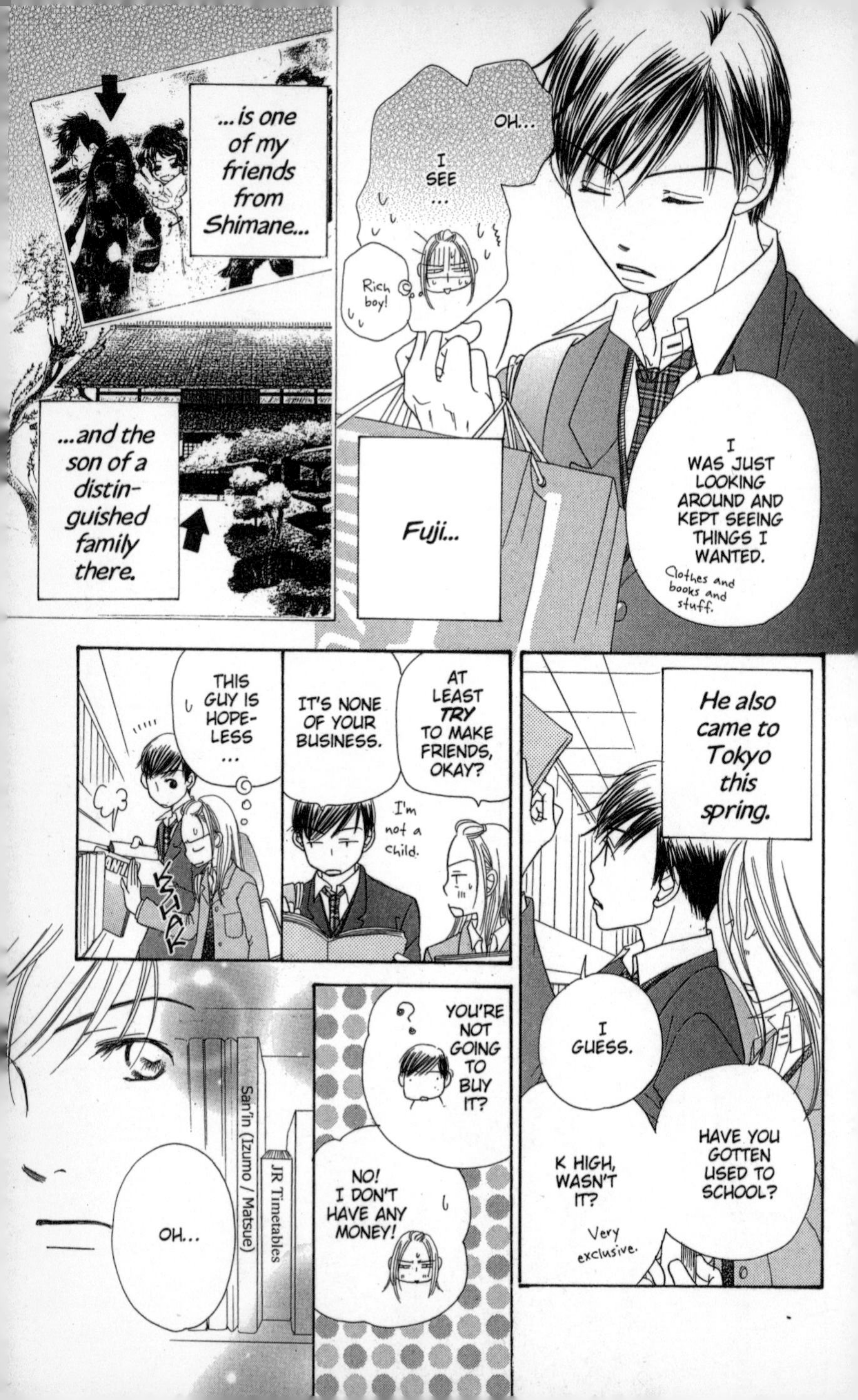
OH...
I SEE...
Rich boy!
I WAS JUST LOOKING AROUND AND KEPT SEEING THINGS I WANTED.
Clothes and books and stuff.
Fuji...
...is one of my friends from Shimane...
...and the son of a distinguished family there.
He also came to Tokyo this spring.
HAVE YOU GOTTEN USED TO SCHOOL?
K HIGH, WASN'T IT?
Very exclusive.
I GUESS.
AT LEAST TRY TO MAKE FRIENDS, OKAY?
I'm not a child.
IT'S NONE OF YOUR BUSINESS.
THIS GUY IS HOPELESS...
YOU'RE NOT GOING TO BUY IT?
NO! I DON'T HAVE ANY MONEY!
JR Timetables
San'in (Izumo / Matsue)
OH...

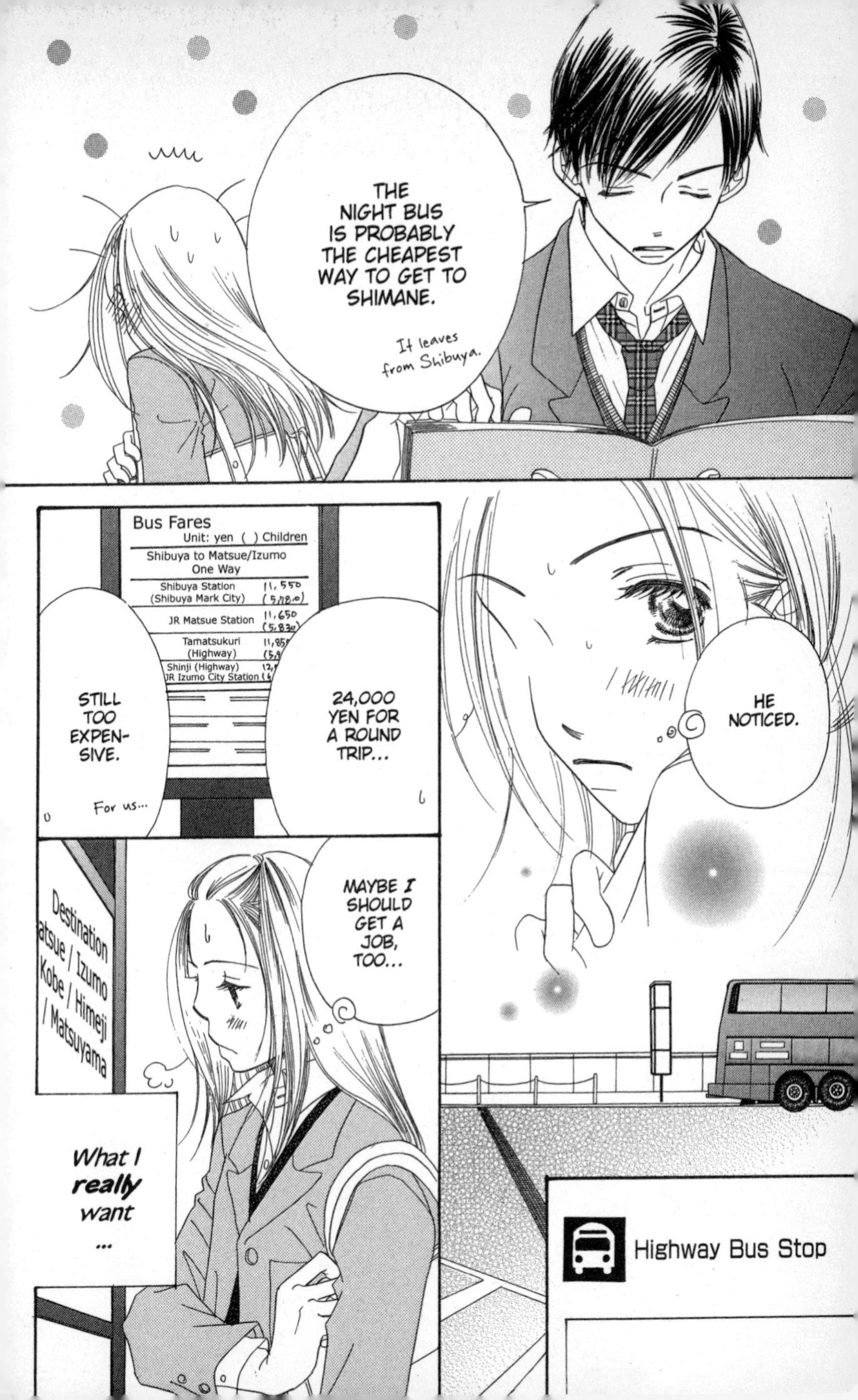

THE NIGHT BUS IS PROBABLY THE CHEAPEST WAY TO GET TO SHIMANE.
It leaves from Shibuya.
HE NOTICED.
Highway Bus Stop
Bus Fares
Unit: yen ( ) Children
Shibuya to Matsue/Izumo One Way
Shibuya Station (Shibuya Mark City) 11,550 (5,780)
JR Matsue Station 11,650 (5,830)
Tamatsukuri (Highway)
Shinji (Highway)
JR Izumo City Station
24,000 YEN FOR A ROUND TRIP...
STILL TOO EXPENSIVE.
For us...
MAYBE I SHOULD GET A JOB, TOO...
Destination
atsue / Izumo
Kobe / Himeji
/ Matsuyama
What I really want ...

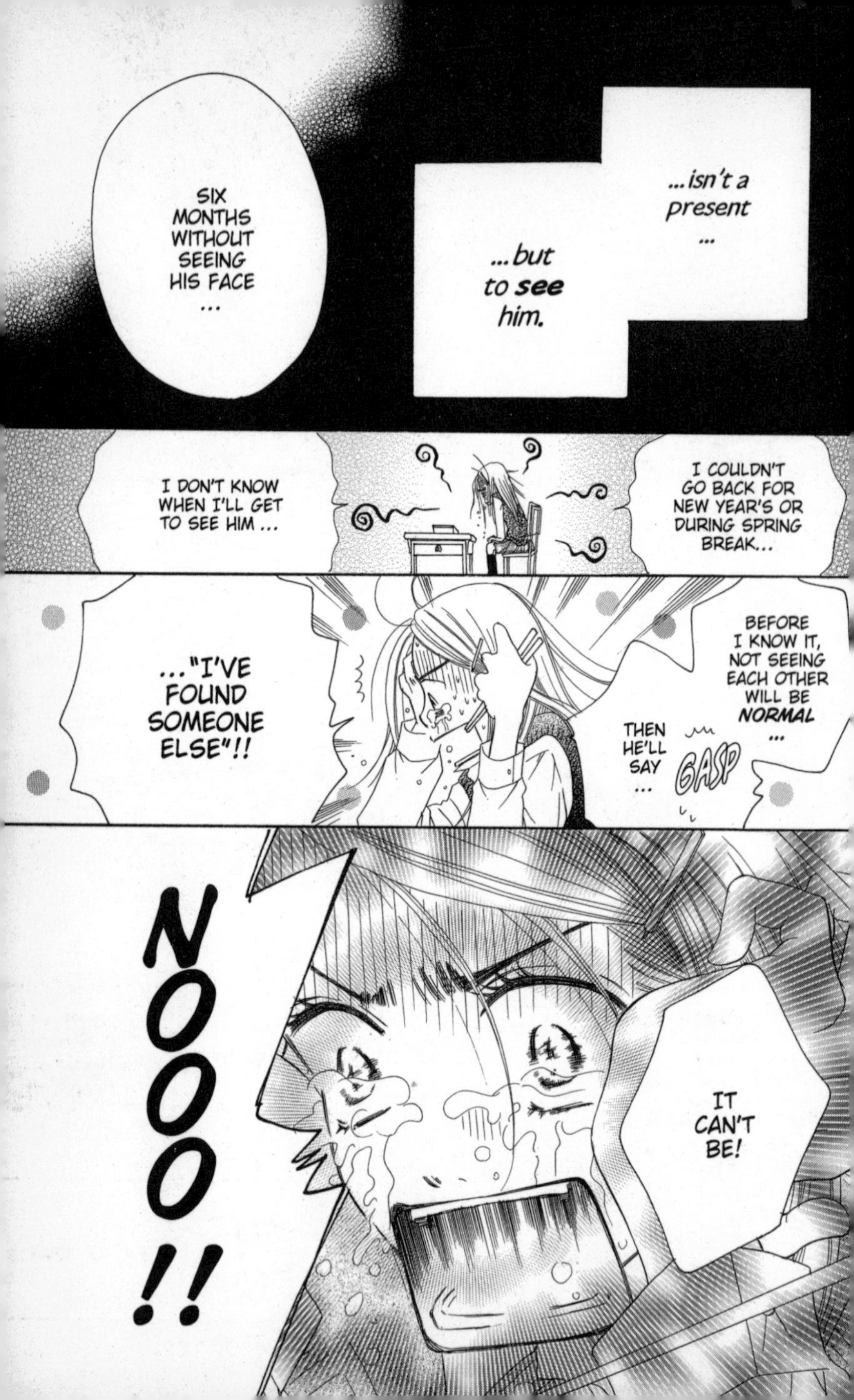
...isn't a present ...
...but to see him.
SIX MONTHS WITHOUT SEEING HIS FACE ...
I COULDN'T GO BACK FOR NEW YEAR'S OR DURING SPRING BREAK...
I DON'T KNOW WHEN I'LL GET TO SEE HIM ...
BEFORE I KNOW IT, NOT SEEING EACH OTHER WILL BE NORMAL ...
GASP
THEN HE'LL SAY ...
..."I'VE FOUND SOMEONE ELSE"!!
IT CAN'T BE!
NOOO!!

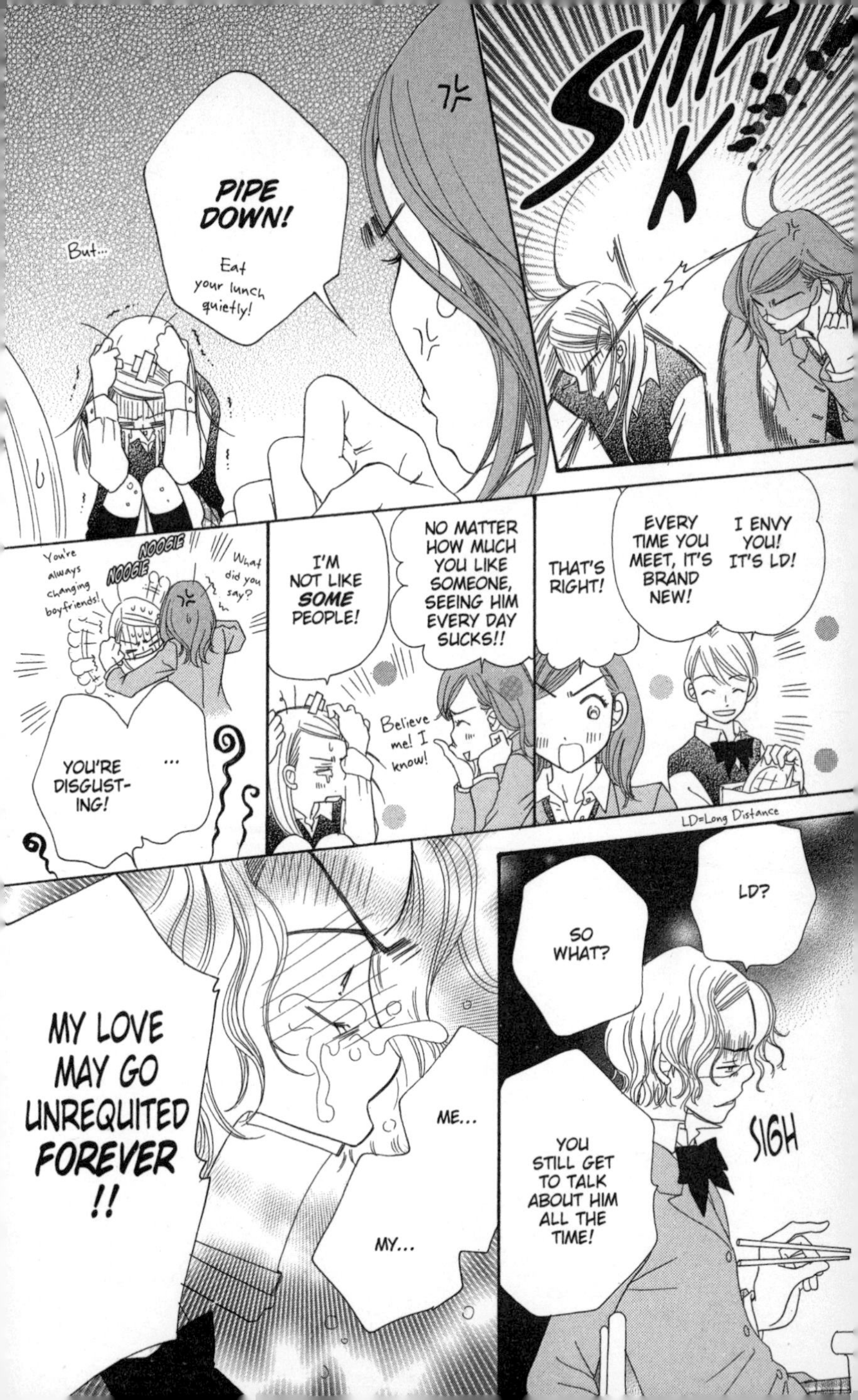
PIPE DOWN!
Eat your lunch quietly!
But...
I ENVY YOU! IT'S LD!
EVERY TIME YOU MEET, IT'S BRAND NEW!
THAT'S RIGHT!
LD=Long Distance
NO MATTER HOW MUCH YOU LIKE SOMEONE, SEEING HIM EVERY DAY SUCKS!!
I'M NOT LIKE *SOME* PEOPLE!
Believe me! I know!
What did you say?
NOOGIE
NOOGIE
You're always changing boyfriends!
...
YOU'RE DISGUSTING!
LD?
SO WHAT?
SIGH
YOU STILL GET TO TALK ABOUT HIM ALL THE TIME!
ME...
MY...
MY LOVE MAY GO UNREQUITED FOREVER!!

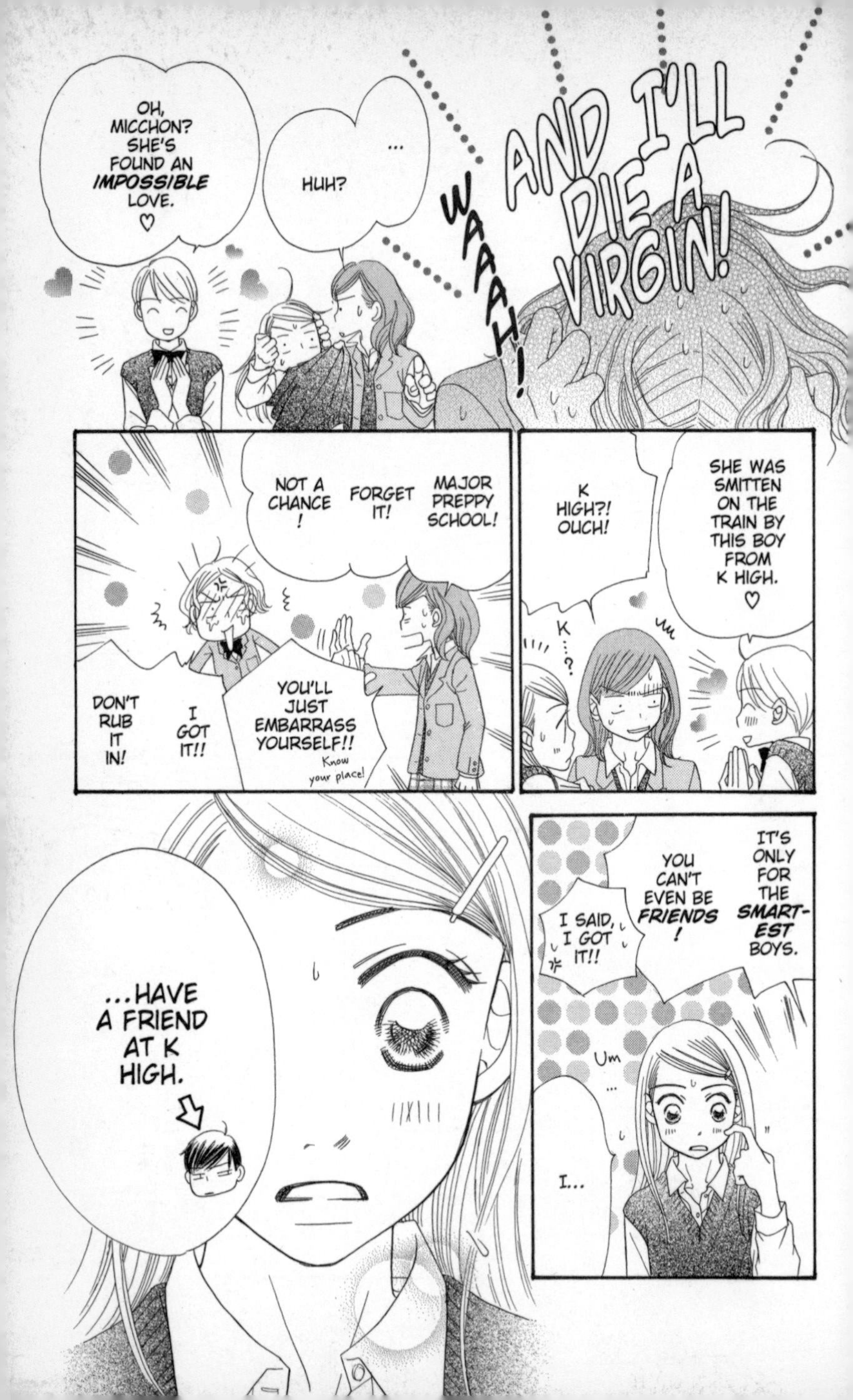
AND I'LL DIE A VIRGIN!
WAAAAH!
... HUH?
OH, MICCHON? SHE'S FOUND AN IMPOSSIBLE LOVE. ♡
SHE WAS SMITTEN ON THE TRAIN BY THIS BOY FROM K HIGH. ♡
K HIGH?! OUCH!
K...?
MAJOR PREPPY SCHOOL!
FORGET IT!
NOT A CHANCE!
YOU'LL JUST EMBARRASS YOURSELF!!
Know your place!
I GOT IT!!
DON'T RUB IT IN!
IT'S ONLY FOR THE SMART-EST BOYS.
YOU CAN'T EVEN BE FRIENDS!
I SAID, I GOT IT!!
Um ...
I...
...HAVE A FRIEND AT K HIGH.

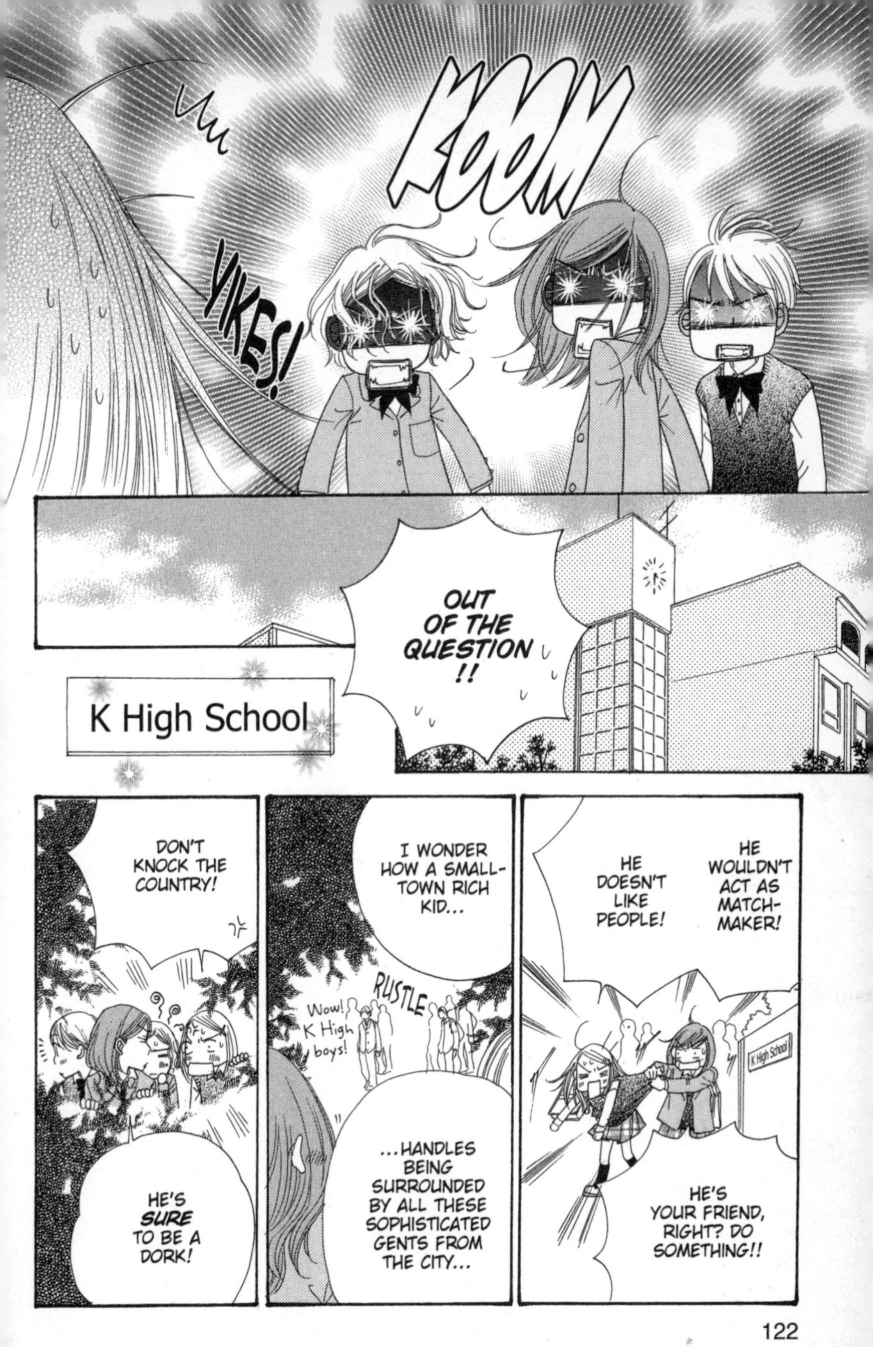
KOOM
YIKES!
Uu
OUT OF THE QUESTION !!
K High School
HE WOULDN'T ACT AS MATCH-MAKER!
HE DOESN'T LIKE PEOPLE!
K High School
HE'S YOUR FRIEND, RIGHT? DO SOMETHING!!
I WONDER HOW A SMALL-TOWN RICH KID...
RUSTLE
Wow! K High boys!
...HANDLES BEING SURROUNDED BY ALL THESE SOPHISTICATED GENTS FROM THE CITY...
DON'T KNOCK THE COUNTRY!
HE'S SURE TO BE A DORK!

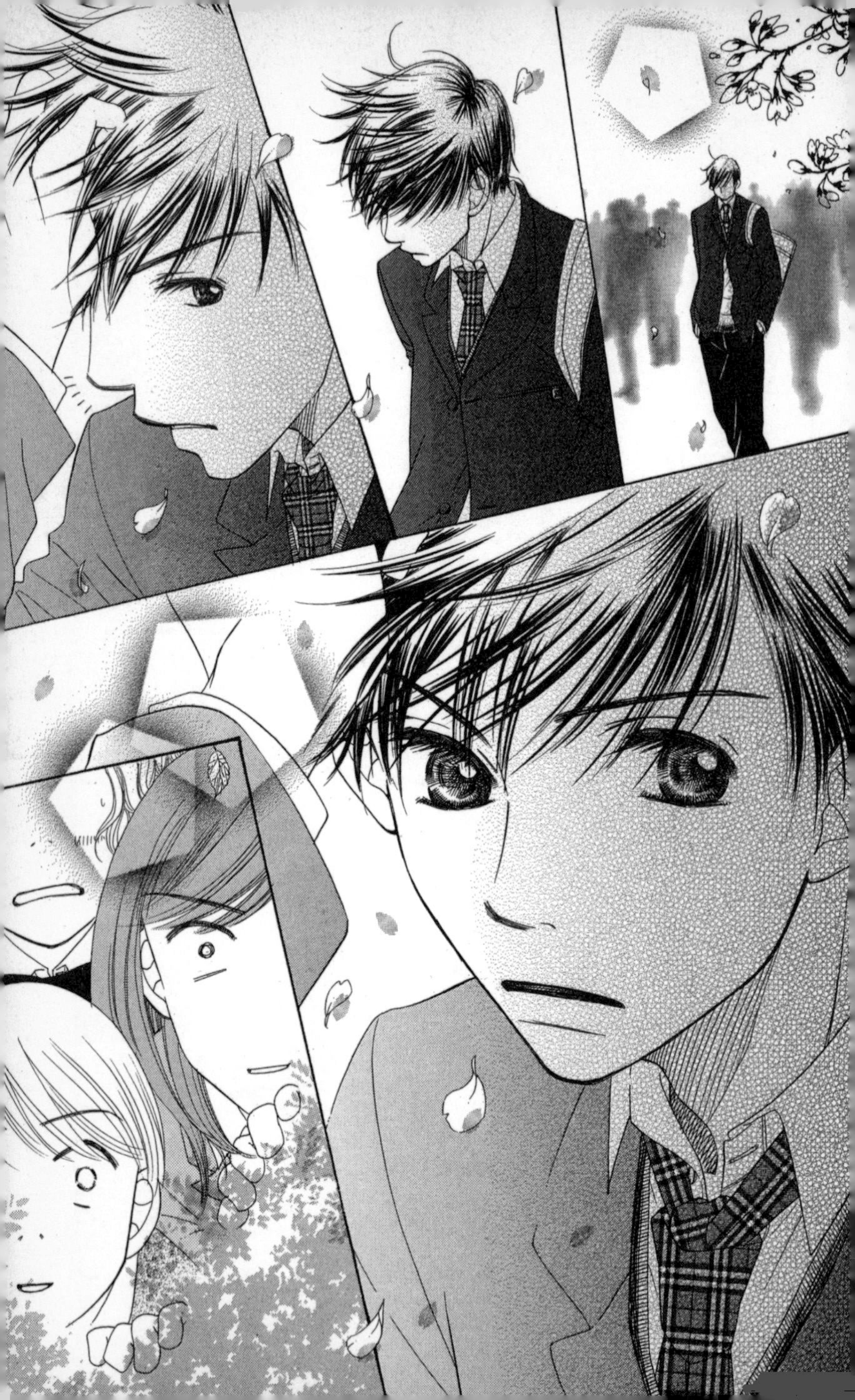

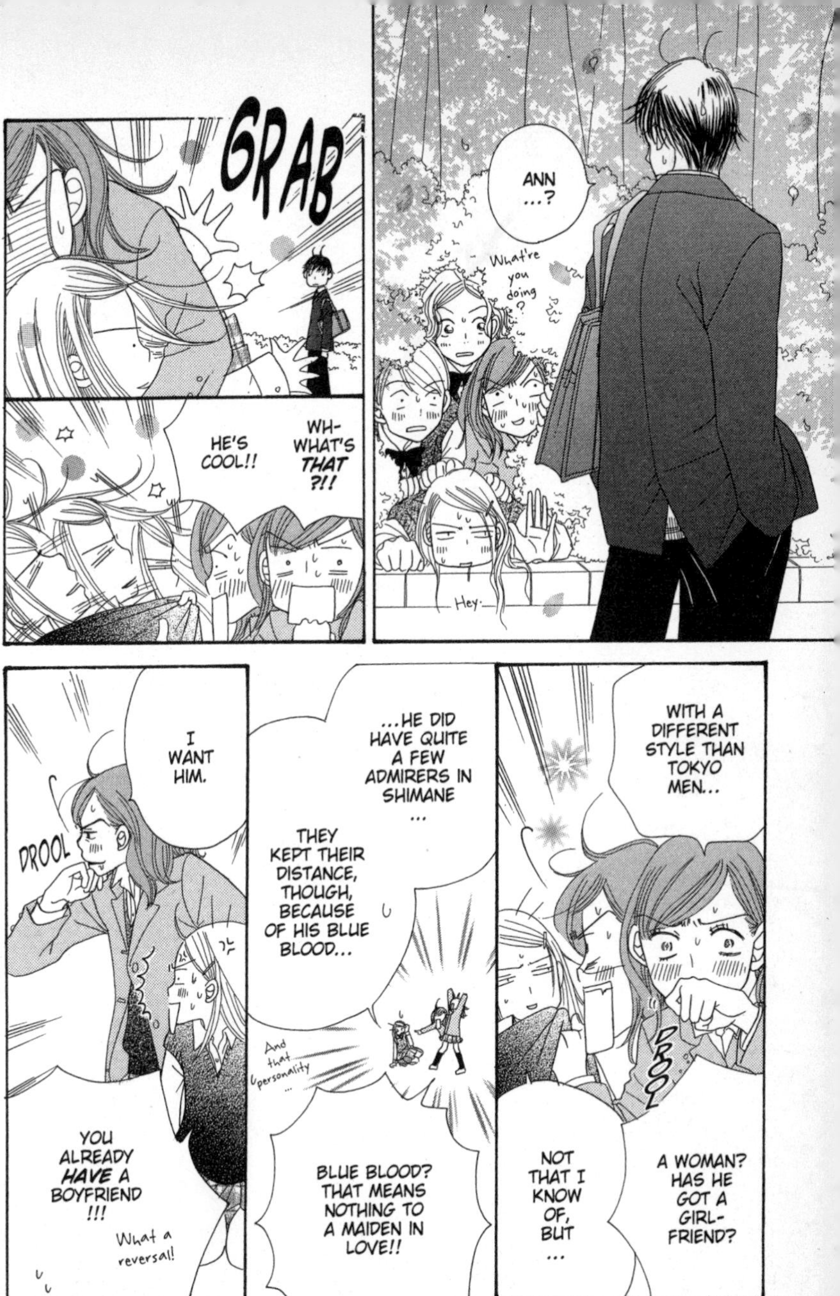
ANN ...?
What're you doing?
Hey.
GRAB
WH-WHAT'S THAT?!!
HE'S COOL!!
WITH A DIFFERENT STYLE THAN TOKYO MEN...
DROOL
A WOMAN? HAS HE GOT A GIRLFRIEND?
NOT THAT I KNOW OF, BUT ...
...HE DID HAVE QUITE A FEW ADMIRERS IN SHIMANE ...
THEY KEPT THEIR DISTANCE, THOUGH, BECAUSE OF HIS BLUE BLOOD...
And that personality ...
BLUE BLOOD? THAT MEANS NOTHING TO A MAIDEN IN LOVE!!
I WANT HIM.
DROOL
YOU ALREADY HAVE A BOYFRIEND !!!
What a reversal!

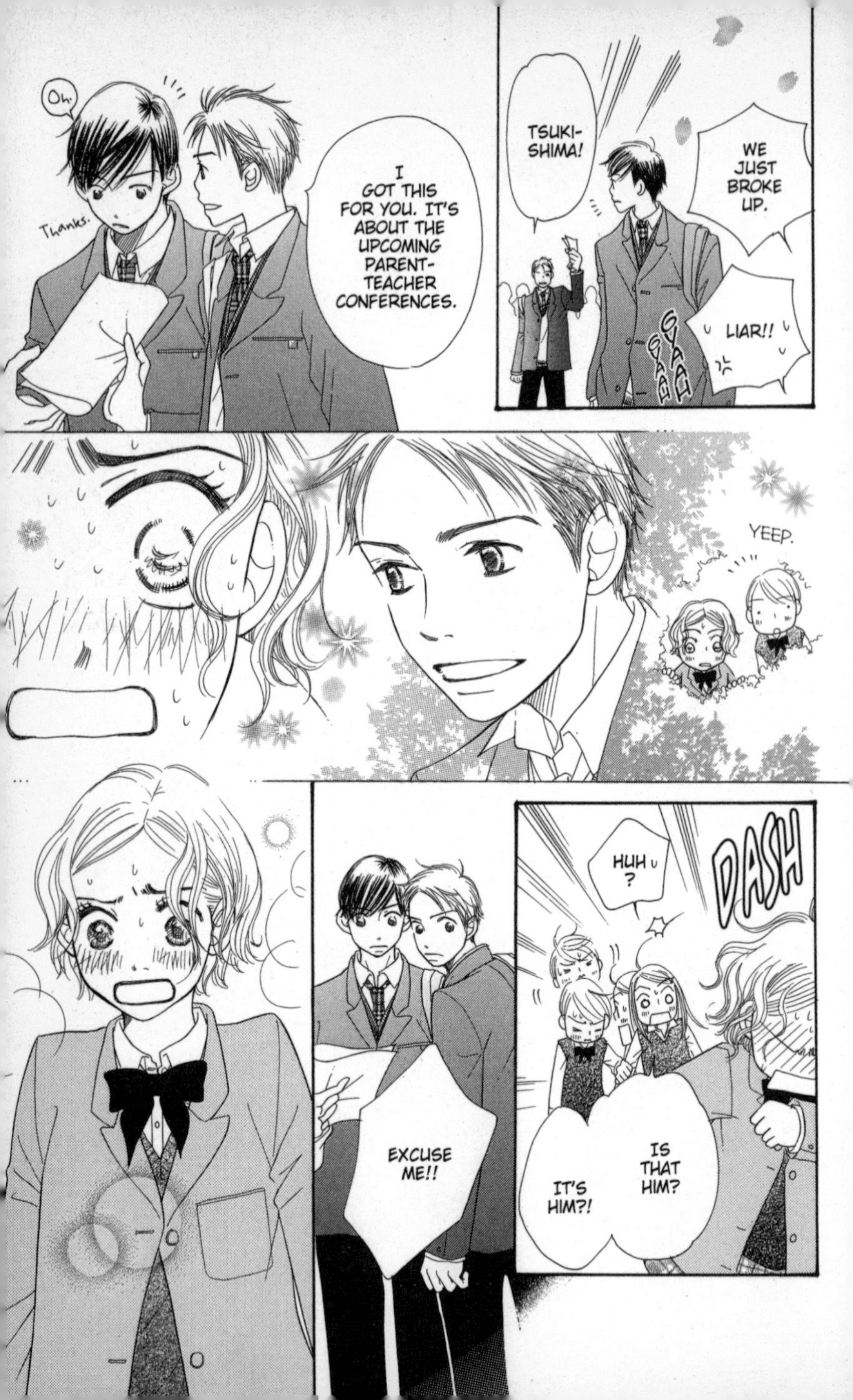
WE JUST BROKE UP.
TSUKI-SHIMA!
LIAR!!
GYAAH GYAAH
I GOT THIS FOR YOU. IT'S ABOUT THE UPCOMING PARENT-TEACHER CONFERENCES.
Oh.
Thanks.
YEEP.
DASH
HUH?
IS THAT HIM?
IT'S HIM?!
EXCUSE ME!!

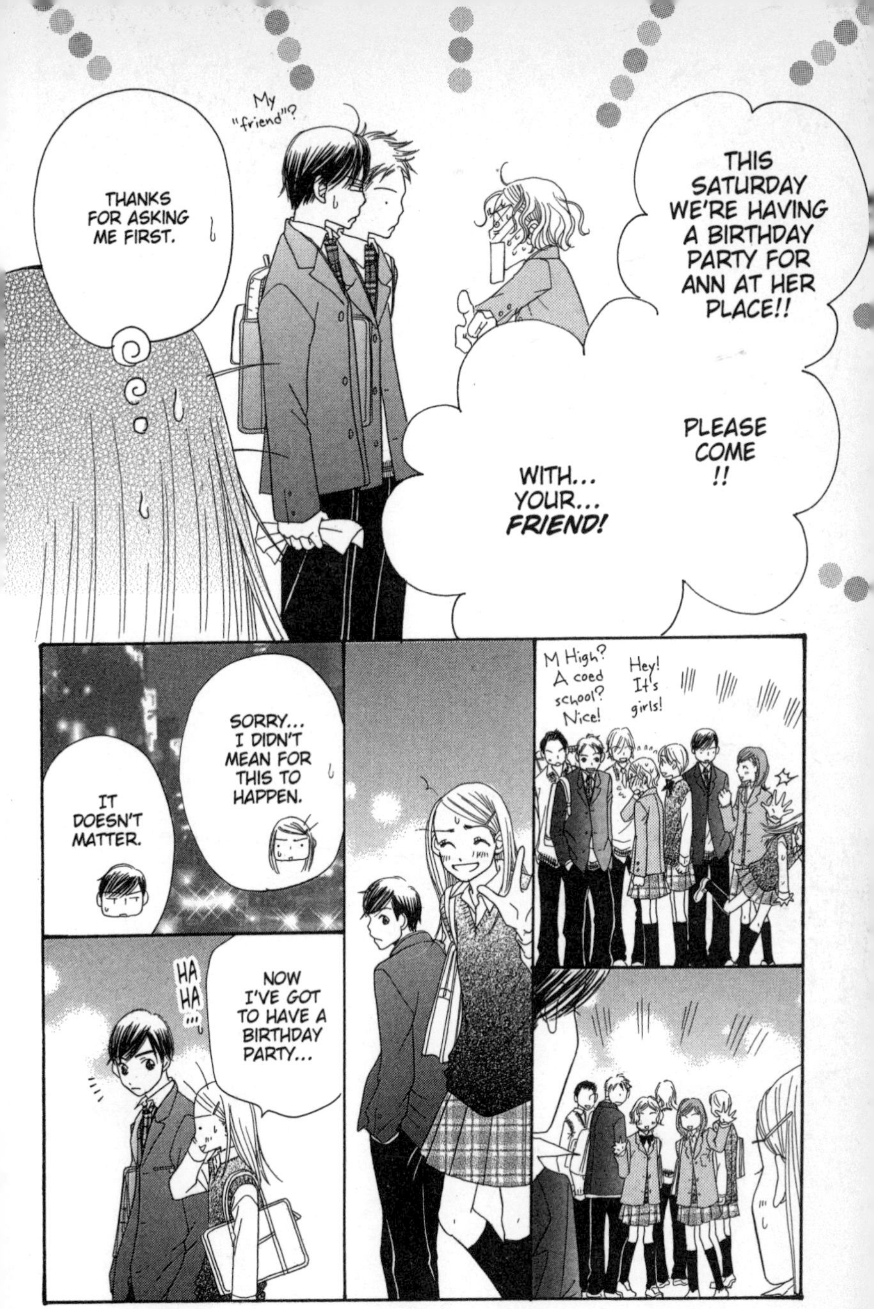
THIS SATURDAY WE'RE HAVING A BIRTHDAY PARTY FOR ANN AT HER PLACE!!
PLEASE COME !!
WITH... YOUR... FRIEND!
My "friend"?
THANKS FOR ASKING ME FIRST.
Hey! It's girls!
M High? A coed school? Nice!
SORRY... I DIDN'T MEAN FOR THIS TO HAPPEN.
IT DOESN'T MATTER.
NOW I'VE GOT TO HAVE A BIRTHDAY PARTY...
HA HA...

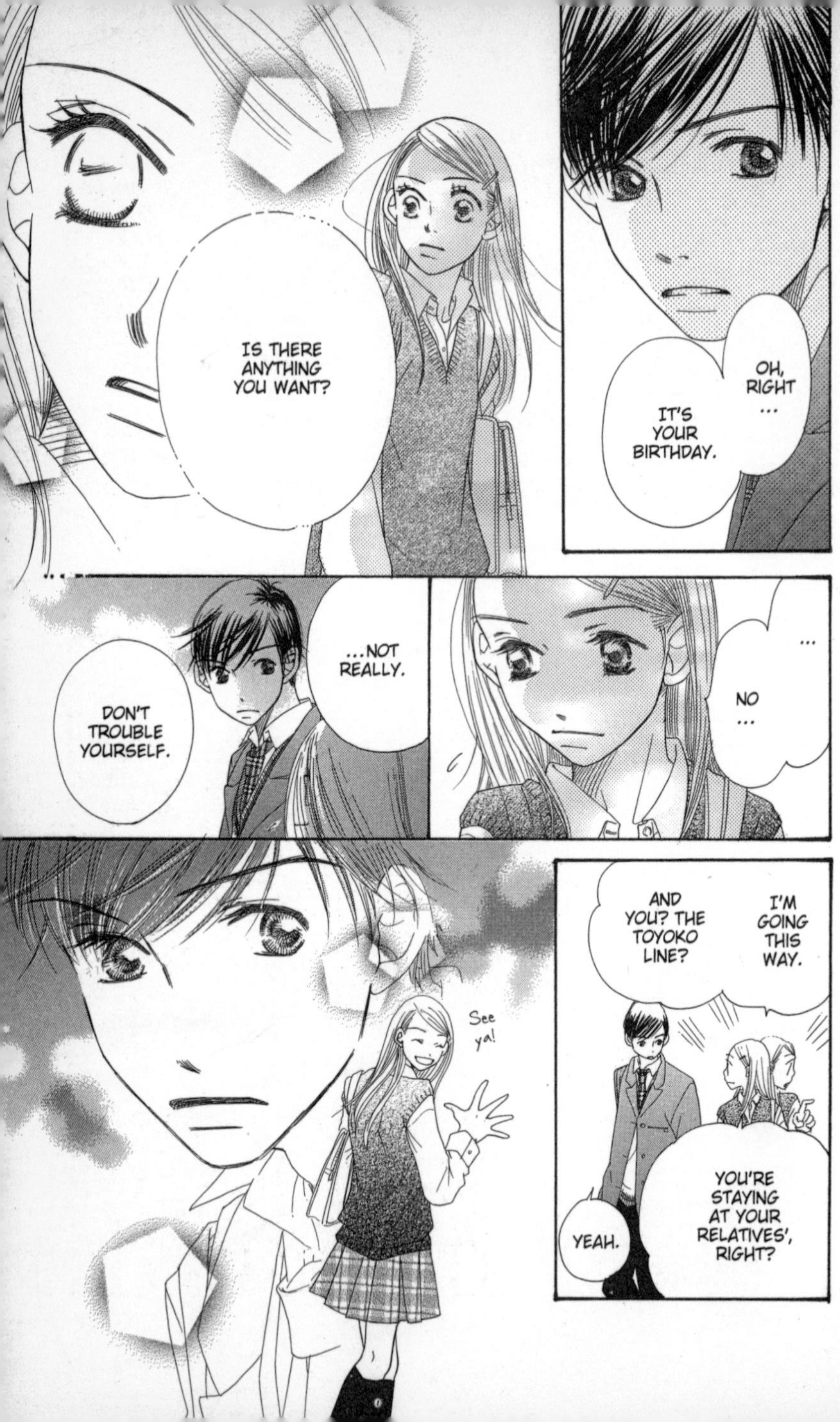
OH, RIGHT ...
IT'S YOUR BIRTHDAY.
IS THERE ANYTHING YOU WANT?
...
NO ...
...NOT REALLY.
DON'T TROUBLE YOURSELF.
I'M GOING THIS WAY.
AND YOU? THE TOYOKO LINE?
YOU'RE STAYING AT YOUR RELATIVES', RIGHT?
YEAH.
See ya!

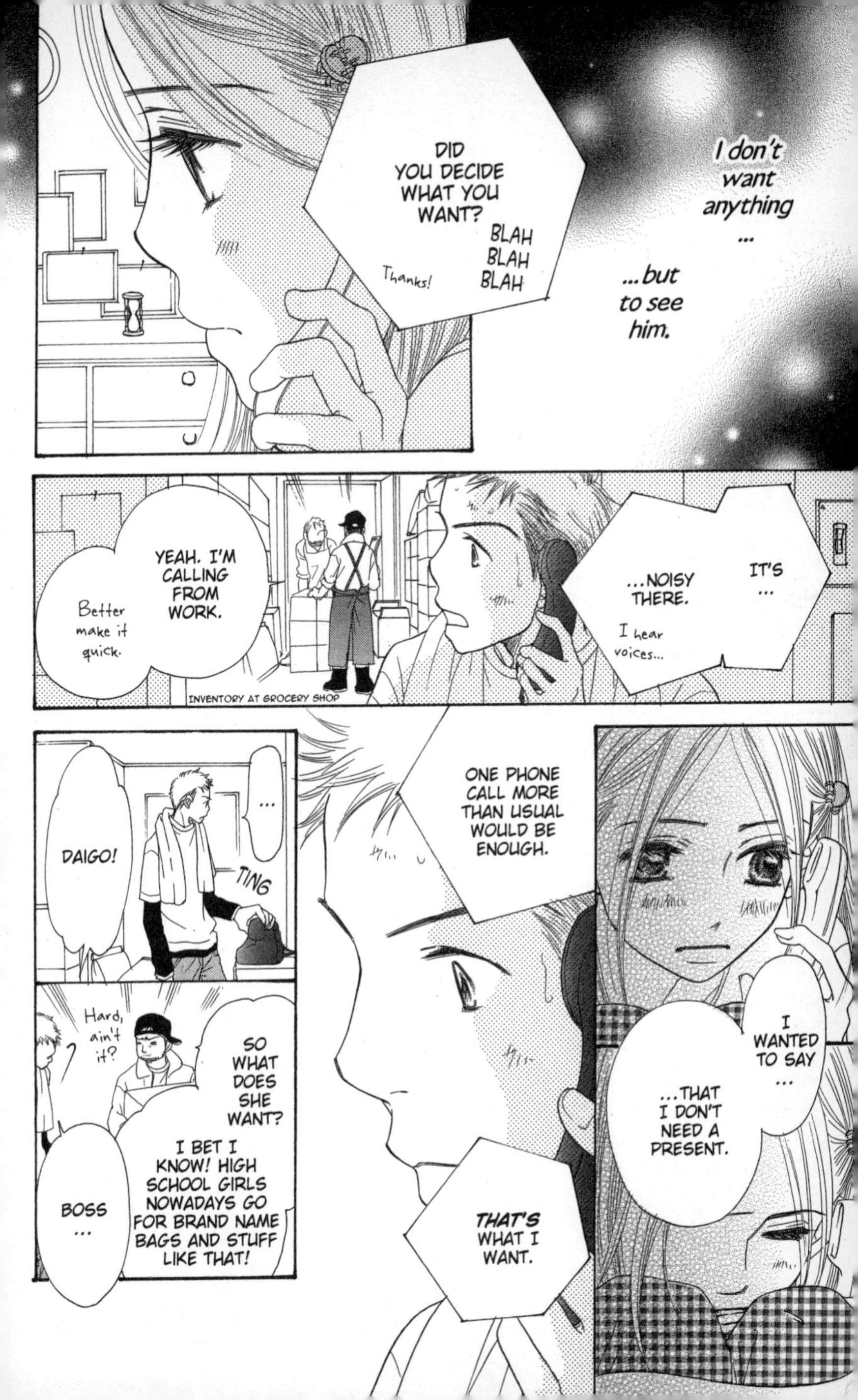
DID YOU DECIDE WHAT YOU WANT?
BLAH BLAH BLAH
Thanks!
I don't want anything ...
...but to see him.
IT'S ...
...NOISY THERE.
I hear voices...
YEAH. I'M CALLING FROM WORK.
Better make it quick.
INVENTORY AT GROCERY SHOP
I WANTED TO SAY ...
...THAT I DON'T NEED A PRESENT.
ONE PHONE CALL MORE THAN USUAL WOULD BE ENOUGH.
THAT'S WHAT I WANT.
...
DAIGO!
TING
SO WHAT DOES SHE WANT?
Hard, ain't it?
I BET I KNOW! HIGH SCHOOL GIRLS NOWADAYS GO FOR BRAND NAME BAGS AND STUFF LIKE THAT!
BOSS ...

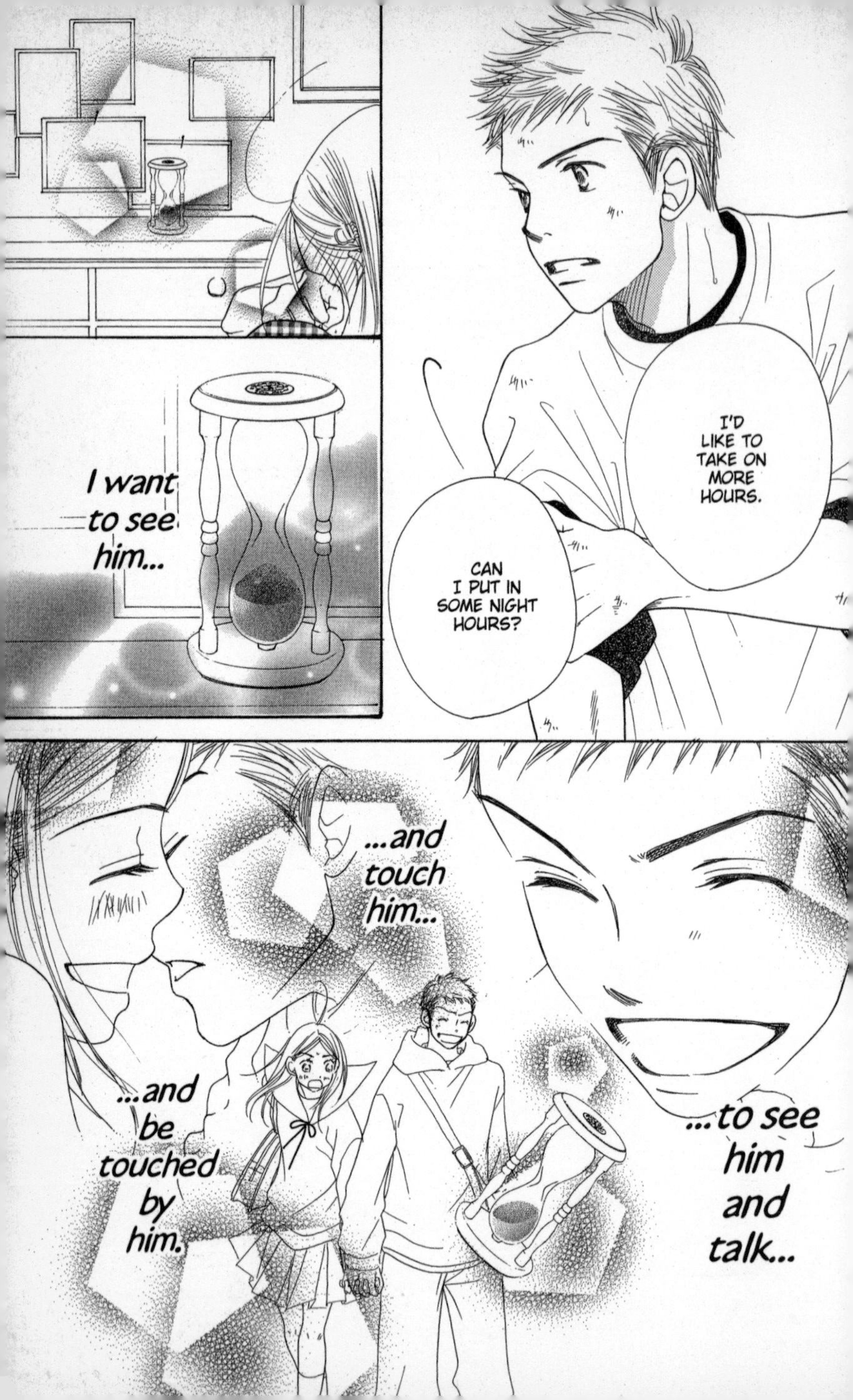
I'D LIKE TO TAKE ON MORE HOURS.
CAN I PUT IN SOME NIGHT HOURS?
I want to see him...
...to see him and talk...
...and touch him...
...and be touched by him.

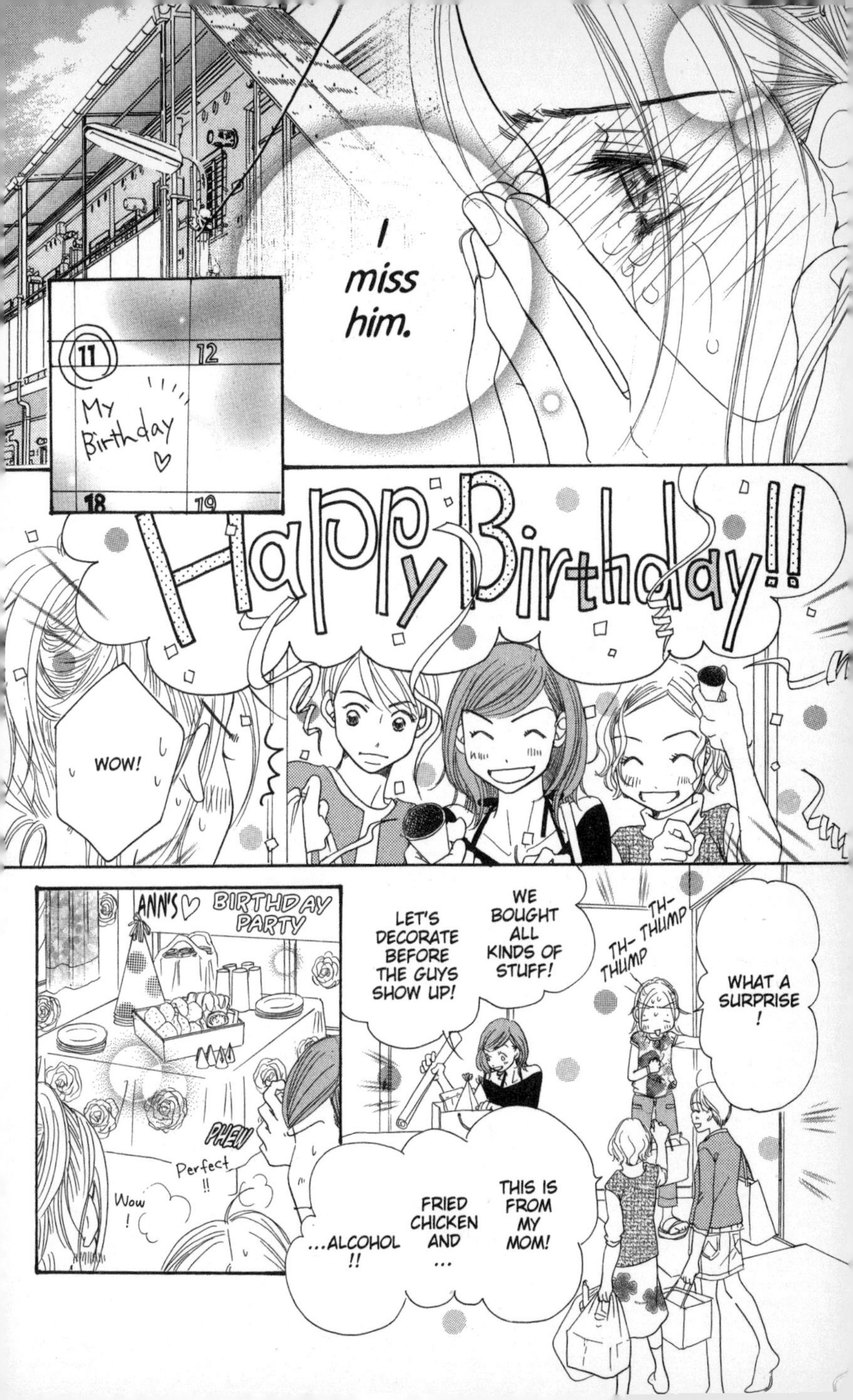

I miss him.
11
My Birthday ♡
12
18
19
Happy Birthday!!
WOW!
WHAT A SURPRISE!
TH- TH- THUMP THUMP
WE BOUGHT ALL KINDS OF STUFF!
LET'S DECORATE BEFORE THE GUYS SHOW UP!
THIS IS FROM MY MOM!
FRIED CHICKEN AND ...
...ALCOHOL!!
ANN'S ♡ BIRTHDAY PARTY
PHEW
Perfect!!
Wow!

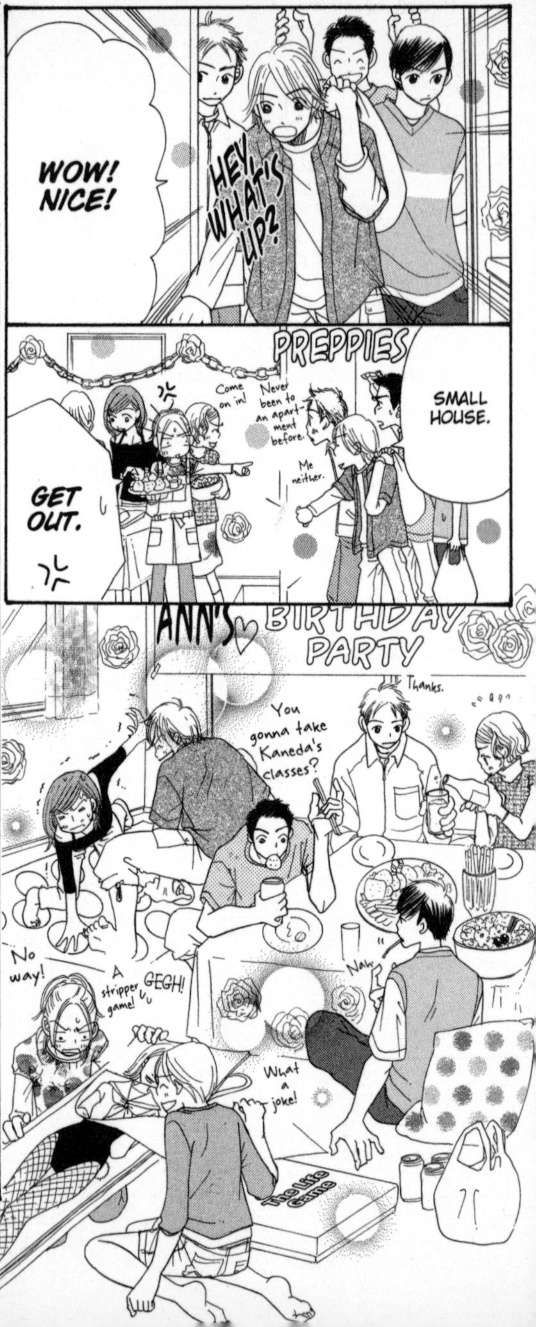
HEY, WHAT'S UP?
WOW! NICE!
SMALL HOUSE.
PREPPIES
Never been to an apartment before.
Me neither.
Come on in!
GET OUT.
ANN'S BIRTHDAY PARTY
Thanks.
You gonna take Kaneda's classes?
Naw
GEGH!
A stripper game!
No way!
What a joke!
The Life Game

Spring, Age 16:
Cherry Blossoms

When it comes to cherry blossoms, most people think of the Somei Yoshino variety. I do, too. Maybe it's because of school entrance ceremonies, but they make me feel nostalgic.

There is a line of cherry trees all the way from the place where I live to the station, and when they're in full bloom they are really pretty.

However...

Last year the season overlapped with some deadlines so I only got a few glimpses while flying by on my bicycle at Mach speed. And this year... when I got back to my hometown all of the blossoms had already fallen. It must be fate...

This time, Ann, Daigo and Fuji have finally entered high school. I plan to take them at age 16 all the way through spring, summer, fall and winter. I hope you will keep reading!

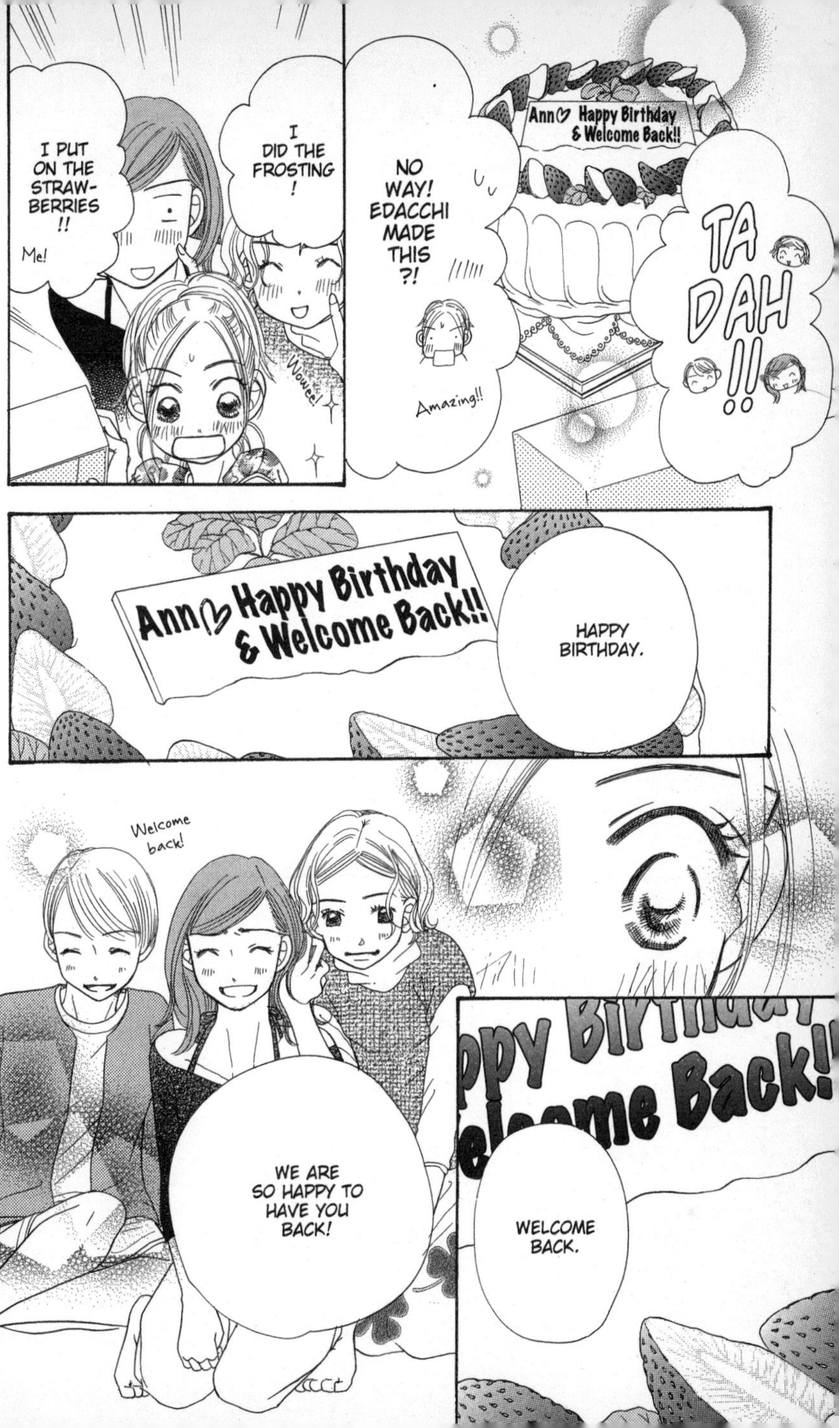
Ann♡ Happy Birthday & Welcome Back!!
TA DAH!!
NO WAY! EDACCHI MADE THIS?!
Amazing!!
I DID THE FROSTING!
I PUT ON THE STRAWBERRIES!!
Me!
Wowee!
Ann♡ Happy Birthday & Welcome Back!!
HAPPY BIRTHDAY.
ppy Birthday
elcome Back!!
WELCOME BACK.
Welcome back!
WE ARE SO HAPPY TO HAVE YOU BACK!

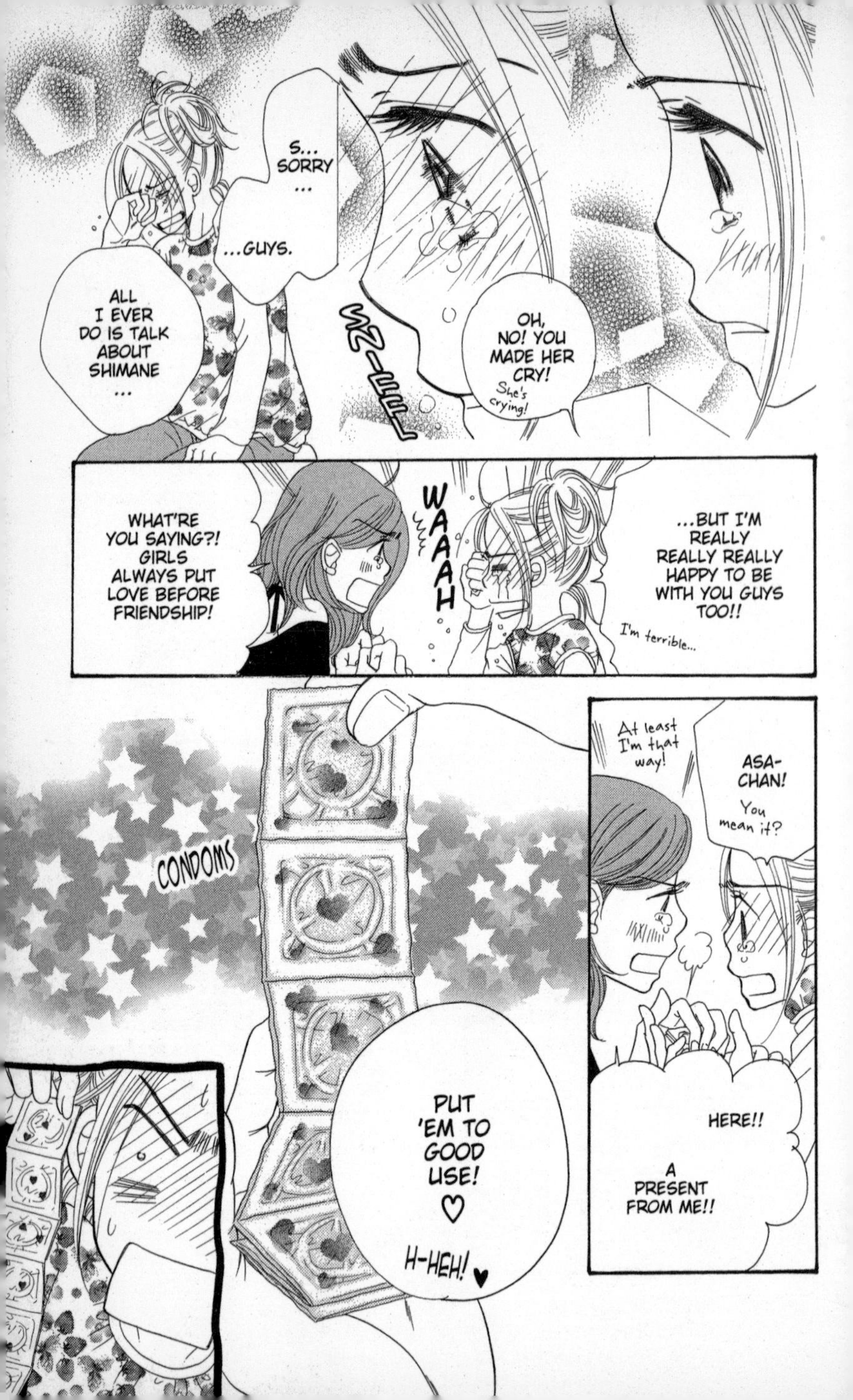
OH, NO! YOU MADE HER CRY!
She's crying!
S... SORRY ...
...GUYS.
ALL I EVER DO IS TALK ABOUT SHIMANE ...
...BUT I'M REALLY REALLY REALLY HAPPY TO BE WITH YOU GUYS TOO!!
I'm terrible...
WAAAAH
WHAT'RE YOU SAYING?! GIRLS ALWAYS PUT LOVE BEFORE FRIENDSHIP!
ASA-CHAN!
You mean it?
At least I'm that way!
HERE!!
A PRESENT FROM ME!!
CONDOMS
PUT 'EM TO GOOD USE! ♡
H-HEH! ♥

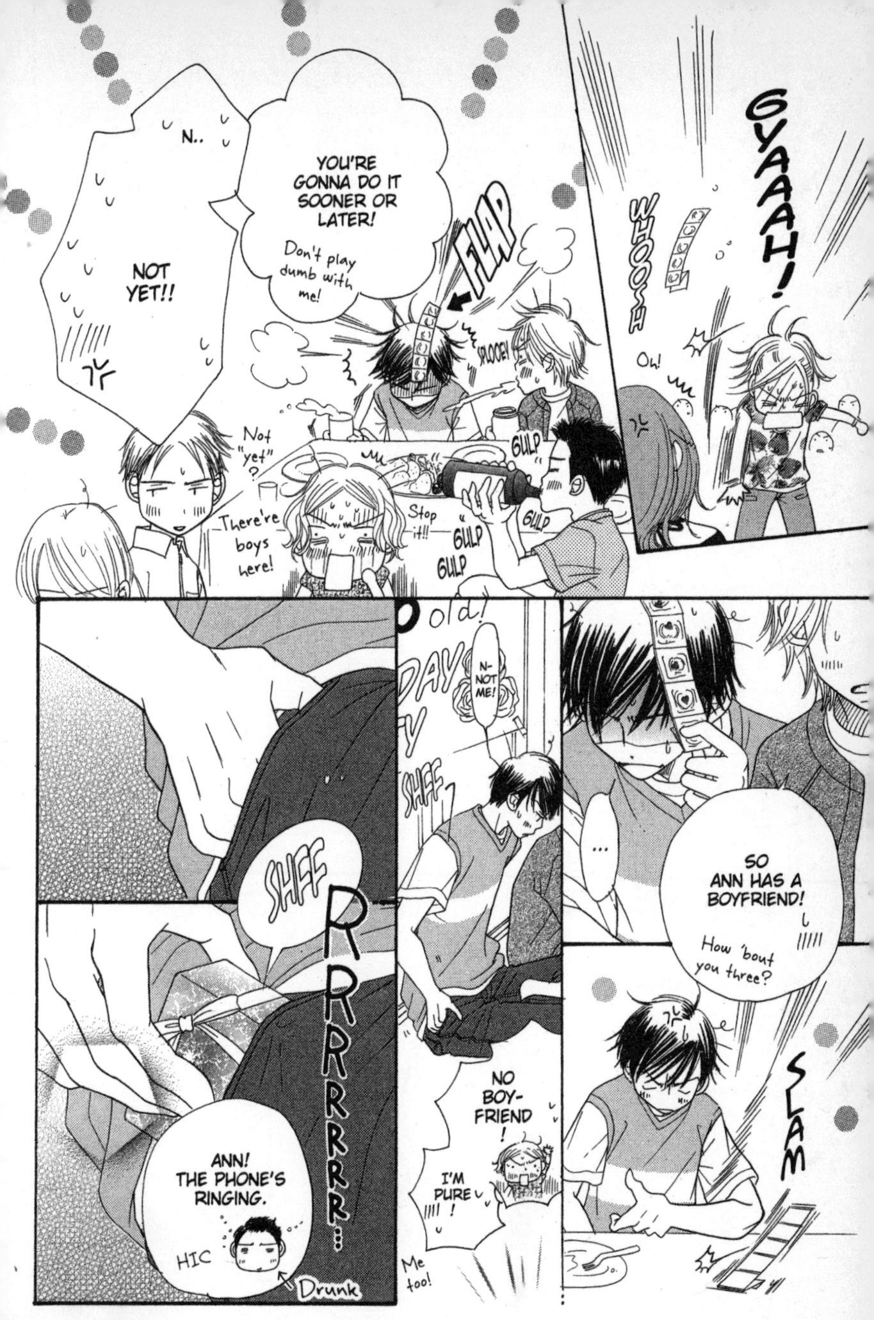
GYAAAAH!
WHOOSH
Oh!
FLAP
YOU'RE GONNA DO IT SOONER OR LATER!
Don't play dumb with me!
N..
NOT YET!!
SPLOOEY
GULP
Not "yet"?
Stop it!!
GULP
GULP
GULP
There're boys here!
...
SO ANN HAS A BOYFRIEND!
How 'bout you three?
SLAM
N-NOT ME!
SHFF
NO BOY-FRIEND!
I'M PURE!
Me too!
SHFF
RRRRRRR...
ANN! THE PHONE'S RINGING.
HIC
Drunk

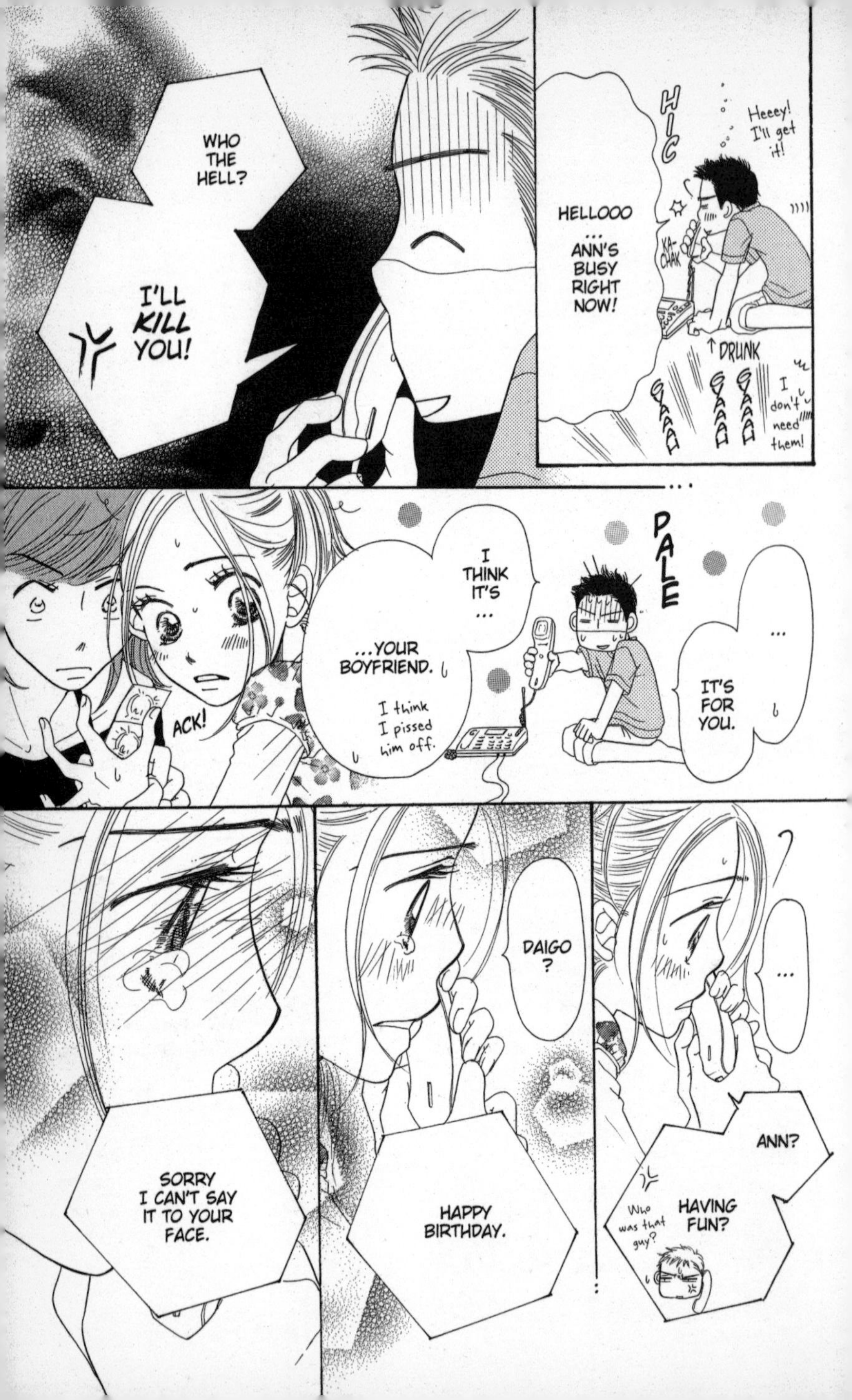
Heeey! I'll get it!
HIC
KA-CHAK
HELLOOO ... ANN'S BUSY RIGHT NOW!
↑DRUNK
GYAAAH GYAAAH GYAAAH
I don't need them!
WHO THE HELL?
I'LL KILL YOU!
...
PALE
... IT'S FOR YOU.
I THINK IT'S ...
...YOUR BOYFRIEND.
I think I pissed him off.
ACK!
...
ANN?
HAVING FUN?
Who was that guy?
DAIGO?
HAPPY BIRTHDAY.
SORRY I CAN'T SAY IT TO YOUR FACE.

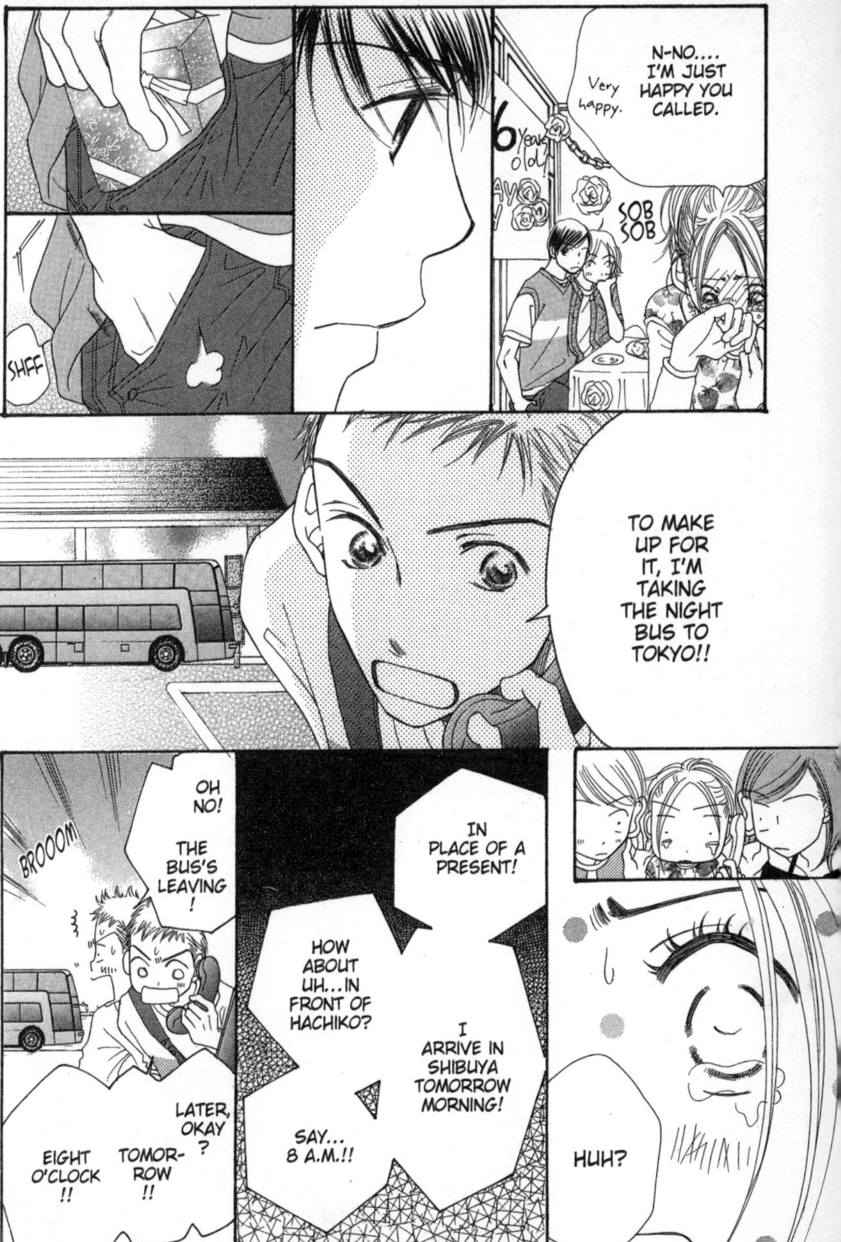
N-NO.... I'M JUST HAPPY YOU CALLED.
Very happy.
SOB SOB
SHFF
TO MAKE UP FOR IT, I'M TAKING THE NIGHT BUS TO TOKYO!!
HUH?
IN PLACE OF A PRESENT!
I ARRIVE IN SHIBUYA TOMORROW MORNING!
HOW ABOUT UH...IN FRONT OF HACHIKO?
SAY... 8 A.M.!!
OH NO!
THE BUS'S LEAVING!
BROOOM
LATER, OKAY?
TOMOR-ROW!!
EIGHT O'CLOCK!!

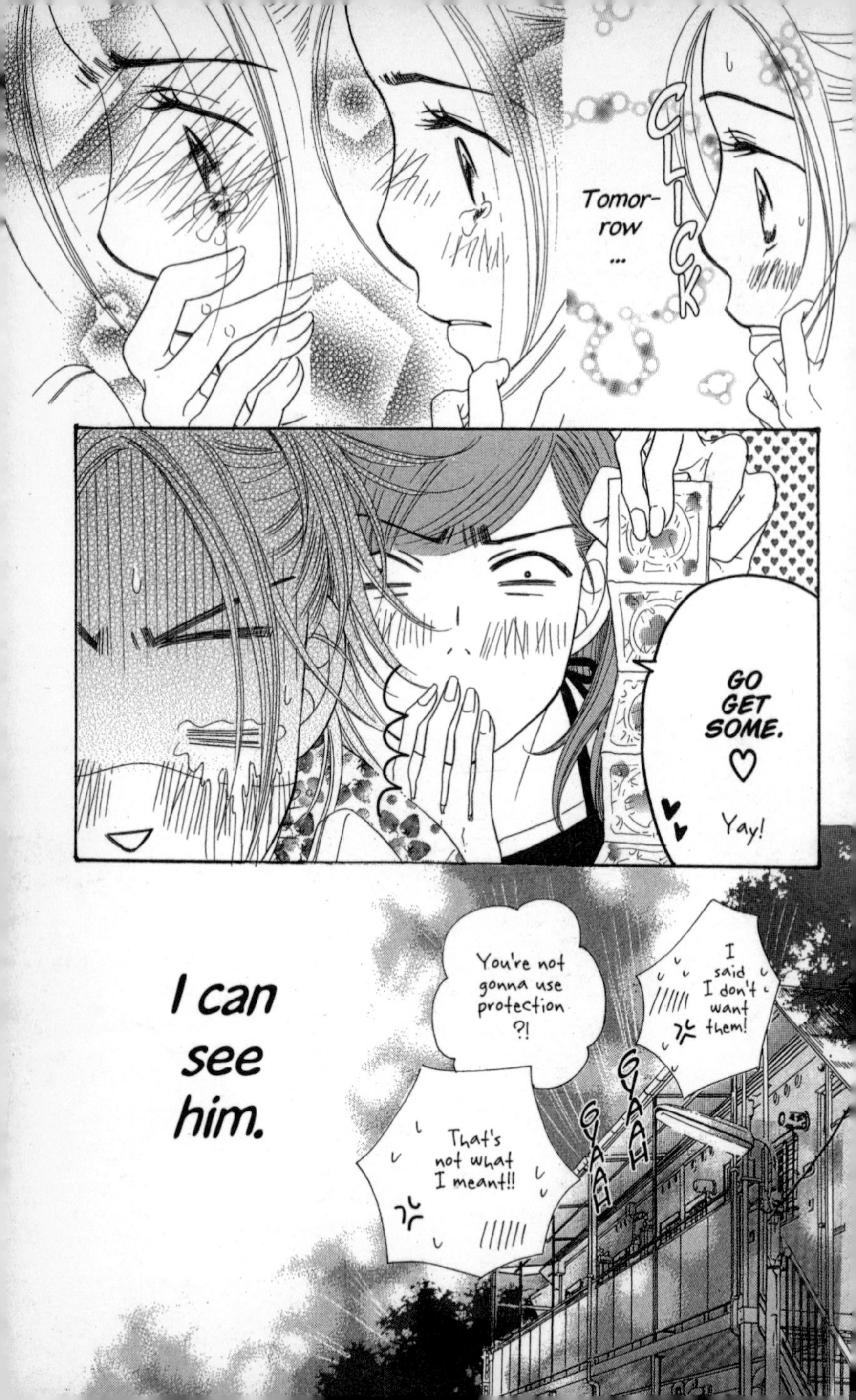
CLICK
Tomor-row ...
GO GET SOME. ♥
Yay!
I said I don't want them!
You're not gonna use protection ?!
GYAAH GYAAH
That's not what I meant!!
I can see him.

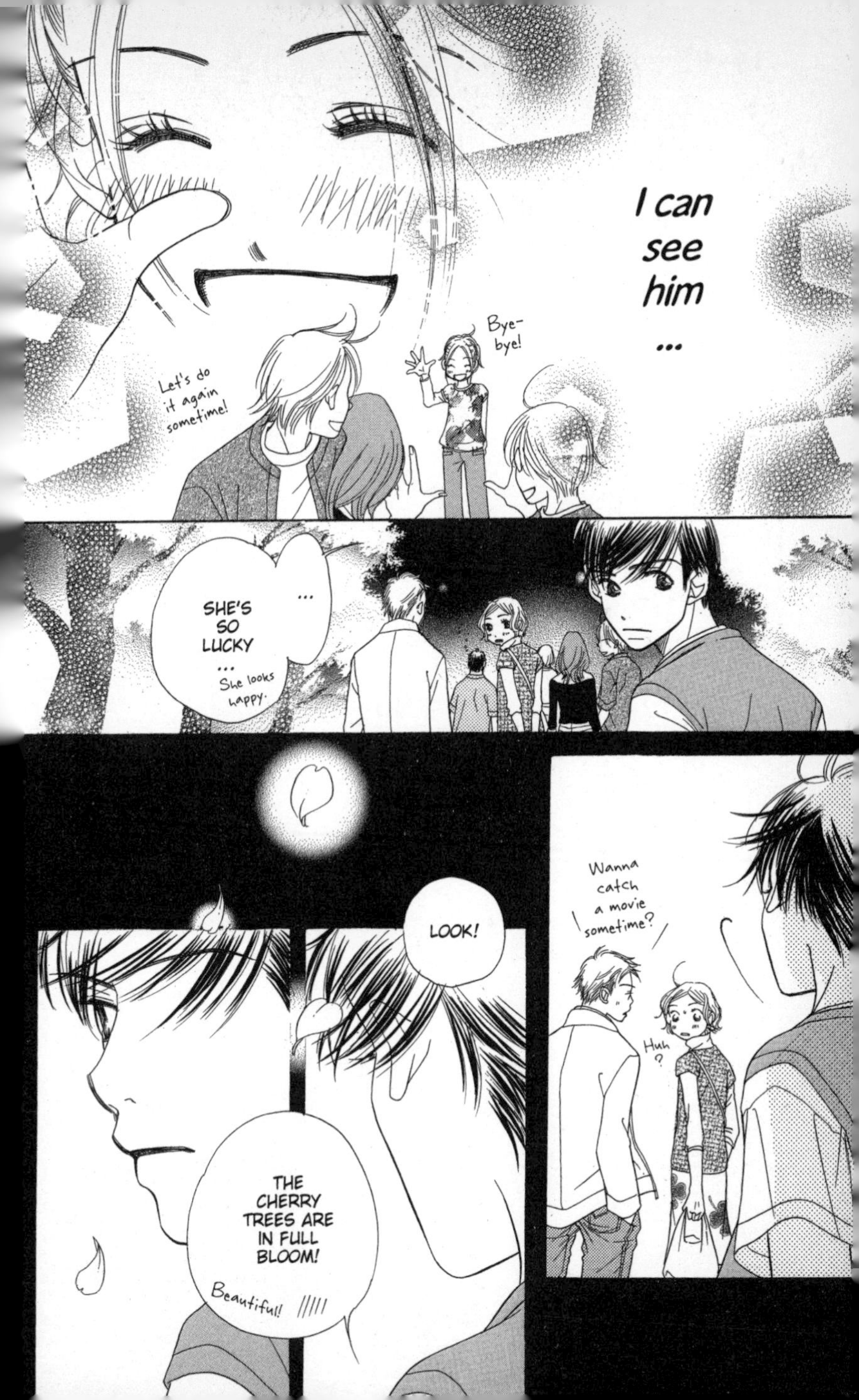
I can see him ...
Bye-bye!
Let's do it again sometime!
...
SHE'S SO LUCKY ...
She looks happy.
Wanna catch a movie sometime?
Huh?
LOOK!
THE CHERRY TREES ARE IN FULL BLOOM!
Beautiful!

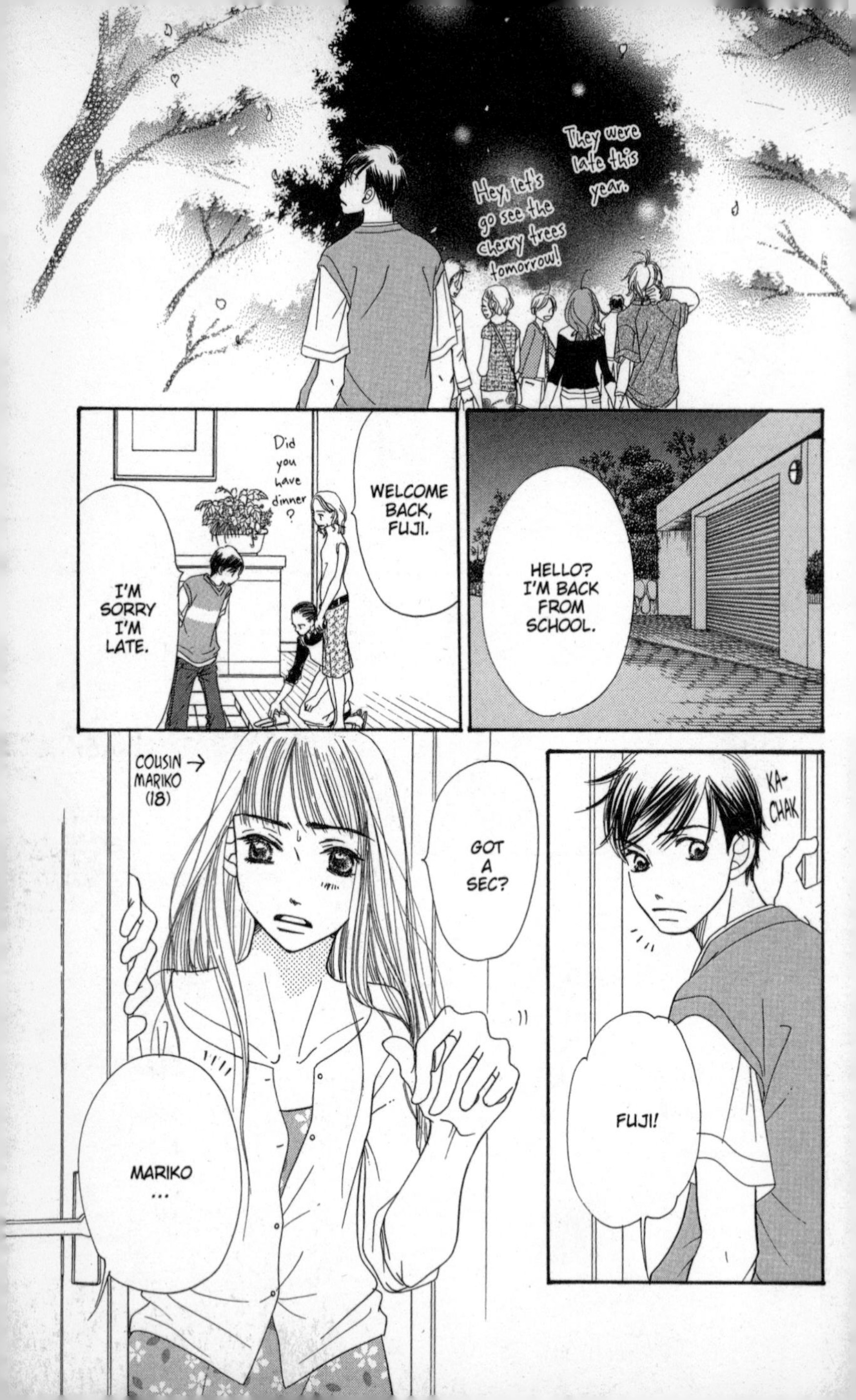
They were late this year.
Hey, let's go see the cherry trees tomorrow!
HELLO? I'M BACK FROM SCHOOL.
WELCOME BACK, FUJI.
Did you have dinner?
I'M SORRY I'M LATE.
KA-CHAK
FUJI!
COUSIN → MARIKO (18)
GOT A SEC?
MARIKO ...

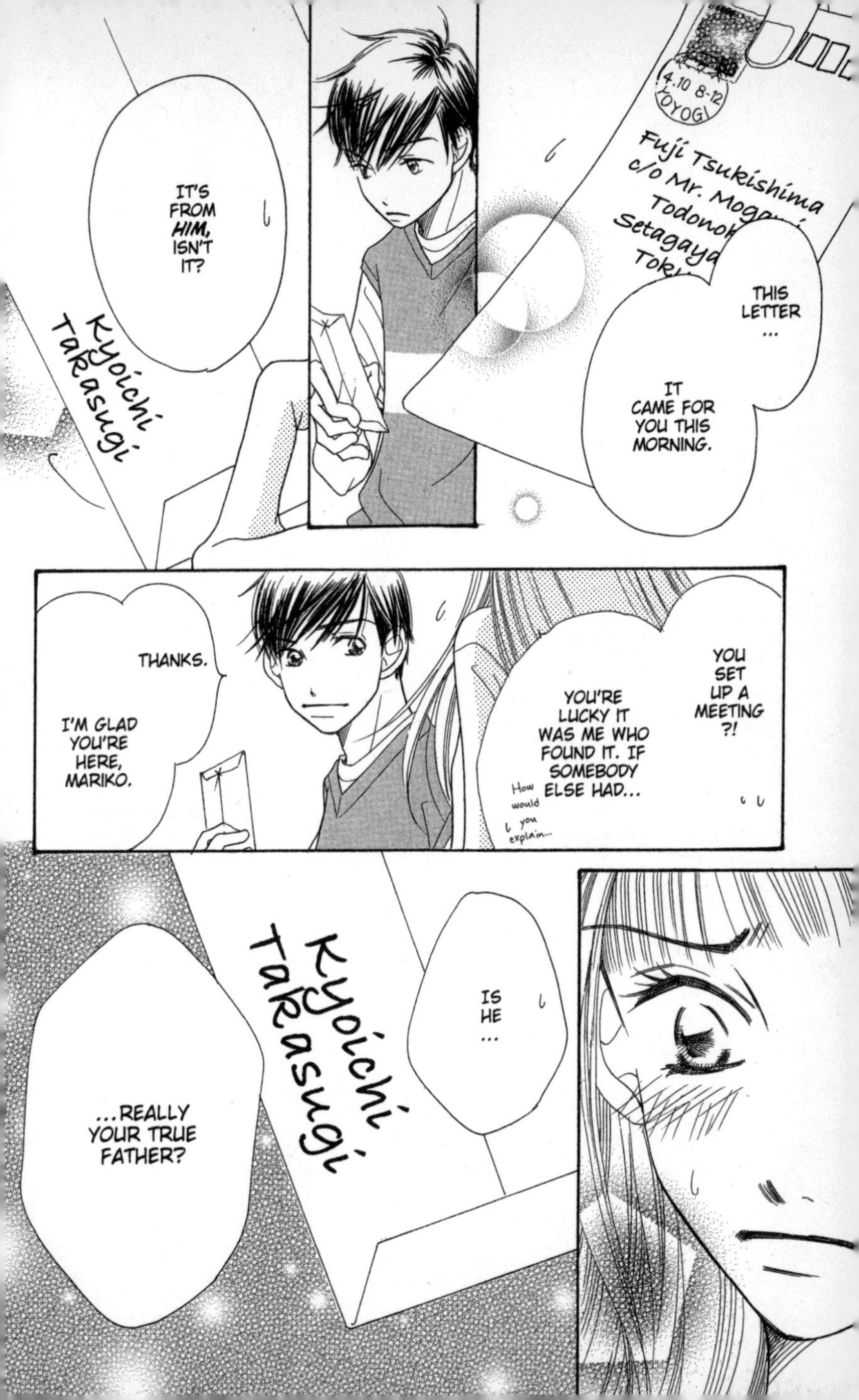
4.10 8-12
YOYOGI
Fuji Tsukishima
THIS LETTER...
IT CAME FOR YOU THIS MORNING.
IT'S FROM ***HIM,*** ISN'T IT?
Kyoichi Takasugi
YOU SET UP A MEETING?!
YOU'RE LUCKY IT WAS ME WHO FOUND IT. IF SOMEBODY ELSE HAD...
How would you explain...
THANKS.
I'M GLAD YOU'RE HERE, MARIKO.
IS HE...
Kyoichi Takasugi
...REALLY YOUR TRUE FATHER?

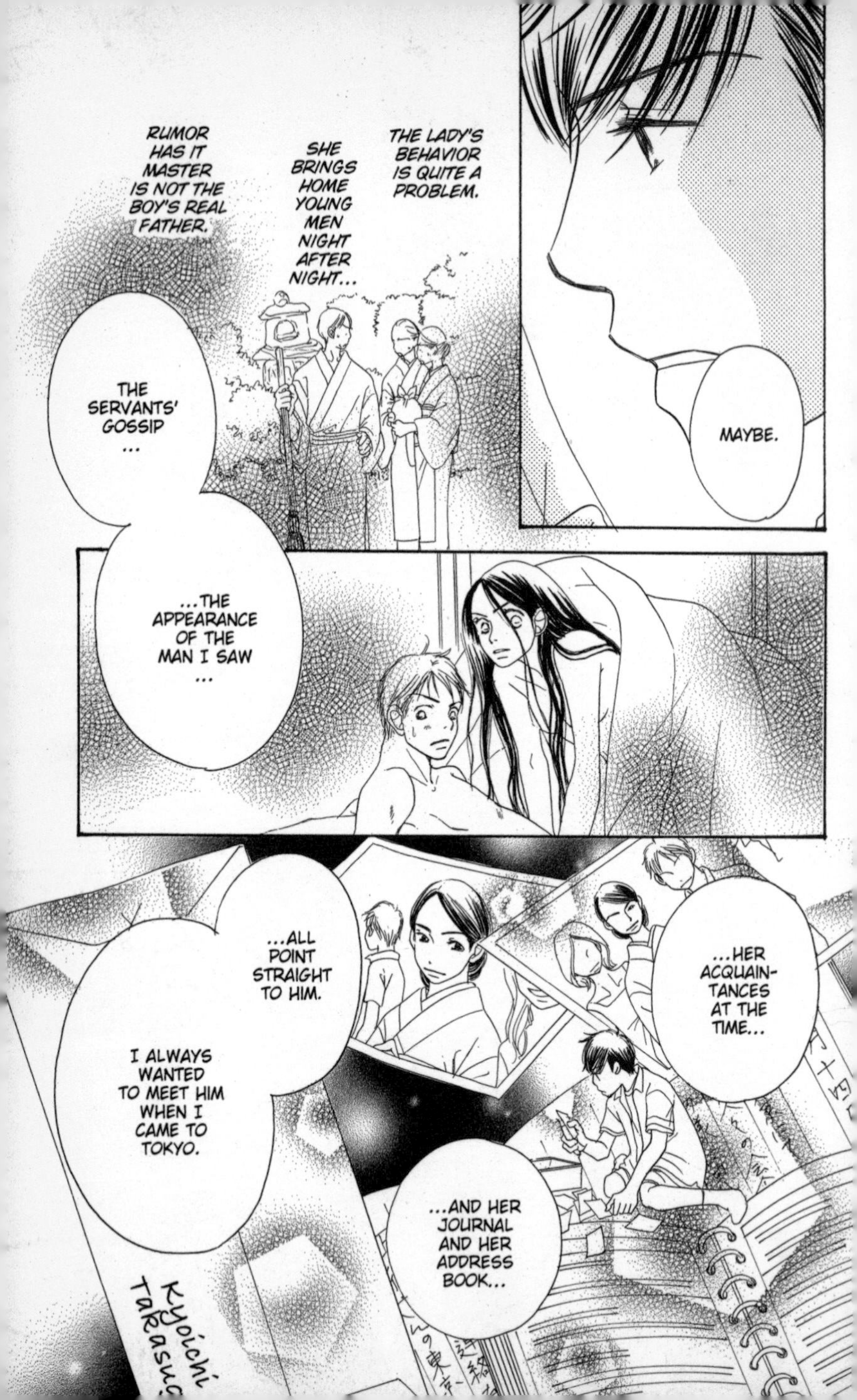
MAYBE.
THE LADY'S BEHAVIOR IS QUITE A PROBLEM.
SHE BRINGS HOME YOUNG MEN NIGHT AFTER NIGHT...
RUMOR HAS IT MASTER IS NOT THE BOY'S REAL FATHER.
THE SERVANTS' GOSSIP...
...THE APPEARANCE OF THE MAN I SAW...
...HER ACQUAINTANCES AT THE TIME...
...AND HER JOURNAL AND HER ADDRESS BOOK...
...ALL POINT STRAIGHT TO HIM.
I ALWAYS WANTED TO MEET HIM WHEN I CAME TO TOKYO.
Kyoichi Takasugi

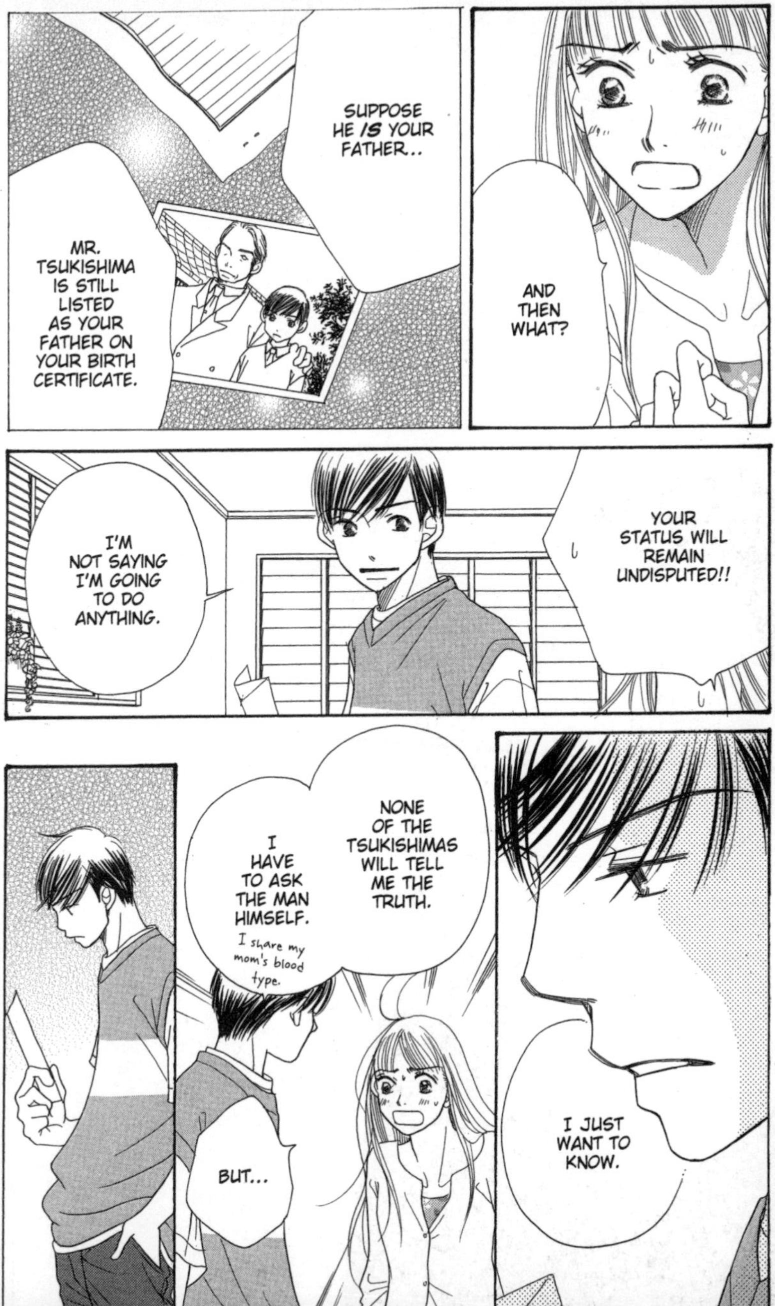
AND THEN WHAT?
SUPPOSE HE *IS* YOUR FATHER...
MR. TSUKISHIMA IS STILL LISTED AS YOUR FATHER ON YOUR BIRTH CERTIFICATE.
YOUR STATUS WILL REMAIN UNDISPUTED!!
I'M NOT SAYING I'M GOING TO DO ANYTHING.
I JUST WANT TO KNOW.
NONE OF THE TSUKISHIMAS WILL TELL ME THE TRUTH.
I HAVE TO ASK THE MAN HIMSELF.
I share my mom's blood type.
BUT...

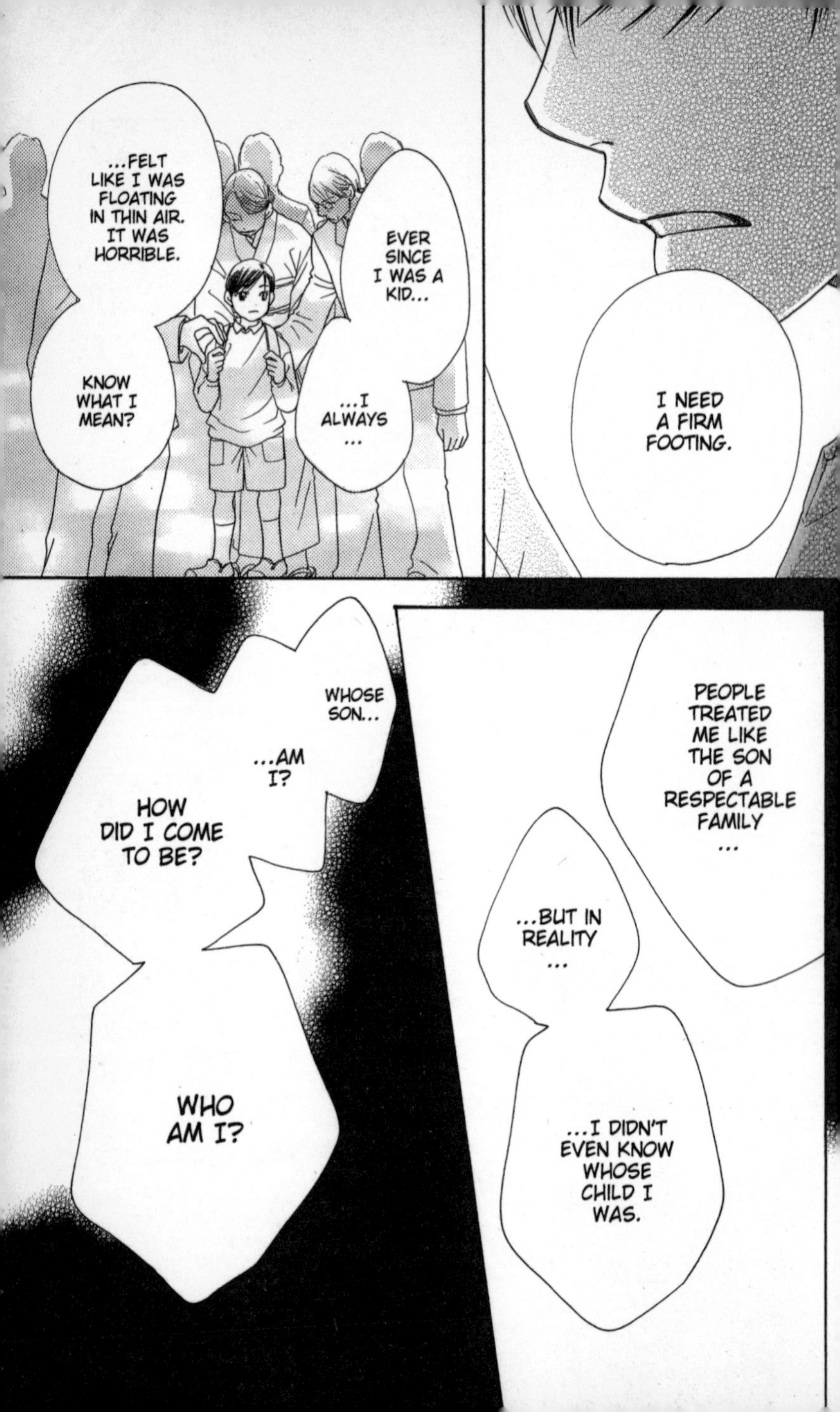
I NEED A FIRM FOOTING.
EVER SINCE I WAS A KID...
...I ALWAYS...
...FELT LIKE I WAS FLOATING IN THIN AIR. IT WAS HORRIBLE.
KNOW WHAT I MEAN?
PEOPLE TREATED ME LIKE THE SON OF A RESPECTABLE FAMILY...
...BUT IN REALITY...
...I DIDN'T EVEN KNOW WHOSE CHILD I WAS.
WHOSE SON...
...AM I?
HOW DID I COME TO BE?
WHO AM I?

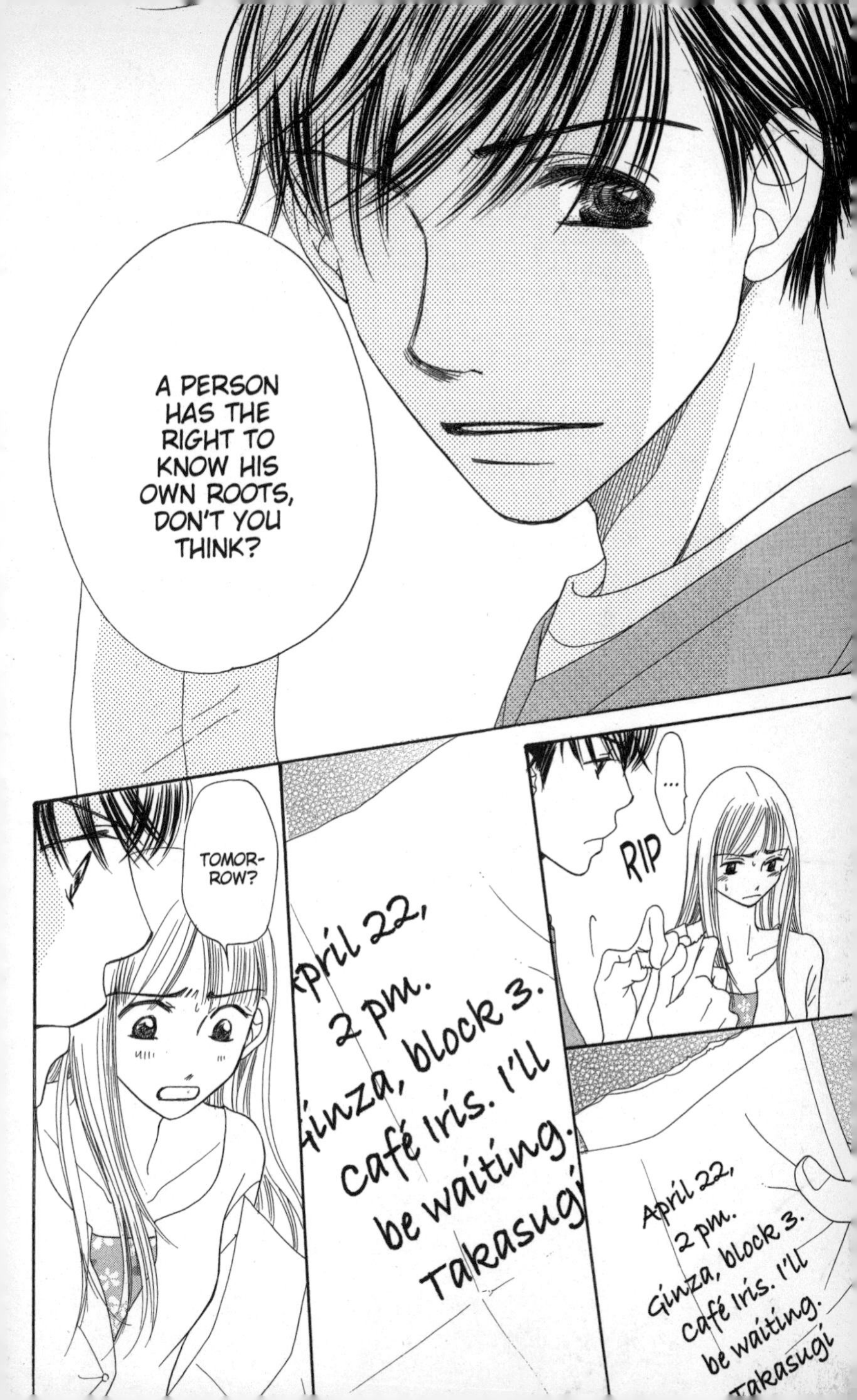
A PERSON HAS THE RIGHT TO KNOW HIS OWN ROOTS, DON'T YOU THINK?
...
RIP
April 22, 2 pm. Ginza, block 3. Café Iris. I'll be waiting. Takasugi
pril 22, 2 pm. inza, block 3. Café Iris. I'll be waiting. Takasugi
TOMOR-ROW?

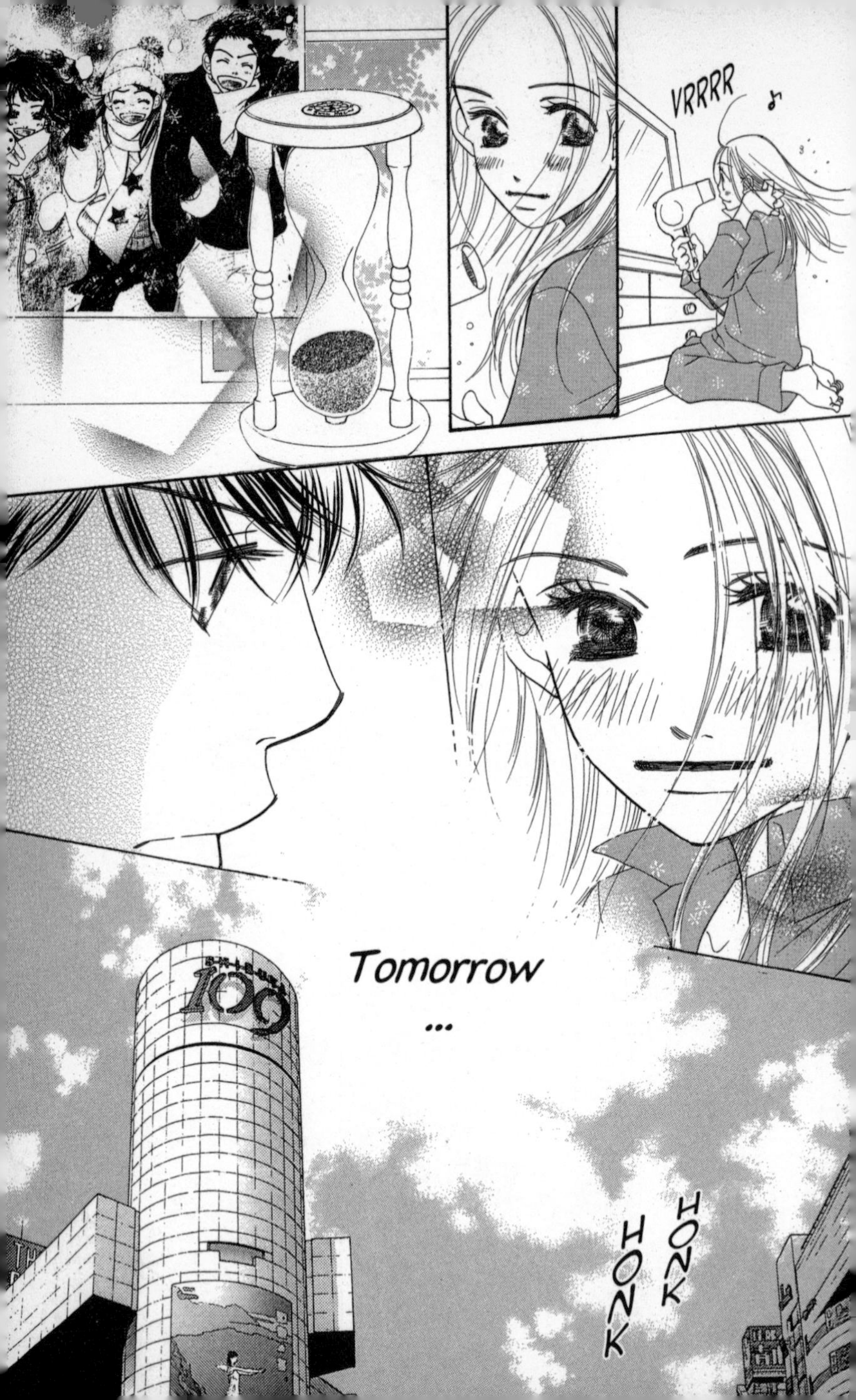
VRRRR
Tomorrow
...
HONK HONK

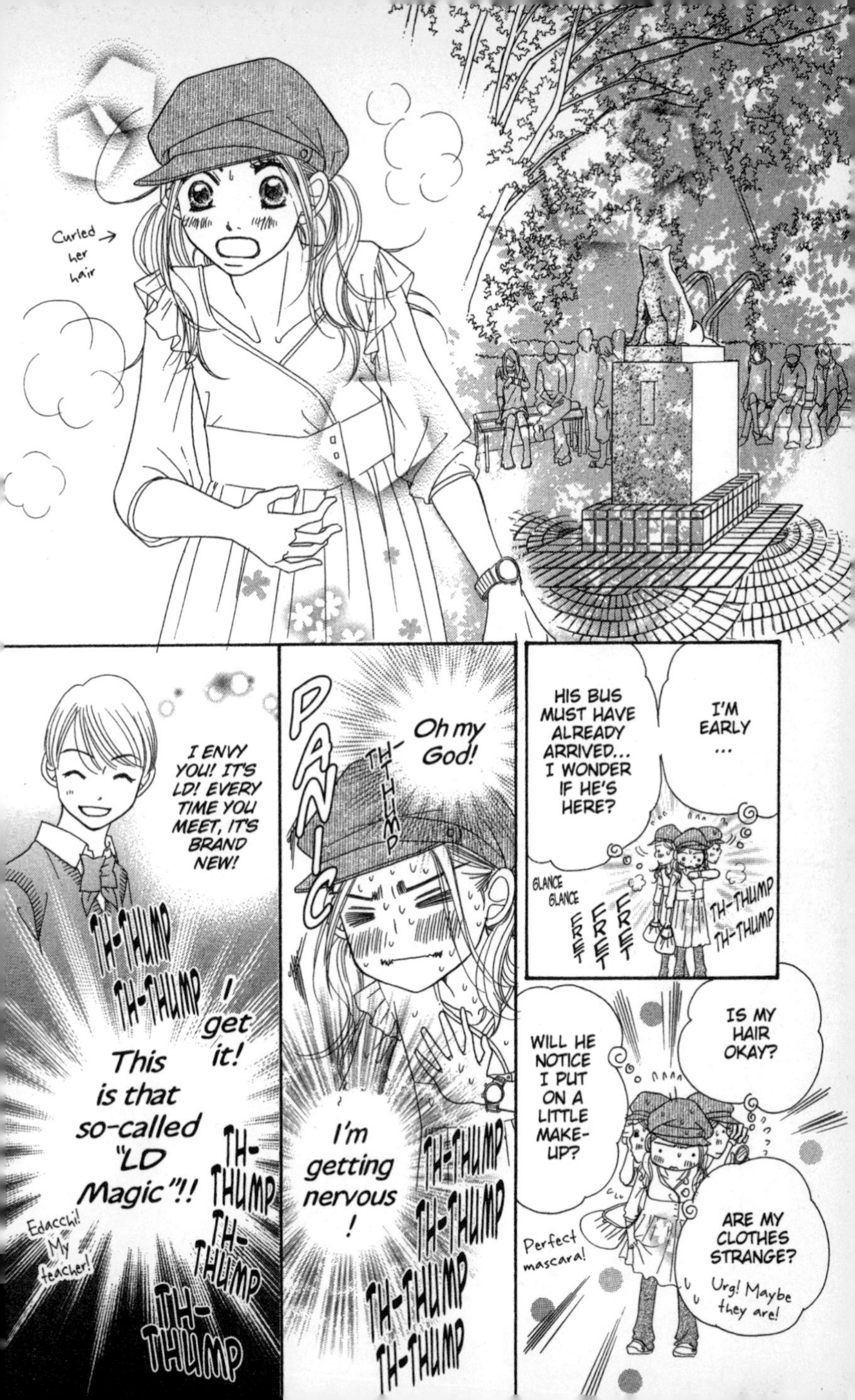

Curled her hair
I'M EARLY ...
HIS BUS MUST HAVE ALREADY ARRIVED... I WONDER IF HE'S HERE?
GLANCE GLANCE
FRET FRET FRET
TH-THUMP TH-THUMP
IS MY HAIR OKAY?
WILL HE NOTICE I PUT ON A LITTLE MAKE-UP?
ARE MY CLOTHES STRANGE?
Urg! Maybe they are!
Perfect mascara!
Oh my God!
PANIC
TH-THUMP
I'm getting nervous!
TH-THUMP TH-THUMP TH-THUMP TH-THUMP
I ENVY YOU! IT'S LD! EVERY TIME YOU MEET, IT'S BRAND NEW!
TH-THUMP TH-THUMP
I get it!
This is that so-called "LD Magic"!!
TH-THUMP TH-THUMP
Edacchi! My teacher!
TH-THUMP

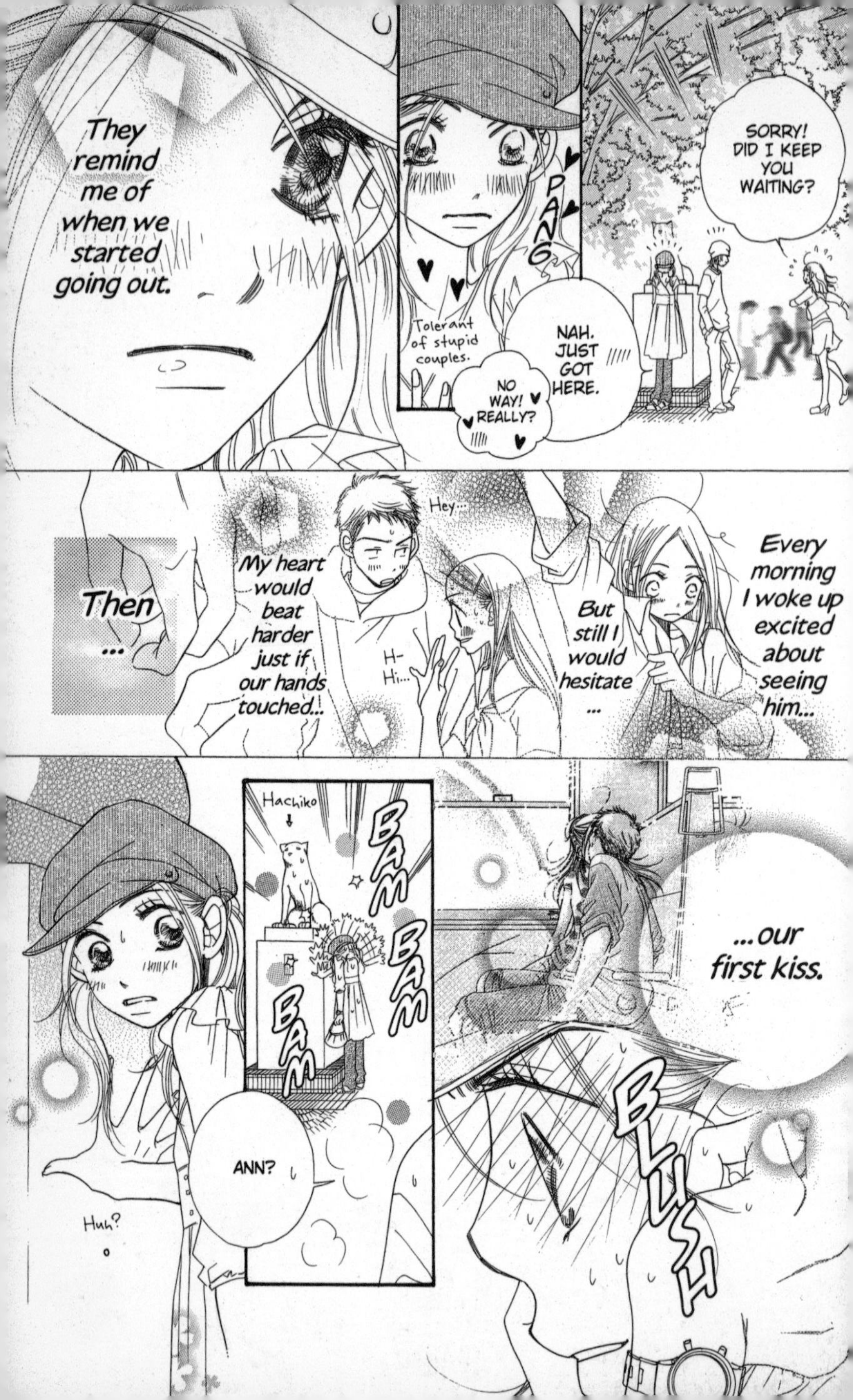

SORRY! DID I KEEP YOU WAITING?
NAH. JUST GOT HERE.
NO WAY! REALLY?
PANG
Tolerant of stupid couples.
They remind me of when we started going out.
Every morning I woke up excited about seeing him...
But still I would hesitate...
Hey...
H- Hi...
My heart would beat harder just if our hands touched...
Then...
...our first kiss.
BLUSH
Hachiko
BAM BAM
BAM BAM
ANN?
Huh?

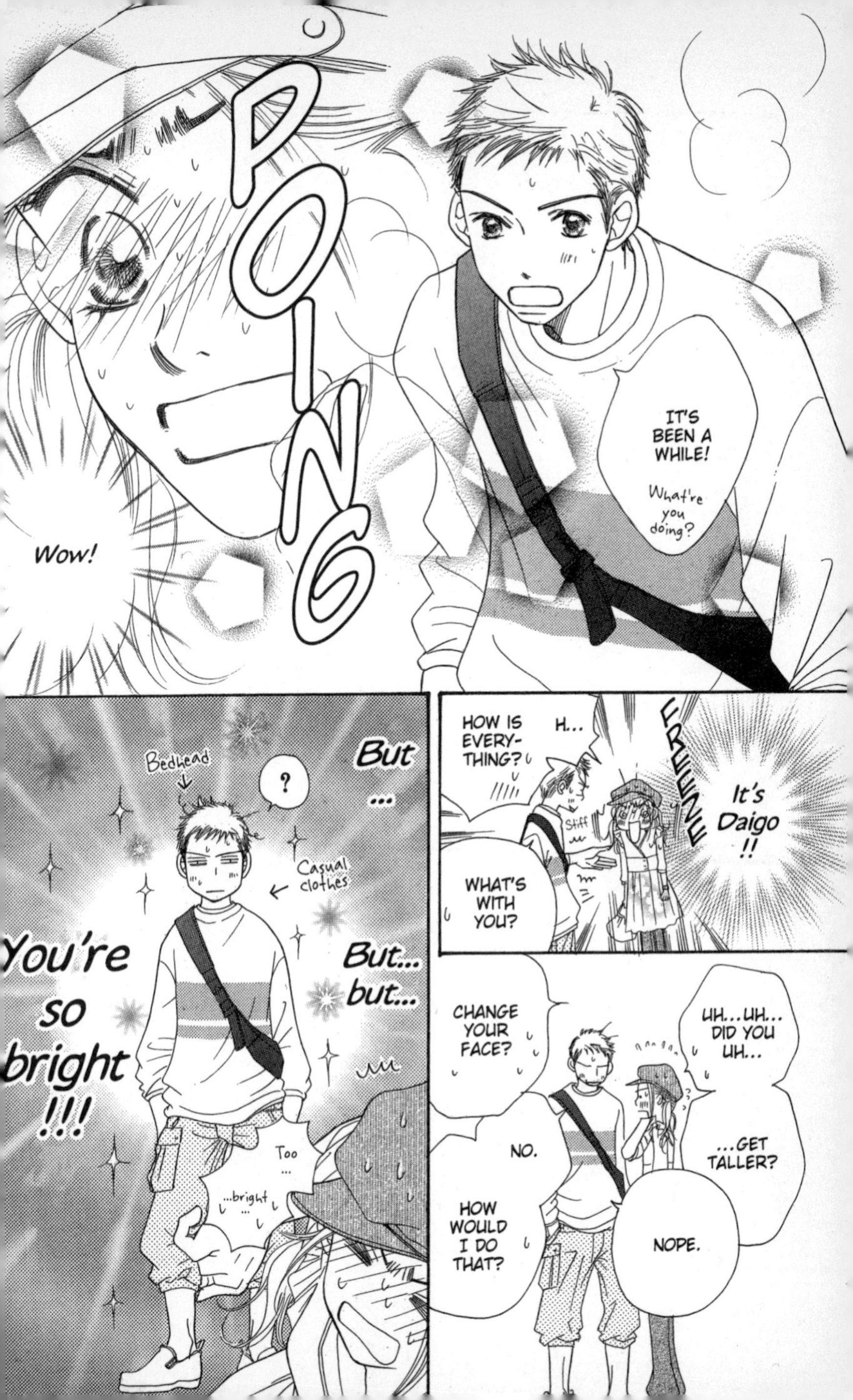
IT'S BEEN A WHILE!
What're you doing?
POING
Wow!
FREEEZE
It's Daigo!!
H...
HOW IS EVERYTHING?
Stiff
WHAT'S WITH YOU?
UH...UH... DID YOU UH...
CHANGE YOUR FACE?
NO.
...GET TALLER?
NOPE.
HOW WOULD I DO THAT?
But...
?
Bedhead
Casual clothes
But... but...
You're so bright!!!
Too...
...bright...

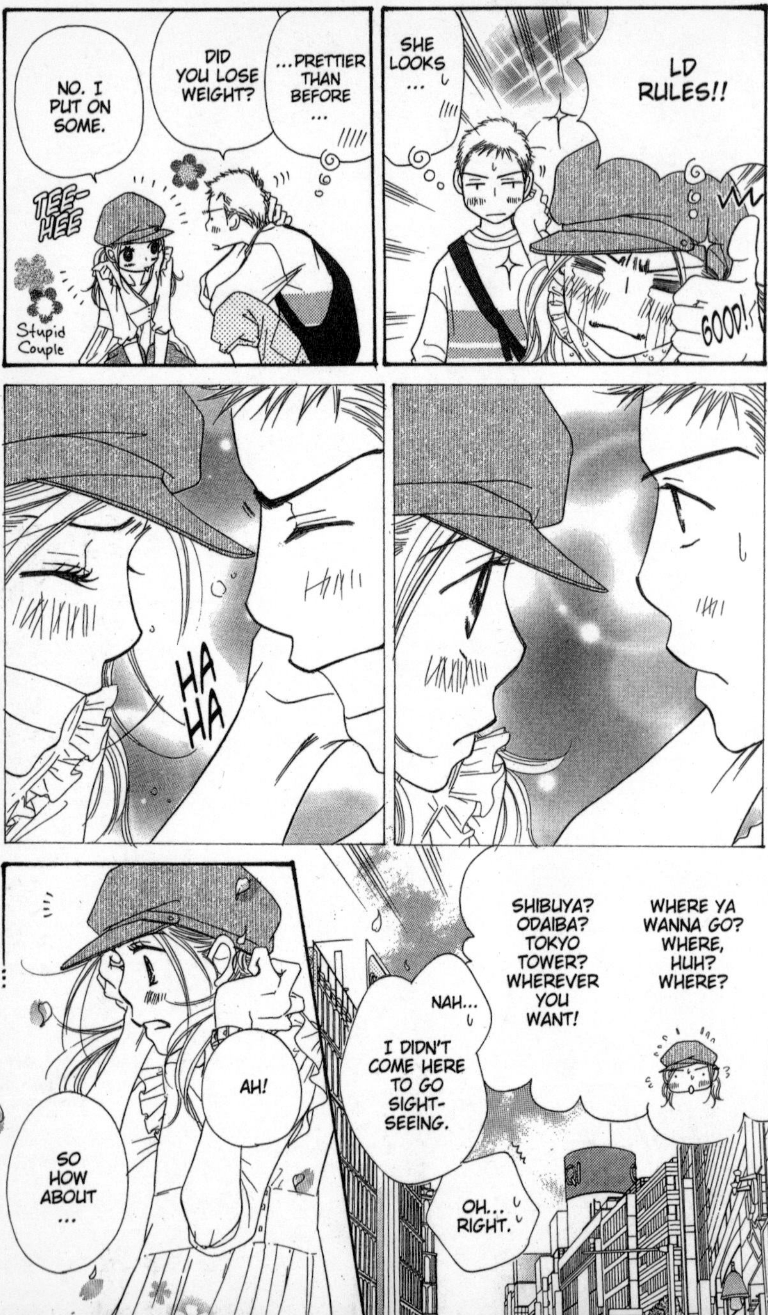
LD RULES!!
SHE LOOKS ...
GOOD!
...PRETTIER THAN BEFORE ...
DID YOU LOSE WEIGHT?
NO. I PUT ON SOME.
TEE-HEE
Stupid Couple
HA HA
WHERE YA WANNA GO? WHERE, HUH? WHERE?
SHIBUYA? ODAIBA? TOKYO TOWER? WHEREVER YOU WANT!
NAH...
I DIDN'T COME HERE TO GO SIGHT-SEEING.
OH... RIGHT.
AH!
SO HOW ABOUT ...

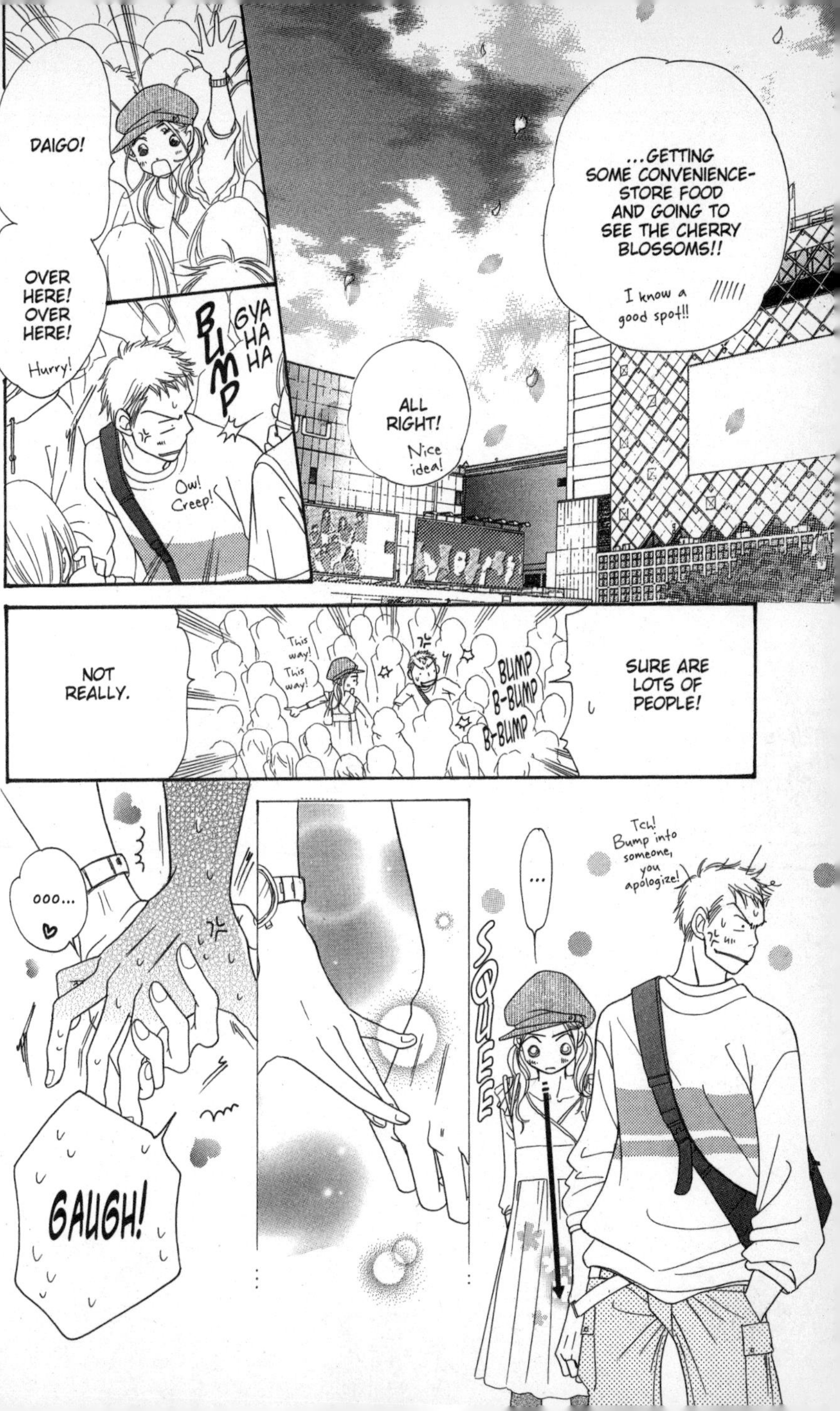
...GETTING SOME CONVENIENCE-STORE FOOD AND GOING TO SEE THE CHERRY BLOSSOMS!!
I know a good spot!!
ALL RIGHT!
Nice idea!
DAIGO!
OVER HERE! OVER HERE!
Hurry!
BUMP
GYA HA HA
Ow! Creep!
SURE ARE LOTS OF PEOPLE!
This way! This way!
BUMP
B-BUMP
B-BUMP
NOT REALLY.
...
Tch! Bump into someone, you apologize!
SQUEEE
ooo...
GAUGH!

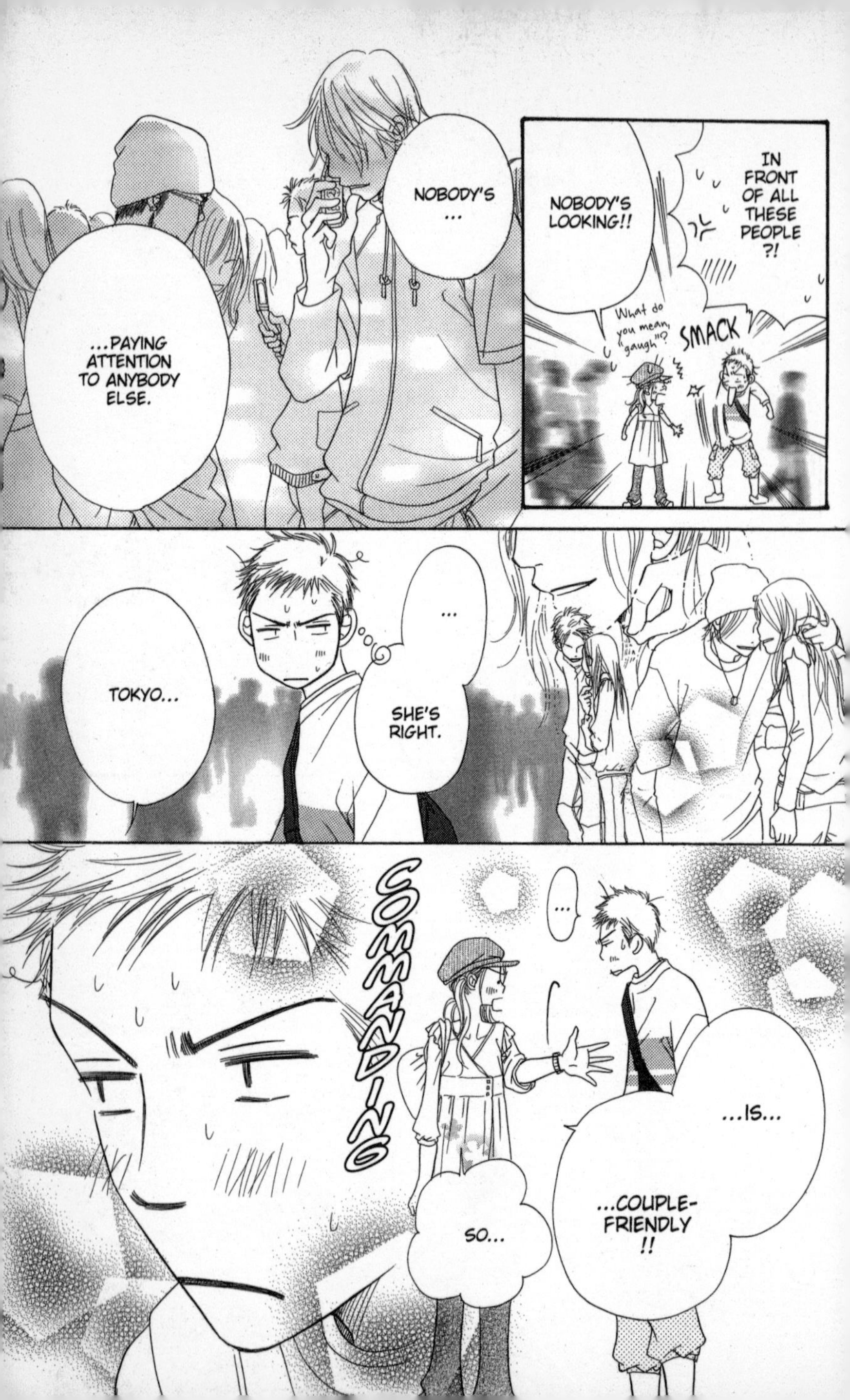
IN FRONT OF ALL THESE PEOPLE ?!
NOBODY'S LOOKING!!
What do you mean, "gaugh"?
SMACK
NOBODY'S ...
...PAYING ATTENTION TO ANYBODY ELSE.
...
SHE'S RIGHT.
TOKYO...
...
COMMANDING
...IS...
...COUPLE-FRIENDLY !!
SO...

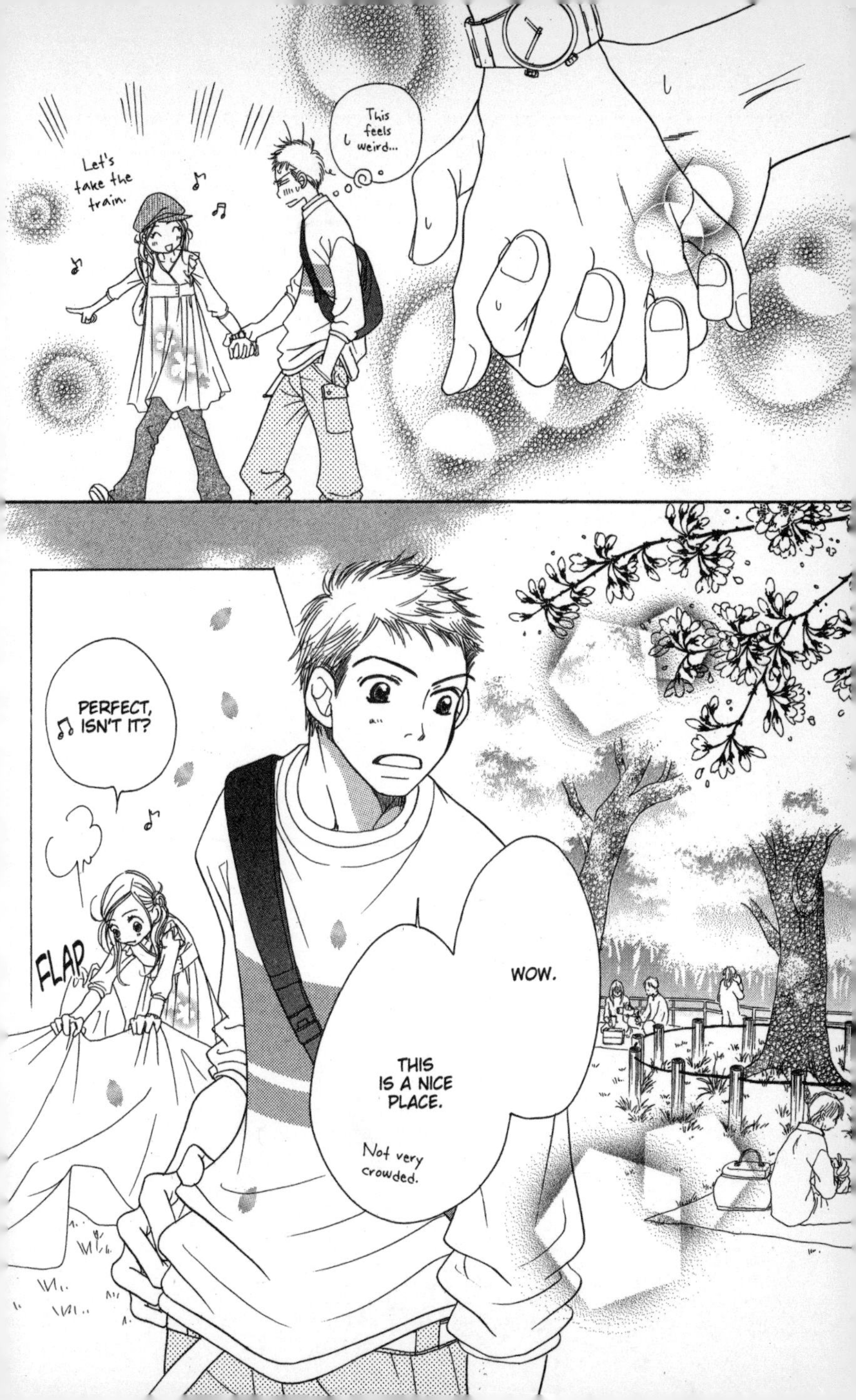
This feels weird...
Let's take the train.
WOW.
THIS IS A NICE PLACE.
Not very crowded.
PERFECT, ISN'T IT?
FLAP

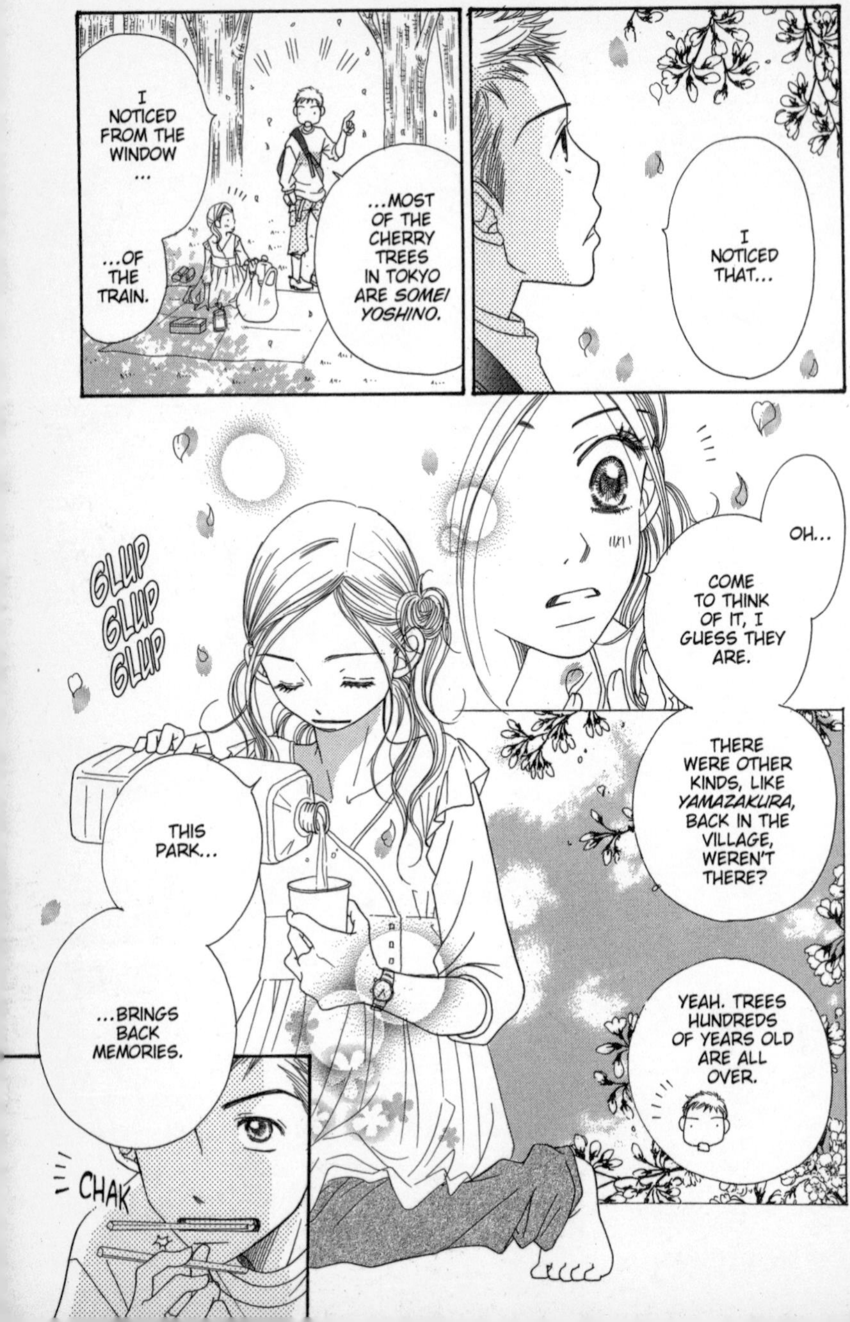
I NOTICED THAT...
I NOTICED FROM THE WINDOW ...
...OF THE TRAIN.
...MOST OF THE CHERRY TREES IN TOKYO ARE *SOMEI YOSHINO*.
OH...
COME TO THINK OF IT, I GUESS THEY ARE.
THERE WERE OTHER KINDS, LIKE *YAMAZAKURA*, BACK IN THE VILLAGE, WEREN'T THERE?
YEAH. TREES HUNDREDS OF YEARS OLD ARE ALL OVER.
GLUP GLUP GLUP
THIS PARK...
...BRINGS BACK MEMORIES.
CHAK

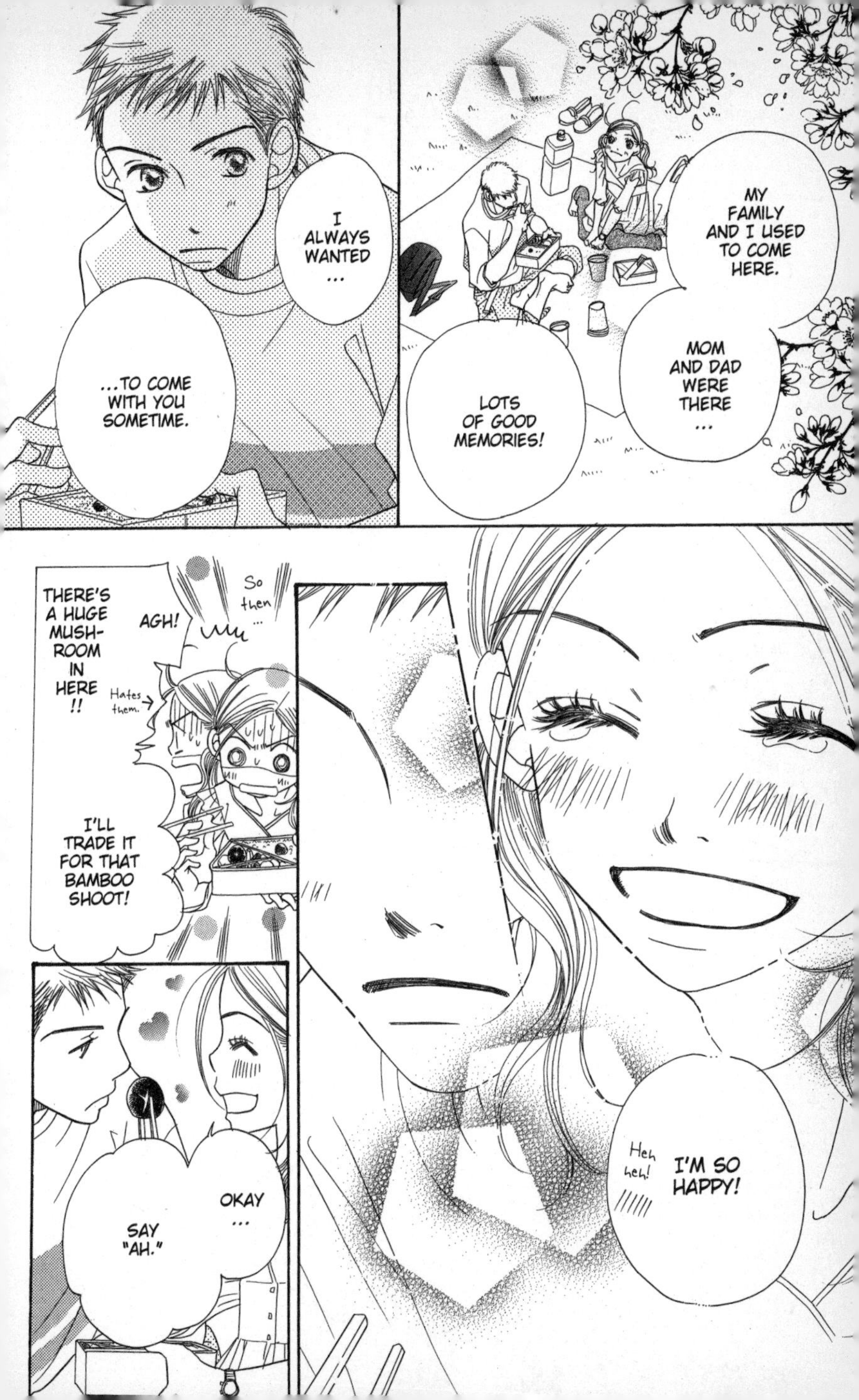
MY FAMILY AND I USED TO COME HERE.
MOM AND DAD WERE THERE...
LOTS OF GOOD MEMORIES!
I ALWAYS WANTED...
...TO COME WITH YOU SOMETIME.
Heh heh!
I'M SO HAPPY!
So then...
AGH!
THERE'S A HUGE MUSH-ROOM IN HERE!!
Hates them.
I'LL TRADE IT FOR THAT BAMBOO SHOOT!
OKAY...
SAY "AH."

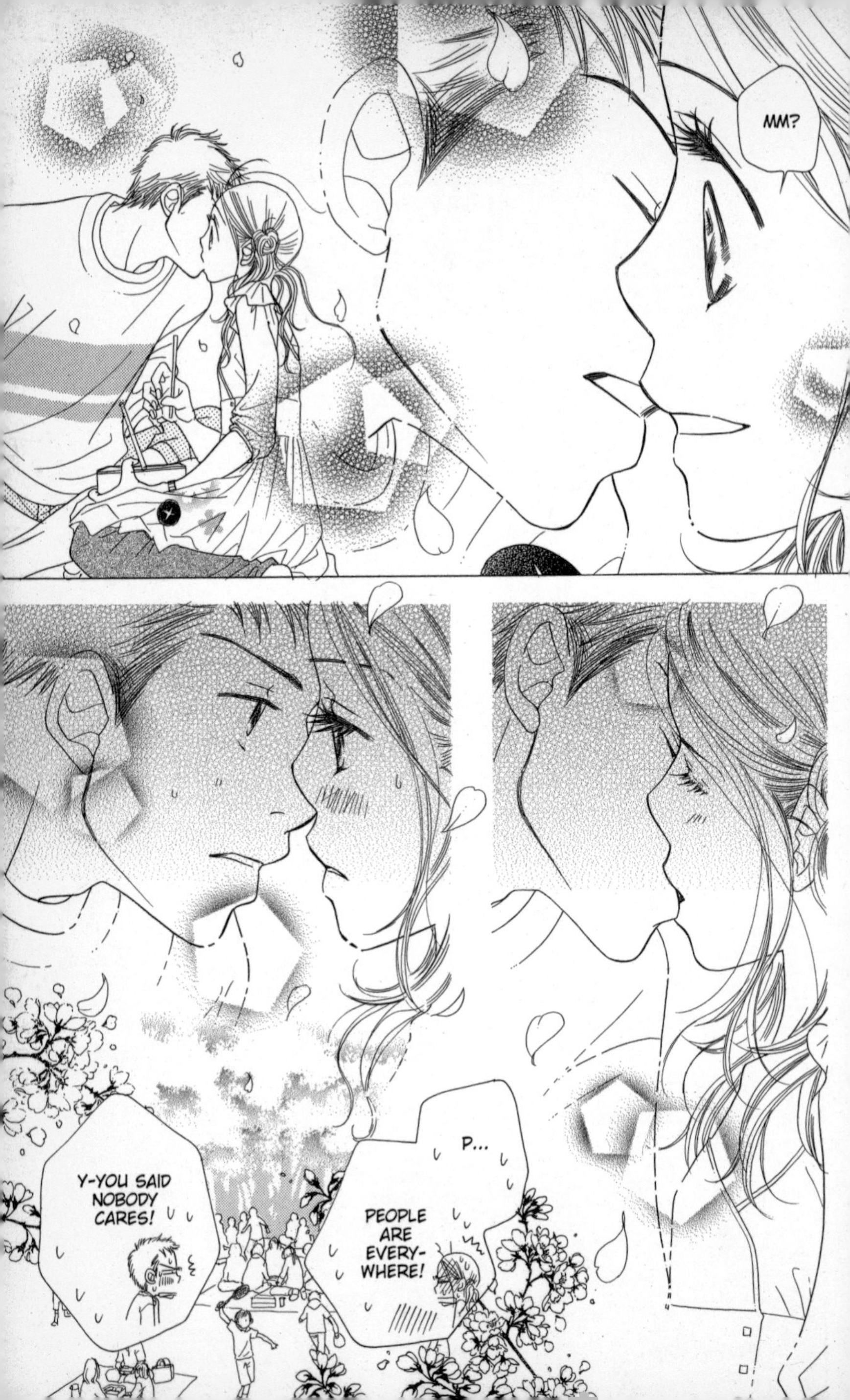
MM?
P...
PEOPLE ARE EVERY-WHERE!
Y-YOU SAID NOBODY CARES!

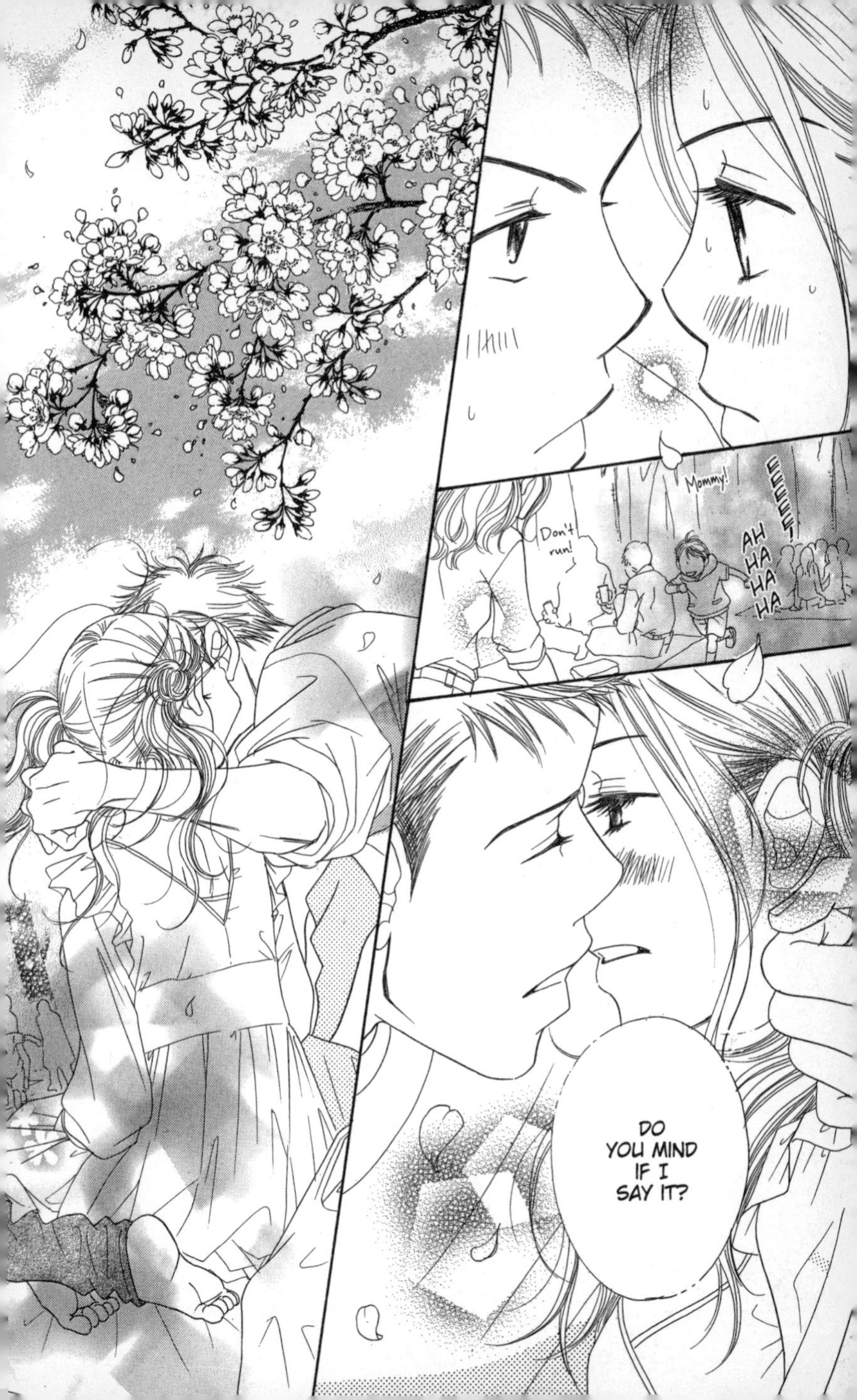
EEEEE!
Mommy!
AH HA HA HA HA
Don't run!
DO YOU MIND IF I SAY IT?

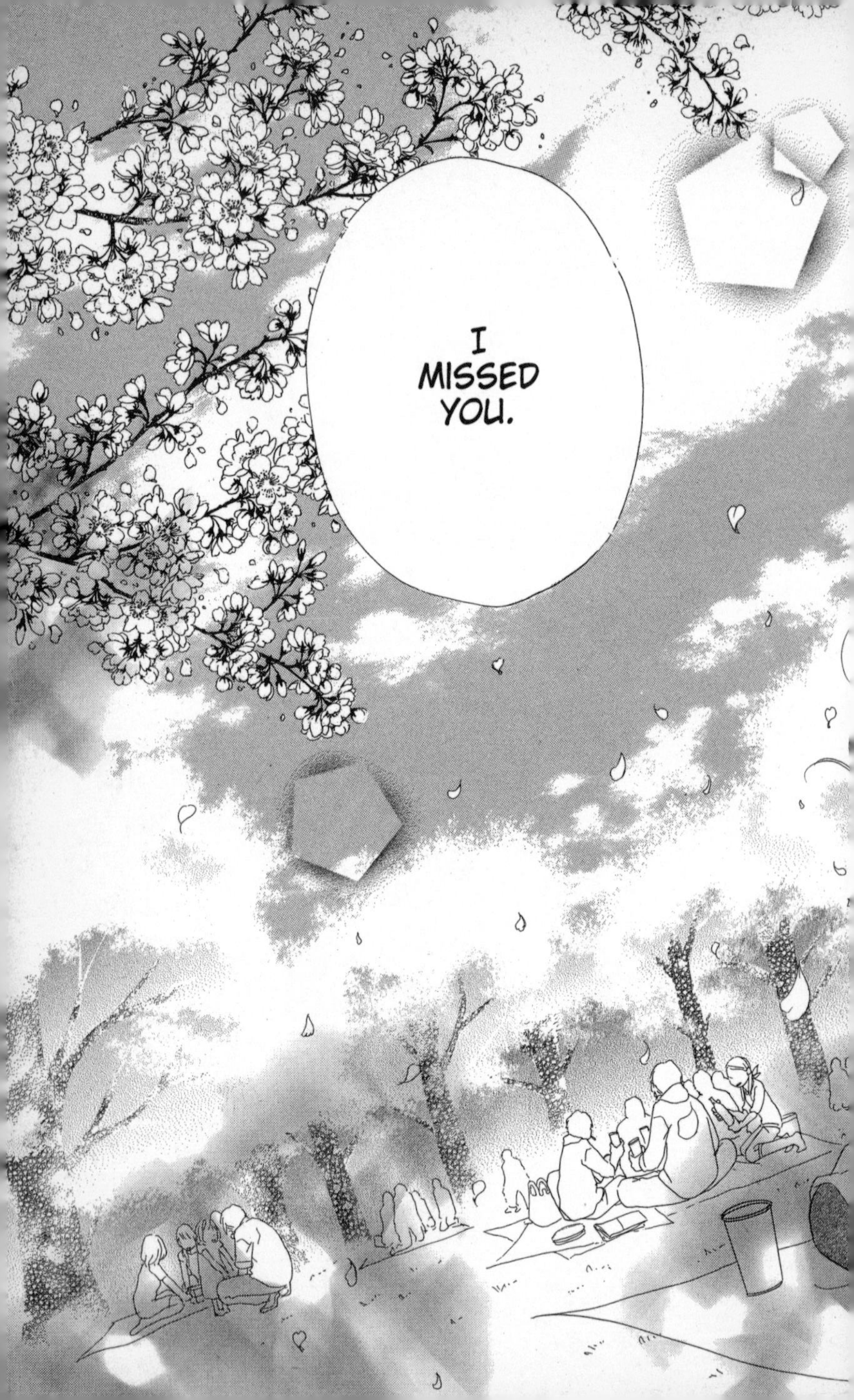
I MISSED YOU.

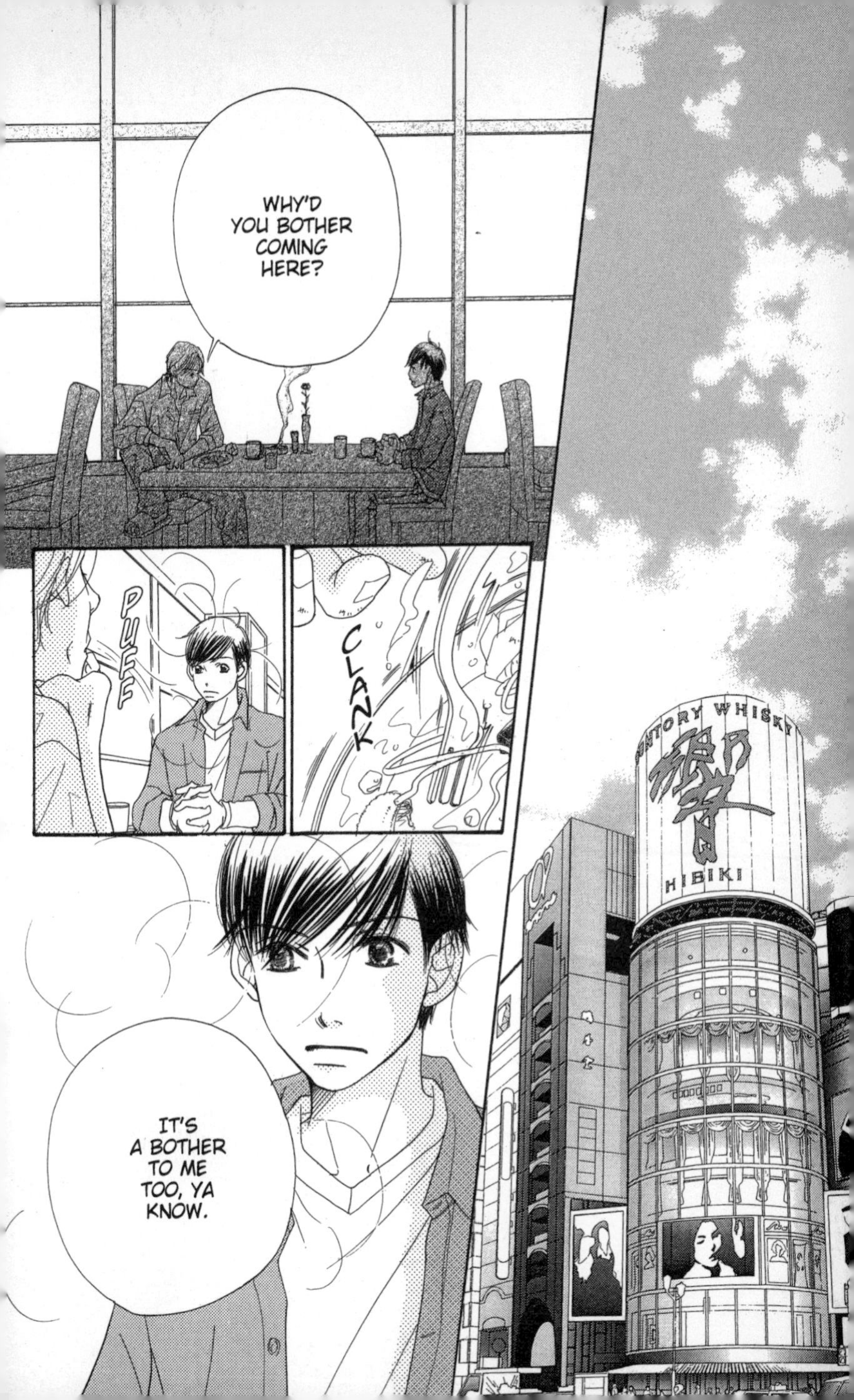
WHISKY
HIBIKI
WHY'D YOU BOTHER COMING HERE?
CLANK
PUFF
IT'S A BOTHER TO ME TOO, YA KNOW.

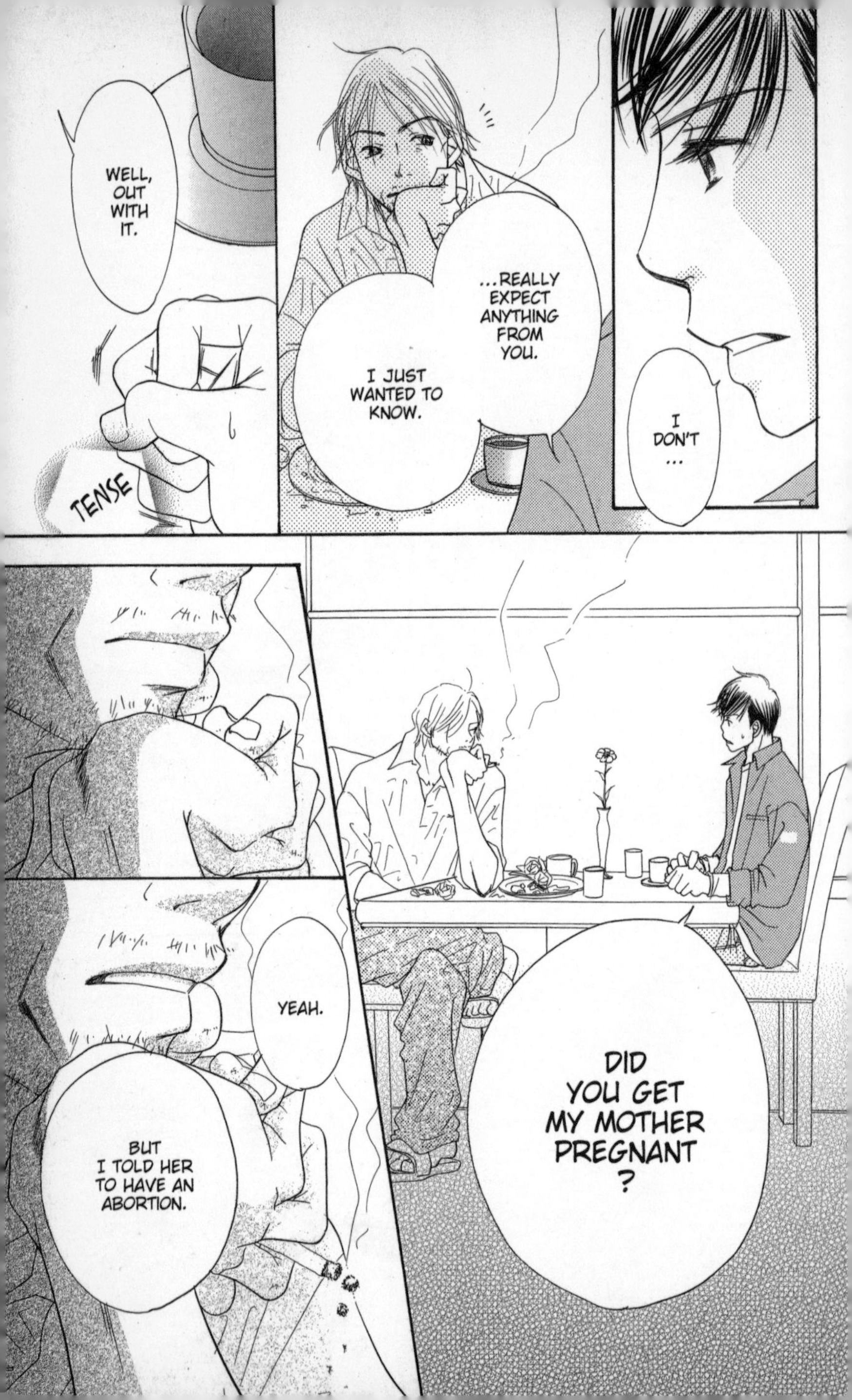
I DON'T ...
...REALLY EXPECT ANYTHING FROM YOU.
I JUST WANTED TO KNOW.
WELL, OUT WITH IT.
TENSE
DID YOU GET MY MOTHER PREGNANT?
YEAH.
BUT I TOLD HER TO HAVE AN ABORTION.

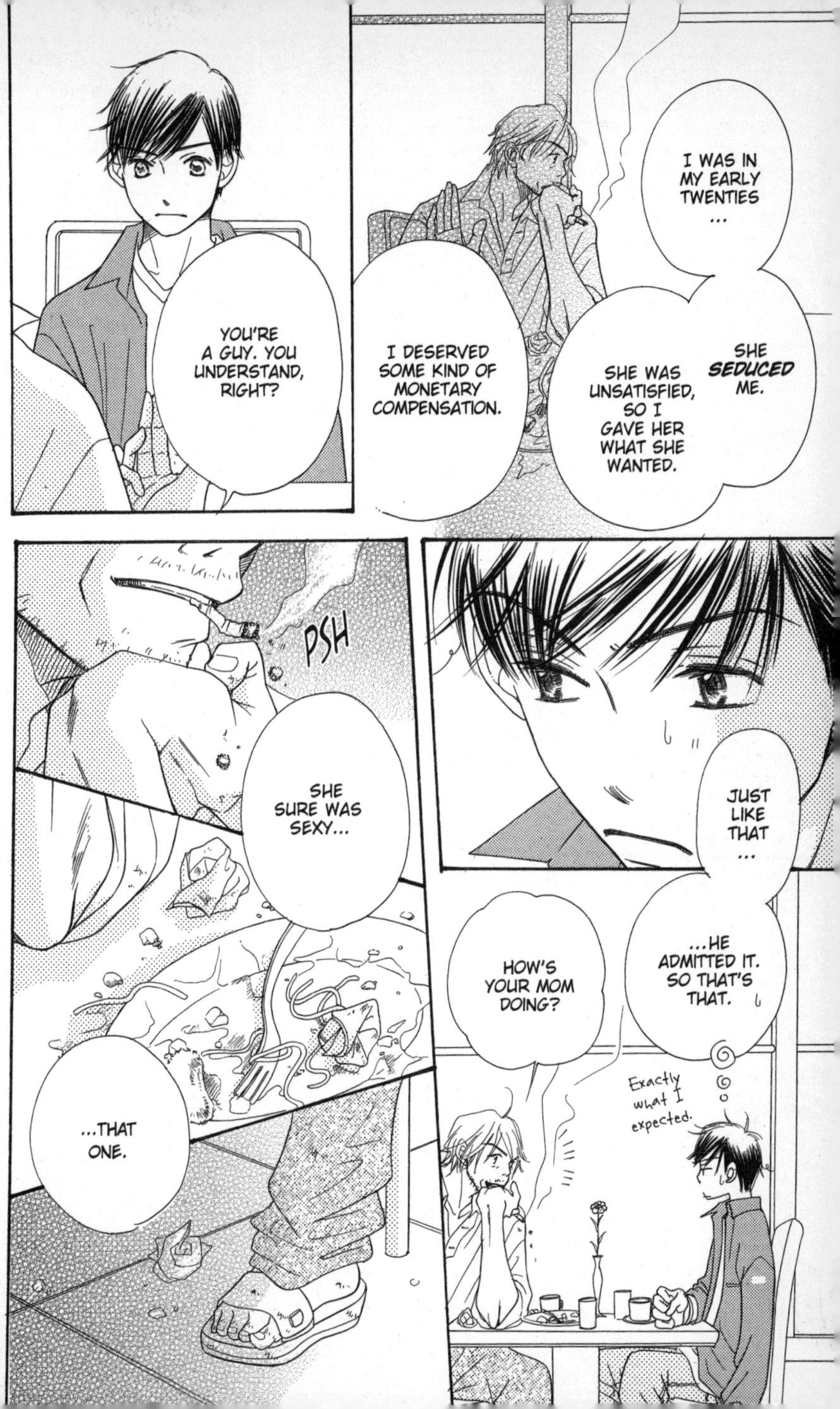
I WAS IN MY EARLY TWENTIES ...
SHE *SEDUCED* ME.
SHE WAS UNSATISFIED, SO I GAVE HER WHAT SHE WANTED.
I DESERVED SOME KIND OF MONETARY COMPENSATION.
YOU'RE A GUY. YOU UNDERSTAND, RIGHT?
JUST LIKE THAT ...
...HE ADMITTED IT. SO THAT'S THAT.
HOW'S YOUR MOM DOING?
Exactly what I expected.
PSH
SHE SURE WAS SEXY...
...THAT ONE.

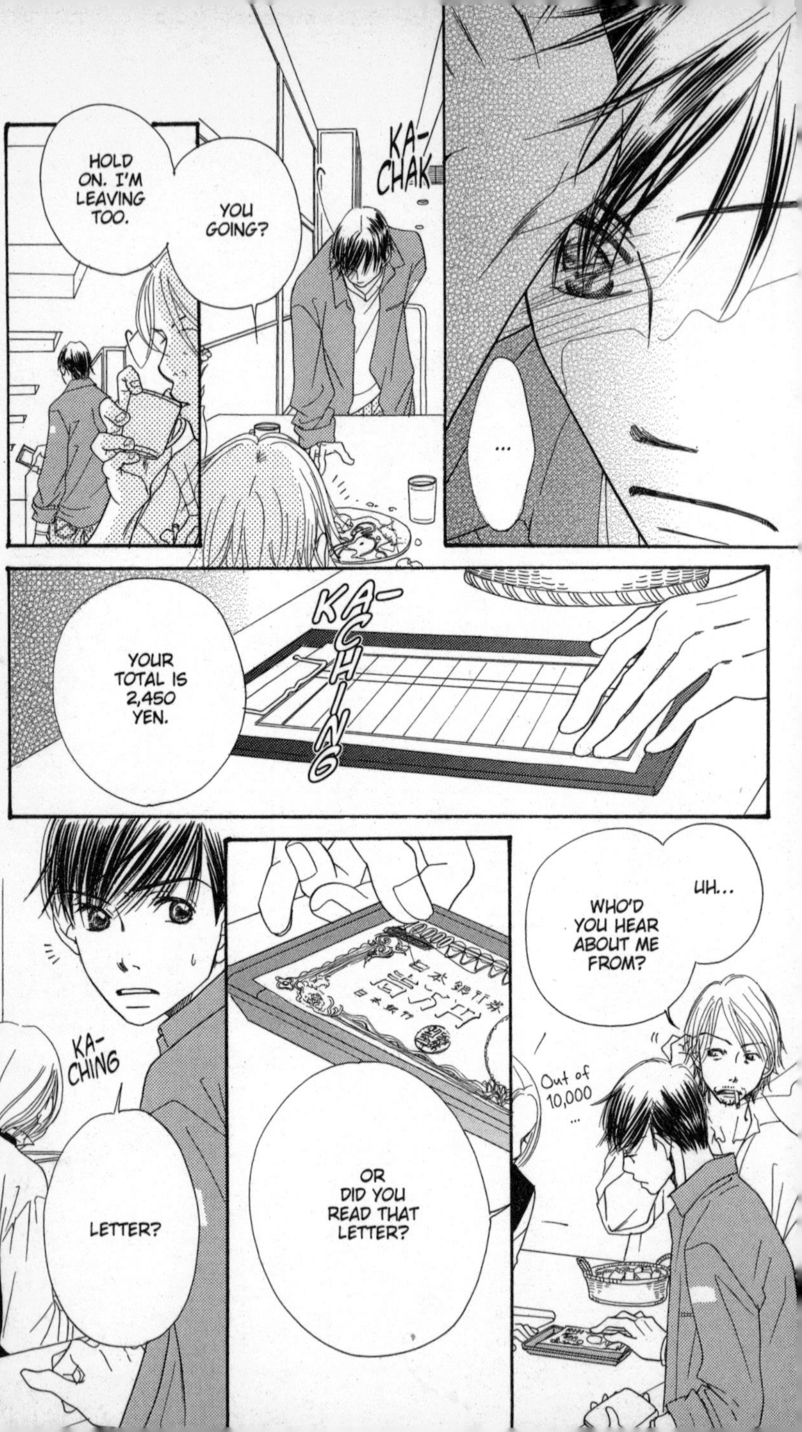
...
KA-CHAK
YOU GOING?
HOLD ON. I'M LEAVING TOO.
KA-CHING
YOUR TOTAL IS 2,450 YEN.
UH...
WHO'D YOU HEAR ABOUT ME FROM?
Out of 10,000 ...
OR DID YOU READ THAT LETTER?
KA-CHING
LETTER?

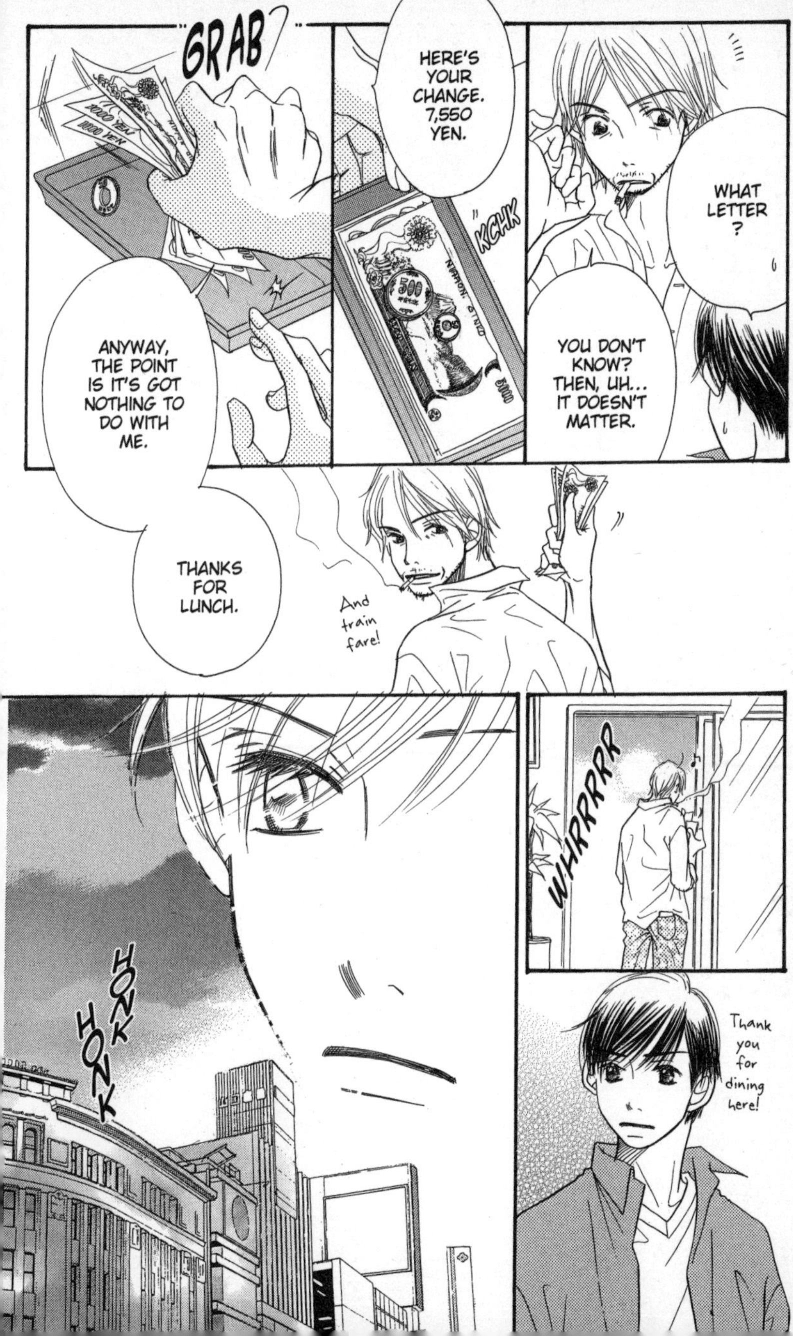
WHAT LETTER?
YOU DON'T KNOW? THEN, UH... IT DOESN'T MATTER.
HERE'S YOUR CHANGE. 7,550 YEN.
KCHK
GRAB
ANYWAY, THE POINT IS IT'S GOT NOTHING TO DO WITH ME.
And train fare!
THANKS FOR LUNCH.
WHRRRRR
Thank you for dining here!
HONK HONK

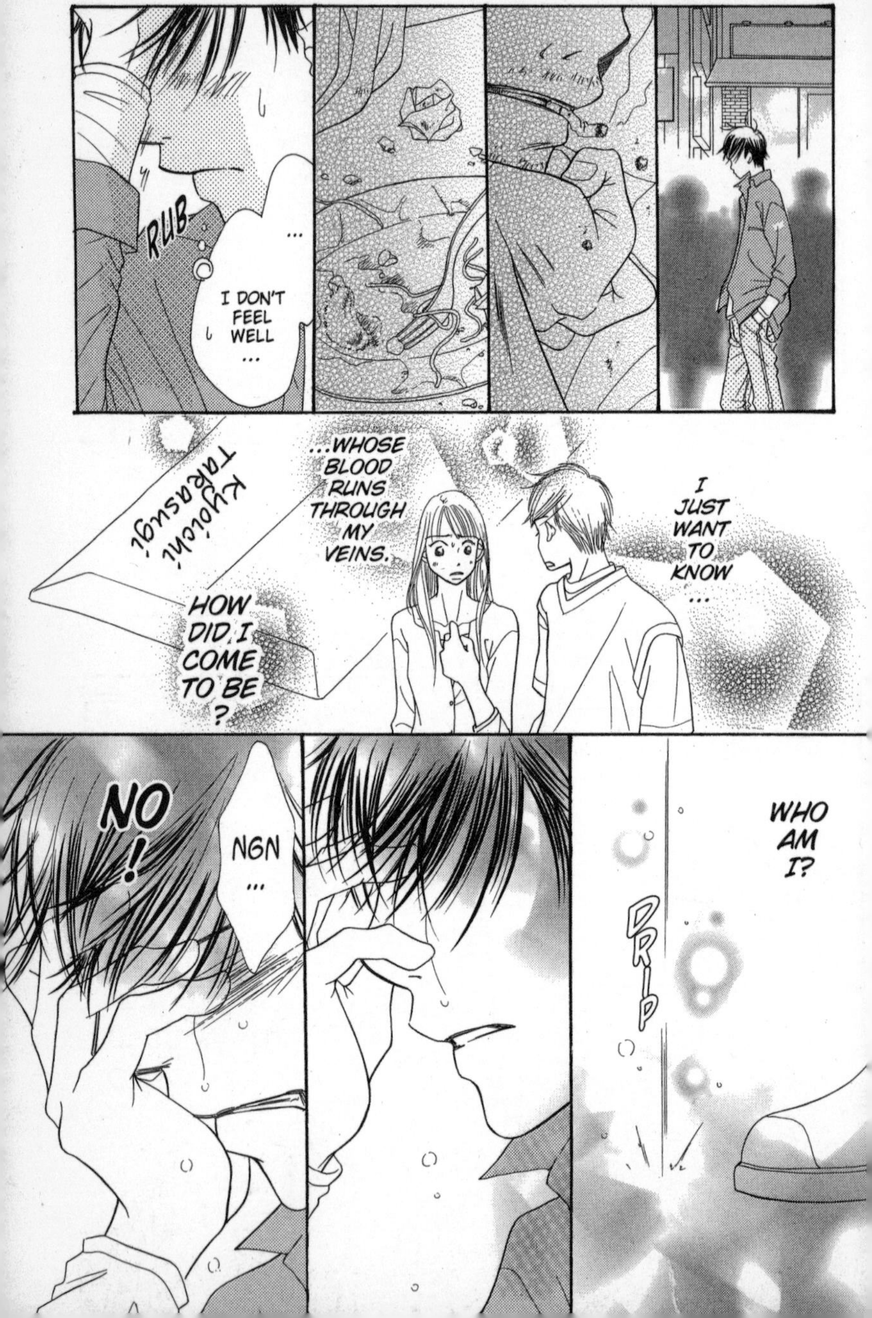
...
I DON'T FEEL WELL ...
RUB
I JUST WANT TO KNOW ...
...WHOSE BLOOD RUNS THROUGH MY VEINS.
Kyoichi Takasugi
HOW DID I COME TO BE?
WHO AM I?
DRIP
NGN ...
NO!

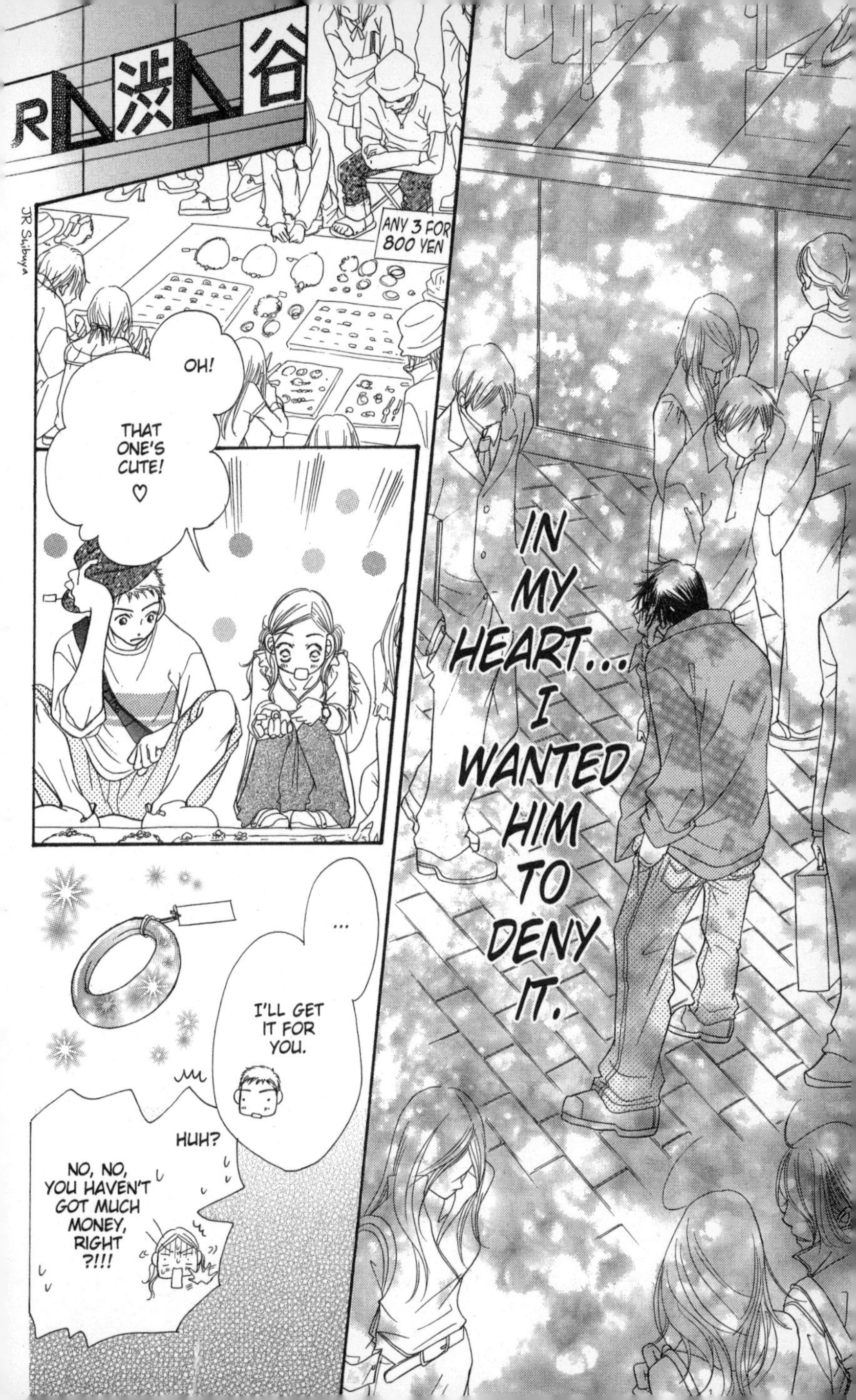
IN MY HEART... I WANTED HIM TO DENY IT.
渋 谷
JR Shibuya
ANY 3 FOR 800 YEN
OH!
THAT ONE'S CUTE! ♡
...
I'LL GET IT FOR YOU.
HUH?
NO, NO, YOU HAVEN'T GOT MUCH MONEY, RIGHT ?!!!

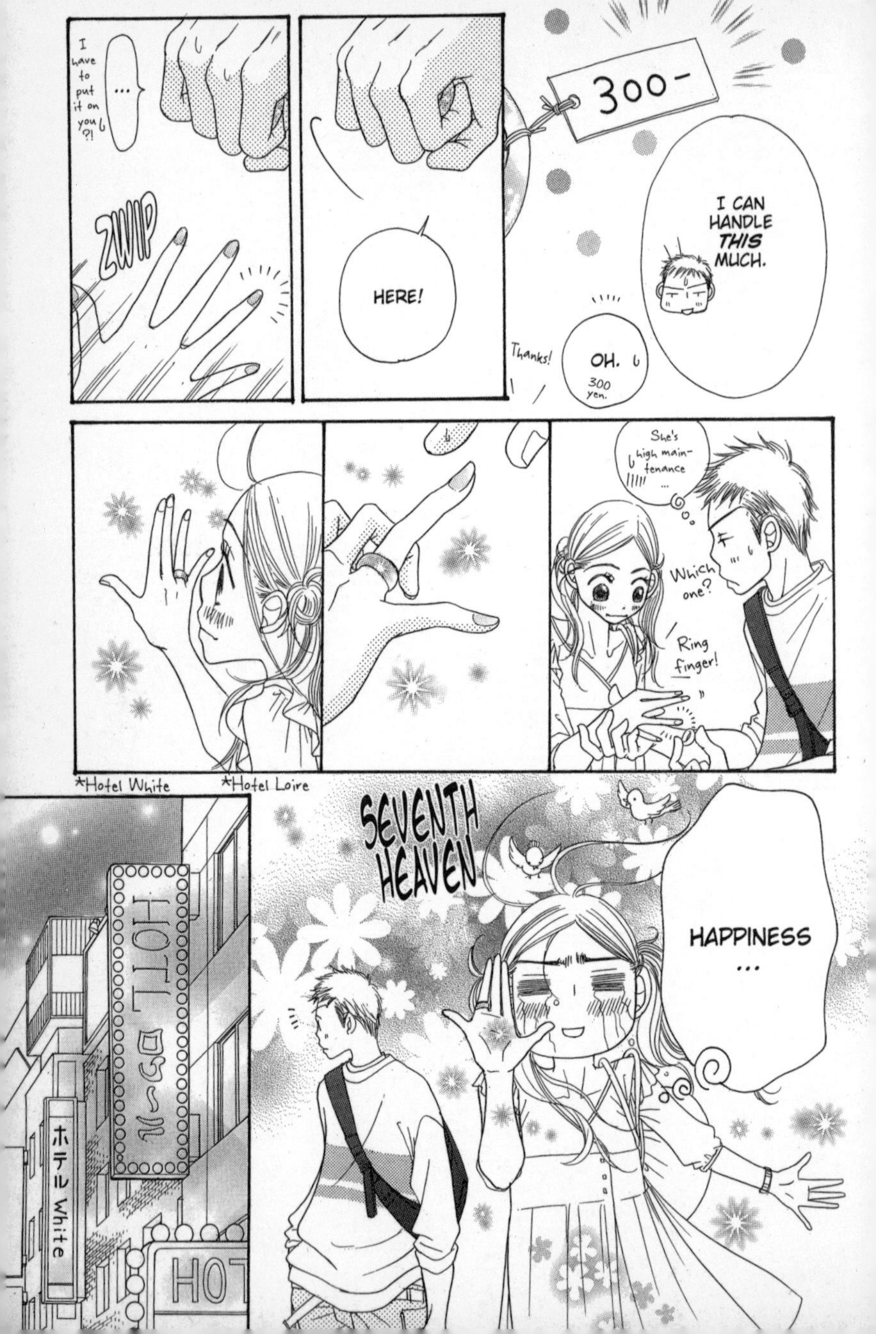
300-
I CAN HANDLE THIS MUCH.
OH.
300 yen.
Thanks!
HERE!
I have to put it on you?!
...
ZWIP
She's high maintenance...
Which one?
Ring finger!
HAPPINESS...
SEVENTH HEAVEN
*Hotel Loire
*Hotel White
HOTL ロワール
ホテル White
HOT

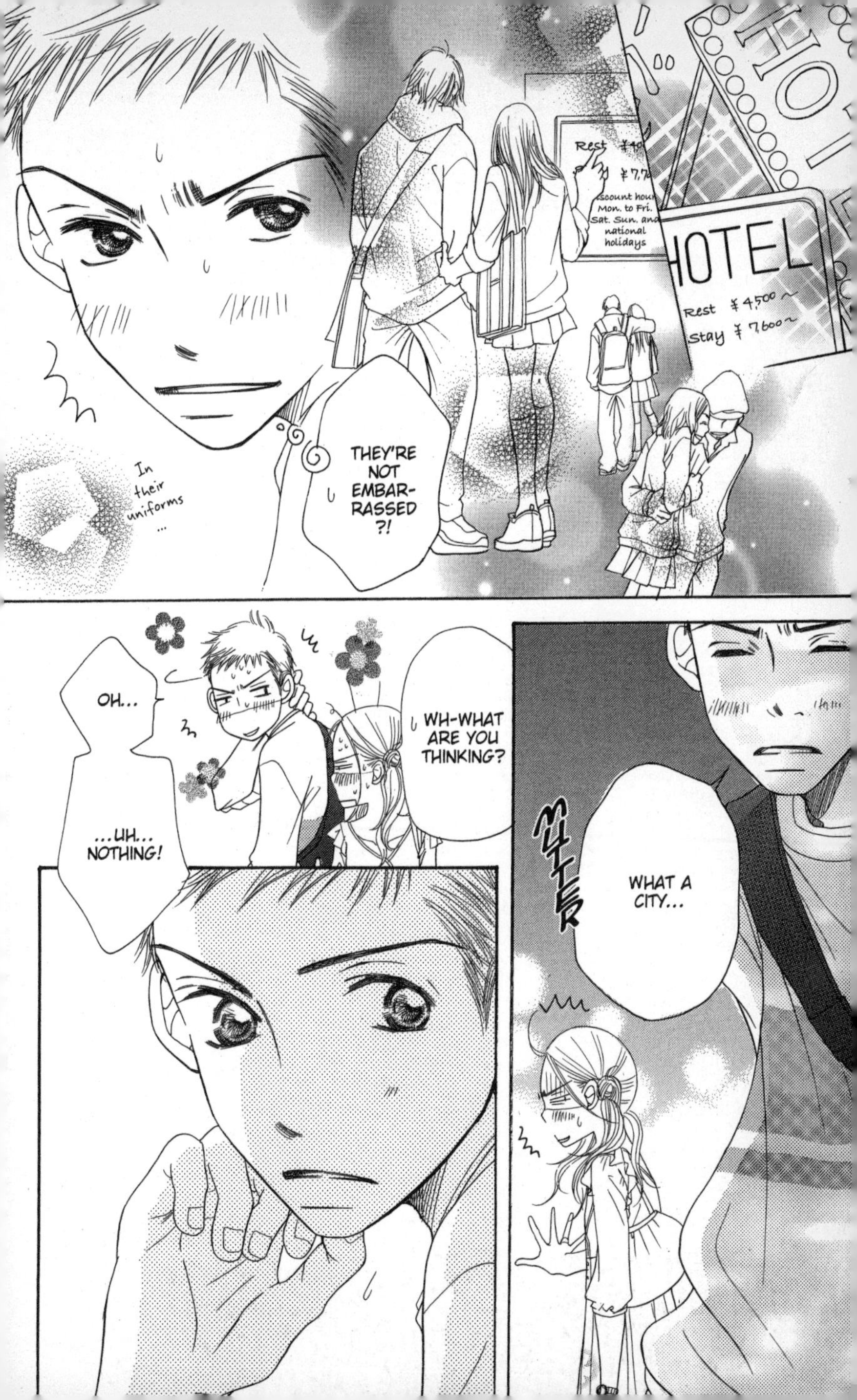
HOTEL
Rest ¥4,500~
Stay ¥7,600~
Mon. to Fri.
Sat. Sun. and national holidays
THEY'RE NOT EMBARRASSED?!
In their uniforms...
MUTTER
WHAT A CITY...
WH-WHAT ARE YOU THINKING?
OH...
...UH... NOTHING!

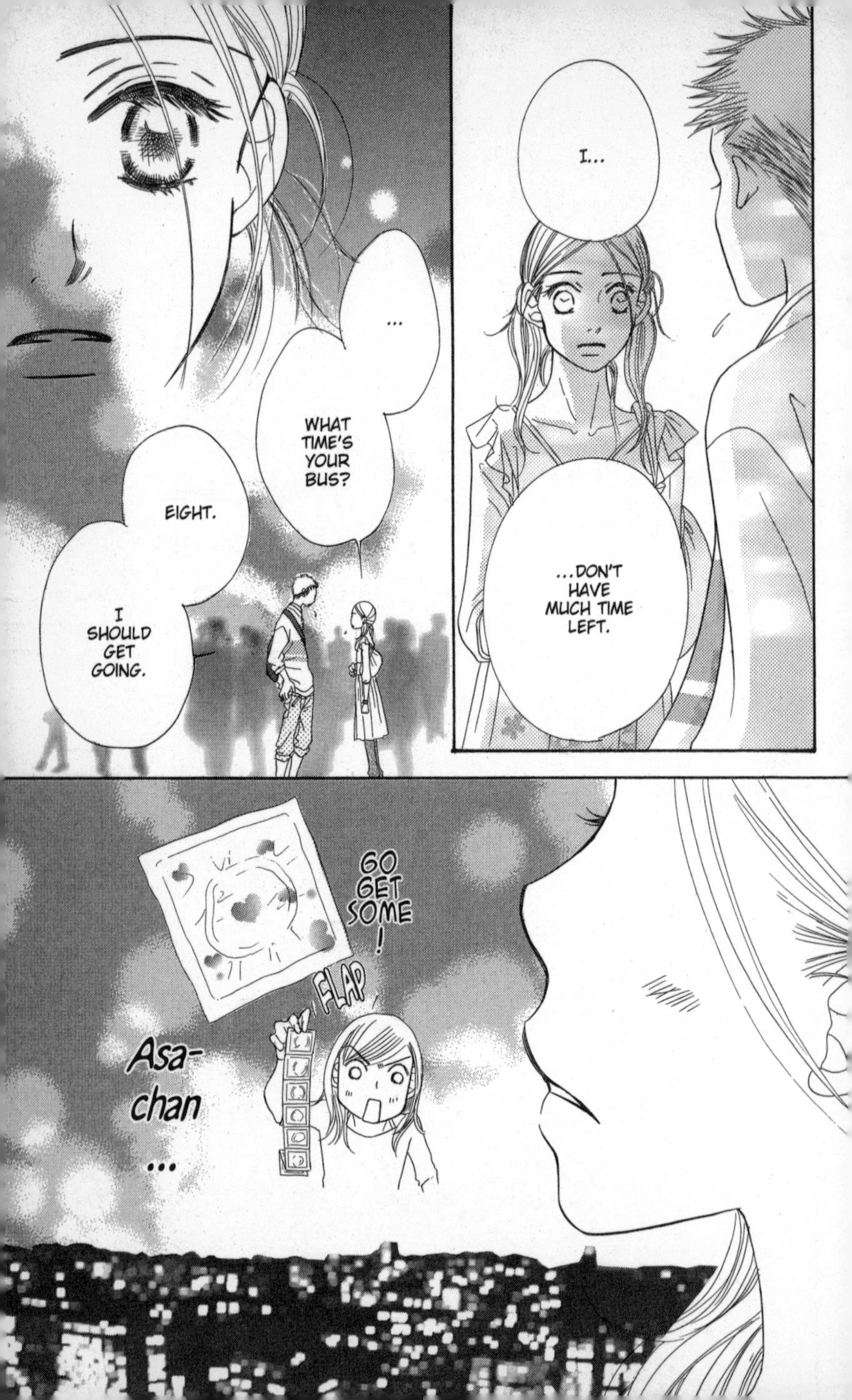
I...
...DON'T HAVE MUCH TIME LEFT.
...
WHAT TIME'S YOUR BUS?
EIGHT.
I SHOULD GET GOING.
GO GET SOME!
FLAP
Asa-chan ...

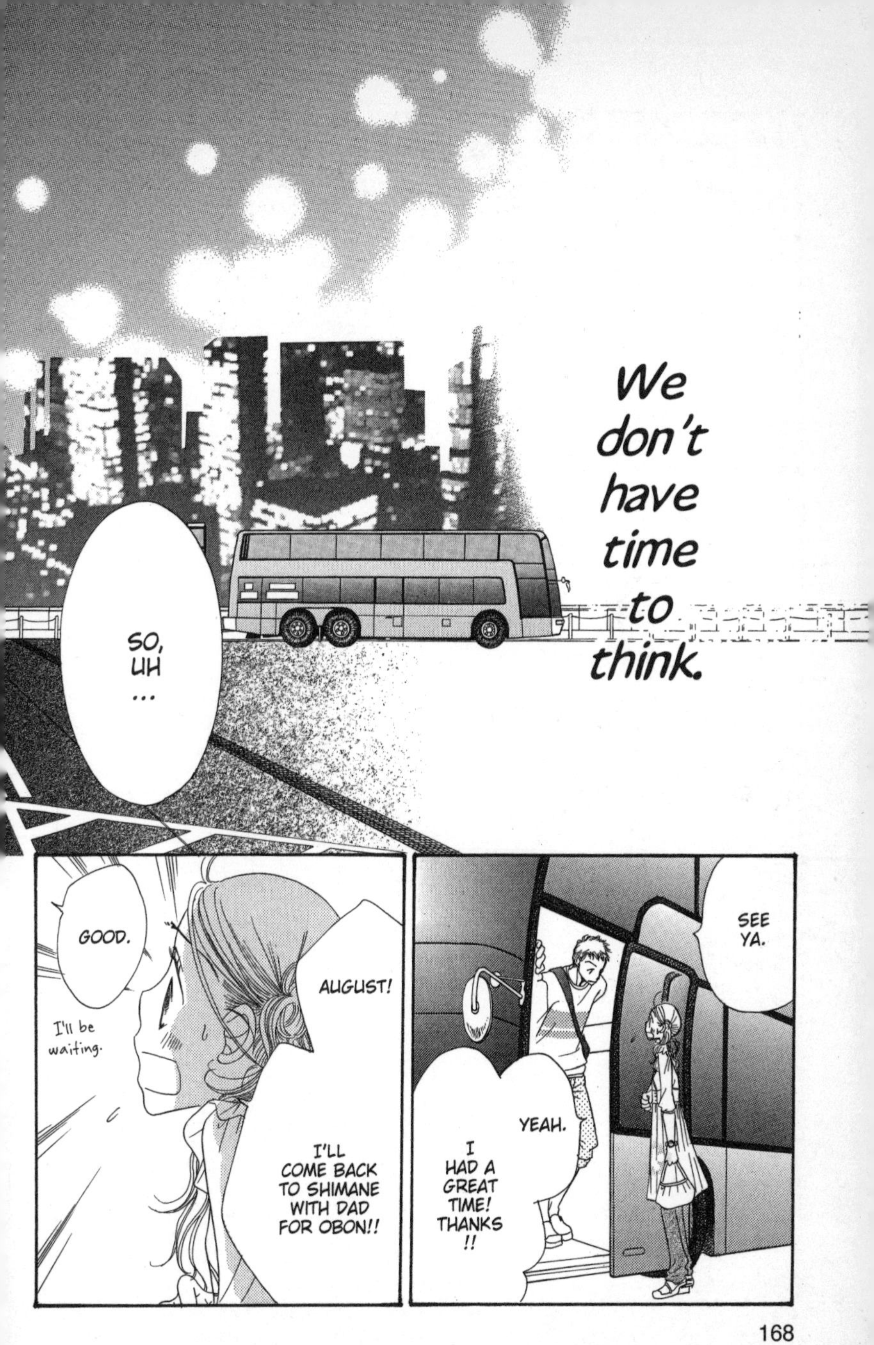
We don't have time to think.
SO, UH ...
SEE YA.
YEAH.
I HAD A GREAT TIME! THANKS!!
AUGUST!
I'LL COME BACK TO SHIMANE WITH DAD FOR OBON!!
GOOD.
I'll be waiting.

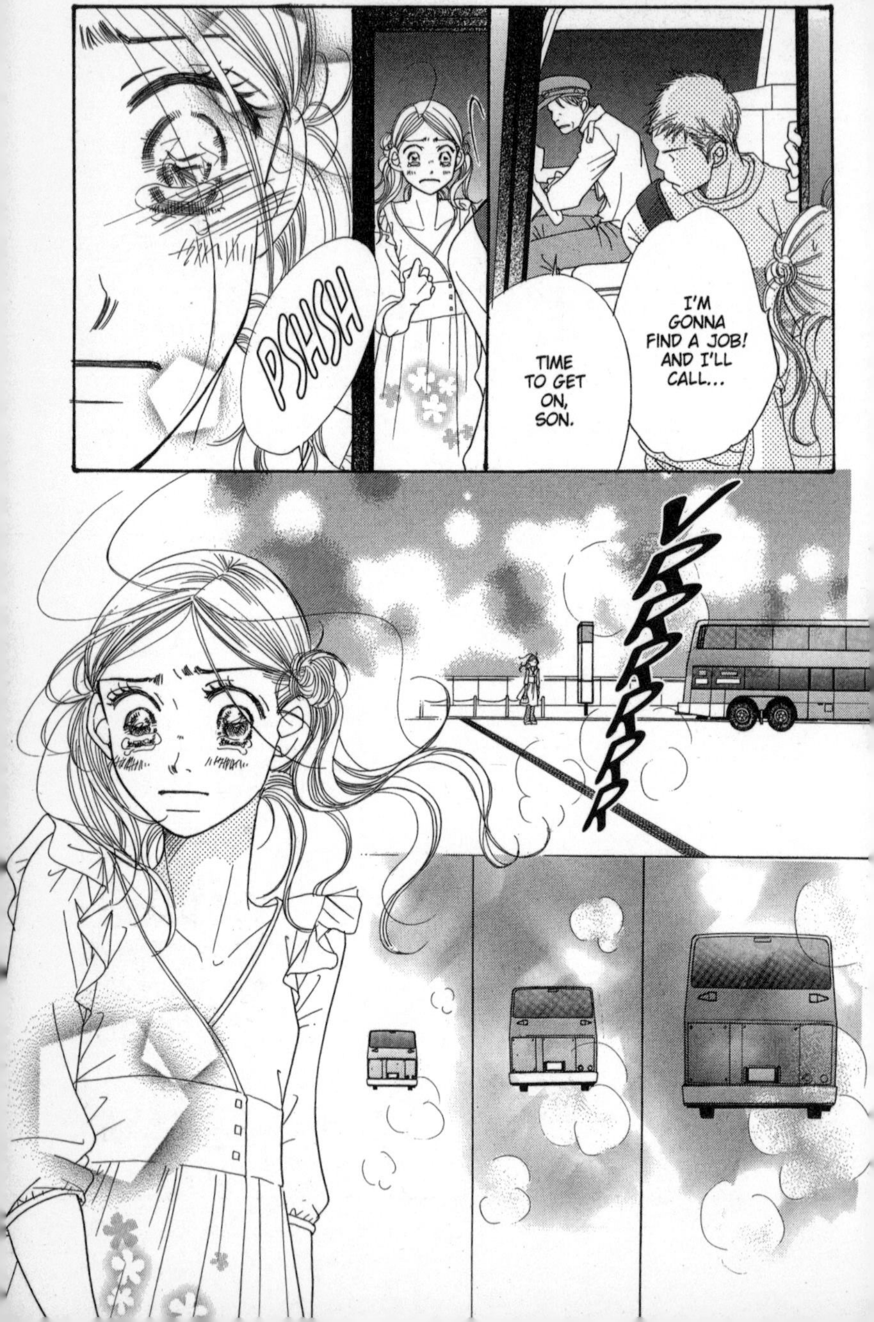
I'M GONNA FIND A JOB! AND I'LL CALL...
TIME TO GET ON, SON.
PSHSH
VRRRRRRR

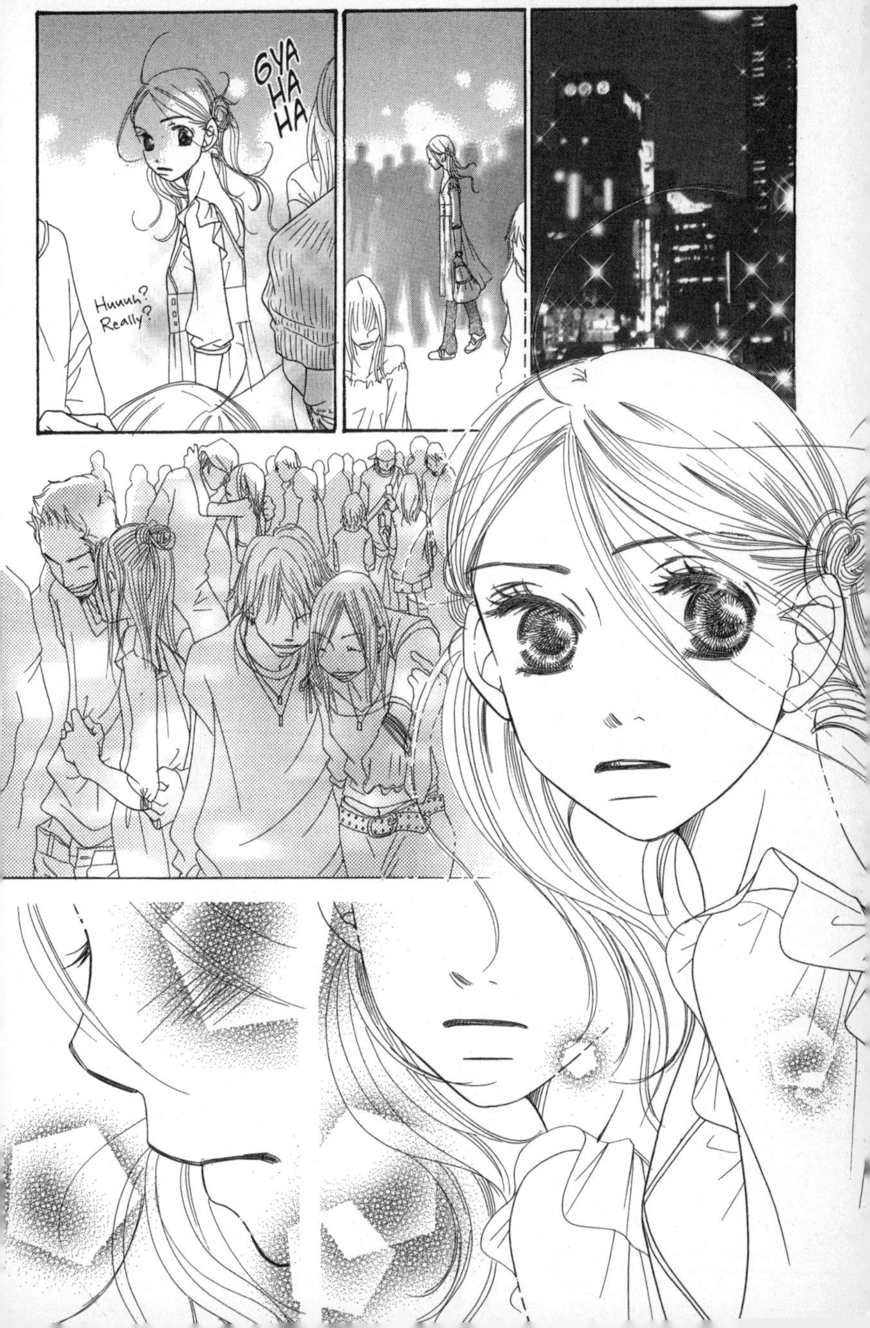
GYA HA HA
Huuuh? Really?

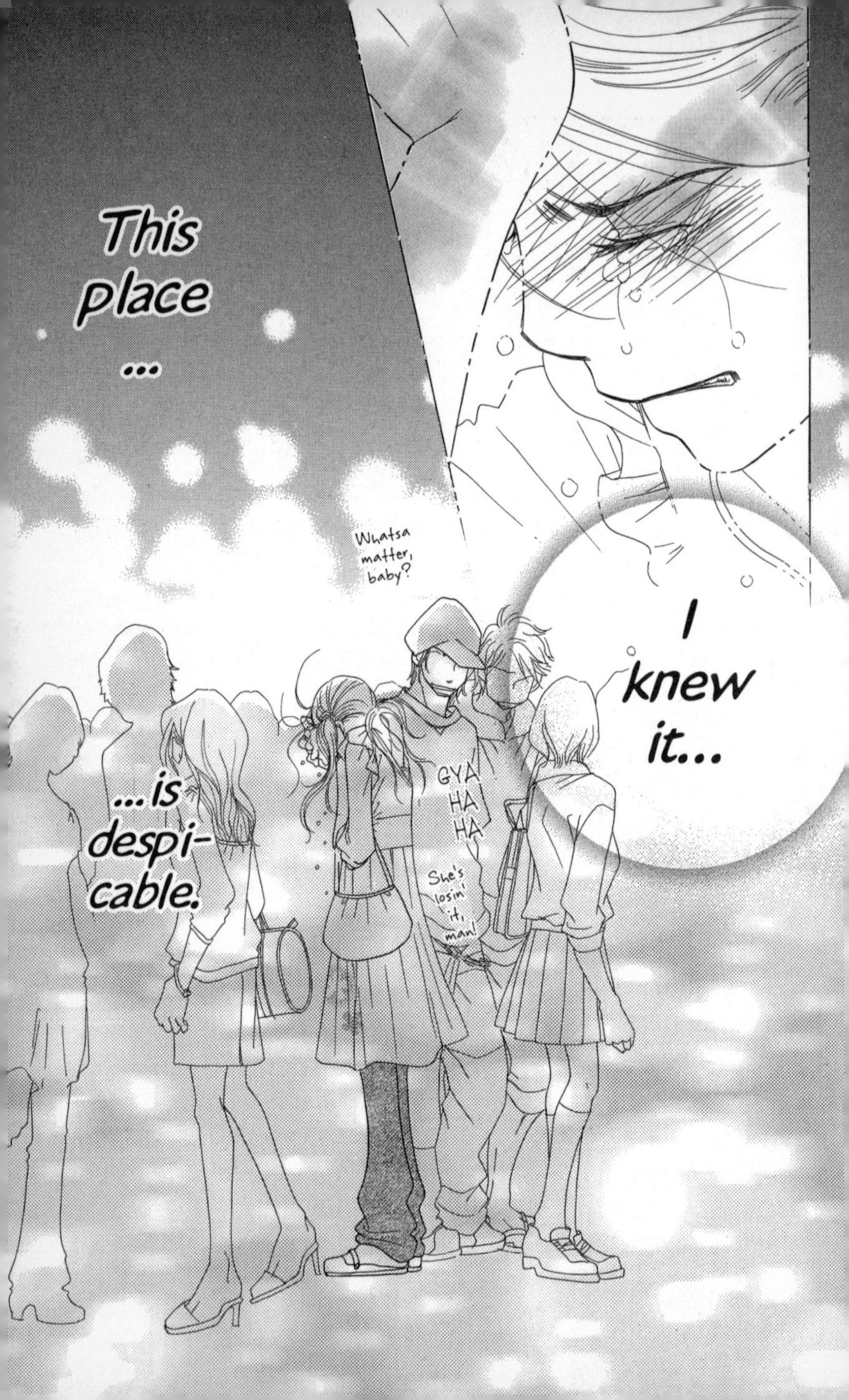
I knew it...
This place ...
Whatsa matter, baby?
GYA HA HA
She's losin' it, man!
... is despicable.

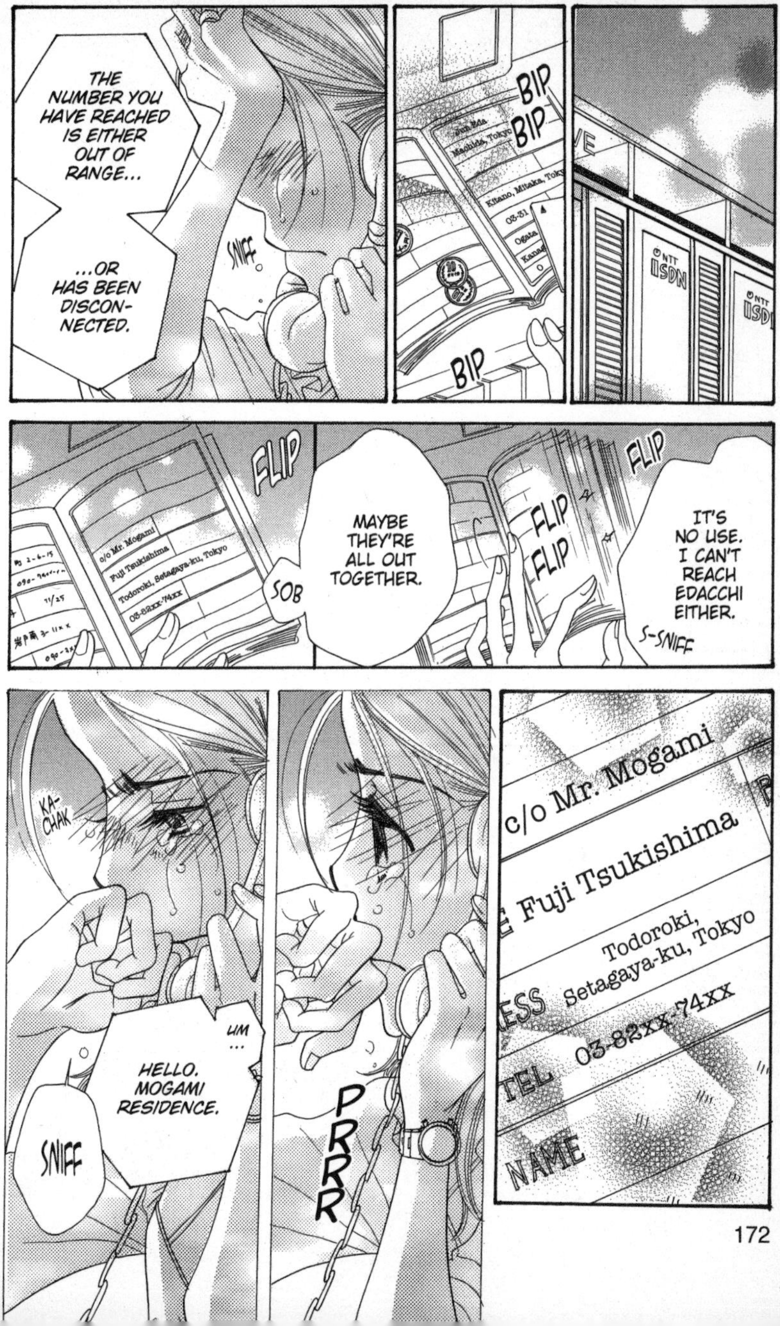
NTT ISDN
NTT ISDN
BIP
BIP
BIP
THE NUMBER YOU HAVE REACHED IS EITHER OUT OF RANGE...
...OR HAS BEEN DISCONNECTED.
SNIFF
FLIP
IT'S NO USE. I CAN'T REACH EDACCHI EITHER.
FLIP
FLIP
S-SNIFF
MAYBE THEY'RE ALL OUT TOGETHER.
SOB
FLIP
c/o Mr. Mogami
Fuji Tsukishima
Todoroki, Setagaya-ku, Tokyo
03-82xx-74xx
c/o Mr. Mogami
Fuji Tsukishima
Todoroki, Setagaya-ku, Tokyo
TEL 03-82xx-74xx
NAME
PRRR
KA-CHAK
UM...
HELLO. MOGAMI RESIDENCE.
SNIFF

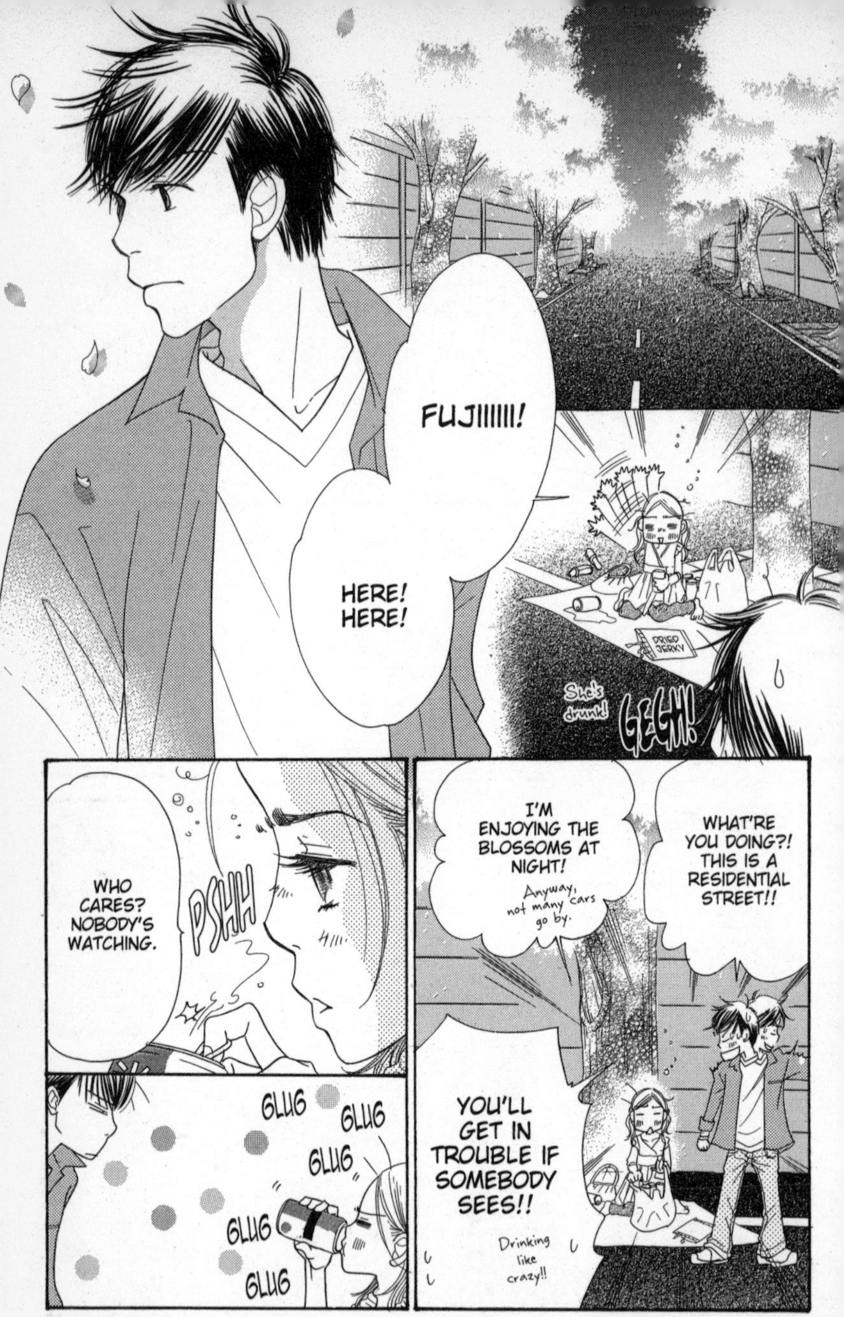
FUJIIIIII!
HERE! HERE!
She's drunk!
GEGH!
WHAT'RE YOU DOING?! THIS IS A RESIDENTIAL STREET!!
I'M ENJOYING THE BLOSSOMS AT NIGHT!
Anyway, not many cars go by.
YOU'LL GET IN TROUBLE IF SOMEBODY SEES!!
Drinking like crazy!!
WHO CARES? NOBODY'S WATCHING.
PSHH
GLUG GLUG GLUG GLUG GLUG

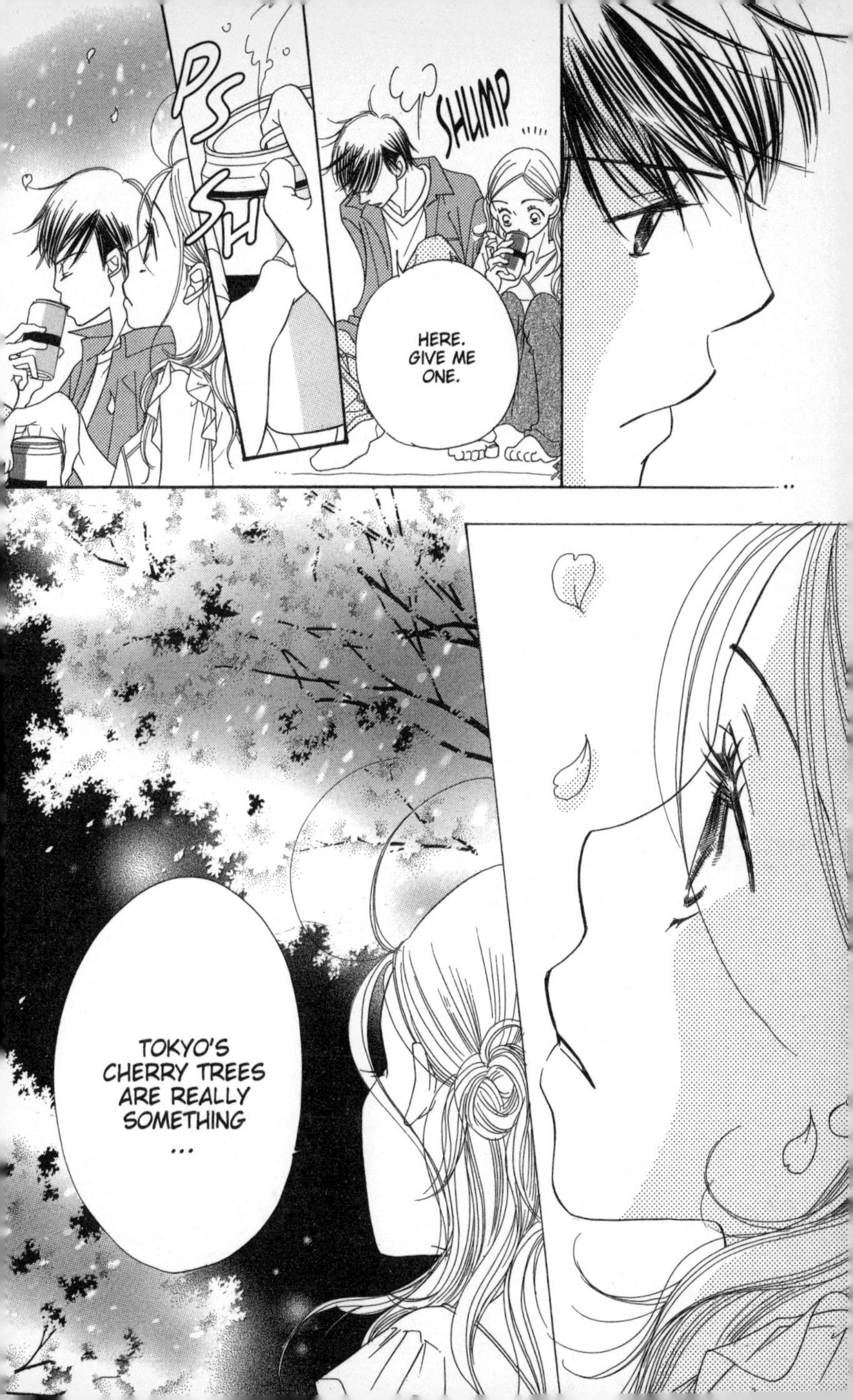

SHUMP
HERE. GIVE ME ONE.
PSSH
TOKYO'S CHERRY TREES ARE REALLY SOMETHING ...

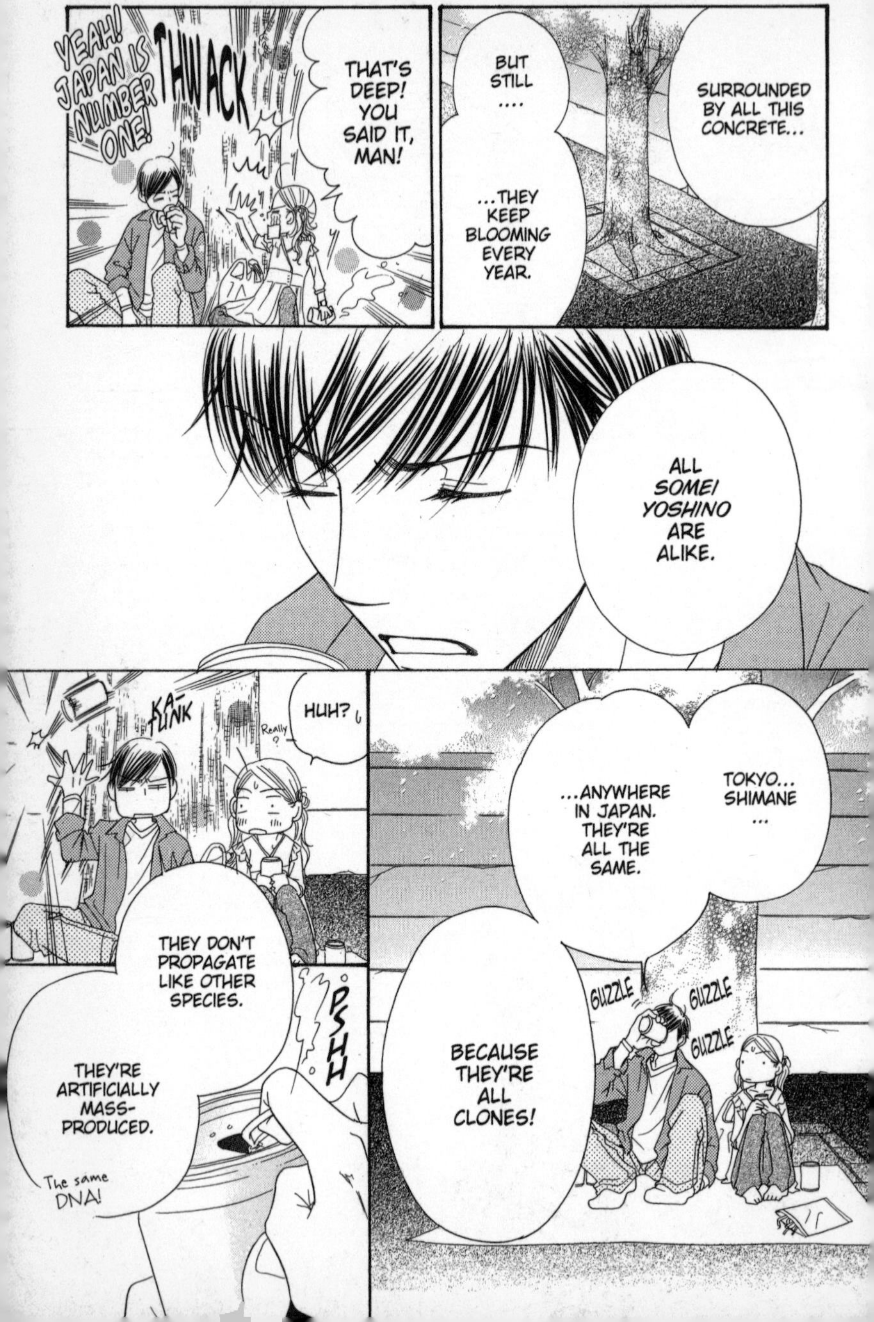
SURROUNDED BY ALL THIS CONCRETE...
BUT STILL ....
...THEY KEEP BLOOMING EVERY YEAR.
THAT'S DEEP! YOU SAID IT, MAN!
THWACK
YEAH! JAPAN IS NUMBER ONE!
ALL SOMEI YOSHINO ARE ALIKE.
TOKYO... SHIMANE ...
...ANYWHERE IN JAPAN. THEY'RE ALL THE SAME.
GUZZLE
GUZZLE
GUZZLE
BECAUSE THEY'RE ALL CLONES!
HUH?
Really?
KA-TUNK
THEY DON'T PROPAGATE LIKE OTHER SPECIES.
PSHH
THEY'RE ARTIFICIALLY MASS-PRODUCED.
The same DNA!

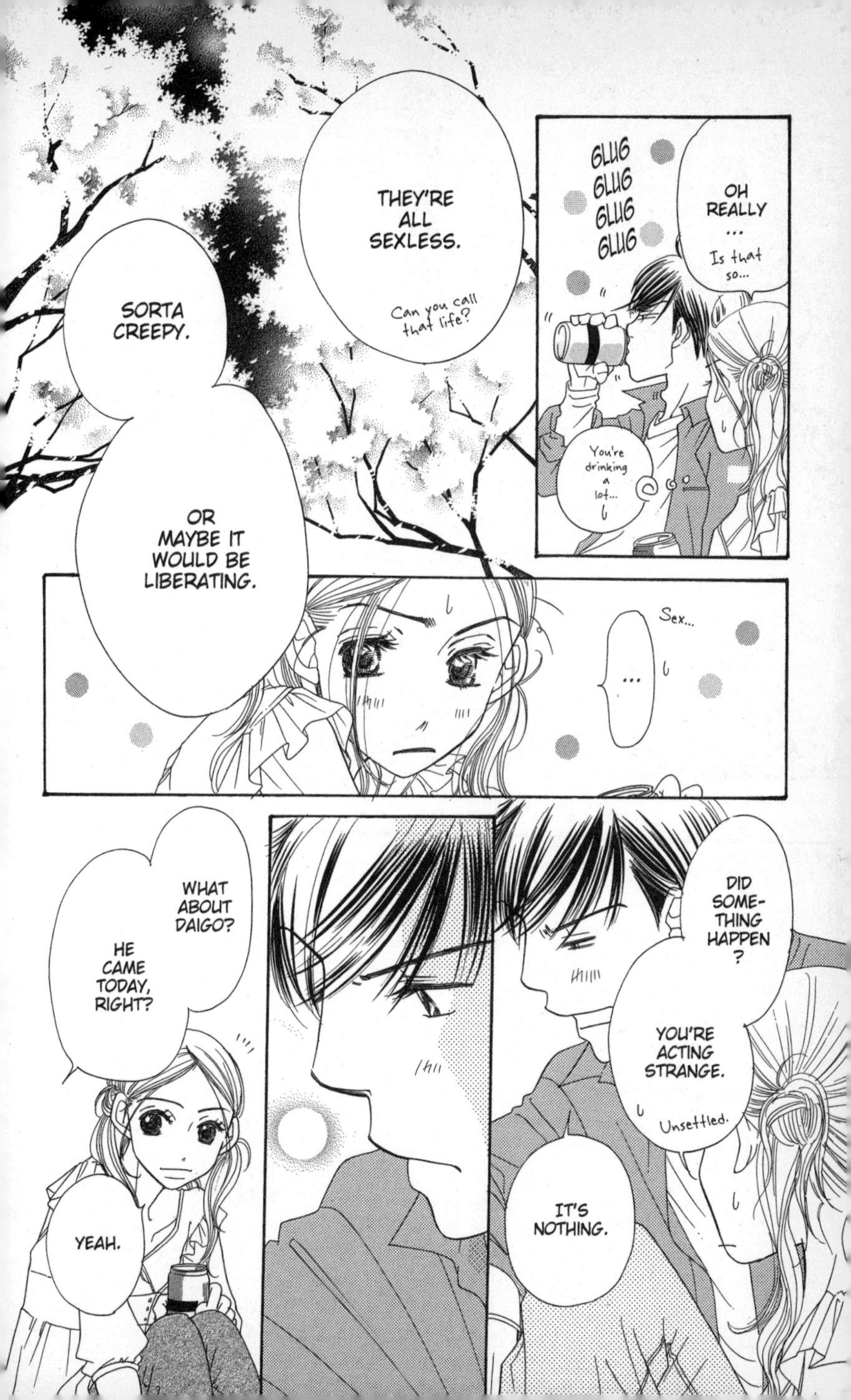
GLUG GLUG GLUG GLUG
OH REALLY ... Is that so...
You're drinking a lot...
THEY'RE ALL SEXLESS.
Can you call that life?
SORTA CREEPY.
OR MAYBE IT WOULD BE LIBERATING.
Sex...
...
DID SOME-THING HAPPEN?
YOU'RE ACTING STRANGE.
Unsettled.
IT'S NOTHING.
WHAT ABOUT DAIGO?
HE CAME TODAY, RIGHT?
YEAH.

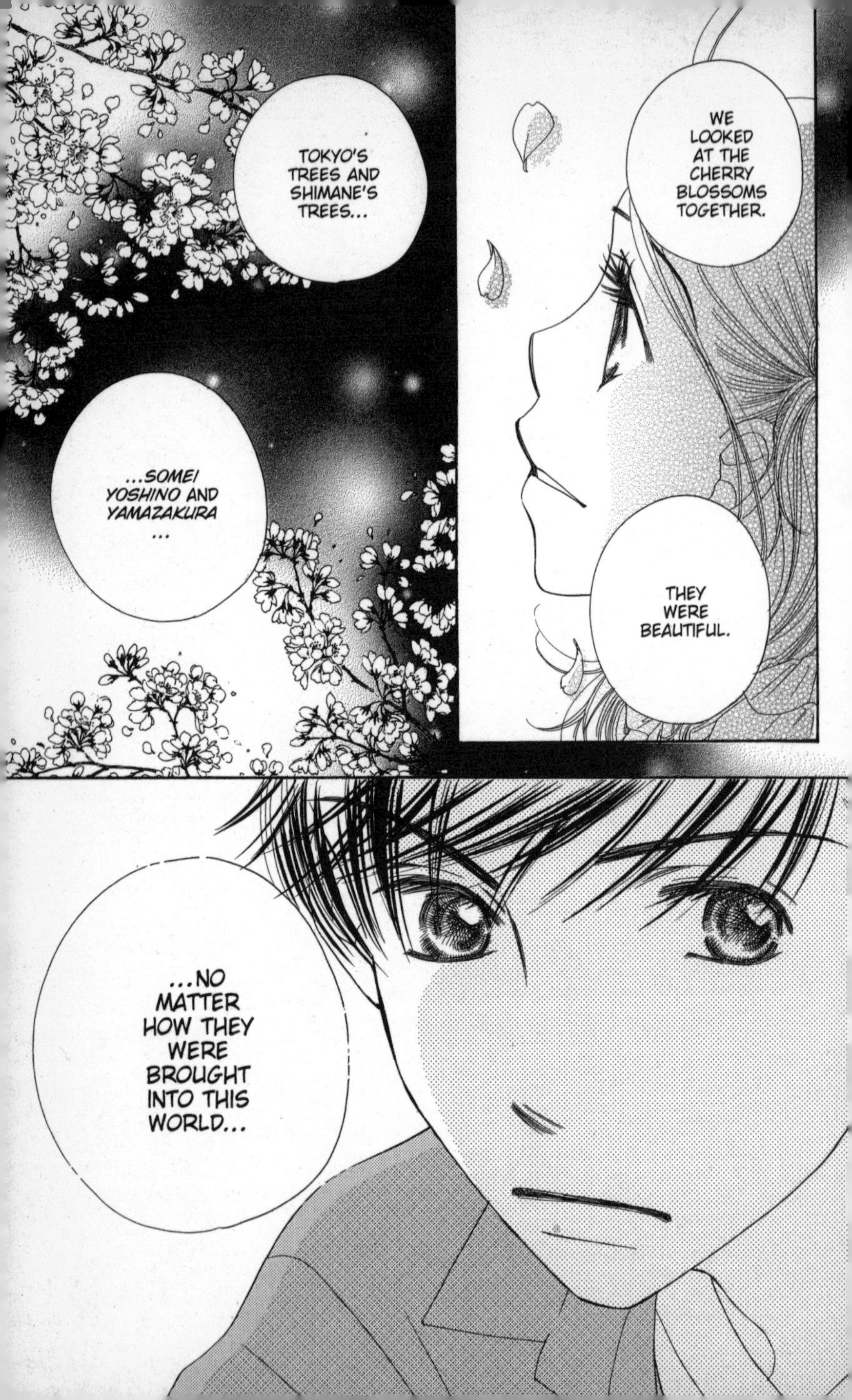
WE LOOKED AT THE CHERRY BLOSSOMS TOGETHER.
THEY WERE BEAUTIFUL.
TOKYO'S TREES AND SHIMANE'S TREES...
...SOMEI YOSHINO AND YAMAZAKURA ...
...NO MATTER HOW THEY WERE BROUGHT INTO THIS WORLD...

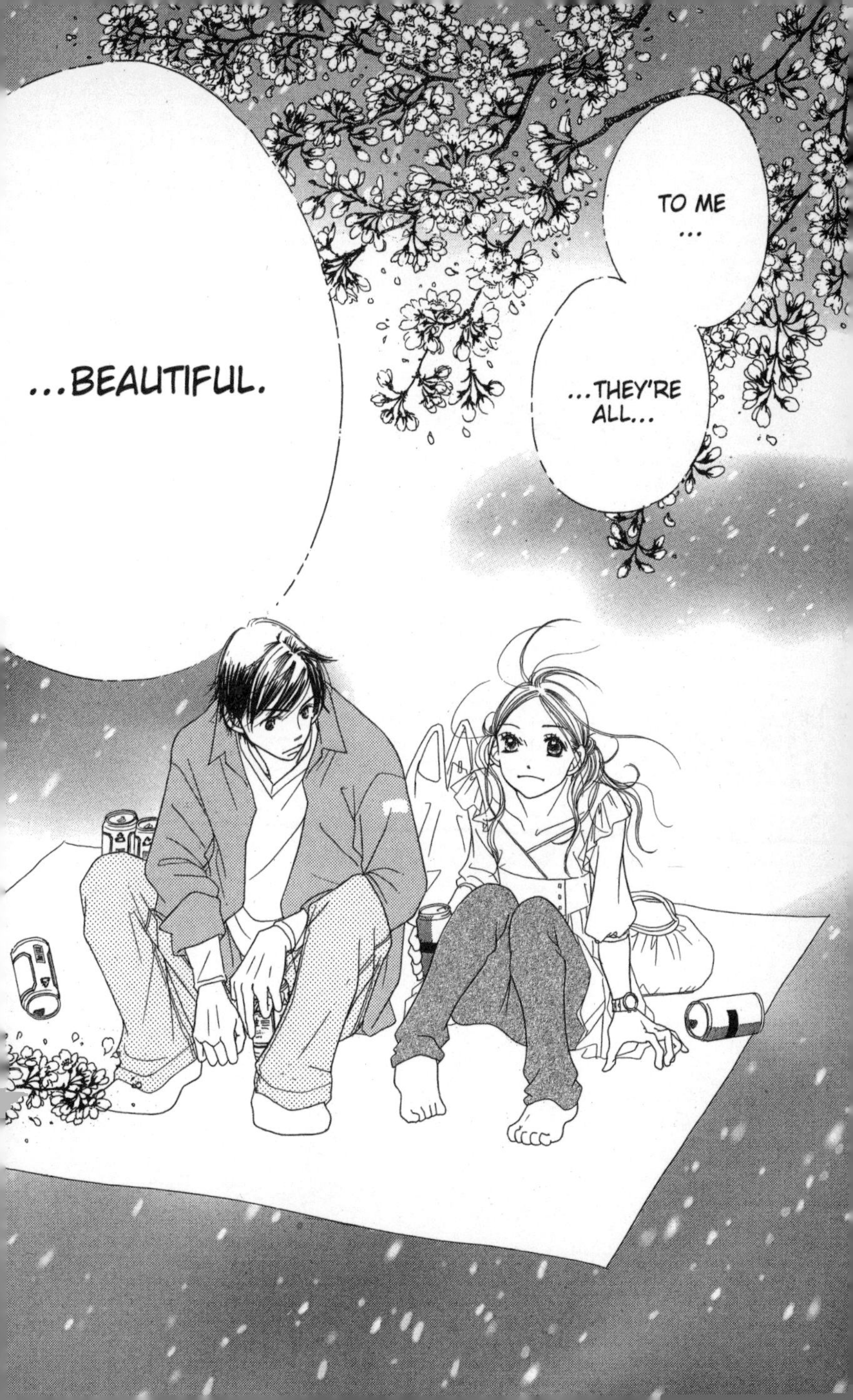
TO ME ...
...THEY'RE ALL...
...BEAUTIFUL.

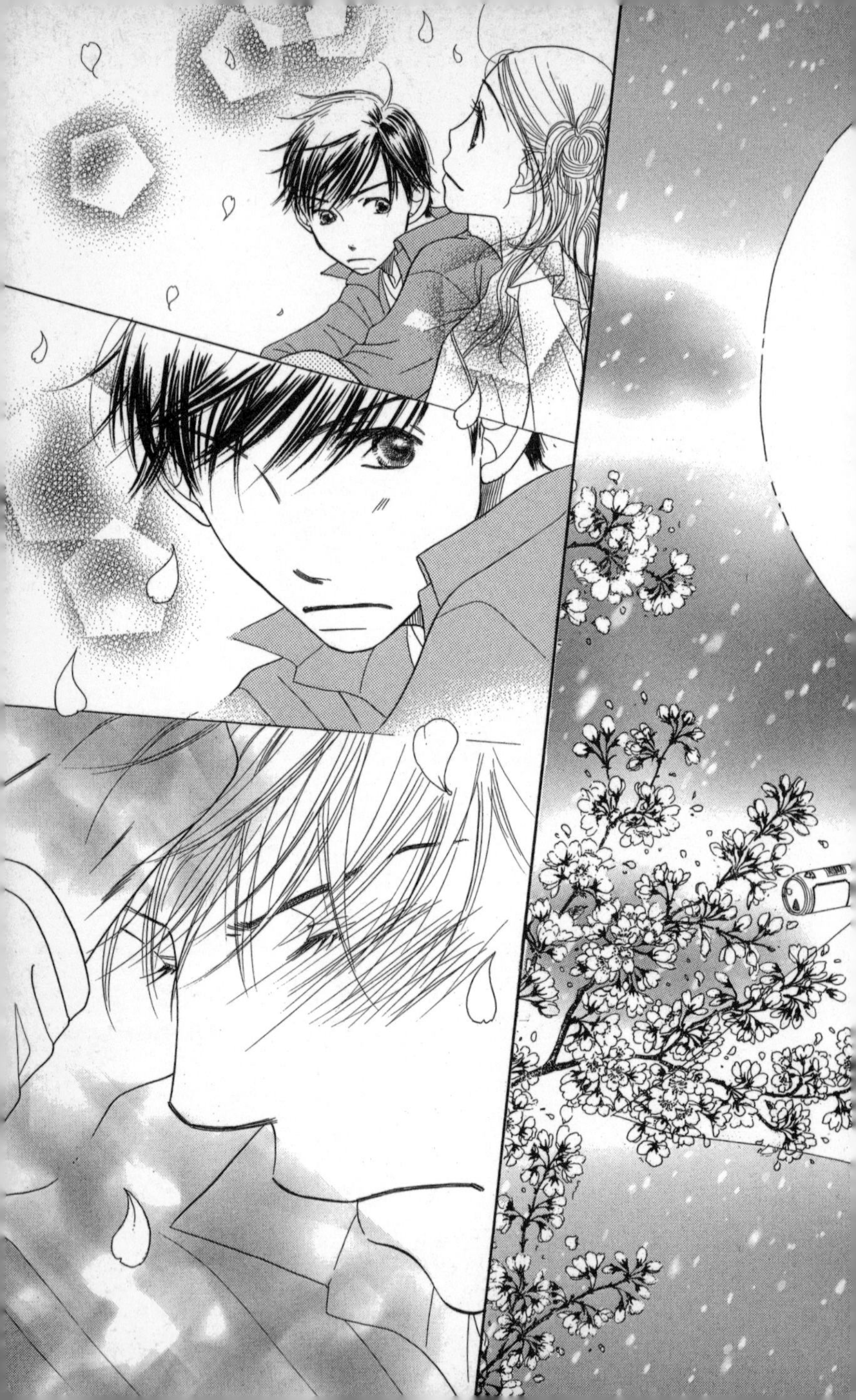

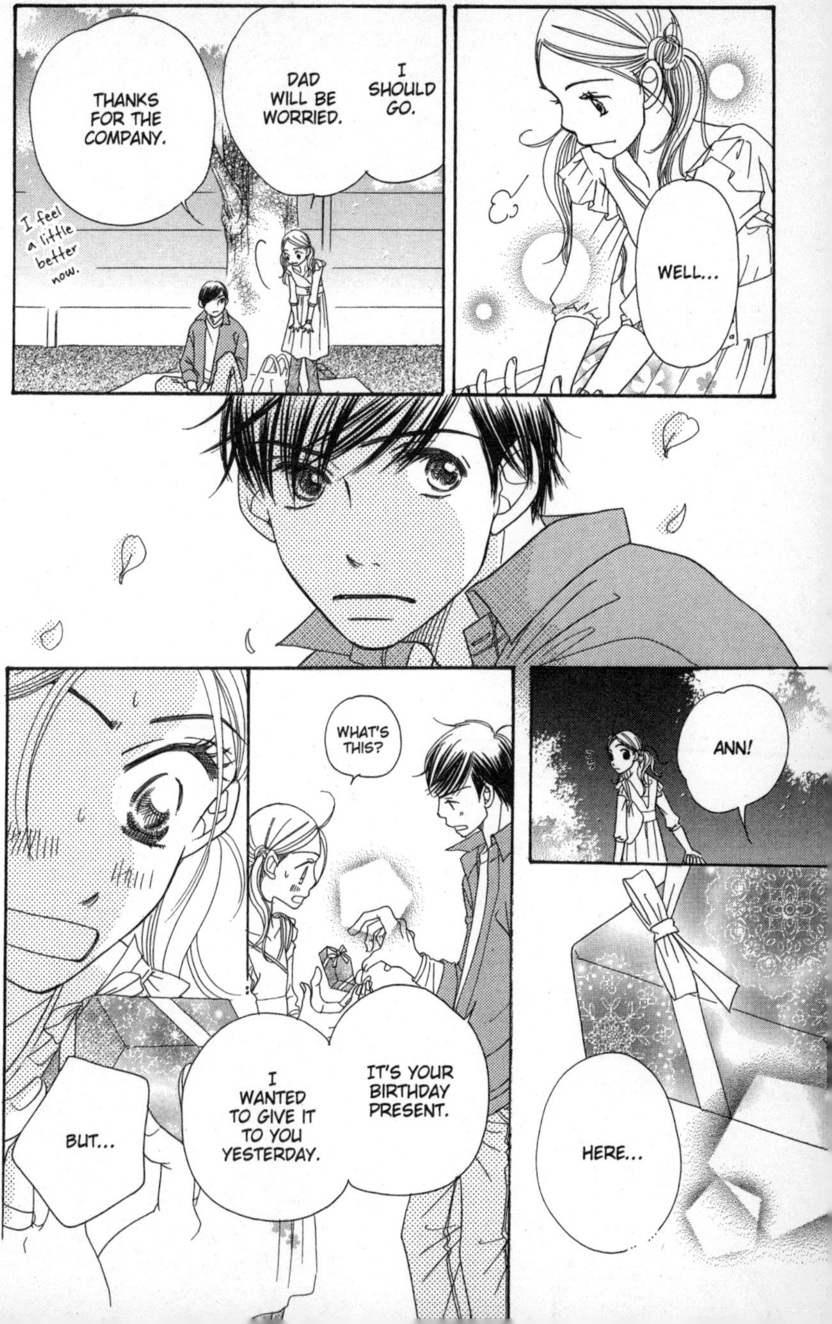
WELL...
I SHOULD GO.
DAD WILL BE WORRIED.
THANKS FOR THE COMPANY.
I feel a little better now.
ANN!
HERE...
WHAT'S THIS?
IT'S YOUR BIRTHDAY PRESENT.
I WANTED TO GIVE IT TO YOU YESTERDAY.
BUT...

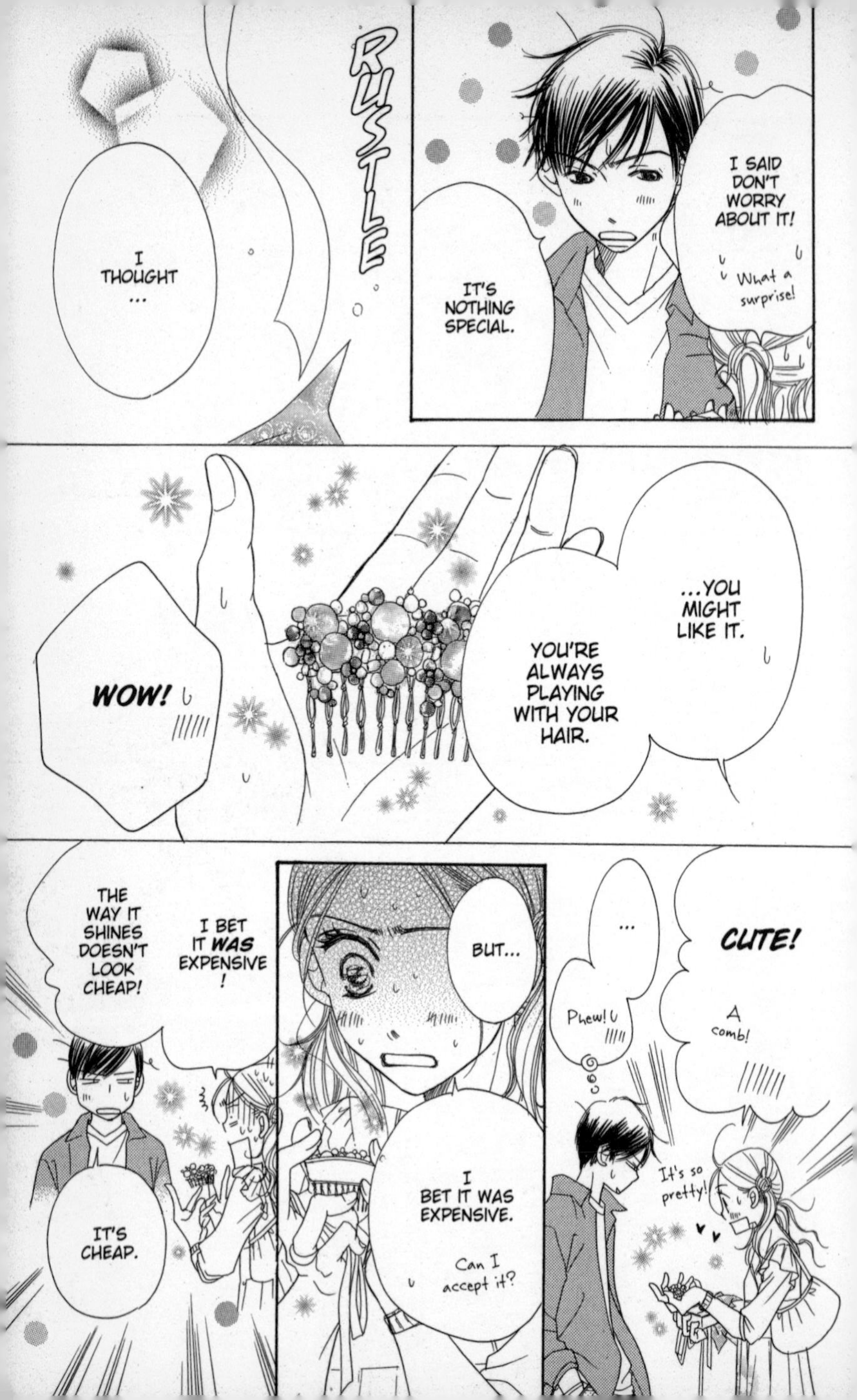
I SAID DON'T WORRY ABOUT IT!
What a surprise!
IT'S NOTHING SPECIAL.
RUSTLE
I THOUGHT ...
...YOU MIGHT LIKE IT.
YOU'RE ALWAYS PLAYING WITH YOUR HAIR.
WOW!
CUTE!
A comb!
...
Phew!
It's so pretty!
BUT...
I BET IT WAS EXPENSIVE.
Can I accept it?
I BET IT WAS EXPENSIVE!
THE WAY IT SHINES DOESN'T LOOK CHEAP!
IT'S CHEAP.

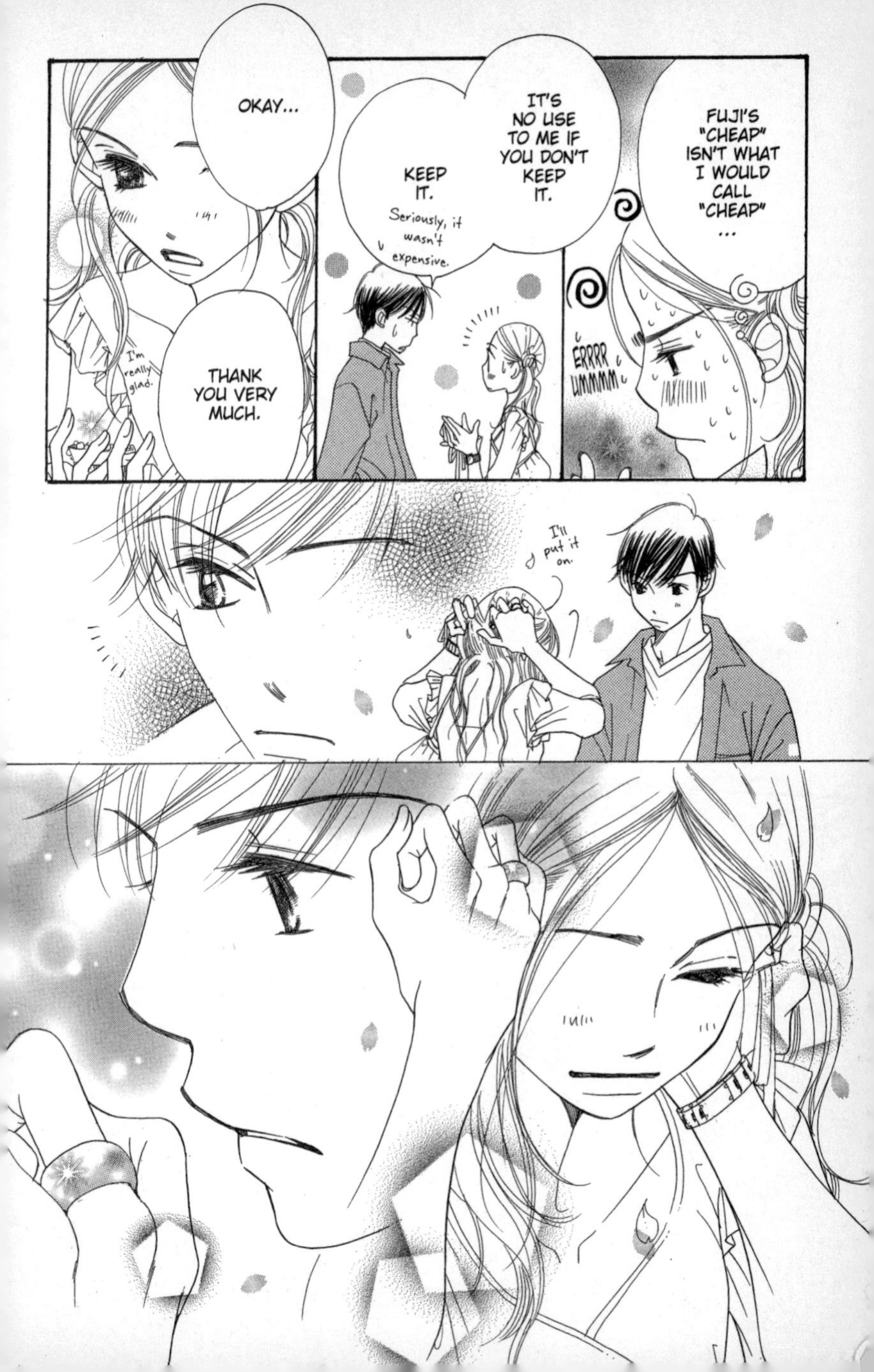
FUJI'S "CHEAP" ISN'T WHAT I WOULD CALL "CHEAP" ...
ERRRR UMMMM
IT'S NO USE TO ME IF YOU DON'T KEEP IT.
KEEP IT.
Seriously, it wasn't expensive.
OKAY...
I'm really glad.
THANK YOU VERY MUCH.
I'll put it on.

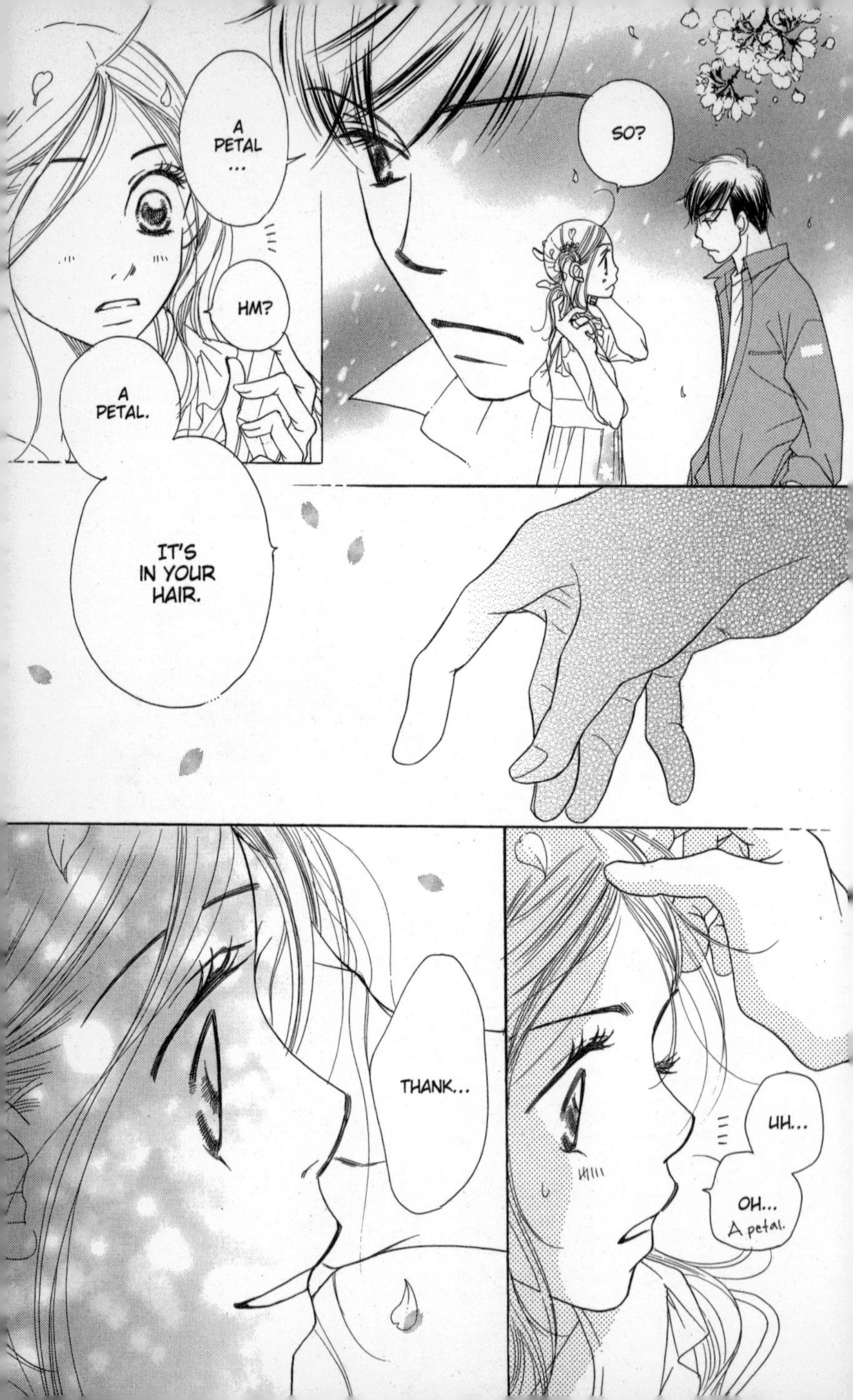
SO?
A PETAL ...
HM?
A PETAL.
IT'S IN YOUR HAIR.
UH...
OH... A petal.
THANK...

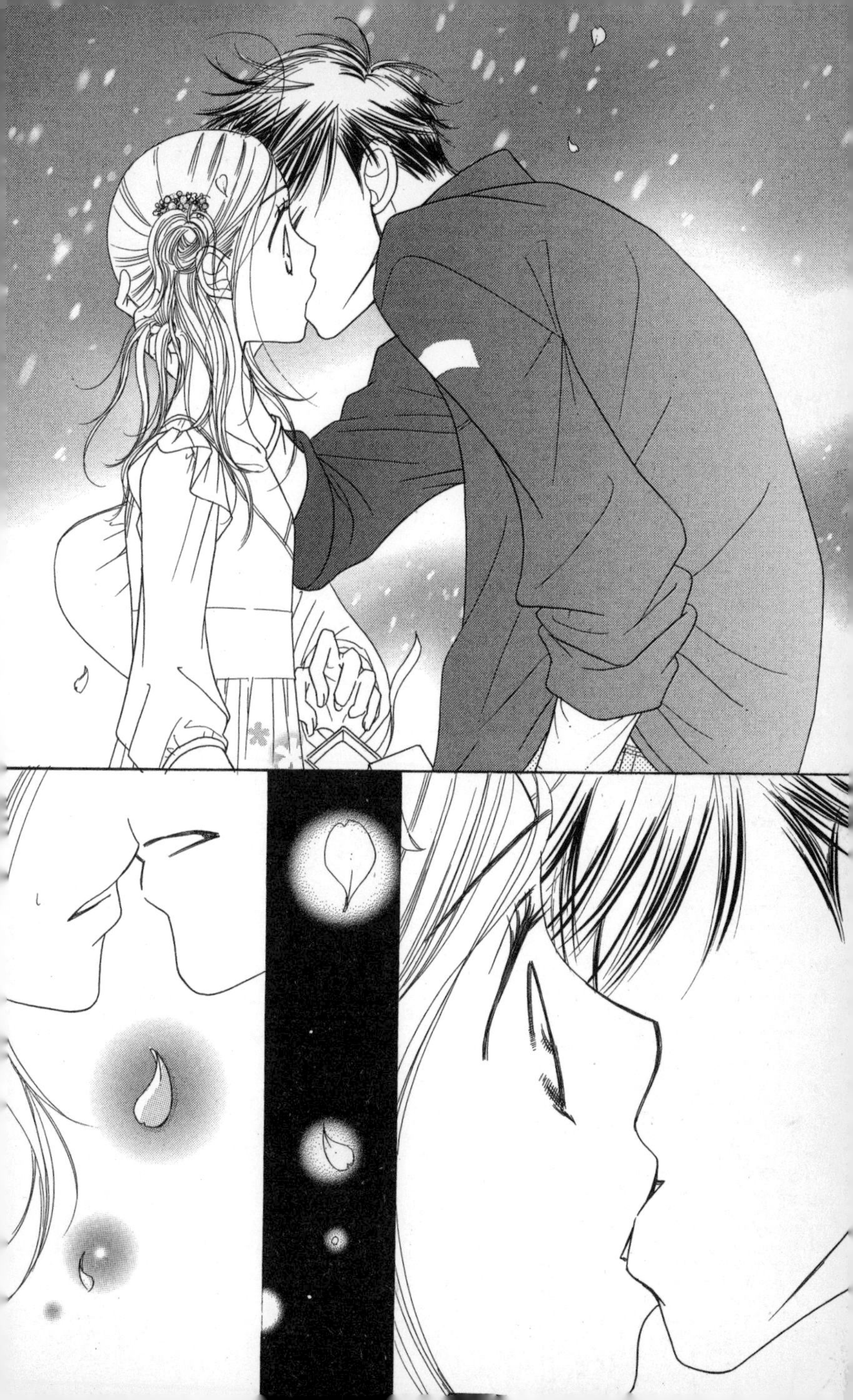

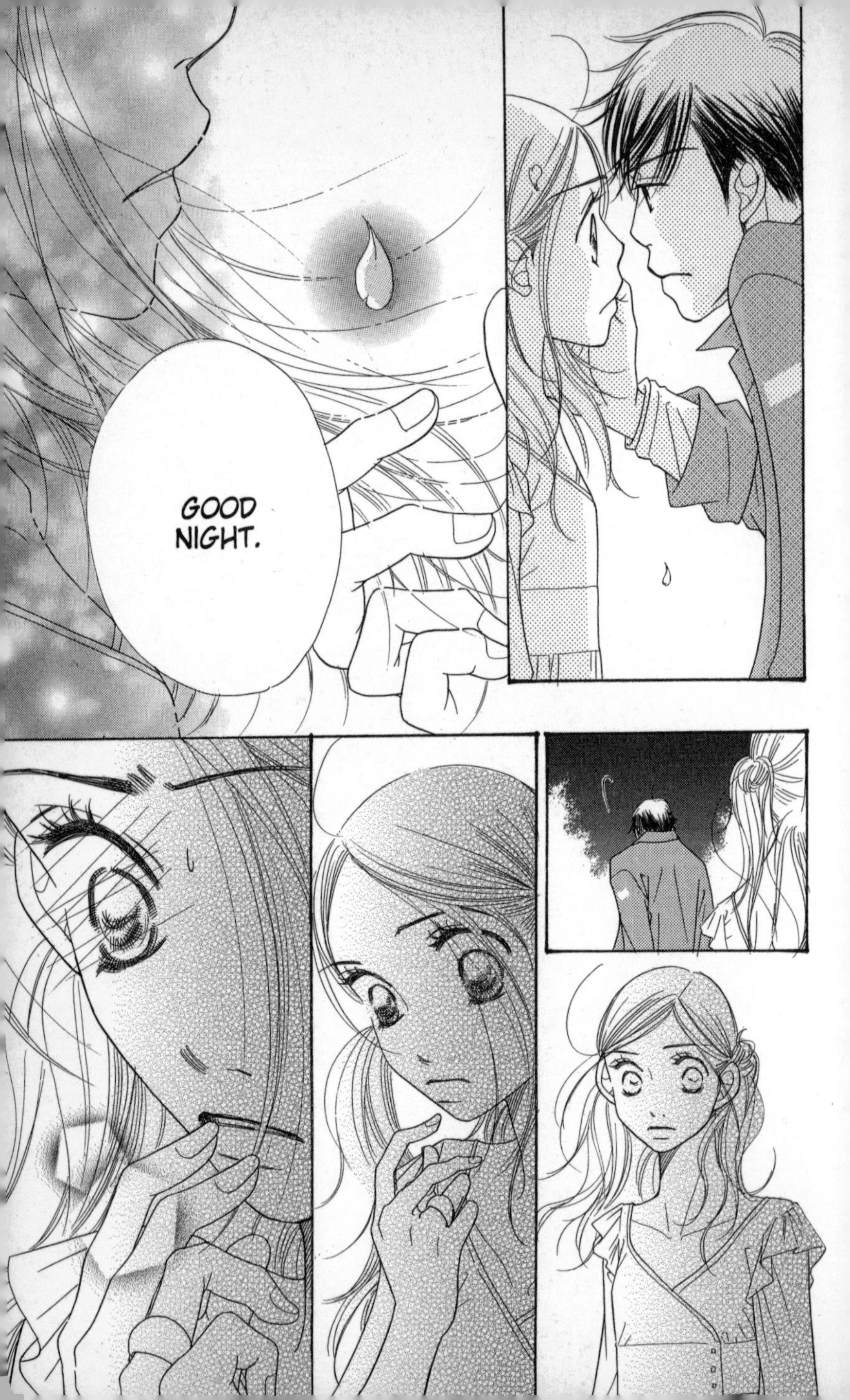
GOOD NIGHT.

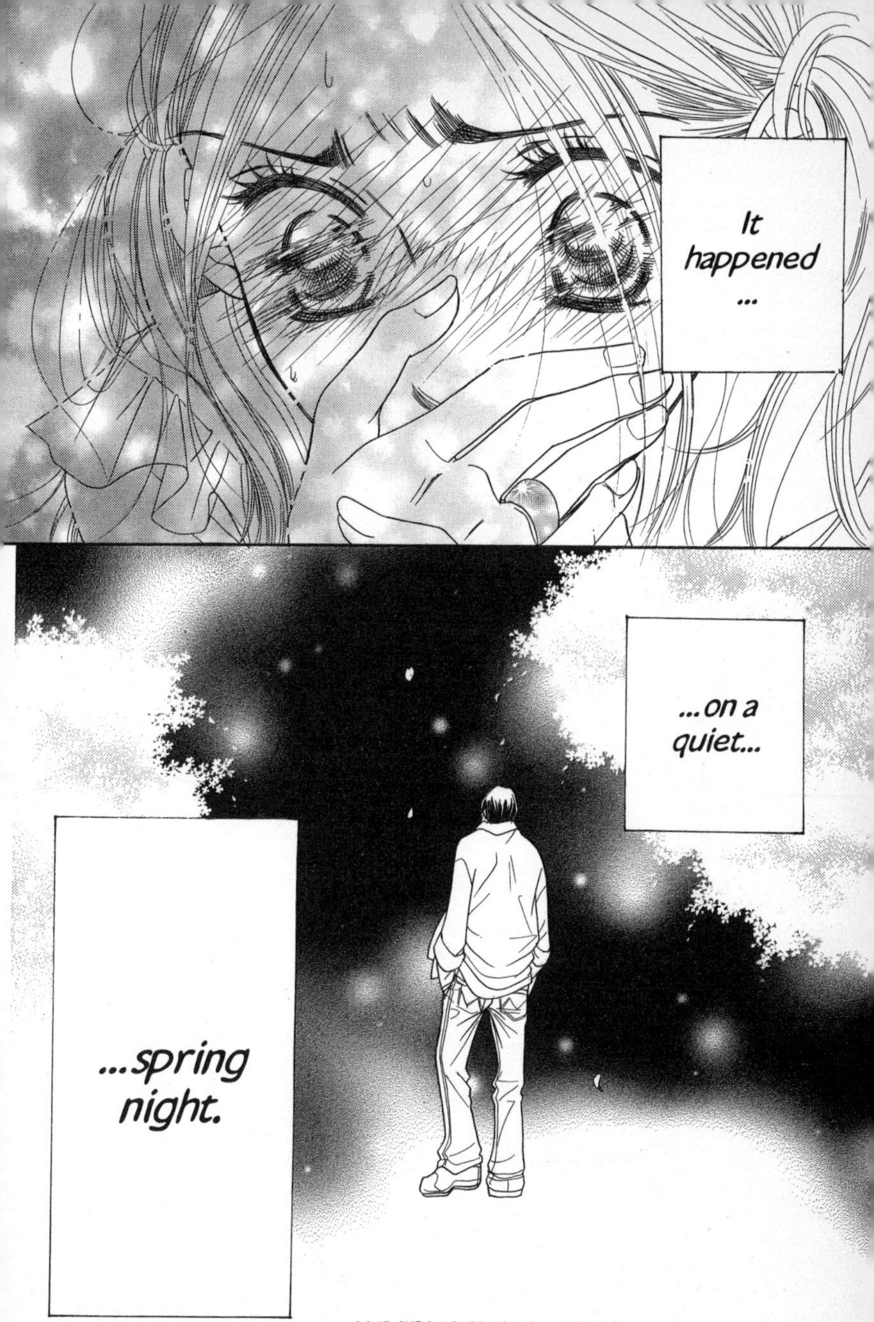
It happened ...
...on a quiet...
...spring night.

SAND CHRONICLES VOL. 2 — THE END

THANKS TO YOU, IT
LOOKS LIKE THIS SERIES
IS GOING TO CONTINUE
FOR A WHILE. THANK YOU
SO MUCH FOR READING!

TEARS
OF JOY

I LOOK FORWARD
TO YOUR CONTINUING
SUPPORT. SEE
YOU IN VOLUME 3.

'03. 11. 20   HINAKO ASHIHARA

Glossary

If only adolescence came with an instruction manual.
We can't give you that, but this glossary of terms might
prove useful.

Page 23, panel 6: Incense stick
To offer an incense stick is to pay tribute to
the deceased.

Page 24, panel 2: Salt
Salt is used to purify in the Shinto religion.
Ann's grandmother is implying that Ann's
father is an unwelcome guest and that she
must purify her house of his presence.

Page 33, panel 2: Who is that?
The 2,240th poem from Man'yoshu. The
author is unknown. There is a double
meaning at work in this poem: "Who is
he (Ta so kare/tasokare)?" and "twilight
(tasogare)." The popular interpretation of
this poem is "You cannot see my face in
the gloom. But please do not be curious as
to who I am. I'm just waiting for my lover
in the twilight, drenched in September's
dew." Twilight came to be called *tasogare*,
because you cannot see a person's face
clearly in the twilight's gloom.

Tasokare (Who is that?) was actually once
used in place of *tasogare* (evening). In the
Japanese he literally asks her, "Have you
learned that word (tasokare) at school?"
It works because the phrase "ta so kare"
(Who is that/he?) was actually a word used
for "evening." "Who is that?" is not one
word in English and could never substitute
for "evening," so we have smoothed over
this in the English dialogue here.

Page 64, panel 2: Studio
In Japan, this is called a 1K (1 room with
kitchen). In reality, a narrow kitchen area, a

galley big enough for one person to stand in,
and a very small bathroom/shower. There is
room to stand and cook. That's all. As far as
apartments go, it doesn't get much smaller.

Page 64, panel 7: House of trash
In real life, there are news stories about
people who haven't taken out their trash
in years, so their house is full of rubbish.
The smell causes a lot of trouble in the
neighborhood and gets a lot of media
attention.

Page 65, panel 2: Futon
Japanese futons are different from the
folding couches we are used to in the West.

Page 79, panel 3: Shimenawa
Shimenawa is a rice-straw rope used to
designate items, places, and spaces as holy
in Shinto. One can often see them tied
around trees at shrines or adorning shrines
and their gates.

Page 80, panel 1: Dedicated
The dedication at the top of this sign
indicates that this torii was donated/
dedicated to Yaegaki Shrine by some
individual, company, or group, or bought
with donated monies.

Page 80, panel 2: Yamata-no-orochi
Yamata-no-Orochi is an eight-headed
snake in Japanese mythology sometimes
simply called Orochi, or Eight-Forked
Serpent, in English. Many renditions
of Japanese myths on the Net and in
academia preserve the longer name.

Page 81, panel 3: Sobagaki
A side dish of buckwheat that is watered down and flavored with soy sauce.

Page 83, panel 4: Izumo Taisha Prayer
One usually only claps twice when praying at a shrine, but Izumo is more important than other shrines.

Page 95, panel 3: Love knot
En (relationship)-musubi (tie): In Japanese, the *musubi* (tie/knot) refers to what the item as a whole is and does, and has very little if anything to do with the actual knot that appears on this charm.

Page 113, panel 2: Train your mind
This phrase comes from Buddhism. In certain states of mind you will not be influenced by external circumstances. Ann's father has put up this sign to help him get by without using the air conditioner.

Page 120, panel 3: LD
The Japanese term is *en-ren*, which is short for *enkyori* (long distance) and *ren'ai* (love relationship).

Page 131, panel 3: Stripper game
Yakkyuuken: A game in which everyone sings a song. When the song stops you play Rock-Paper-Scissors and the loser has to take off an article of clothing. Then the process is repeated. Here they intend to take clothes off this picture rather than themselves.

Page 131, Sidebar: Somei Yoshino
Somei Yoshino is a nearly white kind of sakura. It was developed in the mid to late 19th century and is the most popular type of cherry blossom in Japan. It is the kind most often depicted in movies and other visual media.

Page 136, panel 8: Hachiko
Hachiko is a statue at Shibuya Station. It is often used as a meeting spot, so much so that many people now avoid using it because finding the person you're trying to meet can turn out to be extremely difficult. As a country boy, it's the first and only place Daigo can think of to meet.

Page 168, panel 3: Obon
Obon, an event held in mid August, is a holiday when it is customary for people to return to their hometowns and tend to their family's graves. Many people get time off from work for Obon.

Profile of Hinako Ashihara

This is volume 2. It contains stories about fall and spring. Fall brings to mind colorful leaves, and spring brings to mind cherry blossoms. I went with my friends from my school days to see the cherry blossoms the other day. We actually only looked at them for about the first five minutes…after which we devoted ourselves to our food. But then the cold got to us and it wasn't long before we left. We're the worst…
—Hinako Ashihara

Hinako Ashihara won the 50th Shogakukan Manga Award for *Sunadokei*. She debuted with *Sono Hanashi Okotowari Shimasu* in Bessatsu Shojo Comics in 1994. Her other works include *SOS*, *Forbidden Dance*, and *Tennen Bitter Chocolate*.